PRAISE FOR *66 LOVE LETTERS*

"My longtime friend and colleague, Larry Crabb, has always had a way of getting to the heart of the matter in people's lives and in the Bible too. He is a master at it, blessed by God in it. In this book he brings the story and message of the Bible, book by book, into the story of our lives. The books are many, but the story is one, and the life story of each of us fits into it. This is the story that explains our stories. Larry shows how that is true, and I personally thank him for it."

—RICHARD E. AVERBECK
PROFESSOR, OLD TESTAMENT AND SEMITIC LANGUAGES,
TRINITY EVANGELICAL DIVINITY SCHOOL

"From a counseling perspective, there is nothing more important than feeling that you are loved. In *66 Love Letters* Dr. Larry Crabb not only points us to but also walks with us through an exploration of the only true source of pure, unconditional love: the love of God. A uniquely fresh approach to Scripture, you will find and experience—maybe even for the first time—the amazing love story that is all about God and you."

—DR. TIM CLINTON
PRESIDENT, AMERICAN ASSOCIATION OF CHRISTIAN COUNSELORS

"Larry Crabb holds that our stories—yours and mine—are part of a bigger story: God's. Walking us through the sixty-six books of the Bible, he invites us into the conversations we might have with God. Insightful. Helpful. Honest. Human. Pivotal. Larry pulls back the curtain on His Story and invites us to participate in the drama that is biblical life."

—ELISA MORGAN
PUBLISHER, FULLFILL™; AND AUTHOR, *She Did What She Could*

"Larry Crabb carefully examines each of the sixty-six pieces of the biblical jigsaw puzzle and then fits them together, revealing a stunning picture of God's grace. I think this might be his magnum opus. I know it is a must-read for anyone who doesn't see God's love in every book of the Bible."

—GARY W. MOON, PHD
VICE PRESIDENT, RICHMONT GRADUATE UNIVERSITY;
AND AUTHOR, *Apprenticeship with Jesus*

66 Love Letters

Also by Dr. Larry Crabb

SPIRITUAL GROWTH BOOKS

Becoming a True Spiritual Community

Connecting

Finding God

God of My Father

Inside Out

Marriage Builder

Men & Women

Real Church

Shattered Dreams

Silence of Adam

SoulTalk

The PAPA Prayer

The Pressure's Off

Understanding People

Understanding Who You Are

AUDIO CDs

A Liberating Look at Gender

Chess Players or Poets

Christian Counseling and the New Way

Experiencing the Trinity

Freedom Series

The Church I Want to Be Part Of

The Unique Value of Small Groups

To the Children

What Every Christian Counselor Needs to Know

A Christian Response to Homosexuality

How Not to Become an Atheist

SoulTalk

To the Husbands

Unpacking but Never Solving the Mystery of Prayer

COUNSELING SERIES

Basic Principles of Biblical Counseling

Effective Biblical Counseling

Encouragement

DVD CURRICULUM

The SoulCare Experience

66 Love Letters

A Conversation with God
That Invites You into His Story

DR. LARRY CRABB

THOMAS NELSON
Since 1798

NASHVILLE   DALLAS   MEXICO CITY   RIO DE JANEIRO

Published in Nashville, Tennessee, by Thomas Nelson. Thomas Nelson is a registered trademark of Thomas Nelson, Inc.

Thomas Nelson, Inc. titles may be purchased in bulk for educational, business, fund-raising, or sales promotional use. For information, please e-mail SpecialMarkets@ ThomasNelson.com.

ISBN 978-0-8499-4640-0 (trade paper)

ISBN 978-0-8499-4687-5 (IE)

Library of Congress Cataloging-in-Publication Data

Crabb, Lawrence J.
  66 love letters : a conversation with God that invites you into His story / Larry Crabb.
    p. cm.
  ISBN 978-0-8499-1966-4 (hardcover)
  1. Bible—Meditations. 2. Bible—Outlines, syllabi, etc. I. Title.
  BS491.5.C69 2010
  242'.5—dc22

                                        2009040819

                        Printed in the United States of America
                        HB 05.01.2017

To my daughters-in-law,
Kimmie and Lesley,
whose hunger to know God through His Word
inspired me to write this book

We ask, "Where does God fit into the story of my life?"
when the real question is,
"Where does my little life fall into the great story of God's mission?"
—CHRISTOPHER J. H. WRIGHT

Contents

Acknowledgments

It normally takes me about twelve months to write a book. This one took three and a half years. If reading *66 Love Letters* provides you with even a fraction of the benefit that writing it provided me, join me in thanking:

- the Thomas Nelson publishing team. You've put your hearts into this project.
- the prayer team my wife, Rachael, organized to make sure I was prayed for every day as I read, studied, prayed, reflected, and wrote my way through each book of the Bible. Your prayers were felt.
- the more than three-thousand prayer partners across the world who receive Rachael's prayer initiative for NewWay Ministries. You have prayed for everything we do, including writing this book. I am grateful.
- the spiritual formation group I have been part of for five-plus years. Thanks for knowing me and still believing in me.
- Andi, director of operations for NewWay Ministries. Your passion, ideas, and loyal love keep our ministry moving ahead. You're in a class by yourself.
- my family: Ken and Lesley, and Kep and Kimmie. You make parenting, in-law parenting, and grandparenting a sheer delight.
- Special thanks to Kep, NewWay Ministries executive director, who also is my literary agent and typist. He actually wanted to transcribe my penned scribbles and offered a steady stream of rich encouragement and counsel.
- Special thanks also to Rachael, who deserves more credit than anyone (except God's Spirit) for her intimate support, tested and proven patience, and sacrificial companionship in God's call on our lives. Honey, you're an unmatched treasure!

Prologue: Finding Your Place in God's Story

True Christianity is turning the possible into the actual.
—JAMES HOUSTON

This book had its beginning in the early spring of 2006, at two o'clock in the morning. I'd gone to bed early the night before but couldn't sleep. So by one thirty, I gave up.

Without any sense of gratitude for being awake and alive, I climbed out of bed, grabbed my Bible more from instinct than desire, and stumbled downstairs to my favorite sulking spot, a comfortable chair in front of our gas log fireplace. I turned it on and sat down, feeling a mixture of three ounces anger for being awake when I wanted to be asleep and a half-ounce gratitude for the instant warmth from the fire that required no work on my part. The possibility of more gratitude was smothered by my sense that if I couldn't sleep, I at least deserved warm feet.

In this mood, I arranged myself in the chair, feet propped on the cushioned hearth, the floor lamp casting soft light over my left shoulder, dreaming that someone would bring me an extra hot latté.

For thirty minutes I whined, I suppose to God. He was the only one listening, and I wasn't convinced that He knew how justifiably miserable I felt, given some rough things going on in my life. Surely, if He knew, He would do something about it.

When I got tired of my whining, a verse came to mind. It's in the fifth chapter of Hosea, the last part of verse 15: "in their misery they will earnestly seek me."

I felt a hint of intrigue. Was God speaking to me? I picked up the unopened Bible I'd earlier deposited on the hearth, turned to that verse, and stared at those eight words for at least a minute.

Okay, I thought, *I've mastered the first half of that verse. I'm miserable. Now how do I move to the second half? How do I earnestly seek God?* The question itself jarred something loose in me. I realized I had been assuming it was His job to seek me. I was the lost sheep, baa-baaing alone in the night. Isn't that the cue for the Good Shepherd to leave the ninety-nine and come looking for me? (Matthew 18:12).

I could feel the angry, spoiled-brat passivity behind that assumption. A flame of hope began to melt the ice covering my heart. He had already come after me, and He had come a long way. The incarnation was a big trip. He had come here and had already found me. He was now close enough for me to hear Him speaking. Maybe seeking Him during misery did not mean that I was to wait for Him to do something—He had already done quite a lot; some would say everything. Maybe it meant aggressively listening and, yes, waiting, not for Him to do more but rather for me to listen well, to better hear the story He was telling.

That shift in perspective changed my attitude. It kicked my mind into gear. I remember thinking, *Perhaps my responsibility is to believe He is speaking right now, and perhaps my job is to listen, maybe to see. I'd love to see Jesus right now in a vision. An angel would do if Jesus happened to be busy with some other lost sheep.*

Heck, I'd even settle for audibly hearing His voice. Abraham heard God speak. Why couldn't I? *Show me! Speak to me! I'm all eyes and ears. I'm seeking You, God. C'mon. I'm miserable, and I'm earnestly seeking You. Let me see You. Let me hear You.*

My whining had matured into pious demanding. That realization stopped me. The truth flame burned a bit brighter. God had already revealed Himself to me in His Son, and He had written a whole book to introduce His Son to me. And He was right now actively speaking to me in the Bible. That's why Christians everywhere for a long time have referred to the Bible as the *Word of God*—the speech of God, the revelation from God of Jesus Christ by the Holy Spirit.

What that means is similar to what I had already known and experienced. I met my wife when we were both ten. We had our first "date" at age twelve. Somehow we knew that we were an item, a long-term item. From twelve to twenty-one, when we married, we wrote hundreds of love letters to each other. We still have them, forty-plus years later, stored in a dozen boxes.

She lived a couple of hours away, and we couldn't afford many phone calls, so letters were the preferred mode of communication. This was before some intruder into the slow-paced life replaced rocking chair conversations with e-mail. I can remember eager trips to the mailbox, hoping to see the upside-down stamp (which back in our day was a code meaning "I love you") fastened to an envelope addressed to me.

Rachael's words were the letter. As I read those words, I could hear Rachael speaking to me. Was it really true that the words in the Bible are actually *God's* words, and that I could hear God speaking to me if I learned to read His love letters properly, as I more easily learned to read Rachael's?

I made a choice. It was now about 2:40 a.m.. Rather than sit with closed eyes, waiting to see God with my spiritual eyes (whatever that means), and rather than take advantage of early morning silence and solitude by quieting my inner world enough to somehow hear God in my soul (however you do that), I decided to explore how I might hear Him speak to me from the Bible. I didn't merely want a verse to stir me. I wanted to hear God tell me His story.

A series of questions began to pour out of me: *God, why did You write Genesis? What do You want me to hear You say in Leviticus? Could You tell me why I should bother to read, let alone study, Obadiah? I think I have some idea what Romans is about, but how are You talking to me in Jude or Revelation?*

Now that I've brought up Revelation, do You mind if I ask You something? Couldn't You have finished off the Bible with something a little easier to understand? I know scholars call it apocalyptic *literature, but all that means to me is that it's intentionally confusing.*

God, why did You write Revelation? Come to think of it, why did You write each of the sixty-six books? That last question changed my half-ounce of gratitude for warm feet into a pound of praise for what I found myself anticipating: maybe God would actually answer me. Maybe He and I could have a conversation that invited me into His story.

From my earliest days, I've been fascinated by the Bible. I think my fascination has something to do with watching how my dad read it. He sometimes, and not infrequently, would spend a whole evening reading through Leviticus when there were perfectly good shows on television. That made no sense to me. But it got me thinking, *what's in that book?*

As a teenager, I sat through several Bible conferences every year. When I was sixteen, I listened to a great preacher named S. Lewis Johnson preach five consecutive nights from Zechariah. I can still recall some thoughts he developed from the third chapter. And they still give me goose bumps.

When Dr. Johnson walked to the pulpit, he would position himself behind it, arrange his Bible and notes, then look up and say, "Take your Bibles and turn to Zechariah." I pictured a train leaving the station. I imagined Dr. Johnson shouting, "All aboard! This train is heading for mountain peaks you've never seen before. Are you ready?" I was in the front row every night, on the edge of my seat.

The Bible fascinated me, but it also confused me. I couldn't fit the sixty-six pieces of the jigsaw puzzle together. I couldn't see the picture they were forming. I couldn't hear the story the sixty-six books were telling. The sixty-six dots were hard to connect.

In my graduate studies in psychology, I learned that nonsense syllables, like *bas* and *alk*, are hard to remember. Real words are easier to recall, especially if they fit together into a meaningful sentence. Try to remember these four words: *cat*, *the*, *saw*, and *I*. It will be much easier if you arrange them into a sentence: *I saw the cat.*

I wanted to do something similar with the Bible. I wanted God to give me a sentence—or two or three—that would make sense of Genesis, that would let me know what He wanted me to hear Him say as I read that book. I wanted a sentence, or two or three, for each book of the Bible that I could string together in a sequence that would tell me the one continuous story into which I could fit my life. I wanted to arrange summary sentences of each book into the story God was telling in the Bible. I wanted to know the plot and to see how each chapter (each of the sixty-six books) advanced the plot.

It was now almost three o'clock. My excitement was mounting. The train was leaving the station. And I was on board. I pictured my father in his chair in front of our coal-burning fireplace reading Leviticus while Red Skelton was beginning his monologue. It began to make sense.

"Dad, Red Skelton's on."

"I'm going to skip it tonight, Larry. I'm into something else."

Dad feasted on the Bible. He chewed on different parts of it every day.

Several times, with the passion of a young man the day before his wedding, he told me, "The Bible is a love story that begins with a divorce. Everything from the third chapter of Genesis through the end of Revelation is the story of a betrayed lover wooing us back into His arms so we can enjoy the love of family forever."

Dad's favorite verse, at least the one he quoted the most, was John 6:68. Jesus had just been saying tough things that didn't sit well with most of His followers. When many of them decided to turn away to an easier life than He was talking about, Jesus looked at Peter and asked, "You do not want to leave too, do you?" Peter's reply was Dad's favorite verse: "Lord, to whom shall we go? You have the words of eternal life."

All this came back to me as I sat by the fireplace that early spring morning of 2006. With fresh impact, I realized God was telling a story, a love story, that begins in chapter 1 (Genesis), continues for sixty-four chapters (Exodus through Jude), and reaches its climax in chapter 66 (Revelation). And I prayed, "God, will You tell me what You want me to hear in each of those chapters? I want to know Your story. I want to be a part of Your story. I want to feel passion about Your story."

I visualized each chapter as a love letter from God to me, His fickle friend, His cheating spouse, His spoiled child. He still wants me. He paid a huge price to get me. He has already found me. And now He is telling me the whole story of how I messed up our relationship and how He is putting it back together. And He's letting me know how it's all going to turn out. Every word in the Bible I could now see as a word of life. No wonder Dad loved that verse.

I grabbed a pen and pad of paper. Calling on more than forty years of reading and pondering and studying and teaching the Bible, I turned to Genesis and asked myself, *What do I know about this book that might help me grasp why God wrote it? What is He saying in this first love letter that He wants me to hear? How does His story begin? Can I express in a couple of sentences what I hear Him telling me in Genesis? God, let me hear You speak to me through Your Word.*

I leave it to scholars to understand what only scholars understand and to add depth or correct misdirection in what I've come up with in this book. That early morning I saw myself as I really am, a mere Christian, a hungry follower of Jesus who desperately wants to hear whatever God is telling me, a man in misery who wants only one thing, not relief from misery (although that would be nice), but hope—hope of intimacy and meaning and joy forever, in relationship with God.

To sharpen my focus in what I was aggressively (and dependently) listening for, I indulged in a brief fantasy. Suppose the renowned British author C. S. Lewis came to my home for dinner. After getting beyond intimidation and awe (which would take awhile), I imagined myself pouring him a glass of port and, warming ourselves by my fireplace, asking him, "Professor Lewis"—I couldn't even dream he would invite me to call him Jack—"why did you write each of your books? What did you hope a reader like me would come to know or see more clearly if I read *The Screwtape Letters* or *The Great Divorce* or *Mere Christianity*? Can you answer the question in a sentence or two or three, per book?"

I pictured myself audiotaping his replies so I could write them down accurately and ponder them before I read each of his books again.

That's what I was asking for from God that early morning. But it wasn't a fantasy. God was there, in my living room. He was inviting me to call Him Abba, Lover, Friend. And He was speaking, in sixty-six love letters.

By five thirty, I received what I had asked for. Almost. I had scribbled on three sheets of paper the beginnings of what I believed God wanted me to hear in each of the thirty-nine chapters that make up the first part (the Old Testament) of His story. It remained for a later time to hear sentences conveying God's point in each of the twenty-seven chapters in the rest of His story (the New Testament).

Only then did it occur to me: if I shared with others what I think God wants all of us to hear in each of the Bible's sixty-six books, perhaps a serious, growing problem in the church might move toward a solution. Most Christians don't know the Bible well. Many wish they did. But not everyone is convinced they need to know it. Inspiring music, some biblical tips for living, a few interesting Christian books, and occasional serious study are too often seen as sufficient for living the *Christian* life people want to live.

I'm troubled by how fond we've become of receiving visions and hearing prophetic words, what we assume are direct communications from God that bypass the Bible and diminish the importance of knowing its content. We feel moved by short passages as we meditate on them and we sense internal impressions and experiences that we attribute to the Holy Spirit, but with little understanding of the larger story of the Bible. We try to reach the heart of God without listening to the Word of God. When I couldn't see Rachael, I discovered her heart by reading her words. That's a good plan to follow with God.

With a growing awareness of the biblical narrative and a deep commitment to always knowing more, visions and prophetic words and impacting passages and inner sensations have their place. But without that awareness and commitment, these avenues of communication from God might instead become opportunities for self-serving imagination. It is not a good idea to stare at a couple of jigsaw puzzle pieces and assume you see the picture all sixty-six could form. It is not a good idea to feel inspired and be instructed by a couple of good Bible lessons and assume we know what we need to join the story of God.

My purpose in writing this book is to help you see, as I'm being helped to see, the picture that comes into focus when all sixty-six pieces of the biblical jigsaw puzzle are fitted together. Then we can better look carefully at the unique coloring and texture of each piece, and do serious study.

I want you to hear, as I long to hear, what God is saying to us in each of the sixty-six love letters He has written. When you weave them together into the whole story, you will hear the greatest love story ever told. You will be swept off your feet. No matter what doubts or disappointments or disasters come your way, you will pick up your Bible and rediscover hope. With the apostle Peter and my father, and now with me, you will say, "Lord, to whom shall we go? You have the words of eternal life." It's the life we want. And you will be able to glean from the Bible the wisdom you need to live your life well, in any circumstance.

Well, I think by now you're getting a good feel for what this book is about. A few more comments will wrap up this prologue and get you ready for what follows.

First, each chapter is short. That's by design. This book is not meant to be anything close to a comprehensive analysis of the books of the Bible. In the first love letter (Genesis), I write out the sentence that I believe simply expresses what God wants us to hear when we read through Genesis. I write in the first person, as if God Himself is speaking directly to us, which perhaps He is. Whether I've accurately heard Him or not is up to you to decide.

Second, I add several paragraphs of what I think God would add if He were asked, "Could You unpack Your summary sentences a little, and give me a brief, simple overview of how this chapter communicates what You want me to hear?"

Finally, for each chapter, I indicate what happens in me—what I think and feel—as I listen to God tell me what He wants me to hear. You might want to notice your own reaction.

In the epilogue, I fit together the sixty-six jigsaw puzzle pieces. I string the sixty-six summary paragraphs of each love letter into one continuous story. I want you to see, and I want to see, at least a glimpse of the beautiful picture God is forming from all the pieces. And I want you to feel, and I want to feel, the compelling wonder of the love story God is telling. It really is the greatest love story ever told. And we're in it.

One final thought. I've studied psychology at the doctoral level. I've counseled literally thousands of people struggling with every problem imaginable. I'm familiar in an unscholarly sort of way with great philosophers such as Blaise Pascal. I've read great novelists such as Fyodor Dostoyevsky. I've spent hours soaking in the wisdom of great minds such as C. S. Lewis and great mystics such as John of the Cross and great theologians such as John Owen.

I've concluded one thing: if you face yourself honestly, if you look through a clear lens at your life in this world, hearing God speak to you in the sixty-six love letters that make up the Bible will do you more good than anything else.

I hope this book helps you, as it is helping me, to see the incomparable beauty God is creating out of some rather ugly material. And I hope that together we hear the unequalled love story He is telling.

Nothing will change you more deeply or sustain you with more hope than hearing God speak to you in the Bible. True Christianity turns the possible into the actual. As the biblical ax breaks the frozen sea within us and releases the warm current that flows from our God-invaded center, we become the persons we were meant to be. We can live the *new way* of the Spirit, the *new way* that values loving God and loving others above

everything else, the *new way* that lifts first things into first place and puts
everything else into second place where everything else belongs.

The Bible tells the story of how that happens. You *can* hear God speak.
You *can* know who He is and what He's up to and where He's going. And
you *can* join Him in the story He is telling.

Now you know how this book came to be. Before you dig into it, I want
to make clear how this book can speak to you. Hearing what God is saying
in the letters He's written could change the way you think about life and
transform the way you live your life. That's what's been happening to me.
I want the same for you.

How this Book Can Speak to You

Your life is part of a larger story. Everything you do, from ordinary activities like waiting in long checkout lines to serious responsibilities like handling a family crisis, is part of that story. Everything that happens to you—wonderful things, terrible things, and everything in between—advances the plot.

The trick is to know the story, grasp its plot, and remember it every day. That's difficult to do. But it's the only way you can decide to intentionally join the larger story. It's the only way you can feel the transcendent joy of moving the story forward no matter what is happening in your life, in the smaller story that so easily grabs most of your attention.

The older I get, the more I believe that a larger story, a really good one, is being told right now in the middle of whatever mix of good and bad is going on in each of our smaller stories. But we've twisted the story out of shape; we've changed the plot to accommodate how we, from our limited perspective, want our lives to turn out.

I'm referring to Christians—not all of us but most of us. And non-Christians too. We tend to tweak our understanding of the meaning of life to accommodate our felt desires. We change the plot of life into a drama that satisfies the longings of our hearts—for intimacy, respect, fullness, and comfort—more quickly than the original script calls for. The effect is disastrous.

Our quick-fix, feel-better, make-life-work-for-us, we-want-it-now-and-we're-entitled-to-have-it-now culture has wrenched our understanding of the Christian story into something that it is not and never was. Believe the lie, and you become what no person, especially a Christian person, was meant to be. Twist the story, and you degrade the human spirit.

If you assume that Christianity means satisfaction in this life of all your desires, including the ones that lie deepest in your heart, then you live as no person was meant to live. You demand satisfaction. You live for it. You feel entitled to it. You become incapable of real love, only self-centered passion.

It's completely natural when something goes wrong, when you fail life or life fails you, to want to know what to *do* rather than how to *think*. You scramble, you churn, you try to come up with some plan of action that will control the damage, relieve the discomfort, and restore some level of personal peace.

It's hard to set aside the panic, to move through the pain, to delay gratification, to live feeling empty, worthless, betrayed, and to ask, "So what's the big picture here? What kind of person do I want to be, for my kids, my friends, for me, for God, in the middle of this mess? What values do I want to uphold? What matters the most at any cost to me? What is my life really all about right now, and what fire is still burning in me that can keep me moving toward something truly good? What difference does the sure hope of heaven make right now on my attitudes, passions, and choices?"

It's natural when life throws us a curve to ask, "What can I do to make my life better? To protect myself from more pain?" But it's more human to ask, "What story is my life telling?"

When we manage to ask the more human question, science moves to the back row, and religion and philosophy step forward: *Here's the way to think. These are the beliefs to hold. Tell this story with your life, and you'll be on your way to meaning and hope and happiness.*

But honest people know, if they have lived long enough, that nothing works as it should, and it never will, not in this life. We will always have problems and unsatisfied desires in this life. I've been a psychologist for forty years—a pretty good one—and I've never cured anyone. I've helped lots of struggling people, but even the ones I've helped the most still struggle with something.

The simple truth is, life is hard. It will never be as good as we want it to be, and it will inevitably become painfully difficult for everyone before it's over.

So the question is, what story should we tell with our lives? To achieve what? My life is telling a story. Your life is telling a story. If there is a good story to tell, one that gives us solid hope through bad times that good times lie ahead, and one that releases us to live with joy and purpose now, we want to know it and live it.

Christianity is the story told in the Bible. Christian churches exist to tell that story. Too often Christian churches do lots of good things without telling the good story that makes good things good. In churches across the world, hurting people are encouraged; wounded people are healed; eager people are challenged; addicted people are set free; misguided people are given biblical principles to follow; stubborn people are confronted; selfish people are challenged to feed the poor, build homes for the homeless, and provide medicine to HIV patients; fearful people receive reassurance; bereaved people are comforted; shame-filled people are warmly embraced; and drifting people who would otherwise waste time with too much television are kept busy with meaningful activities.

But the point of all these good things, the real reason to do them and the real good that is done through them, is easily missed. When that happens, Christianity gets reduced to an opportunity to get the most out of life now and to become the happiest and healthiest and most fulfilled person you can be. I call it "good-enough Christianity."

If you believe the Bible and have a basic grasp of its storyline, you know that the real story of life began a long time ago at a family gathering. The plot unfolded during a family split, two splits really: the first in Eden, the second on Calvary. And the story will climax, not when you move into your new house or marry off your kids or celebrate fifty years of a great marriage or look back on a life lived sacrificially for others but at another family gathering in another world—this one, a dinner party where the family will be much larger and where the satisfaction you longed for but never fully experienced in this world will begin and never end.

If you focus on the smaller story of your life from your natural birth to your natural death, you will misunderstand everything that matters. You'll mistake your joys and sorrows for the fullness of real joy that lies ahead and of real sorrows that you'll never experience. Things that feel awful to you will be seen as nothing other than tragedies to reverse if possible, endure if necessary, and at all costs prevent from happening again.

Good things that come your way, things that bring you legitimate pleasure, and the good things you do, acts of decency and sacrificial kindness, will be more valuable in your eyes than, in fact, they are. You'll cling to them as a miser clings to gold. They will mean too much to you. You will live in fear of losing them. You'll live with a demanding spirit of entitlement that will justify doing whatever is necessary to keep them, to preserve them for your well-being. You will live a life "curved in on itself," to quote Augustine.

But when you hear the Master Storyteller tell His story, a shift happens in the center of your heart. You pause in the middle of terrific blessings or terrible trials or maybe just everyday life and you say, "So *that's* what life is all about!"

Pastors who more clearly hear God's story preach their sermons for different reasons. Husbands and wives and parents and friends who understand the story relate in a different way, aiming toward different goals. Business and professional people define success differently. Hospital patients view their diseases differently and face disability or death differently.

Everything you formerly called a disaster you now see as a painful but strangely welcome opportunity to tell more of His story, not because you have to but because you want to. And every good thing you used to cling to you come to see for what it is in reality: a mere drop of pleasure in an ocean of joy, a drop you can lose without really losing anything.

This good story is not told on cable news or in newspaper headlines. It's not told in most institutions of higher learning. It's not always told in churches or seminaries. And it can never be fully told in poetry, novels, paintings, musical compositions, or movies though sometimes these art forms provide windows into God's story and glimpses of its wonders.

The larger story I'm talking about is told accurately and fully (as much as human beings can take in) in only one place, the Bible. And it requires all sixty-six books to tell the story. Each one has a necessary and vital place. It follows, of course, that the better we understand what the Storyteller is telling us in each of the sixty-six chapters He wrote, the better we will know the story and be able to live it.

I'm discovering that the more I long to hear what God is saying in the Bible through each chapter (and by chapter, I mean book), the more I get to know God and to realize He can only tell a good story. He is incapable of telling a bad one. As you see the drama unfold from Genesis to Revelation, you realize that the Dramatist is so generous and jolly that He makes Santa

Claus look stingy and morose. You look instead to Mother Teresa or Billy Graham to get a better idea what the Dramatist is like, and you realize even their exemplary lives pale by comparison.

As you hear the story, you feel the Storyteller's strength, next to which Superman's is puny. The man of steel is exposed as a boy of Jell-O. You tremble when you recognize the Storyteller's impossibly high and unbending standards until you realize they are not the impositions of a tyrant requiring that you do things His way, but they are rather the call of a lover inviting you to enjoy His perfection.

The more deeply you understand and enter the story told in the Bible, the more you hear a story of love unmatched in all of history, in all literature and film. It portrays a kind of love that Shakespeare could not imagine, a pure love that Hollywood's best imitation badly mangles.

Our lives—yours and mine—are part of the story, either as little villains or as little heroes. There is a supervillain, the source of evil, and one Supreme Hero, the source of all goodness. We never play more than a bit part, but the part we play matters. It matters greatly. It therefore matters that we get the story straight, that we grasp its plot so that we can flow with, not against, its current.

After forty years of counseling (and more of trying to get my own life sorted out), I am persuaded that the best thing I can do for people who are struggling with life and for those who are complacent and prematurely happy is to tell the story of God as best I can. The key to living the good life that is available now is to join God's story, to see life as He sees it and learn to live it as He wants it lived.

But first we must know it. We must together hear it, told not by me or by any other human but by God Himself. We need to hear the Master Storyteller tell His story. And that means reading the Bible and listening as the storyline unfolds and develops in all sixty-six chapters.

I've been reading the Bible for more than half a century, never as a scholar—I make no claim to technical knowledge—but always as a seeker. I am a seeker after God, a man who knows that neither memorizing verses nor agreeing with doctrine taught by respected scholars, though both have their place, is ever enough. Neither is meditatively reflecting on certain passages or pondering inspiring stories scattered throughout the Bible's pages. These good activities are not enough to lift me into the larger story in the way I live and think and relate. More is needed.

I like how N. T. Wright, a man who is a biblical scholar, expressed it in an interview: "It's possible to tick the boxes that say Trinity, Incarnation, Atonement, Resurrection, Spirit, Second Coming, and yet it's like a child's follow-the-dots. The great story—and after all the Bible is fundamentally a story—we've got to pay attention to that, rather than abstracting dogmatic points from it. The dogmas are true, they matter, but you have to join them up the right way."

My life is a story that belongs in a larger story. So does yours. I see that more clearly now in my sixties than I did in my fifties or before. I suppose I'll see it more clearly as more time carries me nearer the end of my smaller story, which I'm coming to see is really quite short. With N. T. Wright, I want to weave the many truths revealed in the Bible into the one true story that I've been invited to join. I want to connect the dots the right way.

There are many larger stories to choose from, many religions and philosophies that intelligent, decent people accept as the context to give meaning to their lives. But I want to know and join the story told only in the Bible. I believe God is the Master Storyteller and that He wrote the Bible. I am coming to see the sixty-six books of the Bible as sixty-six love letters God has written to us to tell us His story and to let us know how we can become a good part of it.

But there is a problem. You've felt it, and I have too: *the letters are hard to understand.* They seem disconnected from each other, like sixty-six jigsaw puzzle pieces that don't easily fit together into a picture. What does Haggai have to do with Philemon? I can read Nahum or Galatians in one sitting and close my Bible having no idea what I was supposed to get out of it. How does the story of Ruth tie in with the stories Luke tells in Acts? I have trouble connecting the dots.

And since we're being honest, let's admit that these love letters can be tedious, even boring. When's the last time you got a rise out of reading Leviticus?

Thousands of books, many by scholars and some by amateurs like me, have been written to help us read the Bible well. But none that I'm aware of has suggested in a few sentences what God wants us to hear in each book of the Bible, sentences that if we put them together in a long paragraph, represent the essential story God is telling. That's what I intend to provide in this book as best I can.

For now, let me simply invite you into the greatest love story ever told. If you hear it, you'll want to be a part of it. You might dismiss it as lovely fiction or religious rhetoric, or you may see it as one larger story among many to choose from to fill your smaller story with importance and hope.

But the Bible's story just might ring true as it does for me. It is a story that will take you further down than you ever wanted to go and lift you higher than you ever imagined you could travel. It is a story that provides the power not to give you everything you want in this world but to transform the little story of your life in this world into part of a meaningful and wonderfully, larger story that is the only one worth telling now while you wait for the satisfaction of every desire in the next world when you meet the Storyteller.

A strong suggestion: *don't try to read this book straight through in a week or two, the way you would read a novel or a good Christian book on how to follow Christ.*

If you're a structured type, read one chapter per week. In sixty-six weeks, you'll develop a feel for the story of God. If you're more the artistic type, follow your own pace. In either case, read each chapter slowly. See where you identify with my doubts and struggles and longings. If possible, take the time to read the love letter itself. Only what's written in the Bible is God's Word. What I've written is what I hear God saying to me in each letter.

Read each letter in sequence. Don't skip ahead to John if you feel bogged down in Numbers. Underline sentences that jump out at you. Go where the Spirit takes you, perhaps to what God is saying directly to you in the specific challenges you're facing.

Another strong suggestion: *discuss each chapter in a small group.* That's what I'm doing. If you meet weekly, in less than a year and a half, you'll have a feel for the story God is telling that will draw you into its incredible life-changing drama. If you meet monthly, commit yourself to staying with it. The discipline is worth the reward.

One more strong suggestion: *let the study guide I've written guide your personal reflection and your group discussion.* For each love letter, I've capsulated its message into one key thought and offered a few questions to help you apply that thought to your life. You can download the study guide for this book at www.newwayministries.org.

Well, enough preparation. Let's listen to the story unfold now, one chapter at a time.

PART ONE

A Fall, a Promise, and the Story Begins: Genesis Through Deuteronomy

What's wrong with the world? Something is. That's for sure. But what is it? Philosophers and politicians and religious leaders and ordinary people like you and me have been wrestling with that question for centuries.

Another question follows quickly on the heels of the first one: what is the solution?

Can either question be answered with any real authority?

For as many centuries as those questions have been asked, a significant number of intelligent, thoughtful, and self-aware people have looked to the first five books of the Bible for at least a beginning answer. They have believed that the root of all that's wrong with the world and with you and me is a turning away from God, a turning that first happened in the first garden by the first man and woman.

And on his own, no one since has wanted to turn back to God. So God has turned toward us with a promise that begins His love story.

Love Letter One: Genesis

I Have a Plan: You Are Invited to My Party

G od, what are You saying to me in Your first love letter, Genesis?"

"What I'm saying and what I want you to hear is this:

You've made a mess, but I have a plan!

"In Genesis, I begin telling the story of how everyone fails and I succeed. I want you to know how much of a mess you've made out of all the beauty I created. Nothing works as it should anymore. But I have a plan that your failures cannot destroy. There is a capacity for beauty in your soul that I will restore. That's a promise. I give you a glimpse into how I will carry out My plan in this first love letter."

"God, could You say a little more? How do You make that message clear in Genesis?"

"I don't want you to be afraid of failure, or you will live for success. And I don't want you to be afraid that things in your life will go wrong—they will—or that you will feel empty—you will. If you fear problems or emptiness, you will live for comfort and fulfillment. And that will just complicate the mess you've already made.

"Did you ever stop to ask *why* I made everything; *why* My Spirit,

My Son, and I created the stars, moon, planets, and *why* We made paradise on earth? The three of Us were making preparations to throw a party, to invite others to a dance, to the dance We've been enjoying since before time began. But there were no 'others' to invite.

"So at a family council, We decided to create people, human beings just like you whom We could enjoy as they enjoyed Us and all the beauty We had made. That's why We created Adam and Eve with desires that only We could satisfy. Plans for the party were under way.

"But the story got off track. We knew, of course, that it would. Adam and Eve foolishly decided they could be happier looking out for themselves than trusting Us. They did exactly what you would have done had you been there. They chose to throw their own party, without Us. That's as foolish as trying to breathe in a room without air or trying to sing when you have no vocal cords. It can't be done. There is no party without Us, only the prison of loneliness.

"Adam and Eve made the same choice you've been making since you were a kid, to protect yourself from pain and to be in control of your own pleasure, to negotiate with Me to get what you want out of life. That decision messed up everything in Eden, just as it still is messing up your life. Adam and Eve felt insecure and began to fight. Their son Cain experienced jealousy—an emotion that earned Lucifer a place in hell—and killed Abel.

"A few generations later, things got so bad, so out of sync with Our design, that I felt nothing but pain as I watched what was happening. So I drowned everyone, except Noah and his family. I wasn't about to let My plans for a party degenerate into a violent orgy that would only get worse, where people would use each other for their own pleasure and never love anyone. That would be hell. My plan was heaven. I spared those people from descending even deeper into hell on earth.

"But I wasn't about to give up on My great plan. I knew that one day I would look down on a community of people that I would re-create and feel deep pleasure, and again be able to say, 'This is good. This is *very* good!'

"Then Noah got drunk, his kids got in trouble, and their descen-dants—a capable bunch who developed civilization with the arts, industry, and agriculture—became proud. Drawing from the same energy with which Adam and Eve ate the forbidden fruit, they set about to build their lives into a satisfying, organized existence without Me in the center.

"So they erected this silly tower to rally everyone together. Their goal was unity with each other without union with Me. They thought they could become friends with each other before first becoming friends with Me. It can't be done. To make the point, I ruined their plans by making them speak different languages; I interfered with a plan that would never work.

"Once again, things were a mess. Everyone was living to succeed, to make their lives comfortable and fulfilling. No one was paying attention to My design for the truly good life.

"But I had a plan. I always do. I chose Abraham, just one ordinary, God-dishonoring man, to begin a whole new civilization, a new kingdom, to become a new kind of person to form a new kind of community—a *listening* community made up of people who would know Me, people who would hear Me and relate to others in order to love, both to receive and to give.

"Of course Abraham failed, like everyone, like you. That's why I told you not to fear failure. If you do, you'll live for a success you can never achieve. But I succeeded. I gave Abraham the kind of faith that you must *want*, that you *need*, to join My story. That's what I want you to hear as you read about My friend Abraham.

"Isaac comes next. I saw to it that he be born to Abraham and Sarah when, according to natural law, they could not bear children. And I did that to make one point: *no one joins My story in his or her own power.* I want you to know that.

"And then comes Jacob. He was a self-centered, manipulative, insecure mess from day one. Oh, he was resourceful, clever, and full of ambition, the kind of man who would have made it big in your world. But those talents were not what it takes to make it big in My story. So I went to work on him. I revealed Myself seven times to Jacob, to let him know he needed Me if his life was to amount to anything. He's a good picture of how I change people, slowly, through problems in their lives and failures on their part and an infinite amount of patience and grace on My part.

"Read the story of Jacob and take heart: I can transform anyone into the likeness of My Son. But the process is never easy or short. It took nearly 150 years filled with terrible family problems to change Jacob into Israel, into a man who learned to trust Me in the struggles of life. But I got the job done. I always do.

"I close My first love letter talking about Joseph. As you read what happened in his life, I want you to hear that even people who serve Me well struggle greatly. But never without purpose though the specific purpose will often remain obscure until you're dancing with Me at the eternal party—and you really won't care then. Every moment of suffering you endure is part of the good story I am telling. I don't want you to be surprised when after years of following Me closely, you still run into trouble.

"When you finish reading My first love letter to you, I want you to realize that I never underestimated how thoroughly you'd mess up your life or how painfully you would struggle and suffer, and I don't want you to underestimate your failures or struggles either. They're all part of the story I'm telling.

"But neither have I underestimated My determination or ability to enter the mess you've made and the pain you feel and turn everything around. I can, and I will, make everything good again. Never, *never* underestimate Me. I have a plan, a very good one, and it will move ahead to completion. Guaranteed! Trust Me. Why? Because I love you even when you're messing up badly. I love you in the middle of your pain even though I don't relieve it as quickly as you wish. I am worthy of your trust, no matter what happens in your life. I have a good plan, and nothing will stop Me from carrying it to completion. You must live now in the tension between anguish and hope.

"That's what I want you to hear when you read Genesis."

"God, may I tell You my honest reaction to Your first love letter?"

"Of course! I always want you to be honest with Me. I already know all that is happening inside you, but you will experience My love more deeply when you share your heart with Me."

"Okay, then, here goes! Genesis leaves me confused and frustrated. I really don't get why You killed everyone in the Flood. Did they all go to hell? And weren't the people *after* the Flood just as bad as those *before*?

"You tell me not to be afraid of failure or of pain and emptiness. Well, I *am* afraid, more afraid of my life going badly than of anything else. You tell me that You made me with desires only You can satisfy. Then why aren't You satisfying them?

"I don't think I'm wrong to want satisfaction. You put the craving in me. Are You telling me that my deepest longing is for You, and that I'm to wait until heaven for that desire to be fully satisfied? And in the meantime, I'm to obey and trust You? That's hard!

"I don't think I have the kind of faith Abraham had. I can't bear the thought of losing either of my sons, let alone plunging a knife into one of them because You told me to.

"I do believe I'm a child of promise, like Isaac. I know it's a miracle that I've been born again. But my identity is wrapped up in so many other things than my status as Your son.

"Jacob's life does give me hope. Maybe I will become the person I long to be, but why does it take so long? That frustrates me.

"And Joseph! So much trouble before blessing. Does it have to be like that? And I don't think You even guarantee the blessings I want, at least not in this life. Joseph made it to a throne in Egypt and became a hero to his restored family. I don't think You promised me anything similar.

"God, I don't want to underestimate either my sin and struggle or Your power and love. But I so naturally deny the evil in me and the pain I feel just to emotionally survive, and I have a really hard time seeing Your power and love when so many things go wrong.

"You told me to be honest. God, I'm not really all that warmed by Your first love letter though the promise of restored beauty does stir something deep. I think I need to read more. Thanks for listening."

"I *always* listen. And I'll never turn away from you. Yes, keep reading."

Love Letter Two:
Exodus

YOU MUST KNOW ME TO TRUST ME

*G*od, what do You want me to hear as I read Exodus?"

"Hear this above all:

I will do whatever it takes to carry out My plan!

"I didn't create you to be miserable or empty. My plan was, is, and always will be that you would share My joy. But you got yourself in such bad shape, so far away from Me, that you had no hope of real happiness. I couldn't bear to leave you in that condition.

"So I revealed My *power* by setting you free, My *holiness* by letting you know how you must live to stay close to Me, and My passionate *love* by moving in with you. All of that is in Exodus."

"You've got to help me here, God. If that's what Exodus is all about, why didn't You just say that simply and clearly as You just did, rather than write such a long letter?"

"Listen carefully: until you hear My message wrapped up in the stories of real people, you won't trust that My power could enter your story. And until you imagine what it was like to begin life in the desert by hearing Me lay down laws nobody could keep, you won't feel the crushing weight of My holiness. But you must feel that weight to understand all that's involved in letting unholy people get close to Me. And what's involved is pictured carefully and powerfully in the tabernacle.

"The drama of the first eighteen chapters of My second love letter shows the lengths to which I must go in order to free weak and helpless people from bondage to an evil power greater than themselves. Ask any sex addict what I'm talking about. Or consider it this way: I can and I will detach you from everything that numbs your sacred hunger for Me and makes you feel hungrier for something other than Me.

"But you will never on this earth depend fully enough on My power to live exactly as I want you to live. That's why I had Moses write out the Ten Commandments and all those other rules, not to beat you down into self-hatred over never getting it right, but rather to lift you up into the liberating experience of looking bad in the presence of love. When you read Exodus 19–24 and see how particular I am about all the rules you should obey but never do, let the weight of My holiness draw you into the delights of My love. I still want to be with you.

"Don't ever forget: *I do have a plan*, a plan to make you deliriously happy in the circle of My love. As you read Exodus 25–40 where I record all those architectural details about the tabernacle, realize the lengths I'm willing to go to be with you. Imagine Me, the God of the universe, clothed in splendor and arrayed in glory, living in, by My standards, a simple tent set up in a barren wilderness. Sure, it was fancy, but compare it to what you imagine heaven to be. But that's where I lived, just to be near people like you.

"As you read about the Exodus from Egypt that I made happen, as you consider all the laws I gave that you've never kept, and as you see My willingness to go camping to be with My people, know this: *I will do whatever it takes to fully restore My family and to be with them forever.*"

"God, as You tell me all this, here's what I'm thinking.

"First, I can't get my mind off problems in my life that You aren't doing anything about. And You won't promise to deal with them to make my life better. I think I understand that the Exodus from Egypt is a picture of my being rescued from the kingdom of darkness, but I'm more interested in being rescued from my pain and problems. Maybe that's why I'm not really all that impressed by how You're using Your power.

"Second, I think I've lowered Your standards so I can reach them. Reading all those laws You gave through Moses helps me see how holy and strict You are, but it arouses in me a feeling that I don't like, the feeling that I might as well do what I want since I can't do what I should. I teach about brokenness a lot, but I must not experience it much because I still think I'm entitled to things going well for me or, at least, better than they are.

"And third, I'm having trouble connecting what You're saying in the tabernacle to the pressures and problems I face every day. You tell me that You're with me, but if You know what I'm going through, then why don't You help more? I think I need to keep reading. Right now, I wish the plan You're committed to carrying out were a little different. What am I missing?"

"A great deal. Be patient with how little you know and how slowly you learn. I am. I've written sixty-six love letters. You've read only two. The third reveals what's most wrong with you that blocks your joy. You have more to read, much more to learn."

Love Letter Three: Leviticus

HOLINESS COMES BEFORE HAPPINESS: HOLINESS *IS* HAPPINESS

God, Your first two love letters were at least interesting. You're going to need to really help me with this third one. Why on earth did You write Leviticus when You could have written something more useful, more practical—like how I can get closer to my wife or how I can build up my self-esteem so I don't wrestle with as much insecurity and fear?"

"You must not try to fit Me into your plans. Your plans are too small. You must fit yourself into Mine. Remember, I do have a plan. And it's a good one! I've written Leviticus to tell you one thing:

The toughest part of My plan, the part that's costliest to Me, is to make you holy.

"You want Me to solve your problems, but you don't know what your worst problem is, the one responsible for all the others. You don't yet realize that distance from Me is the most lethal problem you have.

"You assume we're doing just fine together while you run off trying to make life work for you. And you expect Me to cooperate. When you read Leviticus, notice that I never solve anyone's secondary problems. In all those verses about skin infection, for example, I never prescribed ointment or simply cured the disease, which I easily could have done. I simply told people they couldn't enter My Presence with an oozing sore. The issue was worship and intimacy with Me, not health, wealth, or personal comfort.

"All twenty-seven chapters of Leviticus are written to let you know that relationship with Me is *always* the issue that trumps every other concern, and that relating to Me will always, *always*, be on My terms. So many people miss that—they identify their needs, then view Me as a God who wants them satisfied and happy before I deal with their unholiness.

"But because I love them—and you—I've made a way for you to revolve your life around Me as your *first thing*. Everything else—your marriage, your checkbook, your self-esteem, your cancer—is a *second thing*. When the *first thing* (namely, *Me*) is in first place in your life, every *second thing* will be yours to enjoy. And that will be when you're home, not until.

"You've got a long way to go before that's true in your life, but I have a plan to get you there, to make you holy. And that's what Leviticus is all about: the requirement that you be holy in order to be close to Me."

"I think I hear what You're saying. But can You tell me how You say all that in Leviticus? It can be a pretty slow read."

"I really enjoyed writing Leviticus. Every theme in the letter highlights My Son. By the way, He was all through Genesis and Exodus as well. Did you see Him there? He is also in every other Bible book you'll be reading. As you read Leviticus, it's especially important that you not force the book into a tight outline. Just feast on the pictures of Jesus.

"The first theme—*offerings*—is covered in the first seven chapters. They're all about how Jesus is the only way to Me. Think of the *burnt offering* as a picture of My loving Son giving Himself fully to Me on the cross. Let the *grain offering* remind you that Jesus was a perfect man, what I had in mind for every human being to be. He was the perfect person, willingly, voluntarily, gladly offering Himself for imperfect people, to please Me. What a Son!

"And now, because He offered Himself to Me for you, we can get along. I'm no longer mad at you for your sin, and you no longer hate Me. All of that is represented in the *peace offering*. Know, too, that these first three offerings are a sweet fragrance to Me. Every time you celebrate the Lord's Supper, I delight in a special way in My Son's devotion to Me. I love watching you love Him.

"The last two are different. The *sin offering* tells you that My lovely Son became sin. That thought still appalls Me. It's not a sweet fragrance. But the results are incredibly sweet. And the *trespass offering* reflects the value of My Son's death every time you sin. And you still do, every day. Cling to Jesus as you face what you've done, and we will stay in close touch with each other.

"The next three chapters (8 through 10) are all about the priesthood. Aaron is a picture of Jesus. (Melchizedek is a better one. You can read about him in Genesis 14:18–20 and Hebrews 7.) Here's one little detail you might not notice. It's in Leviticus 8. In verse 12, I had Moses anoint Aaron with oil *before* a bull was slaughtered for the sin offering. Aaron's sons were then sprinkled with blood and anointed with oil (along with Aaron) *after* the sin offering (in verse 30). Aaron, a picture of My Son as high priest, needed no cleansing before My Spirit anointed him. Jesus was sinless, no cleansing needed, just Spirit-anointing.

"But Aaron's sons, representing you as a priest in My family, needed forgiveness before I could anoint them. Then, with Jesus sinless and you forgiven, you're both anointed together for priestly work, my Son as the Great High Priest and you as a not-so-great low priest commissioned to draw others into My Presence by the holiness of your life.

"I wrote about that in Hebrews 2:11: 'Both the one who makes men holy and those who are made holy are of the same family.' I love painting portraits of My glorious Son. Leviticus is full of them. Read and worship! Adore My Son! I do.

"Other themes include the need to be *clean*; the requirement that every offering be sacrificed on the *altar* (symbolizing Calvary; only blood shed there by My Son has life-giving power); the provision of *feasts* that would infect people with My holiness as they celebrate Me as their *first thing;* and guidance for living in the *Promised Land* (Canaan), a picture of My plan that you would live holy lives in an unholy world.

"Stay focused on the core message of Leviticus, that My plan is to make you holy, and you'll see My love—and My Son—all through the letter. My Spirit will help."

"Maybe I'm beginning to hear You a little more clearly, God. Let me tell You what happened this morning.

"I woke up with my mind focused on a personal concern. Somewhere in the back of my mind, I could sense that I thought You should be doing something about it that You weren't doing. I was a little ticked. But I had read Leviticus straight through last night before going to sleep. (I think it helped put me to sleep.) I skimmed the verses about split hooves and skin infections, but I read it to hear what You wanted to say to me. And the message came through: *You want me to be holy in any situation more than You want me to figure out what to do to improve any situation.*

"I realized this morning I was trying to fit You into my plans, to use You like I use my car, a vehicle to get me where I want to go. I focused instead on what it would mean to be holy, putting You first, revealing Your character. I thought about the offerings and what they said about Jesus, about my status as a cleansed priest, about how thoroughly clean I am after my bath in Christ's blood, and about my opportunity to dine with You at a feast and to live for You in this frustrating world. The peace that I felt was palpable. The energy was real. I felt alive.

"Well, there are sixty-three more love letters to read. I think I need a break. The first three were a full meal. I'll keep reading but maybe not right away."

"Digest what I've said. When you are ready, I will be here to give you more. Much more."

Love Letter Four: Numbers

Making You Holy Is Hard Work for Both of Us

*G*od, what do You want me to get out of this fourth love letter?"

"You'll hear My Son make the message very clear in Matthew 7:13–14, but I'm saying it now in Numbers, in story form. Here's the message:

You will experience terrible failure and crushing conflict on the road that leads to where I'm taking you, but it is the right road even when it feels like it's killing you.

"In My fourth love letter, I make clear that the road to life is rough. You will begin every new adventure in life with naïve hope and excitement. Every wedding will begin with passion then move into problems. Every decorated nursery will receive a baby that will present unanticipated challenges. Every church plant, every new ministry, every small group that starts with happy hopes—everything you do, no matter how well organized and well intentioned—will run into trouble. If you are in touch with what I created you to enjoy, everything in this life will disappoint you, even the best spouse, the best kids, the best job, the best church, the best vacation.

"And that disappointment will lead you to wonder if you've missed the right road, if perhaps there is a better, more satisfying, less bumpy road through your life. There isn't, not one that leads to real joy. I wrote Numbers to tell you that. The road to life will expose you to terrible failure and crushing conflict. But only *that* road leads to the life you want, the life I give you."

"But God, that's not what I'm hearing from some pastors of really success-ful churches. And lots of books by people who love You teach that the right road isn't nearly as difficult as You're making it out to be. Are they false prophets? Have they missed what You want us to hear in Numbers?"

"Spiritual leaders who teach that I am here to solve your problems and make your lives comfortable and prosperous do what I told you never to do. They underestimate the energy (and badly misunder-stand the nature) of unholiness in the human heart that I must severely deal with to get you to My party. And that underestimation leads them to underestimate the severity of My love. My servant C. S. Lewis got it right: I'm *not* safe, but I am good. I will not coddle you any more than a good surgeon only hugs a cancer-stricken child. I will not coddle you, but I will purify you. And that takes more, though not less, than a hug.

"My fourth love letter begins with My telling Moses to 'number' the people and get them organized for a trip. I ended Exodus when I came to live in the tabernacle. Then for two months (that's the period of time covered in Leviticus), I had the people sit tight while I made them aware that their holiness was My number-one concern. Numbers begins with Moses preparing the people for a trip to joy that would have taken eleven days if they had taken Leviticus to heart and con-cerned themselves more with holiness than comfort.

"More than two million people set out, excited and happy. A short blast on two silver trumpets got them together, then one long blast got them marching. Everything was in place, everyone had a job, just like a happy family driving to Disney World or a growing church meeting for the first time in their new building. From its start-ing point, the road to joy looks smooth as far as the eye can see.

"Did you notice that 603,550 men over age twenty—the soldiers who were to defeat Israel's enemies, protect their women and children, and defend their property—began their march to Canaan with real confidence? *We're on our way. We can do it.*

"But 603,548 of them never made it. They wandered for forty years in the wilderness, and all of them died in the wilderness. Only two of the original bunch, Joshua and Caleb, entered the Promised Land. Do you know why?

"Everyone else was *presumptuous* and *unbelieving*. Read 1 Corinthians 10:1–12 and Hebrews 3:7–19, where I talk about that. My people *presumed* that careful planning, good organization, and the symbol of My Presence (remember the ark of the covenant?) would guarantee good things. They never looked deep enough inside to see what was terribly wrong in their own hearts. Presumption that everything that looks okay on the surface is okay blinds you to your real problem.

"And they wouldn't *believe* I could overcome every problem, the ones inside as well as the difficulties in their circumstances that stood in the way of real joy. So they refused to walk the narrow road of belief that welcomes exposure of failure and conflict, knowing that I have a plan to overcome them.

"Don't be shocked when you read how severely I dealt with them because of their presumption and unbelief. I hate sin, and I will punish sinners. That's part of My plan. But know this: I only kill to resurrect. Everything in you that's bad I destroy in order to release everything in you that's good. And I know goodness is in you, lodged deeper in your heart than badness. I know because I put it there. *It's the goodness of My Son.*"

"God, I just read Numbers again. And after hearing You tell me what You want me to hear in this fourth love letter, I have three thoughts:

"First, having You for their God caused Israel a lot of trouble. I think I can understand why they wanted to run back to Egypt and forget You and Your wonderful plan for their lives. The world's way of thinking assumes life should be more comfortable and much easier. No wonder so many Christians—like me—are drawn to that thinking and try to convince themselves that the ways of the world are okay for Christians to follow if we just 'Christianize' them a bit.

"Second, I really do complain a lot, just like Israel grumbled about their hard life. I do that too. I can sit in a hot tub at a fancy resort and find something to gripe about. That scares me. Maybe You want me scared over how badly I don't measure up to Your standards, so I can understand what Your perfect love casts out.

"Third, when things go wrong in my life, especially my inner life, I easily assume there must be a way to follow You that will make things better. But what I hear You saying in Numbers is that the road to life, to the life I really want, is difficult and long.

"I think I'm getting the idea that trusting and following You is a big deal, the biggest deal of all. That's something I need to remember."

"Yes, you do. And I've written My next love letter to help you do exactly that. Read on."

Love Letter Five:
Deuteronomy

You Fail Me, but I Never Fail You

*T*his one, God, this fifth and final book of Moses, really bothers me. Moses is preaching his last sermon—Your whole letter to me is his sermon—*and nobody gets it!* What do You want me to get out of this love letter?"

"When you listen to men and women who know Me well, people who have been through it all, who have faced themselves and others honestly, who have looked life in the eye and found it bewildering and disappointing, but have still looked toward Me; people who have admitted how confused and troubled they are by how I do things but who through it all have learned to trust Me, these people all say the same thing. And what they say is what I'm saying to you in Deuteronomy. It's what Moses learned through all the trials and blessings in his life. It's what believers down through the ages have learned:

I'm faithful to faithless people. I always keep My word. Believe that, and you will know that through whatever happens I am bringing you nearer to the party. Be faithful to Me, and you'll learn a few dance steps now, right where you are. That's what I want you to hear in My fifth love letter."

"But God, I can't imagine Moses was dancing. You told him that while he was preaching his last sermon, his congregation was already planning to rebel, and that after he died, they would go against everything he said. And I'm not sure reading Deuteronomy will get me dancing either. What confidence can I have that the spiritual direction I receive from books, sermons, and conversations will go any deeper into my heart than it went into the hearts of the Israelites through Moses?"

"Let Me explain Deuteronomy to you. Remember, I unfold My plan slowly. In this love letter, I make three things clearer than in My first four letters.

"First, I am the only true God. There is none other. When you don't like what I'm doing, there is no plan B. That's in Deuteronomy 6:4–5.

"Second, I brought you *out* to bring you *in*. You were locked in the prison of self-centeredness, just as Israel was in painful bondage to Egypt, where all they could think about was themselves—how can we get a better life, not how can we love God. I brought you out of that prison to bring you into the freedom of love. Love has no meaning unless it remains alive when the one you claim to love seems distant and unresponsive. If you love Me only when I immediately satisfy your desires, your love is merely one more form of self-centeredness. Your love becomes trust only when you choose to believe that I brought you out of something bad to bring you into something good *before you experience that something good.* Then your love is sustained by confidence in My character, not by enjoyment of current blessings. Read what I said about that in Deuteronomy 6:23.

"Third, I ask nothing of you but that kind of love, which includes respecting Me for who I am, following Me wherever I lead, serving Me with your whole heart, and obeying every command I give. That's what I asked of Israel in Deuteronomy 10:12–13. And that's what I ask of you.

"But that's asking something neither you nor Israel could give. You are not capable of loving Me like that. I told Israel they needed to cut away all the stubborn self-centeredness that covered their hearts so that they could love Me as I commanded. That's in Deuteronomy 10:16. But they couldn't even do that. So I revealed for the first time

My plan to do it for them. In Deuteronomy 30:6, I made it clear that *I would change their hearts so they could love Me as I asked.*

"Remember how Israel promised to love and obey Me back in Exodus? 'We will do everything the LORD has said.' That was their promise in Exodus 19:8. In Deuteronomy 5:28–29, I told Moses that their intentions were good, but I was deeply grieved that their motives were still self-centered. They wouldn't, they *couldn't*, keep their promise. They needed a changed heart, a circumcised heart where the thick cover of self-centeredness would be recognized, repented of, and cut off. They needed a new heart. But they had no power to provide one for themselves. So I promised to give them one.

"Read Deuteronomy and realize that no one can please me unless I put the life of My Son, who *always* pleases Me, into their hearts. And that's what I promised to do. That's what I have done. I'm faithful to faithless people. Believe that, and know that now you *can* be faithful to Me, not perfectly, but you *can* learn to live in rhythm with My Son, a little more gracefully each day."

"That helps, God, a lot. But can I ask one more question? How did Moses feel when You told him that forty years of faithful service to Israel on his part wouldn't result in faithfulness on Israel's part? I know two pastors, one who served his church thirty years, the other for eleven, and both their churches turned on them. They both got booted out. It's been devastating for them. How was it for Moses?"

"You must see the larger story or the smaller one will make no sense. At times, it will be nothing but awful. Moses was the only person I ever personally buried. And I put him in a private grave that no one could find. Did you ever wonder why I mentioned that in Deuteronomy 34:5–6?

"My plan was that he wouldn't stay there long. Sure, he was discouraged with Israel when he died, and he was disappointed I wouldn't let him into the Promised Land. But Satan knew what I was up to. He knew I had plans to let Moses and Elijah meet My Son when He revealed His glory to Peter, James, and John on the Mount of Transfiguration. That's what My angel Michael was fighting with Satan about: the buried body of Moses. (I mention that in Jude 9.)

"When Moses and Elijah were talking with My Son about the real exodus, about *His* death and resurrection, that put everything in perspective for Moses. What My Son accomplished in the real exodus made it possible for My Spirit to circumcise people's hearts, to incline people to love Me, even when I don't satisfy them, because they have hope in My character. They know I'll get everybody to the party that I invite to come. That's My plan. How do you think Moses felt when he saw My plan and realized the part he had already played in it? He was pretty excited."

"Oh, God, if only what You're saying would get all the way into my heart. If it did, I think I'd be a new person."

"That's My plan. Keep reading."

PART TWO

History Gives Away the Plot: Joshua Through Esther

In the next twelve love letters, the plot more than thickens. It gets heavy, confusing, encouraging, and depressing from one letter to the next. But a theme emerges: *we're in trouble, and God wants to rescue us.* But we can't be rescued until we know we need rescuing and until we know what's so wrong with us that needs rescuing.

As you read this next part of the story, realize that the severity of what's wrong with us only highlights the wonder and enormity of what God must do to move His love story along to its terrific conclusion.

Get ready for a roller-coaster ride. Your emotions will sink to new lows and then rise to new heights. Because we're so out of sync with God's plan, that's what has to happen. But hang on. We're heading toward a high that will never quit.

Love Letter Six:
Joshua

LEARN TO HATE SIN MORE THAN SUFFERING

*G*od, there's so much bloodshed in Your sixth letter. What do You want me to hear You say as I read about Israel entering the Promised Land under Joshua, killing so many of the people already there and then moving into their houses? Is this really a love letter? It sounds more like a call to fight."

"It *is* a call to fight. Loving Me and becoming holy requires that you realize there is an enemy *within* you who will cause you more trouble than all the enemies *outside* you, than even the devil. I want you to fight, but I want you to fight the right battle. Here's what I want you to understand as you read My love letter about Joshua leading the people into Canaan:

Loving Me and being faithful to My plan requires hating everything in you that is opposed to Me, everything about you that wants someone or something besides Me to have first place in your life. You'll need help discerning what that is."

"How do You say that in Joshua?"

"To hear what I'm saying in Joshua, you must avoid two mistakes.
"First, never mistake Canaan for heaven. The Promised Land in

Joshua's day symbolizes the life I promise you *before* you get to heaven while you're still living here. My promise to you when you get to heaven (which, by the way, will be this earth restored to full beauty) is that there will be no fighting, only harmony; no failure, only fullness; and complete joy, your best life forever. My promise to you for now is that you can move toward Me and become like My Son, but it will involve exhausting battle and humbling failure.

"Second, never mistake the enemies in Canaan for only those things that are wrong in the world around you. There is much that is wrong in the world. And you must stand against it. But your worst enemy is in you. And I don't mean the devil. I mean your tendency to want what you want more than what I want and to think that's perfectly okay with Me. It isn't. When I had Joshua kill the terribly wicked people in Canaan, I was more concerned with the tendency in My people to feel attracted to the self-protecting, pleasure-seeking ways of the Canaanites. I wanted My people, whom I chose to be holy, to make no provision for the flesh within them, for that unholy inclination to use Me to make their lives work rather than trusting Me to accomplish My plan of love through blessings *and* hardships.

"I tell Joshua's story in three parts. First, he led the people to *enter the land.* That's the story of the Jordan crossing that I tell in Joshua 1–5. Second, Joshua led the people to *defeat the enemies* in the land, enemies who were capable of no worse evil than My people. That's in Joshua 6–12. And third, he led the people to *enjoy the provisions* of the land, which represent a mere taste of what I have in store for My family at the eternal party I'm throwing. All of that is narrated in Joshua 13–24.

"Notice that entering the land—crossing the Jordan—involved no conflict, only trust. But once in the land, there were battles to fight. Invite Christians to live for Jesus and imply that the Christian life is all about blessings, about entering a land filled with milk and honey with no real battles, and they'll all come forward. Churches that never deal with the real fight that following My Son requires often grow large but mostly with small Christians.

"Defeating their enemies involved conflict for Israel, failure, and the need for discernment, just as it does in your life. Israel had to fight real battles with real swords that shed real blood. Some of the people, like Achan, preferred blessings to battle. That preference led to failure as it will in your life.

"Discernment, too, is hard to come by. Even Joshua mistook an enemy for a friend, a terrible lack of discernment. You can read about that incident in chapter 9.

"And despite Joshua's best efforts, My people sometimes squabbled over their enjoyment of blessings. Pay attention to that. A spirit of entitlement and jealousy will plague you until you die. You'll need discernment to identify it, recognize it as wrong, and know how to navigate your way through it.

"Your leaders, all of them, are imperfect, but you will need them to more effectively fight the real battle, to resist compromise and deception, and to enjoy your blessings without the spirit of entitlement corrupting your gratitude. Substantial victory is available in this life but only with struggles that remain until heaven. That's what I want you to hear Me say in Joshua."

"Well, here's my reaction, God, or at least a strong one that comes to mind. I love the part where, after You told Joshua to circumcise all the soldiers (strange preparation for taking on Jericho) and after all Israel celebrated the Passover, You immediately stopped sending down manna. After forty years of nothing but manna, Your people enjoyed bread and corn, food from the Promised Land.

"It makes me think: if I stay in the wilderness of weak belief and comfort-driven commitment, my food from You will be manna, and I'll want to eat more pleasurable meals that I can get elsewhere. I'll want to go back to Egypt. But if I get serious about radically believing everything You say and really trusting You with my life, if I cross the Jordan and engage my real enemy, then You'll supply the 'rich fare' You talk about in Isaiah 55:2. I've tasted that food, only nibbles, but it is *good*.

"And if I kid myself that I'm really committed to You but refuse to engage the battle going on in me as well as around me, I'll starve, and end up gorging on the cotton candy available in good-enough Christianity.

"God, I want to eat whatever rich food You provide now, knowing it's only a taste of what You'll serve at the party. I think I'll reread Joshua. I want to better understand what battle I need to fight within me and how to go about fighting it."

"Remember that I said your worst enemy is in you. Reread Joshua to better understand that you are in a battle. Then read My next letter to more clearly recognize your worst enemy."

Love Letter Seven: Judges

SIN IS IN YOU, LODGED DEEP

*G*od, life is confusing enough without having to read Judges. The stories are all about people's lives going well for a while, then bad, then they go better, then bad again. And You make it very clear that You're behind it all, arranging the bad times when Your people don't live as You want them to, then bringing in good times when they repent. Is that what You want me to get from this seventh love letter? That if I'm bad, You'll see to it bad things happen in my life; but if I repent and behave well, You'll make things go more smoothly for me?"

"No. My people in Judges never repented."

"Oh? I thought they did, and that's why You blessed them. Well, I have to admit I'm glad to hear You say that being good doesn't guarantee that good things will always happen. That is what You are saying, isn't it? I've certainly seen bad things happen to good people and vice versa. So trusting You to bless me with good things when I live well isn't Your point. I'm glad about that. I couldn't stand the pressure to be good although I would like the control. But living good to have a good life isn't Your point. So what is?"

"I want you to realize that your problem is the same as the problem you can see in My people in all the stories I tell in Judges. Your problem is the same, as bad and as deep. And I want you to see that no system of reward and punishment changes what is so terribly wrong, in you or in them."

"God, I know I'm far from perfect and that punishing me when I'm bad and rewarding me when I'm good, though it seems necessary with little kids, doesn't really change whatever keeps me from being good more often. But I'm not all that clear on what my real problem is. And reading Judges doesn't help. You describe some guy who cuts his dead mistress into pieces and sends her body parts to the twelve tribes and thinks he's communicating some God-honoring message. I can't relate to that. If You want me to see what's so terribly wrong with Your people that's just as wrong with me, I need some help. Will you make it clear in Judges?"

"Do you want Me to?"

"I think so. But as You ask me that question, I feel afraid that I won't be able to recognize what my deepest problem is. Is it sin? Fear? Shame? Insecurity? But I'm even more afraid You'll make it clear. And that I'll be blown away. I guess that scares me because Your track record in Judges of making bad people good is spotty at best. Most everyone got worse. I know You said that no system of reward and punishment changes what's really wrong with people, but it seems to me that You didn't do an especially good job with that approach. You handled Your people the way a weak father might handle a spoiled brat. You kicked them to the curb when they didn't do things Your way, and You did it in anger. And then, when they bellyached loud enough, You gave in to their whining. That approach would make any kid worse. So I'm left with the question: will You really change me? If I face what is so awful about me, will You fix it? And if so, how?"

"I can and I will, in My way and in My time. I AM able."

"God, I know I've got fifty-nine more love letters to read after this, so I don't expect to see the whole picture yet. But what am I supposed to see in Judges? What are You saying to me in this confusing, discouraging letter?"

"Hear this as you read the stories I tell in Judges:

My people never looked deeply into themselves to identify what they most deeply feared. They never realized that there's something worse than a difficult life, than feelings of inadequacy and insecurity, than discomfort and pain. The worst fear they faced was the loss of the blessings that were providing them with comfort and a sense of personal well-being. That's why they paid no attention to Me when life was pleasant. They took Me for granted when their lives were going well. And when life became painful, when their fear of lost blessings was realized, they returned to Me—not for relationship with Me, but only for the good life they believed was their greatest good."

"God, Your love letters are making me redefine the word *love*. You're sure that Judges is a love letter?"

"A physician must convince you that your disease is serious before you'll cooperate with radically invasive treatment. I offer nothing less than heart transplant surgery. That is My plan because that is your only hope.

"I never heal superficially. Many of My people wish I did and think I do. I don't. My plan is to change you from the inside out, to change your *motives*—why you do what you do—and to change your *impact* on people so that how you relate to others will make them thirsty for Me and will draw them into desperate, grateful dependence on Me.

"When you love Me above all else, what you do will bring Me pleasure because your motives, though never pure, will be holy. And when you love others with an authenticity and passion that draws them toward Me, you will feel a little of the pleasure I feel. Yes, Judges is a love letter. Think of it as a disturbingly clear MRI that prepares you to submit to the healing skill of a caring and gifted surgeon who guarantees a good result."

"God, can You tell me how You get all that across in Judges? I read the book, but I'm not sure I heard what You've just told me is there."

"I raised up and supernaturally equipped twelve leaders—I called them *judges*—to rescue My people from misery. But I tell the stories of only six: Othniel, Ehud, Deborah, Gideon, Jephthah, and Samson. Pay special attention to them. Like always, I work through imperfect people to advance My plan until the perfect Man comes. Then I complete My plan.

"You'll notice a weary cycle is repeated with no visible progress. Things actually get worse. My people forget Me because they focus on the good life more than on the One who provides it for them. That's the first stage in the cycle. Then I get angry and take their good life away. That, of course, gets their attention. They remember Me and plead for relief, asking Me to bring back the good life they think is the source of their greatest joy. And that's what I do. I raise up and equip judges, deliverers really, to defeat their enemies and provide My people with the pleasant life they so badly want. Then the cycle repeats itself. After a while, they forget Me because they really don't want *Me*; they want the good life I can give them. Then I become angry, and we go through the whole sequence again.

"Don't make the mistake of overlooking or softening how angry I became. *You must feel My wrath before you will appreciate the extent of My love.* Six times I specifically record that in My anger I took away the good life My people were enjoying. Look it up: Judges 3:8; 3:12; 4:2; 6:1; 10:7; 13:1. But remember this: wrath is not My bottom line. The center of My heart is love. Always has been. Always will be. What I inspired the writer to the Hebrews to say of Me is true: 'God is doing what is best for us, training us to live God's holy best.' That's in Hebrews 12:10 in a version you call *The Message*. And remember this too. *Holiness consists of loving Me and not demanding to use Me as you see fit; and of loving others, of sacrificing your well-being for theirs.* Holiness is your path to joy, the only path. If you grasp that, you'll understand that all sixty-six of My letters to you, including Judges, are love letters.

"I wrote Judges to make this clear: *only when people look deeply into themselves will they truly repent.* My people in Judges never repented. They remained in love with their own sense of well-being, with no understanding that love, real love, the love that defines Me, involves suffering the loss of well-being for the sake of another.

"That lack of understanding is epidemic, not only in culture but in churches today. And it is in you. You and everyone else are inclined to depend on Me for the good life of blessings *and to mistake that dependence for love.* You're more afraid of losing the good life than of losing (or never gaining) a close relationship with Me. You do not yet see that being with Me is your greatest blessing, no matter what else may be happening in your life.

"As long as your terror of misery (which is *not* sinful) drives you above all else to secure the blessings of life for yourself (which *is* sinful), you'll remain unrepentant, distant from Me, and incapable of love. And no arrangement of bad times or good will change you, any more than it changed My people in Judges.

"You wonder how you can read Judges as a love letter and delight in the reading? Do as I do. Keep your attention focused on My Son. Because of Him, you now can love Me rather than demanding to use Me; you can trust My love even when life is unspeakably hard. That's what My Son made possible when the soldiers were pounding spikes into His hands and feet. His motives are now in you. And you can impact others as He did, at least a little."

"God, I guess I do have something in common with the people whose stories You tell in Judges. I really do want to use You to get the life I want. It's so hard to see that my wrong motives can spoil my impact on people. But if that's true, something much more relational must take place between You and me, something different than reward and punishment, something as deeply personal as sex is physical. You've got to get *in* me and pour Your life into mine so that Your motives, the way You love, reach deeper inside me than my sometimes well-disguised motivation to use You. Am I hearing You, God?"

"There's so much more you need to hear before My plan to change you will be realized. Read My next love letter. Through Ruth, Naomi, and Boaz, you'll see a picture of what you could become."

Love Letter Eight:
Ruth

I HAVE THE CURE

*G*od, I'm pretty sure I get the book of Ruth. I think I finally know what You're trying to say to me in one of Your love letters before You tell me. See if I have it right. Ruth is a tender love story about a young woman who, even after her husband dies, sticks with her mother-in-law, who has lost not only her own husband but also her two sons. Then You step in and arrange for Ruth to meet and marry Boaz, a rich relative of Naomi's who solves all Ruth's and Naomi's problems. And because this they-all-lived-happily-ever-after story takes place during the awful days of the Judges, You're telling me to look for divinely arranged beauty in the middle of human ugliness. And maybe, too, You're letting me know that You do get some people out of trouble who, unlike those ingrates in Judges, appreciate what You do and stay faithful to You. Did I get it?"

"Does that message stir you?"

"Well, some. It is a heartwarming, sweet message."

"I never merely warm people's hearts with a sweet message. I penetrate people's hearts and transform them with a true message."

"Okay, I guess I didn't quite get it. So what *are* You saying to me in Ruth?"

"I've told you already that your problem runs deep. You value what I can give you more than you value the privilege and delight of knowing Me and being radically changed by the experience. And you use much of what happens in your life to justify and strengthen your upside-down value system. In the story of Ruth, I'm displaying a profound truth:

No matter what happens in your life, I can reach into your heart with the power to form you into someone who values Me above everyone and everything else. I am determined to reverse your values.

"But You do that slowly, right? I mean really slowly, after long seasons of trouble that make it seem as though You're not doing anything, and that leads people to believe You couldn't care less about all that they're going through. I think I let Ruth's story give me false hope by only seeing a sweet romance where a Cinderella figure marries Prince Charming and a dour old mother-in-law gets a cuddly grandson to keep her happy. I want my story to have a happy ending, too, sooner rather than later."

"My plan has a happy ending, a wonderful finale far better than you can imagine, but the happy ending is only for the holy. I am committed to your holiness at any cost to Me, required by My nature, and at any cost to you, required by yours, and on whatever timetable is necessary. There are intractable obstacles I must overcome to make you holy. I deal with three in Ruth: *natural disadvantages* that to you seem more important to overcome than an unholy value system, *shattered dreams* that bring so much pain into your life that it's difficult to welcome the opportunity they provide for new levels of trust, and *material resources* that make it easy to disguise narcissism behind non-sacrificial generosity."

"God, I don't see any of that in Ruth. Show me how this letter communicates those messages. And please, make them clear. I don't know what You're talking about."

"In different ways, each of these three obstacles to holiness (and a thousand others) keeps personal, radical holiness low on your list of priorities. My power in the human heart overcomes them all.

"*Consider Ruth.* She faced overwhelming disadvantages. Poverty. Racism. (Israel hated Moab. Ruth was a Moabitess.) No job prospects. Widowed. *But she valued relationships over advantages.* With only a beginning sense that I was there, her thirst for relating well led her toward loyalty to Naomi and faith in Me. She made choices that, unless I existed and had a loving plan for her, would have been foolish. No one can value relationships over advantages without faith that I am at work, moving toward a happy ending that justifies present troubles.

"*And Naomi.* When her husband moved to Moab with her and their two sons to find work, she fully expected they would all return to their home in Bethlehem when the economy turned around. Her plan seemed reasonable. Mine, as it unfolded, looked terrible. When her husband and then her sons all died, leaving her alone in Moab with two Moabite daughters-in-law, Naomi was miserable, disillusioned, and broke. Good dreams lay shattered all around her. Unlike Ruth, faith wasn't Naomi's strong suit. *But Naomi never gave up.* A flicker of hope that her problems couldn't smother kept her moving, though with no clear idea that a good plan was unfolding. It was bare naked hope, unreasonable hope, hope with no visible support. She didn't know it then, but the grandson she held in her lap at the end of this letter, Boaz and Ruth's child, became the grandfather of David. And that meant that My Son's human ancestry now includes a Gentile, a Moabite woman no less. My plan to reach all nations was on track. Naomi knows all that now. Unfelt but vaguely sensed and unsmotherable hope in Naomi has matured into joy. No shattered dream can block My plan when there is hope.

"*Finally Boaz,* the star of the story, is a picture of My Son. He had wealth that did not numb his heart, desire for love that made money a second thing, and integrity that refused immoral or illegal movement toward satisfaction of that desire. Boaz was a good man. See in him a faint picture of My Son. My Son was wealthy beyond description but gave up everything to become like you, your kinsman; and He paid the price required by My holiness to be your redeemer. Yes, Ruth's life is a they-all-lived-happily-ever-after story, but it is *not* a parable of My power to make life comfortable; it *is* a parable of My power to make people holy. Know this: holiness and only holiness brings joy. No problem in your life, whether difficult problems such as disadvantages and loss or agreeable problems such as wealth, can stop My plan. Faith and hope together release love. And love is holiness. Hear what I'm saying in this love letter: *no matter how dark the world around you, no matter how difficult the world inside you, My plan overcomes all obstacles to holiness.*"

"God, You're saying more in Ruth than I could ever hear without Your help. But what You're saying still isn't reaching me as deeply as I think it should. There are lots of obstacles to holiness in my life that I can't overcome. When I'm rejected, I really don't care about getting holy. I just want to get away or get even. Or I obsess about what I should do, what would be the right thing to do, and I end up feeling guilty, pressured, and inadequate. And when dreams shatter, my faith seems to weaken more than strengthen; not always but especially when life seems so random, so unfair. And when things go well, I want to keep it that way. I worry more about things going bad than about me going bad. Personal holiness really isn't at the top of my priority list. I wish it were. Or maybe I don't. Any thoughts?"

"Keep reading."

Love Letter Nine:
1 Samuel

THE CURE WILL HURT

God, I can sense that Your story is getting some traction now, that things are starting to work the way they should. I like that, I guess, because I want everything to be in place for my life to move in good directions. After those dismal days of Judges, it seems like it's about time for Israel to catch a break. So what is it You want me to hear in this ninth love letter? I'm hoping You'll tell me how I can move through whatever mess shows up in my life in ways that will lead to better times so that I can see the sunrise. Isn't that what happens to Israel in 1 Samuel? Things go really well for Your people in this letter."

"It is true that 'those who sow in tears shall reap in joy' [NKJV]. Someone who returned home after a long exile in a foreign country wrote those words in Psalm 126:5. But it's also true that only tears from the heart release laughter from the belly. And it's that laughter that I want us to enjoy together. What I want to say to you in 1 Samuel is designed to prepare you for real laughter by deepening real tears. Real tears flow not only *from* your heart, but they are also triggered by what's happening *in* your heart. In this love letter I want you to hear Me say:

When things go wrong in your life, or when you fear they might, you'll be tempted to sacrifice ethics for pragmatism. You'll

hear your heart asking, what will work to make things better? You'll not as clearly hear yourself asking, what is holy in this situation that will please the Lord?"

"God, I have no idea what You're talking about."

"I know. Never expect to hear what I'm saying in My letters as long as you read them with your natural agendas in place. You are more Ptolemaic than Copernican. Claudius Ptolemy, a first-century astronomer, thought the sun revolved around the earth. You naturally assume My agenda revolves around yours. Sixteen centuries later, Nicholas Copernicus realized the earth revolves around the sun. It takes a long time to understand that I am not here for you, but that you are here for Me. It takes even longer to enjoy that arrangement. Come to Me in My letters with all your frustrations, hopes, and questions, but do not come expecting that I will advise you on how best to accomplish your agendas. I have a far better plan."

"God, I really don't get it. No, let me say what I mean: *I really don't get You.* Just tell me what to do so that we get along and things go well, and I'll do it. I promise! Why do You insist on telling me all these ancient stories with messages so hidden I can't even hear them? Sometimes I get so discouraged trying to figure out what You're trying to tell me in all these stories about biblical characters like Hannah, Samuel, Saul, and David that I end up closing my Bible and watching television or catching a movie. Those stories I understand."

"Stories made up *by* people never confront what is most wrong *in* people. They flow in directions you're already moving. And those directions are wrong. The stories I tell convey My message only to desperate people, to people miserable enough to realize that their approach to life is horribly and subtly flawed, who want to overcome their biggest flaw more than they want their lives to go well."

"Maybe I'm there. Not completely, I guess. But I've sort of given up on life.

The more I face what I really want from life in this world, the more I realize that I not only don't have it but that I won't get it no matter how well my life might go. And I think I'm coming to see that evil is not only in the world; it's in me. I'm flawed in a way that keeps me from enjoying what You provide, who You are. So maybe I'm ready to listen without my usual agendas in place. Will You tell me again what You're saying in this letter and how You're saying it?"

"I'm aware that things go wrong in your life, that family and friends don't always treat you well, that nothing goes exactly as you want it to. I grieve with you over the pain that life causes you. But our priorities differ. You ask what will work to make your life better, to correct the injustice you suffer, to see to it that more things go as they should in your life. I want you to ask what holiness would look like in your situation, whatever it is; holiness that might not right the wrongs you suffer but that would let us enjoy each other.

"I tell Hannah's story to make that point. Infertile women typically feel the most joy when they conceive, give birth, and rock their healthy newborn to sleep. Hannah was desperate to bear a child, but she was more desperate to be part of My plan than to enjoy motherhood. She sang her song of joy not when she gave birth but when she gave her little boy Samuel to a higher calling. She had no idea what that calling would be, except that it was part of My plan.

"I tell Samuel's story to let you see how Israel's spiritual leaders, when they saw trouble brewing at the end of Samuel's life, forgot Me—no, they *rejected* Me—and honored their own agenda to make life work according to their own wisdom. They insisted Samuel appoint a human king, a king other than Me, to lead them. They wanted to fit in with the way other people ran their lives that seemed to be working for them. Israel had never had a king other than Me. They were not convinced having Me continue as their king would get them what they wanted. You feel the same way every time you handle tensions with a friend by doing whatever it takes for you to get your way. You reject Me and bow down before the prince of this world as though he were a good king who has your best interests at heart, and you don't even realize that's what you're doing. Pastors do the same thing every time they honor a higher agenda than seeing people become more like My Son. They value efficiency and effectiveness more than love and humility as they build their churches.

"It hurts Me to see My people chase after a lesser good than knowing Me. It disturbs Me to watch them follow so-called proven methods to make good things happen and to value those managerial methods more than the holy and self-denying relating that pleases Me no matter what happens. *You will understand My central message in this letter when you understand the tragedy of asking for a king other than Me.* Following the ways of another may work for a season. It often leads to the shallow and short-lived laughter of pride in an accomplished agenda. Following My ways will lead you through trouble and emptiness to real laughter, to the laughter that only persons in holy relationship can enjoy.

"The story of Saul illustrates what I'm saying. Tall and good-looking, Saul began well. For the sake of My people, I empowered him to win a few victories. But he only heard his heart asking what he could do in the moment to make things go better for him. Even during his last days, he never heard his heart cry out for holiness. The truest words he ever spoke were uttered when he realized David, the man Saul wanted dead, was My choice to be king. To David, he said, 'I have played the fool and erred exceedingly' [NKJV]. That's in 1 Samuel 26:21. My plan does not include having a fool for a king.

"And that's why I complete this letter by introducing David. In Deuteronomy 17:14–20, I announced My intention to honor Israel's desire for a king. Everyone wants someone to follow. My plan centers on a king who wants Me more than the perks of power, a man who enjoys My company more than the pleasures of sex, wealth, or achievements, who surrenders his plan to Mine. David pictures that king. David failed, but he was not a fool. He was a man after My own heart but never as completely as the king I had in mind. When He comes (and yes, I'm speaking of My Son), He will bring in a kingdom that neither David nor Solomon could envision, let alone create.

"That day is come. The kingdom is here, not yet complete, but underway—a kingdom with a king who adores Me, who always does things My way—and a kingdom of people is here, people who have the power never to say 'Give us another king,' people who have the capacity to value My agenda of holiness over their agendas of things working as they want. As you read this love letter and ponder the timing of Hannah's joy, the integrity of Samuel, the flawed personality of Saul, and the heart of David, listen to your heart. Because My Son has come and you now belong to Him, you will hear yourself weeping over how you demand that I cooperate with your agenda, and you'll hear the cry for holiness arising from your deepest center."

"God, now I do feel stirred. And convicted. I get in an argument, and I try to prove my point. I commit myself to following You; then something goes wrong: I feel empty, and I'm willing to do whatever it takes to feel better. What I want, whether You like it or not, so often rules as king of my choices. I want to meet Your King, to see Your Son. Could we skip the next thirty love letters and get to the good part of the story, when Jesus comes?"

"You're not yet ready to hear all that He has to say to you. The scalpel must cut deeper before the medicine will heal. That's why the thirty-nine love letters of the Old Testament precede twenty-seven letters in the New. Don't skip ahead. Keep reading."

Love Letter Ten: 2 Samuel

THE CURE WILL MAKE YOU GREAT

God, I know this might be off track, but I want to mention to You a dream I had last night. I read through 2 Samuel before I turned in, and for some reason that incident in chapter 16 stood out to me where some guy named Shimei yelled at David and threw stones at him while David was running for his life away from his son Absalom. What really got me was how David, feeling all the pain of the son he loved stealing the kingdom from him and wanting him dead, treated Shimei as if he were delivering a message from God. I just couldn't see it that way. I wanted David to beat the guy up.

"Then I fell asleep. In my dream, three sassy teenage boys, maybe fourteen or fifteen, saw me walking by myself and began throwing heavy sticks at me, like cut-up pieces of two-by-fours; and they were yelling that I was a loser, a wimp. I immediately charged them, threw the two smaller ones to the ground, then grabbed the biggest one and made him eat dirt. It felt really good. An hour later, they walked by me, and I reached out my hand to the kid I hurt the most and said, 'I'm sorry. I shouldn't have done what I did to you. I was wrong.'

"This morning when I woke up and remembered the dream, I thought of Pascal's line that true religion accounts for both the wretchedness and greatness of people. And that made me think of the story of David as You tell it in this tenth love letter. He was a really great man who did some wretched things. I have no idea where I'm going with all this, but I wonder if it has anything to do with what You're saying to me in 2 Samuel? Do You still speak to people in dreams? I know You used to."

"I speak into the souls of people. The soul is who you are in My Presence."

"When I read through 2 Samuel last night, I was consciously waiting in Your presence, wanting to hear what You were saying to me. Did I hear something in Shimei's story that went into my soul, something that leaked out in my dream?"

"David was a man after My own heart, but like you and everyone else, he was deeply flawed. And still I gave him My word that I would never remove My loving purpose from his life, as I did with Saul, and that I would see to it his dynasty lasted forever. I felt enormous pleasure telling him that because, of course, I was thinking of My Son bringing in a new kingdom that offered people a new way to live in this messed-up world, a way to live that would characterize people who are on their way to the party. As you read the story of David's forty-year reign over Israel, and as you see what kind of man he was, both wretched and great, hear Me telling you this:

Whether you make those who abuse you eat dirt or you forgive them, whether you fail miserably or act nobly, live with this confidence: I will defeat all evil, both the evil in you and the evil in the world. There will be a party. And you'll be there. So will David. I gave My word to him, and I give My word to you."

"God, I need to hear that. It's so easy to lose that confidence when I see everything going on in the world, with the blatant evil of terrorists and the more subtle evil in churches, and in me. The more I recognize evil and realize that no politician, general, pastor, or therapist can defeat it, the more I need to know that Your plan for the party is on course. Tell me how to read this love letter to hear that confidence-building message clearly."

"The best men cannot defeat evil because the best man born in Adam's line is not good enough. In Ezekiel 14:14, I hold up three men as examples of righteous living: Noah, Daniel, and Job. Noah, the most blameless person in his day, the head of the one family I chose not to destroy in the Flood, got drunk [Genesis 9:21]. Daniel, amazingly faithful to Me in a godless culture, confessed wickedness as a citizen of a wicked nation [Daniel 9:5–9]. And Job, after suffering without cause, repented of his demand that I treat him better [Job 42:6]. Even My best people are flawed.

"David too. But as you read his story, I want you to see glimpses of greatness as well as exposures of evil. Realize that though you still fail, you can advance My plan. See how you could dance at the party now, the way David danced before the ark of the covenant. *Worship!* See how You could bring others to the party as David brought Mephibosheth to his table. *Show mercy!* See how, like David in Israel and Mother Teresa in India, you could change a little corner of your world into a dance floor by living a life of *suffering love,* by extending forgiveness to delinquent boys and cheating spouses and sexual predators. And see, too, how you can spoil the party, as David did, by dancing with the wrong woman.

"I don't want you to miss the glimpses of greatness in this love letter that reveal My Son and let you see what a world without evil will one day look like. Here are four:

"First, David grieved—he didn't celebrate—the death of Saul, the man who tried to kill him [1:17]. *That's a new way to live.*

"Second, David waited patiently in Hebron for seven years as king over only one tribe, knowing I had appointed him king over all twelve. He waited for My time to move to Jerusalem, and he won the allegiance of Israel through godly character, not with manipulation, marketing, or better public relations management [5:1–5]. *That's a new way to live.*

"Third, David invited his enemy's descendant, a crippled man named Mephibosheth whose grandfather was Saul, to regularly eat at his table. Imagine inviting the offspring of the defeated rival for president to live at the White House. *That would be a new way to live.*

"Fourth, when Absalom was killed in battle, after deposing his father David from his throne, David cried, 'If only I had died instead of you' (18:33). Paul spoke similarly about his own people who had rejected him: 'I could wish that I myself were cursed and cut off from Christ for the sake of my brothers' (Romans 9:3). Both men were willing to sacrifice their well-being for another's. Love had found a deeper place in their hearts than legitimate concern for themselves. *That's really a new way to live.*

"Yet David added many women to his harem in direct violation of My instructions in Deuteronomy 17:17. And he did so right after I blessed him [2 Samuel 5:13]. Good times can make you feel entitled to more pleasures. Again, in direct violation of My orders in Numbers 4:15, David imitated the godless Philistines when he transported My ark on a new cart. I had been explicit that only Levites were to carry the ark. When I expressed My wrath, David retreated from Me in anger and fear [2 Samuel 6:3–9].

"I recorded David's adultery to let you know two things: one, great men sin greatly, as all people do, so be alert; and two, when things are going well as they were for David, it's tempting to relax your guard and indulge your desires. David should have been leading his army. Instead, he stayed home, seduced a soldier's wife, and then had that soldier killed to keep it a secret.

"And then, like a rich man committed to his ongoing comfort who checks his stock holdings every day, David numbered his army to reassure himself that he could remain in power. For a short season (and more than once), David valued a comfortable life above a holy life and built his house on sand.

"But I never broke My promise to David. And I will never break My promise to you. *There will be a party, and you're both invited.* That's My message in 2 Samuel. It's the covenant I made with David."

"God, I guess I have a long way to go. If You're telling me that whether I make an annoying kid eat dirt or turn the other cheek I'll still get to the party, I'm tempted to be as good as I can for a while then do whatever feels good when I really want to, knowing You'll forgive me and keep Your plan moving ahead in my life. I know my thinking is off, but I'm not sure how to think right. And I know You won't give me some legalistic spiel about doing what I should whether I feel like it or not."

"Troubles come into everyone's life, whether they behave well or not. But troubles that weaken the soul, troubles that are unnecessary in the life of My followers, are a natural consequence of valuing immediate and shallow pleasures available now over permanent and deep pleasures available later. I'll make that clear in My next four letters. Read on."

Love Letter Eleven:
1 Kings

Do Not Make Solomon's Mistake:
Success Is Not Greatness

*G*od, I've lost interest in reading more of Your love letters, at least, for now. I have a bad cold, my head hurts, and I'm way behind in returning phone calls and answering mail. And just yesterday a woman I care about got beat up by a drunk relative. I think she ought to press charges. She isn't sure. I have another friend who was told he has a month to live, maybe two or three. And he doesn't know Your Son. A married couple I know called this morning to tell me their marriage is stuck in a bad place. They want to talk. And I just got word by e-mail that a friend's pastor seems to be on an ego trip that's putting his church in serious debt.

"Reading 1 Kings right now would feel like sitting through a lecture on ancient history when what I need is a nap, a good doctor, and enough time and wisdom to deal with everything that's being thrown at me. I'm afraid that reading this next letter would feel more like I've been wheeled into the emergency room screaming in pain, and You're the doctor, but You ignore my screams and offer me a book to read on the history of diseases.

"Okay, enough metaphors. I know You get the point. What I don't want to do is read this next letter as some sort of religious duty. I want to hear You talk to me in the middle of my life as it really is, runny nose and all. Look, I know there's a time to take a nap or go to a movie or read another book besides the Bible, but I want to know what to do. My life feels unmanageable right now and not a whole lot of fun. What can I hear You say to me in I Kings that I need to hear in the middle of what's happening in my life?"

"You're making Solomon's mistake. You're in danger of losing your center as Solomon lost his. When that happens, things spin out of control."

"So You really think what You're saying in I Kings is something that could help me with all I'm feeling?"

"What I say always speaks to what you need."

"God, I need to know how to manage my life better so I can deal with head-aches and hurting friends and disappointing pastors in ways that please You and keep me sane."

"That was Solomon's mistake."

"What? You've just lost me. I thought his big mistake was to do his dad one better and have sex with lots of off-limits women. But You have aroused my curiosity. What *was* Solomon's mistake, and what does it have to do with me? And how are You telling me all that in I Kings?"

"There are many things I want you to understand as you read this love letter. The most important is this:

Your desire to be effective, to depend on biblical principles for success in your family, church, career, and friendships, is legitimately strong. But when that desire is stronger than your desire to be holy and to depend on My power for becoming more like My Son, whether you succeed or fail in other ways, then you will not advance My plan, no matter how carefully you follow My principles or how much apparent success you enjoy. And you'll be especially vulnerable to serious sin."

"God, I'm not sure what You're saying, and I'm even less sure how You're saying it in I Kings."

"Read Solomon's prayer for wisdom in chapter 3. Solomon had already seen through his older brother's deceitful attempt to steal the throne that David had promised to him. And he had married Pharaoh's daughter to secure an alliance with Egypt. Solomon was not quite twenty and was running a huge country with no experience. He was facing far bigger challenges than you're facing, and he felt overwhelmed and inadequate. So when I asked him what he'd like Me to do for him, he requested wisdom for leadership. He wanted to effectively rule Israel according to My principles. And that was commendable. *But his desire to be effective in handling, as you put it, all that life threw at him, was stronger than his desire to be holy in the middle of his difficult challenges.* That was Solomon's mistake.

"When efficient management, especially when you're good at it, trumps holy living, the lack of holiness is either not recognized or is not seen as a terribly serious problem. Compromise, including using illegitimate pleasure to relieve stress, feels warranted. People with little concern for holiness often manage their families well, they sometimes lead prospering ministries, and many are successful in their careers. But the center of My plan has nothing to do with well-managed families, ministries, or careers. When the center of My plan is not the center of your hope, your interior world is unstable, and your soul is weakened.

"Consider this: Solomon's priority on power made him vulnerable to the demand for pleasure. The power to manage life well never fills the depths of one's soul. It never provides the deep satisfaction I made you to enjoy. Without the hope of holiness filling your soul, the need to fill yourself with something will lead to compromise that will seem necessary, even wise. Solomon married many foreign women and 'effectively managed' those relationships by giving their false gods a place in Israel's worship.

"It was that one sin, which was fertilized in Solomon's desire for wisdom to make his life work, that split the kingdom. You said you feel sick, your friends are hurting, and a few spiritual leaders disappoint you. Solomon faced challenges too. And because he wanted to manage them effectively more than he wanted to be holy in the middle of them, his success disintegrated. His son Rehoboam, following in his father's foolish footsteps, was more interested in managing his inadequacies than becoming holy, and he ended up a fool. Jeroboam, whom Solomon had appointed secretary of labor, turned against Solomon and led a rebellion that divided the kingdom.

"Know this: prioritizing managerial efficiency over personal holiness opens the door to sin spinning out of control. Jeroboam (who committed that same sin) reduced worship to mere convenience, placing two golden calves within the boundaries of his part of the divided kingdom, telling the people he was making it easier for them to 'get to church' when all he was doing was keeping them from traveling to Rehoboam's territory in Jerusalem and perhaps losing their allegiance.

"Both Rehoboam's southern kingdom of two tribes (which were called Judah) and Jeroboam's northern kingdom of ten (known as Israel) began a downward decline from the glory days of Solomon to terrible days of captivity and exile. The lesson to be learned from the wisest of men who became the greatest of fools is this: *leadership without a priority concern for personal holiness over effective management at best produces only outward success. It fails to engage the real battle in the human soul, between losing your life for Me or gaining your life without Me.*

"I could not let this state of affairs go unaddressed. So I raised up Elijah, an irritating misfit in the religious culture of Israel under Ahab, the worst of all Israel's kings. You must be prepared: if you challenge merely effective leaders by the standards of holiness, you will not be well received. John the Baptist was regarded as strange. My Son was declared a heretic. Follow in their ways. Value spiritual formation above successful management. It might get you killed."

"God, I'm glad I listened to what You had to say in this letter. My nose is still running, my head still hurts, and I don't feel adequate to handle all the problems I see in myself and others. I still want to manage my life well—take mega doses of vitamin C, catch a long nap, respond wisely to all of life's challenges—but I think I'm hearing You. If I'm more concerned with letting You form me like Your Son than managing things well, chances are I'll end up gaining wisdom for both. I guess Solomon would have benefited from what You said through James: 'Consider it a sheer gift, friends, when tests and challenges come to you from all sides. You know that under pressure, your faith-life is forced into the open and shows it's true colors. So don't try to get out of anything prematurely. Let it do its work, so you become mature and well-developed, not deficient in any way. If you don't know what you're doing, pray to the Father. He loves to help' (James 1: 2-4 MSG).

"I hear You promising to give me the wisdom I need, not always to make things go as they should or as I want, but to make me develop as I should and as You want. I'm glad I read Your letter, God. What You've said really does change my perspective. I'm still taking Tylenol though. I think it's a good way to manage my cold."

"Your changed perspective is good. Read on."

Love Letter Twelve:
2 Kings

FAILURE IS AN OPPORTUNITY, NOT A DEFEAT

*G*od, reading Your letters feels like riding a roller coaster to nowhere. Your story about David lifts me high, then when he falls, I go down too. Is that what life is like for people who follow You? Solomon brings in glory days then becomes the cause of civil war with his sexual addiction. And then You write 2 Kings. God, this is Your most dismal letter since Judges. What are You trying to say?

"Wait. Before You tell me, let me say this. It just occurred to me. The division of Your people into north and south, the northern ten tribes of the kingdom of Israel and the southern two tribes of the kingdom of Judah, makes me think of the American Civil War. Except there's no Abraham Lincoln. God, where are the heroes? Where's the next Joseph, the next Moses, the next David? If the story You tell in 2 Kings is meant to be some sort of prophecy of how my life will turn out, then reading it makes me feel like I'm going down in quicksand. I can't find a rock to stand on."

"He's coming."

"I know You said You have a plan. But all I can feel right now is swallowing sand beneath my feet. That had to be how Israel felt."

"No one finds the Rock until they sink to the bottom."

"Are You *wanting* Your people to feel really bad?"

"My people must be crushed into hopelessness and helplessness by realizing that they are being swallowed up by evil. Any thought that without Me they can escape from the pit into which they have fallen will keep them depending on themselves, not Me. Very few in any age, even among My followers, have faced the presence of evil within them. When My servant Aleksandr Solzhenitsyn returned to his Russian homeland after a season of forced exile, he was criticized for meeting with former leaders under the evil Communist regime. With wisdom that is largely lost in today's church, he told his critics that the line between good and evil does not run between us and them; it runs through each one of us. He recognized that the saintliest among My people has more in common with Stalin than My Son. I wrote 2 Kings to help you understand the lethal nature of the evil that is in My people and for you to tremble before its power to ruin your life."

"Is there any *good* news in 2 Kings?"

"The sweetest song is sung in the darkest night. As you read this letter of love hear this:

My plan is moving ahead in the worst of times. Don't make it your goal to change bad times to good. Pray for that, of course, and do all you can to improve the world in which you live. But above all else, seek to know Me better and to represent Me well in every circumstance, no matter how you feel."

"Once again, God, I didn't hear anything like that as I read this twelfth letter of Yours. Show me how You get that message across in 2 Kings."

"Remember that My letters combine to tell an epic story. The plot unfolded when evil entered the human soul in Eden. You must understand the deceptive nature of evil. It hides itself and does its destructive work slowly, beneath the disguise of necessity, reasonableness, efficiency, pragmatism, even morality, even goodness.

"Evil, the rebelliously foolish conviction that without living for what *I* want you can dance in the happy rhythm of life, is now the second strongest force in the universe, an almost personal power that is in the bloodstream of every human soul but one. Let Me repeat Myself: very few people, even in the church, believe that. And yet it's true. Unless I intervene, creation itself, along with every person ever born to Adam and Eve, will be carried captive into the isolating power of evil.

"But I have a plan, a plan to restore the beauty of Eden, a plan to create a community of men and women who live their lives in rhythm with My holiness, who dance with Me into joy.

"I chose Abraham to begin that community. He was to draw others to the party by the joy of the dance. He succeeded, but he also failed. I knew he would. He was My friend, but he was not My Son.

"Through Jacob, I formed Abraham's descendants into a nation. When David became king (My choice after Saul, the people's choice), I promised him that through his bloodline would come a righteous king, a man in whom evil would find no foothold.

"But until He came—I am referring, of course, to My Son; He is always My heart's delight—I would permit the power of evil to run the world. Only as My people felt its crushing power would they be humbled enough to hear the good news My Son would bring. My plan was to release evil, though containing it within boundaries that I set to guard My purposes until it gathered its full force in an attempt to ruin the life of the Man in whom I would place all My hope. When you understand My plan, you will tremble as you stand on Mount Calvary, knowing what happened there.

"In the story of My people—as you see first Israel destroyed, then Judah captured—notice this; I make it clear in 2 Kings: *every king who reigned in Judah, good or bad, was from the line of David*. The source of evil, My archenemy, did all he could to destroy that line. He knew (because I told him) that I planned to destroy him through a descendant of David. But not even Satan can stop My plan. *The line of David continued*. My Son was on His way.

"Even when Jehoram became king of Judah and severely grieved Me as he yielded to the force of evil within him, for the sake of My servant David, I was not willing to destroy Judah. *I had promised to maintain a lamp for David and his descendants forever.* You can read about that in 2 Kings 8:16–19.

"And notice Manasseh, the most evil and longest-reigning king of Judah. Only My heart of love endured the length of his wickedness. When I had My fill of him, I sent him off into terrible prison conditions under Assyria's brutal military. But Manasseh, unlike most people in whom evil has taken over, humbled himself greatly. Read about My forgiving love extended to Manasseh in 2 Chronicles 35:10–20. When you find yourself overcome by evil, take heart. Repentance leads to restoration. Manasseh finished his life dancing in My rhythm. He's with Me now.

"Read this love letter and know this: *evil is real, and it is in you.* Evil promises life and delivers death. It destroys everything worth living for. Under its influence and in consequence of yielding to it, My people sank deep into misery, as all people and nations will who value prosperity above holiness. *But I have a plan.* The power of evil cannot stop it. Read this love letter and be filled with hope: the line of David was preserved."

"God, what You're saying is so countercultural, even in the church. We talk more about wounds and the promise of therapy. We see people as more insecure than bad and affirm them to build their self-image. And some self-righteous fanatics, moral idiots really, speak out against sin in others as if it isn't their problem. Uh, I guess I do that too.

"But I hear You telling me to pay attention to how terrible and deep within me is the reality of evil. And You make it painfully clear in 2 Kings that evil unadmitted, unchecked, unforgiven, and unchanged leads eventually to soul-shattering misery, always. As I now read 2 Kings, hearing at least a little of what You're saying, I want to sit down with Jeremiah and cry like an abandoned baby as together we watch even Judah be carried off into Babylonian captivity: 'How lonely sits the city that was full of people' [NKJV]. As I just read those words in Lamentations 1:1, I think I caught a glimpse of the horror of evil and what it can do. It's enough to make me lose hope in Your plan. Don't leave me here!"

"I don't. My next two letters were written to restore confidence in My people that their feet will one day stand on the Rock. So will yours. Keep reading."

Love Letter Thirteen: 1 Chronicles

EMPTINESS NOW, FULLNESS LATER; THAT IS A PROMISE

*G*od, reading this love letter feels like watching a rerun on the History Channel with an hour of credits at the beginning. Those first nine chapters of genealogies provide all the reading excitement of a phone book. And then, in the rest of 1 Chronicles, You tell the same story about David that You already told in Samuel and Kings. Is there anything new You're wanting me to hear in this somewhat tedious retelling of David's story? And do those endless lists of names I can't pronounce have any relevance to where I am in my life?"

"Where are you?"

"Huh?"

"Where are you? What is your experience of yourself, life, and Me at this moment? It's the same question I asked Adam some years ago."

"Well, let me think a minute. I guess I'm feeling a little unbalanced right now. Too much work, too little play. So many people are struggling, so much is wrong, so many conflicts and tensions. My life at this moment feels like jumping into a deep cesspool with one can of deodorant. I do my best, and things are still a foul-smelling mess. And to be honest, I don't see You doing all that I hoped You would. A week in Hawaii sounds really good right now. Maybe a year."

"My people were feeling the same way, discouraged, tired, wondering if I'd abandoned them, wanting more pleasure and satisfaction out of life. I wrote 1 Chronicles to encourage them, to give them the hope they needed to return to the narrow road and stay on it. My message then to them, and now to you, is this:

You cannot now enjoy what you once did. The satisfactions of earlier days are no longer available. Life feels empty. Not much is fun. I invite you to delight in your distress. Nothing else provides the same opportunity to move strongly and joyfully into life on the basis of My promises alone, the promises of My Presence now and My satisfaction forever. Seizing that opportunity will free you to passionately engage life for My purposes with no demands."

"You're saying *that* in 1 Chronicles? Where? How? I don't see it."

"You don't see it because you expect that My letters will be immediately relevant to your desires for a balanced, fulfilling, and satisfying life. You underestimate the obstacle your unholiness presents that I must overcome before you can live the life I want you to live. Because you read My letters with the demand that your emptiness be filled now, you do not see what you truly desire, nor do you thrill in My promise to lavishly satisfy that desire in the next world, beyond what you can now imagine. I'm right now preparing your place at My party. But you are out of touch with those desires that cannot be satisfied till then. You, therefore, reduce My letters to practical tips for satisfying lesser desires now."

"God, I don't want to change what You're saying into what I foolishly want to hear. I know I do that, but I don't want to. I really don't. Tell me what You're saying to me in these genealogies and in this version of David's story."

"You spoke correctly. This is a different version of the story than before. You will not grasp the significance of the differences or, perhaps, even notice them until you realize this: *I am writing to My people in a specific time and in specific circumstances, a time and a set of circumstances that were different from when I wrote to them in Samuel and Kings."*

"God, I need some help here. Once again, I don't know what You're talking about."

"I wrote My earlier four letters soon after My people were carried into exile, forcibly taken from their homes, and relocated in a foreign country under a godless king. Like you, when things go wrong in your life for which you can see no purpose, My people cried, 'Foul!' They felt mistreated, victims of a fate they didn't deserve. They saw themselves as decent people entitled to a better life that I should provide. Because they couldn't fathom that My love had a purpose in mind far greater than their present comfort, they listened to smiling preachers who told them I could be persuaded to turn things around for them before I made them holy.

"In the four letters I wrote to them at that specific time and in those specific circumstances, I detailed their history of moral failure: Saul's weak character, David's unthinkable evil with Bathsheba and Uriah, plus all David's family problems. I recorded Solomon's descent into the emptiness of the good life and his foolish effort to satisfy himself with godless women who led him to honor their godless gods. His ego and lust split the kingdom. I then underlined the evil nature of every king who ruled Israel (the Northern Kingdom) as well as the general spiritual decline of Judah under the nineteen men, some good, most bad, who sat on David's throne.

"My message to those people, in that time, in those circumstances, and with that attitude, was clear. It was a message of hard and humbling love: *You are not entitled to the good life. Stop whimpering as if you deserve what I am not providing.* That is what I still say to people whose resentment over suffering is keeping them from flowing with grateful hope in the stream of My plan."

"But aren't You saying the same thing in 1 Chronicles?"

"No. In Chronicles, both letters, I am writing to My people in a different time and in different circumstances, and I tell the same story differently to make a different point. In 1 and 2 Samuel and in 1 and 2 Kings, I am writing to the *exiled* community. In 1 and 2 Chronicles, I am writing to the *restored* community."

"God, I'm not tracking with You yet."

"Listen carefully. When My people were released from captivity and permitted to return home, they arrived in Jerusalem with one mandate: to *rebuild the temple*. But they had no king, no homes, and limited resources. They were strongly tempted to organize themselves with the wrong priority in mind, to *rebuild their lives*. I told them to first *rebuild the temple*. I understand—and you do as well—how emptiness and hardships can lead people to redefine worship as living right in the hope that life will go right. But I want My people to live right now for the joy of knowing Me and in anticipation of what I yet will do.

"Even when life is so barren and troubled that the demand for relief seems justified, I want My people to know this: *in spite of appearances, the former days of Solomon's splendor are as nothing compared to the glory days ahead.* When you find yourself in the desert, draw near to Me, not with an entitled spirit but in confident hope. You will discover that hope only in My Presence. Therefore, devote your *first* energies to rebuilding the temple, not your lives."

"I think I'm with You now, God. But exactly how are You saying that in 1 Chronicles?"

"To the exiled but still proud community, I underlined sin. To the restored but discouraged community, I aroused hope. All hope centers in My Son. I point to Him through every difference in this version of David's story. Let Me give a few examples. You can find more if you look for them.

"In the Chronicles, I make no mention of David's seven-year wait in Hebron before I seated him on the throne of all Israel. *When My*

Son returns to sit on David's throne, there will be no delay. Every knee will bow, immediately and forever. You will discover that hope in the temple.

"In 2 Samuel, I record David's sin with Bathsheba in shameful detail. In 1 Chronicles, I say nothing about it. I rather present David as a man after My own heart, as an almost-in-focus picture of My coming Son, *the only Man whose heart was fully toward Me, the King in whose heart I find My greatest delight. The perfect King is coming.* You will discover that hope in the temple.

"David's family troubles—incest, murder, rebellion—are detailed in the earlier version of his story and passed over in this one. Again, the difference points to My people's great hope: *when My Son rules from David's throne and My people are themselves My temple, Satan will be banished to eternal darkness, and the kingdom of light—no problems, no pressures—will bless the world, forever.* You will discover that hope in the temple.

"Even the two sins of David that I do mention in 1 Chronicles reveal the hope that My people will discover only when they rebuild the temple. When David repented of transporting the ark of the covenant on a new cart—I had given specific orders that the ark be transported only by Levites—he understood that worship must be carried out My way, not according to cultural fashion or practical expedience. You can read the story in 1 Chronicles 13 and 15:1–2.

"And David's punishment for counting his soldiers, which indicated a proud dependence on his military strength rather than a humble dependence on Mine, led him to repentant worship on the exact site where the temple would be erected. I tell that story in 1 Chronicles 21. But you must read and underline the first verse in chapter 22. I recorded both sins to show the restored community that everything, even their failures, points them to the priority of putting Me first in their lives. *My Son made that possible. He is your ticket to the party.* You will enjoy that hope only in the temple."

"God, something I knew has just taken on new meaning. *I'm the temple!* You want me to become a worshiping person at any cost, to live as You direct, in my relationships and business decisions, whether it seems effective or not in making my life more fulfilling or prosperous. Am I hearing You?"

"Yes, but you must hear Me every day. This message is easily forgotten. When you feel empty tomorrow, when life's troubles and disappointments continue, you will again be tempted to devote more energy to making your life better than to drawing closer to Me. It is not easy to practice the priority of rebuilding the temple over rebuilding your life. And it's difficult even to know when you're violating it.

"And one more thing—a word about the genealogies that you found so dull. The restored community found them invigorating. I traced their ancestry back to the beginning of My plan, starting with Adam, down through Noah, Abraham, Isaac, and Jacob, all the way down to the names of the remnant that I preserved and who were now gathered in Jerusalem. And that remnant included all the people necessary to worship Me in the temple as I had directed. They knew they were part of the plan. I want you to know that too. Because of My Son, you're now in the family. You're coming to the party. You will discover and enjoy real hope only in My Presence. *Rebuild the temple.*"

Love Letter Fourteen:
2 Chronicles

REAL TRUST DEVELOPS IN THE DARK

*G*od, what You're saying is getting more and more difficult to live. No matter what happens in our lives—tornadoes, divorce, cancer, whatever—You want me to think more about how I'm relating to You and others than about how to get my life together. And You want me to look deep inside, into my motives, to see if I'm really looking out for myself when I think I'm living for You. Am I hearing You?"

"Yes."

"Well, that message doesn't sit too well with me when I see real tragedy. I was just watching a television report about a little girl in Jerusalem, maybe six or seven years old, who was severely hurt in a recent bombing. She's going to spend the rest of her life in a wheelchair, unable to move anything below her neck and incapable of coherent speech. The family's enormous medical expenses will be covered for a few months and then, as the announcer said, 'Who knows what will happen to her after that?'

"God, I wanted to scream; I think I wanted to scream at You. If I had the power to fix her life, to see her running around a schoolyard and laughing with her playmates, I'd use it. I'd give her back to her parents as a healthy, happy little girl. You have that power, and You do nothing. Would You *really* tell her brokenhearted parents to think more about worshiping You in the temple than doing all they can to make life better for their daughter? I know that part of worshiping You is taking the best possible care of family and friends, but why should they love You when You could cure their child but don't?

"God, are You there?

"God, answer me, please. I know I'm out of line, but I don't know how else to think."

"My heart breaks as I watch that little girl. I created her to dance."

"Then do something about it!"

"I have. I AM. I will."

"God, I just don't get it. *Explain Yourself!*"

"I owe you nothing. I give you everything. Your desire to fix things, to relieve suffering, to confront injustice, to heal wounds, to end poverty, and to generate joy is commendable. But your desire is too weak and misguided. If I were to fix all you see that is wrong and painful without first destroying evil, no one would dance at My party. No one would want to. In My plan, I must do whatever is necessary to destroy the evil within your depths, where you desire the good life more than you want Me; and I must replace that idolatrous desire with the holy yearning to know Me at any cost in the midst of your worst pain. Only then will eternal joy be possible for that little girl and for you.

"For reasons you have no capacity to understand, I must allow suffering that serves no visible purpose. What I can tell you is this. Listen well. There is an evil greater than bombs, tsunamis, and cancer. Those are *natural* evils. But when people live to get their own way, when they determine what is good for them and live to get it, all hell breaks loose within and between them. Greed, loveless sex, frenzied grabs for happiness with no concern for how others are impacted, more interest in making one's point than listening to another's, an inability to give or receive love, the vicious habit of depersonalizing everyone into a rival, ugly parodies of community-like courtesy without connection, laughter without love, weeping without worship—these are *moral* evils, savage beasts that rise out of the evil sea of willfulness, the demand in everyone's heart to make their lives work [Galatians 5:19–21 MSG; Daniel 7:3].

"Only when you see the moral evil in the human heart will you surrender to the mystery of My plan. In this world, I am destroying moral evil in My people. In the next, I will eliminate natural evil. You are struggling to reconcile the tragedy in that little girl's life with My love. You must trust that I permit such terrible things, natural evil that grieves My heart far more than yours, as part of the process of destroying the moral evil that offends My heart. Do not assume I am punishing that child. In ways you cannot understand, I have the power and wisdom needed to move My plan forward through the evil of bombs and the injustice of suffering."

"God, I guess I hit a hot button. Is any of this in 2 Chronicles?"

"This is what I'm saying to you in My letter you call 2 Chronicles:

No matter how great your pain or how confusing and intense your suffering, live in the mystery of My love. Struggle to trust Me. Do not live with the priority of making your life in this world as good as you can make it. You will suffer, at times unfairly, but you will be given what you need to enter strongly and wisely with supernatural love into every circumstance you face, including a beloved child in a wheelchair. Doing so will be your joy, your hope, and your deepest fulfillment now as you look forward to a world where every child runs and laughs."

"God, how are You saying all that in this letter?"

"Once again, compare how I tell My people's story differently in 2 Chronicles than in 1 and 2 Kings.

"The first nine chapters in this letter focus on Solomon's work to build the temple. It was a magnificent structure. All Israel celebrated

My glory. As My people who were now back in Jerusalem after their long captivity read this history, I was awakening their appetite for the glory yet to come. The splendor of Solomon is nothing compared to the splendor My people will celebrate when a king greater than Solomon takes the throne. By remembering Solomon, My people felt their emptiness in a desolate city; they longed for a satisfaction that only My Son can provide. Suffering is necessary until evil is finally banished. Suffering opens the holy space in your soul that will be filled only when you're dancing with Me at My party. I want My people, you included, to persevere through suffering with the hope of full satisfaction when My Son sits on David's throne and with occasional tastes of that satisfaction now.

"Notice that in this letter, unlike 1 Kings, I mention only one failing in Solomon. It began when he married Pharaoh's daughter to secure an alliance with Egypt that he did not need. You do the same thing every time you indulge in sexual fantasy or try to control how another person treats you. You are looking out for yourself without entrusting your soul to Me, just as Solomon was protecting his kingdom with his own maneuverings. Like you, Solomon knew he was doing something wrong. And again like you, he disguised his compromise in religious clothing—listen to what he said: 'My wife shall not dwell in the house of David king of Israel, because the places to which the ark of the LORD has come are holy' (8:11 NKJV). Solomon was kidding himself, thinking that if he could keep sin at a safe distance, he'd be able to enjoy the pleasures of compromise without cost.

"It wasn't long after that well-disguised compromise that Solomon built places to worship the false gods of the many godless wives he later married, and he built them nearer to Jerusalem. See what I recorded in 2 Kings 11:7–8 about that. I want My people to know this: *if even in small ways you live to 'fix your life,' to arrange for your own pleasure in ways that violate holiness, your love for a better life now will eventually corrupt your love for Me.*

"In this letter, unlike 1 and 2 Kings, I offer no record of the kings in the Northern Kingdom. They were not worth mentioning to My discouraged people because I found nothing in them that reminded

Me of My Son. And in telling the story of the kings of the Southern Kingdom, I emphasized not their military or economic strength but the longing of certain kings for *holiness in the temple*:

❁ Asa did what he could to eliminate false worship [2 Chronicles 15].
❁ Jehoshaphat led My people in temple worship when enemies threatened them [2 Chronicles 20].
❁ Joash, in his earlier days, displayed great zeal in repairing the temple [2 Chronicles 24].
❁ Hezekiah's resolve to live holy in the temple merited three chapters [2 Chronicles 29–31].
❁ Josiah, after discovering My long-neglected instructions for worship, led My people in the greatest Passover ever celebrated [2 Chronicles 34–35].

"What I am saying to you in this letter is hard to hear, even harder to live, but it is vital. I can restate it this way: *don't look for experts to coach you in how to make your life work before you follow elders who will lead you into My Presence.*"

"God, Your instructions are difficult to follow, especially when life is difficult."

"My instructions are impossible to follow."

"Then why do You give them?"

"To prepare your heart to hear My Son. He delighted My heart by following every instruction perfectly, and He did so for your sake. It was part of My plan. My first thirty-nine letters will create space within you that only My Son can fill. Keep reading. I have a plan for you and for that little girl in Jerusalem."

Love Letter Fifteen:
Ezra

I Am Here: I Will Make You Holy and Whole

God, I just finished Ezra, and as I was reflecting on what I heard You saying in this letter, tears began flowing from depths within me I rarely reach. I loved Your phrase in Ezra 6:22: You 'plunged them into a sea of joy' (MSG). That's what I felt You were doing for me. I couldn't stop crying over the hope of actually dancing with You, of feeling the same delight directed toward me that You feel toward Your Son, and of passionately inviting others to the party. I'm not sure what caused this epiphany, but I think I realized how low You had brought me through Your first fourteen letters only to lift me in this one higher than I ever thought possible. In a new way, I understood what my father once told me: 'Sometimes I'm so overwhelmed by what God is pouring into me, I wonder if I should ask Him to shut it off.' God, would You put into words what You're saying in Ezra that plunged me into this sea of joy?"

"You are sharing in the joy I felt as I wrote this love letter to you. What My Son makes possible delights Me to the core of My infinite being: *you will join My party.* You are far more precious to Me than the person you love most on earth is to you. In the book of Ezra, I reveal more of how My plan is underway to release you so you can dance to My Spirit's rhythm. What I am saying, and what you are beginning to hear (thanks to My glorious Spirit), is this:

❀ I will do whatever it takes to release your heart to delight in Me.

❀ I will move in the hearts of ungodly people to serve that purpose.

❀ I will arouse your heart to enjoy worship more than any other blessing on earth.

❀ I will permit strong opposition to oppress you as you walk the narrow road to the party.

❀ At times you will fail—you will choose the easier road that leads to immediate satisfaction; but I will break your heart over your movement away from Me, and I will stir you to ongoing radical repentance.

❀ I will complete the life-giving work in your heart that I have already begun.

❀ You will dance with Me at My party."

"God, I so badly need to hear this and to believe it in the core of my being. After nearly sixty years of following You, I still am influenced, sometimes ruled, by fears that Your love hasn't yet cast out. I so easily violate love for others by relating with my well-being more in mind than theirs. I so often see people as opportunities for me to feel fulfilled rather than opportunities for me to relate with the secure unthreatened love of Jesus. And that depersonalizes them into useful objects that I either appreciate or despise. But when I'm swimming in that sea of joy, *I can love! I'm free!* Please, God, let me hear You speak clearly in this fifteenth love letter."

"You will need a little background to hear Me well in Ezra. Never underestimate the value of *studying* My letters before *meditating* on them. The impact will reach deeper.

"In Jeremiah 29:10, I spoke into the future (which is always *now* to Me) and declared that Babylon would be the dominant world power for seventy years. I did *not* say that My people would be in exile for seventy years. From 606 BC until 536 BC, seventy years, Babylon ruled the civilized world. My people were exiled in 587 BC and returned to Judah in 536 BC, after an exile of fifty-one years. Knowing that bit of history lets you see that older people in their seventies who had seen Solomon's temple before it was destroyed could be (and were) part of the fifty thousand Jews who made the five-month journey by foot from the land of exile to the land of promise.

"I stirred the heart of Cyrus, ruler of Persia when the Medes and Persians united to overthrow Babylon in 536 BC, to release My people to return to Judah with clear instructions to rebuild the temple. I did so by seeing to it that Cyrus read My words through Isaiah where, *two hundred years before Cyrus lived,* I specifically named him three times as the ruler who would release My people from exile. Read these occasions in Isaiah 44:28; 45:1; and 45:13. Learn this: *no matter who is in power in governments across the world, liberals or conservatives, tyrants or compassionate leaders, I not only will prevent them from blocking My ultimate plan but also will use them when and how I choose to further My plan for your life. Celebrate My power. It guarantees your coming to the party.*

"Now, with that background for this letter that was written to My people after the temple was rebuilt in the restored community, you will better hear what I'm saying to you in Ezra. In its first six chapters, I tell the story not of Ezra but of Zerubbabel, whom I chose to lead fifty thousand people back to the land years before Ezra returned. Then in the last four chapters, I tell the story of Ezra—a student of the Scriptures—who led another few thousand Jews to Judah to remind everyone of My primary concern for holiness over prosperity or pleasure. As you read this letter—better named Restoration to the Narrow Road—and as you imagine yourself reading it as a Jew living in the not-so-glorious post-exile days in the land of promise, hear this: it will again release tears of hope in you as I intended it to do in My people.

"Although My people continued to fail, they never again returned to the blatant idolatry of worshiping false gods. *You can come to love Me enough in this life to want Me above all else.*

"The first group of returned exiles was restored to the Promised Land. All movement toward holiness begins from that place. *You, too, are always free to come back to the promise of the gospel, no matter your suffering or failure, to the promise that one day, as holy and happy people, you will dance at My party, forever.*

"As soon as My people were settled in the land of promise, they rebuilt the altar, and they rebuilt it on the same site where the original altar had rested. The altar of sacrifice symbolizes 'yieldedness' to Me. *To return to the narrow road, you need only surrender your will to Mine. Like the Jews, you have seen often enough what happens when you insist on your own way.*

"Four months later under Zerubbabel, My people began to rebuild the temple, the witness to the world that I am with My people to make them holy. Know this: *I leave you in this world, not to retire comfortably but to draw the people in your sphere of relating to Me by the power of your holy, radically self-sacrificing, other-centered love. You are here to live the new way, to draw close to Me in order to be formed into the likeness of My Son.*

"Opposition to rebuilding the temple came quickly, first through an invitation to compromise [4:1–3], then through threats of disruption [4:5], and finally through legal action [chapter 5]. The opposition was effective. Work on rebuilding the temple 'came to a standstill' (4:24). *You, too, will face opposition where the battle to be holy will become so difficult and the narrow road so steep and tough that you will leave the narrow road for a season.* And as my beloved and for so long troubled servant John Bunyan described in *Pilgrim's Progress*, you will take the broad, more comfortable road through 'bypath meadow.' But know this: I will not leave you there!

"I raised up and empowered two prophets, Haggai and Zechariah, not to remove opposition but to exhort My people to keep building in the face of opposition at great personal risk. When life gets rough and a detour through bypath meadow seems reasonable, listen to the faithful men and women who urge you to remain in the battle for holiness no matter how difficult or dangerous.

"My people returned to building, and the temple was completed. Draw courage from this history. I will strengthen you to fight the good fight and to finish well. You will make it to the party. It's My plan.

"Zerubbabel labored for twenty years. When Ezra arrived, sixty years after Zerubbabel's work was completed, many of My people had grown complacent about holiness and were eager for pleasure. They had wandered off the narrow road by marrying foreign women and 'mingled the holy race with the peoples around them' (9:2). And the leaders of My people led the way in their unfaithfulness.

"Hear this: You must remain alert to compromised spiritual leaders who entice you more with the hope of blessings than with the promise of holiness, who lead you to think that My love makes Me more concerned with your present comfort than your eternal joy. Resist them. Leave their churches. Do not attend their conferences or read their books.

"Ezra was deeply distressed by My people's compromise more than by their troubles. His burden for holiness led to tears of repentance and to his refusal to eat or drink as he grieved My people's evil. When they saw the distress of this godly man, My people came together in brokenness and stood in a rainstorm that spoke of My distress over their actions. Radical repentance followed, painful, costly repentance under Ezra's leadership. *There is always a way back from sin. Tears of hope will flow every time you experience My loving mercy when you fail. I still love you. I will not give up on you. I have a plan.*"

"God, I know more failure lies in my path. But as I get to know You better, I find myself focusing more on You and Your plan than on me and my failures. My heart is swelling with gratitude. More tears are arising from my depths."

"Your battle continues but now with hope. Keep reading. Hope is never properly anchored until it is grounded in My Son."

Love Letter Sixteen:
Nehemiah

REMEMBER, SMALL OBEDIENCE IS A GREAT WORK

"Well, God, I think I've come down from the high I felt as I read Ezra."

"It was not a high. It was a glimpse."

"What do You mean?"

"As you studied and reflected on My letter to you from Ezra, My Spirit opened your eyes. You caught a glimpse of My plan, all that I'm doing through My Son to prepare you for the dance. To study My plan is good. To see it is transforming. Your excitement was not merely an emotional reaction; it was the passion that is released every time you see reality."

"But God, the glimpse is gone. I still believe that a really good plan is under-way, but I'm not caught up in it. I'm back to feeling very ordinary, doing very ordinary things in an ordinary world. Some things are good, some bad. I'm up and down and just moving on. Right now, life feels daily—get up, make coffee, do what you have to do, go to bed. Nothing seems to matter all that much. Am I becoming a fatalist?"

"It's time to read My next letter. Nehemiah did little more than build an unimpressive wall around an apparently insignificant city that housed a relatively small population of unimportant-looking people. And yet when people laughed at him for taking on such a trivial project, he replied, 'I am doing a great work' (6:3 NKJV). Read this letter and hear Me say this:

> Whatever anyone does out of a sincere desire to know Me and draw others to Me is a great work. And as you engage in that work, sometimes you will be energized as you catch a glimpse of My plan unfolding. More often you won't. Either way you are doing a great work.

"Every father who repairs a leaky faucet and then prays with his kids before dinner is doing a great work. Every mother who prepares that dinner and joins in that prayer is doing a great work. Every single person who works hard to pay the rent and reads the Bible before bedtime is doing a great work. I see it all. And I am pleased. Their reward is coming."

"Tell me how You're saying that in Nehemiah."

"What stirs you most deeply? Is it advancing your plan for your life or My plan for My world? Is it closing the deal or revealing the character of My Son as you negotiate? Is it finding a way to get your spouse to understand how abandoned you feel or revealing the character of My Son as you deal with your troubled marriage?

"Read what broke Nehemiah's heart in chapter 1. It wasn't the hardship and inconvenience he would face if he left his important job in the Persian king's court to go to Jerusalem. Nehemiah knew he was called to a great work when he heard that My plan was not going forward among My people and *when he realized how deeply that troubled him.* He couldn't get over it. Nearly one hundred years had passed since My people, a small number, had left the relative comforts of Persia and returned to a city in ruins. And the walls and city gates were still rubble. In all that time, My people were not willing to do the hard work of rebuilding the walls to protect themselves from neighboring enemies. They were more concerned to live as comfortably as they could in the immediate than to preserve their destiny, their calling to be a holy nation through whom I would bless the world.

"Nehemiah was offended and deeply saddened. He caught a glimpse of what was at stake. My people were neither honoring Me nor seizing the opportunity I had given them to join My plan. Like you when you catch a glimpse of the battle being fought in the heavenlies and of My ultimate victory, Nehemiah was prepared to do whatever he could at whatever personal cost to honor Me and seize that opportunity and persuade others to do the same.

"As happens in the lives of all My dedicated servants when they undertake a great work, opposition quickly arose. Fear set in. The road to life is narrow; it is bumpy and steep. But it was Nehemiah's awareness that he was doing a great work that kept him going. And the wall was rebuilt in record time, fifty-two days. Imagine Nehemiah's satisfaction when all the people gathered in the safety of the newly protected city and reaffirmed their commitment to follow My plan for their lives that Ezra then made clear to them at a huge Bible conference. Both Ezra and Nehemiah were plunged into that sea of joy. They caught a glimpse of what I was doing.

"But only a few years later, after Nehemiah had returned to the Persian court and then came back again to Jerusalem, My people were not taking worship seriously. My provisions for holiness were being used for personal gain, and My call to holiness was again being violated by their entering marriage with unbelievers. Nehemiah's 'high' was gone. But the glimpse he had seen sustained him. He knew he was doing a great work, just as parents whose children break their hearts must remember that the greatness of their work is not measured by the results they see but by their faithfulness to Me. Whatever is done to know Me and make Me known, to advance My purposes, is a great work. And I will use every great work done by My people, no matter how small it seems, to further My great plan. When you see the fullness of that plan and its end result, you will be plunged forever in a sea of joy. Your experience then will never be mistaken for a high."

"God, my reaction to what You're saying in this love letter surprises me. I feel both flat and exhilarated, both weary and energized. Life still seems mostly ordinary—I need to pick up some dry cleaning today and get started on my taxes—but at the same time I somehow know a much larger story is being told, right now, through my life. And that picking up a couple of laundered shirts can be part of a great work. Am I crazy? Oh, for another glimpse, this one even clearer and longer lasting."

"I see everything. And until I banish all evil and My Son becomes visible as King of kings and Lord of lords, I am both grieved and joyful, both angry and at rest. I see all that is wrong, all that is painful. My heart is offended and broken. I see, too, faithful Nehemiahs in all times across the world, and I see their great works. My great plan began in Eden and will quietly unfold until My Son returns in great glory and power. The next love letter, the story of Esther, will provide another glimpse, if My Spirit opens your eyes. Ask Him to do that."

Love Letter Seventeen: Esther

No One, No One, Can Thwart My Plan

God, after reading Your first sixteen love letters and now beginning to look at Esther, I've got to ask You a question. It's the same question I feel compelled to ask when I see what's happening all over the world today, especially among Your people. Here's the question: *Is Your plan going well or not?* Are Your people becoming more holy or just more noisy? Are they—and am I—even interested in real holiness, in what *You* call holiness? Or are we mistaking tolerance and niceness and spiritual experiences for the deep change in the human soul that You desire? Most of us seem to think Christianity is a moral and social policy to make this life better for people rather than a redemptive plan for making people better in this life.

"It was the reading of Nehemiah that got me asking this question. In that letter, You completed the history of the Old Testament, and it ended with only a handful of Your people being where You wanted them, and the majority of that minority were worshiping You halfheartedly in a second-rate temple. Nehemiah himself was frustrated with their spiritual condition. And after everything You had done for this nation You plucked out of nowhere, I can't imagine how You must have felt.

"And then I read Esther. *God, most of Your people were still in Persia fifty years after You provided the opportunity for everyone to return to Judah.* What's up with that? The only thing I can figure is that Your people then preferred the comforts a well-established secular lifestyle could provide, just like most of us do today. Add a religious veneer on top, and life in Persia must have seemed much better than enduring the hardships of rebuilding a sacred community from scratch. God, how did that make You feel then? How does it make You feel today? It looks to me like Your plan has never been going too well."

"I exist above time, and I engage with all that happens in time. I live in the perfect peace of unthreatened hope, and I feel grieved and angry, every day, and full of joy."

"I'm not sure I follow You there. You are *so* out of my league. But I do have that second part down pretty well. I'm discouraged and mad a lot. It's the peace and hope part I can't seem to get hold of. And that leaves me still asking my question: *Is Your plan going well or not?*"

"I wrote Esther to let you see that everything that happens in time is under My control. I allow nothing to happen that I cannot use for the good of My plan. *How* I use everything is not always obvious. That I *do* use everything is certain. I hate much that I see, much of what goes on grieves and saddens Me and tries My patience, but I use everything to further My purposes. What I cannot use I do not permit."

"So Your plan *is* going well?"

"Of course. It is your spiritual nearsightedness that makes you ask the question. From before time began when My Son, My Spirit, and I conceived Our plan together until the eternal day dawns and the music plays and the dance begins, My plan follows a straight line that no one can bend. When necessary, I miraculously intervene to keep the line straight. More often, I providentially overrule both the natural events of life and the free choices of people to prosper My plan. That is what I did in Esther. But know this. I tell you the truth: *whether through decisive intervention* (as so often in Exodus) *or through quiet overruling* (as consistently in Esther), *I see to it that My plan stays on course. I AM God. There is no other.*"

"God, I caught that in Esther. There is no record of Your doing any miracles, and You never even mention Yourself by name. You remain out of sight, hidden but active. Why? Wouldn't Your people have celebrated You more if they had seen You more clearly? And I'm still curious about how You felt toward all those Jews who didn't celebrate You enough to leave the easier life in Persia, away from Your presence in the temple, for the harder life in Judah where You wanted them to be."

"I will answer your question and satisfy your curiosity. To understand what I am about to say, to hear what I'm telling you in this seventeenth letter, you must become familiar with the story of five people: Xerxes, the unstable Persian king; Vashti, the beautiful, modest, and, therefore, deposed queen; Haman, the demonically inspired Jew hater; Mordecai, the faithful Jewish leader; and Esther, the ravishing Jewish orphan girl I raised from obscurity to rescue My people. As you read the story of these five people, hear Me say this:

Even when you value living comfortably in this world more than worshiping Me in My temple, I still love you. I will still accomplish My ultimate purpose to bring you to the party. I will always protect you (though often through suffering) from anything that would defeat that purpose, but I will not always reveal Myself to you. You will always benefit from My providential care, but you will not always experience the intimate relationship I more often make available to those who seek Me with all their hearts."

"God, I want to experience that union with You. I've tasted it. I want more. I want so badly to hear what You're saying to me in Esther. Show me how You reveal Your message to me in this letter."

"You were correct in what you said earlier. All of My people should have seized the opportunity I provided fifty years before the story of Esther took place, the opportunity to leave Persia and travel the five-month journey to Judah. Only fifty thousand did. Several million did not. My grief was real. They deprived themselves of the enjoyment of My Presence. Wherever My people live in this world, whether in a mansion or a tent, they will suffer, not always, but inevitably. The difference is this: when My people refuse the tent of a pilgrim for the temporary mansion of one whose treasure is in this world, I will continue to be with them, but they will not enter the rest of that reality. The loss will be theirs and Mine. The story I tell in Esther makes that point. Listen.

"King Ahasuerus (his Greek name was Xerxes) was a power- and pleasure-hungry monarch. When his battle against a foreign enemy failed, he offered a reward to anyone who could think up a pleasure he had not yet experienced. If I can use a man like that for My purposes, you need not frantically fear the wrong person gaining power in your government. Personal holiness matters more than political activism.

"When Queen Vashti refused the king's command to parade her feminine beauty before his drunken dinner guests, she was deposed. I didn't cause that, but I used it. With Vashti's throne empty, the even more beautiful Esther became queen, in place to protect My people from Haman's plot to exterminate My people, which unfolded five years later. When someone chooses to follow Satan, he chooses Me for an enemy. That is a bad choice.

"Haman's insane pride, a genetic defect inherited from his father the devil, caused him to hate Mordecai when the Jewish leader refused to pay him homage. In his demonic pique, he unwittingly served the devil's agenda by plotting to destroy the line through which hell's greatest enemy, My Son, would come. When My people learned that Ahasuerus had authorized Haman to kill every Jew scattered throughout all the 127 provinces of Persia, they fasted and wailed and mourned in sackcloth and ashes. *But not once did they turn to Me by name.*

"Haman's plan, of course, backfired as all of Satan's schemes do. Read the story. I used the natural event of the king's insomnia to remind him of an unpaid debt he owed to Mordecai. As he lay awake, a servant read from the chronicles of his reign, and the king heard how Mordecai had years earlier saved his life. The next day he asked Haman what should be done to reward a man worthy of special honor. Thinking the king was referring to him, Haman suggested an extravagant plan to celebrate the worthy person. When he was told the special honoree was Mordecai, Haman was both humiliated and shaken. Later that same day, at a private dinner party arranged by Esther for herself, the king, and Haman, Esther revealed for the first time that she was a Jewess and that Haman's outrageous and evil plan to kill all Jews would mean her death. The angry king stormed out of the banquet room, only to come back a few minutes later to see Haman falling on the couch where Esther was reclining, begging for his life. The king wrongly assumed Haman was forcing himself sexually on his queen and promptly had him hung on the gallows Haman had just built to execute Mordecai. Why do rulers conspire against Me? I laugh at their futile plans. I scoff at them, and I terrify them in My wrath. (To understand this more fully, read the second psalm.)

"Notice that all these events—Ahasuerus's party; Vashti's refusal to demean herself to entertain the king's guests; Mordecai's saving the king's life; Haman's murderous plot; Esther's beauty, position, and courage; and many others—were natural events that I used for My purposes. Haman was killed, My people became strong, Ahasuerus elevated Mordecai to greater prominence, and Esther reigned as queen in Vashti's place. The feast of Purim, which Israel observes to this day, was inaugurated to celebrate My people's good fortune. *But not once is it recorded that they praised Me by name.* In their need, My people did not seek Me by name. In their joy, My people did not celebrate Me by name. My power had protected them, and they celebrated their safety, but they did not draw close to Me in the intimacy of relationship that I designed them to enjoy. That is what I am saying to you, among many other things, in this seventeenth love letter: I care for you. Acknowledge Me by name. See Me in everything, including your worst torment and suffering, with the eyes of faith. And you and I together will enjoy a relationship of love."

"God, I saw none of that in this letter until You showed me. But now that I see it, I realize I sometimes feel like one of Your followers who did return to Judah and who sincerely promised to follow You on the narrow road and ended up on the broad one. Other times I think I'm more like one of Your people who stayed in Persia. I'm too often more interested in how well life is going than whether I'm becoming more like Your Son, and when I think about it honestly, I realize my spiritual life has more to do with enjoying Your blessings than knowing You. Are those my only two options: to slide onto the broad road even though I want to walk the narrow road to knowing You or to live the good life, thinking I'm close to You when I'm really not? I want to leave Persia and cooperate with the straight line of Your plan for me to become holy and be able to dance with You. Is that possible?"

"The story of My people's failures, both in Judah and Persia, is designed to prepare your heart to hear My Son. With Him, it is possible not only to know My providential care but also to trust My abiding Presence and to live an increasingly holy life in whatever circumstances you find yourself. My next five letters were written to tell you how to walk the narrow road through Jordan into the Promised Land of life with Me—a holy life of hope and joy. I now shift from historical narrative to personal guidance. Keep reading."

PART THREE

Living in Mystery with Wisdom and Hope: Job Through Song of Songs

I don't know about you, but after reading all those letters about Israel's history and trying to absorb all that God is saying to us in each one, I'm not feeling better. I don't feel lighter, I don't feel freer, I don't feel encouraged, I don't feel excited, I don't feel warmly loved, and I sure don't feel happier. What I do feel is an urge to put these letters aside and pick up a good novel.

If I heard God correctly so far, I'm left more aware of how important holiness is to Him and more aware of how reliably and miserably unholy I am. Now there's a real self-esteem boost. I feel more judged than loved. I do want to know God. I do want to cooperate with His plan. I do want to dance. I do want to eagerly anticipate the party and all the food He'll spread before me at the banquet.

But I feel heavier and more absorbed with myself than before I read all those letters. And God seems further away. Intimacy with Him seems less available, not more.

I think I prefer sweet Christianity to hard Christianity. But I'm pretty sure the hard version is the true version. And yet it's also true that it's just plain easier to ignore the tough stuff in all God's letters and focus instead on a few watered-down ideas about love and acceptance, sing a few verses of

"Amazing Grace" (maybe skipping that part about God saving "a wretch like me"—better to see the cross as an affirmation of my value, not His holiness), and get on with a positive, upbeat, hope-in-this-life script for the Christian life.

Doing that attracts me and scares me. It's attractive to think I can claim to love Jesus without having to enter a messy battle going on inside me 24/7 and focus instead on enjoying all that's enjoyable in life. But it scares me too. I'm scared I'll miss out on what Jesus meant when He said that He came to bring wonderful news (Mark 1:14). I want what God is giving, all of it. But I'm afraid I'll only get dribs and drabs if I do an end run around the holiness hurdle to pursue my happiness and my enjoyment of life now.

So here's where I am. Reading God's first seventeen love letters has me asking the question, "How am I supposed to live in a messed-up world with a community of messed-up people as a messed-up person?" But as I ask that question, I can almost see God smiling. I can just barely hear Him whisper, *Keep reading. I'm preparing you to hear good news that will blow your mind. Get ready for My Son. He's coming!*

Time to put down my novel and begin reading Job, then Psalms, Proverbs, Ecclesiastes, and the Song of Songs. I'm ready. I hope you are too.

Love Letter Eighteen:
Job

To Rest in Hope, You Must Writhe in Pain

God, I know Your plan is You, not a program or an impersonal idea. I know it's You pouring Your life into me, into all of Your children. And that's holiness. I think I understand that, at least, a little. What I still don't understand is all the suffering You allow and, maybe, even cause. Just this morning at breakfast, a pastor friend told me about one of his faithful church members whose body is filled with malignant tumors. And he fears confinement to a wheelchair more than pain or even death.

"So here's what I don't get. I can see You punishing Your people, as You did in Judges, when we tell You to take a hike then do whatever we feel like doing. But this guy loves You; he's a good man, and You won't even keep him mobile till he dies, which You easily could do and, it seems to me, would do *if* You're both powerful and good. And You are, *so why don't You do it?* I've been reading Job, and the story just adds to my confusion."

"I punish people who reject Me by letting them have their way. Hell is the enjoyment of their own way forever. In this world, having your way can feel good. In the next, it never does. I love those I've invited to My party by permitting suffering that draws them to concentrate on Me as their only source of life. It awakens their taste buds to enjoy the rich food I offer. Heaven is the enjoyment of My way forever."

"God, is that what's happening in Job? You're *loving* him by giving Satan free rein to ruin his life? I don't get it. And I sure as heck don't like it."

"To know Me well, you must first be confused by Me. Only in the mystery of suffering will you stop trying to fit Me into your understanding of life. Learn this as you read Job:

When you stand before Me in mystery, you will eventually rest within Me in trust. When you can't figure Me out, you will give up the illusion of predictability and control and discover the joy and freedom of hope."

"I'm not sure what You mean by standing before You in mystery. But is that what You arranged for Job to do, by not explaining to him what was going on behind the scenes? It's never made sense to me why You let him suffer in ways that to him seemed utterly pointless. Without a purpose, suffering feels cruel."

"Suffering without explanation creates the opportunity for faith in Me, the kind of faith that sees My heart. Suffering with explanation allows you to maintain the false hope of control. In My plan, I remove all sources of hope but Me, thereby revealing the narrow road to holiness, the only road that leads to My party. It's the road of trusting Me in darkness so dark that all reason for trust is obscured. My troubled but trusting servant Søren Kierkegaard put it well: 'As long as there are many springs from which to draw water, anxiety about possible water failure does not arise.'

"He went on to comment that anxiety arises when there is only one source. When I am recognized as a dehydrated person's only spring, the spiritual battle begins. Can I be trusted? Will I be trusted? Those are the questions I forcefully, yes brutally, required Job to answer. If you never are confronted by those questions in the depths of agony, you will never know Me well."

"God, I'm not sure I like where this is going."

"Hear Me say it clearly: I make no promise to provide you with the good things you legitimately want in this world. Do not trust Me for a pleasant, prosperous life. Let Me quote Kierkegaard again. He learned wisdom through pain. 'Nothing is more certain. Coming close to God brings catastrophe. Everyone whose life does not bring relative catastrophe has never even once turned . . . to God; it is just as impossible as it is to touch the conductor of a generator without getting a shock.'

"Learn, too, what My Jewish servant Abraham Heschel discovered: 'God is not nice. God is not an uncle. God is an earthquake.' The world of Christendom, so far removed from Christianity, does not believe that. It does not want to believe that."

"I don't either. Why can't You be nice? Isn't it loving to be nice, to relieve suffering and restore pleasure?"

"Love seeks the deepest well-being of another. If that requires suffering, then love permits and, sometimes, brings about suffering. But love never allows more suffering than is necessary to achieve the well-being of the beloved."

"God, is this what I'm to learn from Your eighteenth love letter?"

"I wrote Job to reveal who I AM, not who you imagine Me to be. I permit suffering but never more, always less, than I experience. Gaze on Calvary. Look at My Son. We are committed to your well-being, to your eternal joy, to getting you to the party. We suffered then in ways you will never experience, and We suffer with you now until the party begins, until the banquet is ready.

"Job's friends reduced Me to a traffic cop. Obey the speed limit, and I let you drive on to the beach. Drive too fast, and I interfere with your plans. That false image of Me gives rise to the cry I hear from many: 'I don't deserve this. I lived well. You owe me a better life.' That cry drowns out the music of heaven; it prevents the one who cries from learning to dance.

"Job knew his friends were wrong. He knew his suffering was not punishment for sin that he could end by living better. But he did not realize the opportunity that his suffering presented for him to see

Me. Job was terrified that I might be powerful but not good. A universe in the hands of an almighty but unloving God is a terrible place to be. Job was compelled to ask deep, hard questions.

"I removed all sources of encouragement but one. I extinguished all the lights that had been guiding Job on a pleasant path through life, not to prove a point to Satan—I owe him nothing but hell—but to gain entrance into Job's heart with the light of My Presence. It was in the darkness of unexplained suffering that Job learned he was not the prosecuting attorney nor I the defendant. My message to him is My message to you: I remain all-powerful and all-good in your darkest night. Trust Me. You don't know enough not to.

"When the lights go out, when suffering brings despair, emptiness, futility, and misery, trust Me. I am removing the scales from your eyes so that you will soon see My light. The morning star is visible when the darkness is deepest. And when you see Him, you will see Me and discover yourself. My Son is coming!

"Listen again to Kierkegaard. He understood what your generation doesn't. 'God punishes the ungodly by ignoring them. This is why they have success in the world—the most frightful punishment because in God's view, this world is immersed in evil. But God sends suffering to those whom he loves, as assistance to enable them to become happy by loving him.' That is what I am saying to you in this letter."

"God, You have more work to do in me, a lot more work. I think I'd rather be like Job when his life was good even though he had only heard of You. I've got lots going for me right now—a great wife, two sons walking with You, two wonderful daughters-in-law, five gorgeous grandkids, a well-received ministry. I really want to keep it that way even if it means not knowing You better than I do now. Well, maybe I don't mean that. Okay, here's my question, now that I've heard what You're saying to me in Job: If I'm willing to die to my blessings as my source of life and if I come alive to You as my only source of life, if I really fall in love with You, what will I experience? What will my life in this world be like?"

"I wrote My next letter to answer that question. Keep reading."

Love Letter Nineteen:
Psalms

ASK YOUR HARDEST QUESTIONS AND SING YOUR LOUDEST PRAISE

*G*od, as I read Your love letters, I get the strange sense that a whole new way of thinking is coming into focus, a way that feels unnatural but full of a new kind of hope. But I also sense that something in me is dying, something I wanted to live."

"What is dying needs to die."

"God, that scares me. The ground I've been standing on is turning into quicksand. I know You've given me no guarantees that You'll protect me from bad things or even that You'll heal my insecurities, only that You'll lead me through them to knowing You better.

"But what I struggle with—and so many others struggle with the same thing—is fear: fear of failure, fear of rejection, fear of bad things happening like the death of a child or loss of a job, fear of disapproval, fear of not having what it takes to relate well or succeed in life, fear of being on the outside, fear of looking foolish, fear of depending on someone and realizing they're not there for me. All kinds of fears and insecurities. It's pretty clear that something's wrong inside me or I wouldn't be so afraid, but I don't know what it is. And I'm not clear what You're doing about whatever it is that's so wrong. I receive counsel and spiritual direction from a few close friends. But even the best conversations seem only to matter for the moment, then whatever it is I'm scared of, whatever demon is still alive, comes back to bite me again. I read books by wise spiritual guides, and I get excited and stirred for a day, a stab of light flashes in my soul, then the fog rolls in again, darker and thicker than before. But I'm still looking to You; I'm crying out to You, maybe because I can't find a better option. And yet I believe, I really do believe, that You're good and that a good plan is somehow unfolding through all the mess of my life. My hope is in You."

"You have just sung a psalm."

"Really? It feels more like a funeral dirge. Something is dying, and it hurts. I feel like someone who wants to follow You but can't find the way."

"The way to what?"

"To life, to the life I want. To emotional stability, to feeling more solid than insecure, to a thrilling awareness that I'm alive with purpose and joy, to a sure hope that gets me out of bed every morning ready to seize every opportunity in the adventure of life."

"Your desire to live is good. My Spirit will keep that desire alive in every circumstance through every dark night. Your understanding of the road to life is bad. It must die. Your foolish understanding is what is most wrong within you. You assume I relieve struggle and replace it with rest. But I use struggle to uncover a rest beneath the struggle that no anguish can destroy. The struggle with fear and pain will continue. Only in the storm will you know there is an anchor."

"God, when I told You about my fears and frustration, You said I was singing a psalm. I know Your nineteenth love letter is a collection of Hebrew poems that were sung when Your people gathered to worship You. And I know they're full of praise and prayer, of complaint and celebration, of every experience Your people went through as You worked Your purposes in them. I guess I've been thinking of the Psalms as a kind of spiritual aspirin, a chance to feel comfort, an opportunity to taste the life I so badly want. I've not wanted an anchor in the storm. I've wanted a quick trip to shore."

"There is no quick trip except death. The Psalms are not an anesthetic. They are not a cup of hot chocolate on a cold night. They are the prayers of someone lost in a dark wood, shivering in bitter cold, unable to stand in fierce wind. They are the praise that flows from that person's heart when he abandons himself to Me for deliverance, when he trusts that My hand has grasped his and that I am leading him home, very slowly but very surely. Job learned that he must die to the hope that darkness and cold and wind were not part of My plan.

"In the Psalms, I reveal what life is like for the person who lives in the storm with his eyes fixed on Me. As you read the Psalms, hear Me say this:

Face the hard questions that life requires you to ask. Gather with other travelers on the narrow road, pilgrims who acknowledge their confusion and feel their fears. Then, together, live those questions in My Presence.

"Your tears will become the melody of a new song. Your darkness will become the window through which new light will appear. Your doubt will become new ground, solid ground, on which to stand. Expect your theological boxes to explode, to lose all false hope in what My love will provide in this life. Expect your personal dreams to shatter, to lose all false confidence in what My power guarantees in this life. Meditate on each psalm, knowing that I am calling you to walk a road that, for long seasons, you will not enjoy. Then decide, again and again: *either cling to Me as I AM or reshape Me into who you want Me to be.* The stakes are high. Either you will find yourself in finding Me as I reveal Myself, or you will lose yourself in creating Me to fit your foolish expectations. Make the right choice. I want you to sing a new song."

"God, just yesterday a pastor asked me my reaction to what the modern church calls worship. I told him that more often than not, I can't stand it.

Where's the struggle? Where's the confusion? Where's the honest admission of emptiness? When I see a pretty girl smiling on cue and singing happily into a microphone, thinking she's leading me into worship, I want to unplug her microphone and slap her face. Am I wrong?"

"Of course. Only My Son can slap a face and remain holy. But your longing to feel your emptiness and ask your questions in My Presence, in the company of other authentic pilgrims, is good. That longing releases true worship and opens your ears to hear the music of heaven and to awkwardly but rhythmically begin to dance. As the Psalms become the standard for worship, the honest community will become the suffering community that sings.

❋ *Your thirst for Me will become all-consuming.* 'One thing I ask of the LORD . . . to gaze upon the beauty of the LORD' (27:4).

❋ *In desperate confusion and anguish, you will know Me in ways no one knows Me in comfort.* 'My life is consumed by anguish . . . but I trust in You, O LORD; I say, "You are my God"' (31:10, 14).

❋ *You will feel desire that nothing in this world can satisfy, and that will make life unbearable. Only then will your options become clear: trust Me and live My way or figure life out and live your way.* 'I call as my heart grows faint; lead me to the rock that is higher than I' (61:2).

❋ *When your soul is troubled, you will hear My voice and find rest.* 'Find rest, O my soul, in God alone' (62:5). 'One thing God has spoken, two things have I heard; that you, O God, are strong, and that you, O Lord, are loving' (62:11–12).

❋ *You will endure seasons when thoughts of Me will deepen your anguish.* 'I remembered you, O God, and I groaned' (77:3).

❋ *But every heartache will create space that I alone can fill. And I will. You will learn to wait in hope.* 'My soul yearns, even faints, for the courts of the LORD . . . Blessed are those . . . who have set their hearts on pilgrimage. As they pass through the Valley of Baca [seasons of weeping], they make it a place of springs' (84:2, 5–6).

❋ *You will become passionate to meet others in their brokenness and to encourage them to wait with you in hope.* '. . . as for me, I will always have hope . . . Even when I am old and gray, do not forsake me, O God, till I declare your power to the next generation' (71:14, 18).

❀ *You will come to love My way, no matter the cost.* 'I rejoice in following your statutes as one rejoices in great riches' (119:14).

❀ *You will know you are known, fully seen and fully loved.* 'O LORD . . . you know me . . . How precious to me are your thoughts, O God' (139:1, 17).

❀ *The more clearly you see Me, the more gladly you will sing a new song that can never be sung by those who live on the broad road of seeking Me for blessings. You will dance before Me with all your might, in moments now, in endless joy forever.* 'I will sing praise to my God as long as I live . . . The LORD reigns forever . . . Praise the LORD' (146:2, 10)."

"God, kill everything in me that keeps me from an authentic encounter with You. Your plan is hard but it is good. You are severe, but You are merciful. *I want to know You.* Shine Your light on the narrow road so I can live in this world the way You want me to live."

"Those who die to every false hope (the message of Job), who come alive to Me as they are and as I AM and not as they think I should be (the message of Psalms), are ready to live My way in this world. I wrote My next letter to reveal what My way looks like in the everyday relating of life. You are now ready to hear My instructions as an invitation to freedom."

Love Letter Twenty: Proverbs

You Must Fear Me to Follow Me

*G*od, You just told me that in this next letter You'd show me how You want me to live in the middle of all that goes on in this world. And You thought maybe I was ready to hear Your instructions, not as some formula for success or as another bunch of rules I couldn't keep, but as an invitation to freedom, an invitation to gladly follow Your way in any situation even when almost everything in me screams to handle things my way. At least that's what I heard. Maybe it's what I wanted to hear. Did You really mean it when You said I might be ready to get serious about real holiness?"

"I never flatter. I encourage only with truth."

"After reading Your first nineteen love letters, I think I might be ready too. But I just read through Your twentieth letter, and I have a problem. Actually, I have three problems. Here's the first: *Your storyline is hard to follow.* You've been saying all along that making us happy in a pleasant world is Your plan for the next life, that making us holy in a messed-up world is what You're up to now. Have I heard you right?"

"Yes."

"Then Proverbs doesn't fit. It takes Your story in an entirely different direction. The first seven verses say it right up front: You wrote this letter to help me live wisely. And nearly every verse after those first seven tell me that if I get wisdom and live wisely, my life in this world will go pretty well. Now I know that Your plan is about a whole lot more than getting me to heaven. You intend to bring heaven's way of doing things to earth, and You want to do that through the likes of me. I think I understand that.

"But what I'm struggling with is what this letter seems to promise, that living wisely guarantees the good life of blessings now. Here's one example. 'Hear, my son, and receive my sayings, and the years of your life will be many' (4:10 NKJV). Does that mean that my friend's daughter who died in her twenties wasn't listening to You? I don't think so. Here's another. 'The fear of the LORD leads to life, and he who has it will abide in satisfaction; he will not be visited with evil' (19:23 NKJV). So when trouble hits my life, it means I haven't been fearing You? But Paul's life was touched by lots of trouble, and he found contentment in the middle of it [Philippians 4:11–12]. So which is it? Which story are You telling? The story of how I can get You to bless my life with peace, long life, and prosperity? Or is it the story of Your plan to make me holy in this life and happily satisfied forever in the next?

"That's one problem. Here's the second. When Solomon asked You for wisdom when You offered him anything he wanted, You were pleased that he didn't ask for money or military power or long life [1 Kings 3:5–15]. But he already had all of that. Well, maybe not long life, but what healthy twenty-year-old thinks about dying? He was King David's son, wealthy, in charge of a strong army, and about to sit on his father's throne. If Bill Gates became president of the United States, I doubt if he'd ask You to double his new salary. What's an extra couple hundred thousand to him? Like Solomon, the one thing he wouldn't be sure he had was the know-how to run a country. Of course Solomon asked for wisdom. And now You want me to get all excited about listening to a guy sitting on top of the world telling an ordinary schmuck like me how to get my life together? We live in two different worlds. It's like conscientious parents with screwed-up kids listening to a famous Christian with six well-adjusted, healthy, godly, successful children tell them how he did it. And then, to make matters worse, after Solomon directs me to follow his lead in resisting lust, he collects more women than Tiger Woods has golf balls.

"And here's the topper, my third problem. This really puts me over the edge. In Your next letter, Ecclesiastes, Solomon admits that his celebrated wisdom left him empty, more miserable than happy [Ecclesiastes 1:16–18]. So why am I supposed to listen to him tell me to go on a diet that he followed and got fat? So that's what I think about as I read Proverbs. I know my thinking is wrong, but I don't see how."

"Your thinking is wrong but hopeful. It's good that you're wrestling with My words. Too many churchgoers read a few favorite verses in Proverbs, such as 'Train up a child in the way he should go, and when he is old he will not depart from it' (22:6 NKJV), and think they've found the manual to make life work, a map to the Promised Land. You have not made that lethal error that only a shallow reading allows. But You have missed two vital truths that I communicate in this letter, two truths that serve as foundation and framework for everything else I say. Hear Me now:

Truth #1: The wisdom I offer you is the wisdom by which I made the world, what little of it you can receive. I made life to work only if lived according to My design.

Truth #2: You will hear and live My wisdom only if first you fear Me, if you fall before Me in desperate terror and draw near to Me in trusting awe.

"Most people who claim to follow Me expect to dance before they tremble. It cannot be done. They want to climb into My lap and call Me Daddy before they bow before Me and call Me Lord. Without terror and awe, worship and love become an illusion that makes foolish living look wise."

"God, this is all very interesting, but You aren't dealing with the problems I face when I read Proverbs. You aren't answering my questions."

"Do you ponder all I have created and recognize a wisdom you lack? Do you observe life and see your God whose sovereign power shuts your mouth, whose uncompromising love opens your ears to hear Me speak? If not, you have no fear of Me. You have not even the beginnings of wisdom."

"Uh, I guess I was out of line demanding answers to my questions. I'm sorry. I think I get your point. Like Job, I hear You, and I'm putting my hand over my big mouth."

"Your error is hopeful. You aren't presuming blessings I have not promised. Continue asking your questions. They are good. But stop demanding answers. Live those questions long enough in My Presence, and you will run out of words. You will then catch a brief glimpse of who I AM that will seal your lips. Unless you then deliberately turn from Me, you will tremble before My power and surrender to My goodness. You will fear Me, and your ears will open to hear My wisdom. I meant what I said: the fear of the Lord is the beginning, though not the end, of wisdom. My Son is the beginning and the end."

"God, I'm listening. Tell me how to hear You speak to me in this letter."

"Then hear this: by wisdom, I created all of life to function together in harmony with integrity in beauty. It is that wisdom I share through My servant Solomon.

"Ever since Eden, the way that intuitively seems right to people—gossip, indulgence, quick speaking, valuing money over right relationships, cutting corners to secure a deal—is reliably wrong. The foolish way ruins harmony, betrays integrity, and soils beauty.

"I gave Solomon the discernment to recognize the way of wisdom and to identify in everyday life the way of foolishness. As you read Proverbs, expect to feel the shame of exposure. Many of your ways are foolish. Expect, too, to feel the appeal of wisdom. I gave you a heart that wants to walk the narrow road.

"But never mistake this letter as a manual for successful living. One day everyone living in the new heavens and the new earth will live the way of wisdom. Life then will be blessed—harmony, integrity, beauty—everywhere. Respect this letter as a guide to skillful living that *may* produce blessings today and *will* produce blessings when My Son returns. And in this life, skillful living will better accomplish My purposes.

"Let every desire for long life, vibrant health, intimate relationships, material comfort, and meaningful activity strengthen your resolve to be holy until the day that a fully holy community will be a fully blessed community.

"Let the wisdom of Solomon guide you to the narrow road that will expose your foolishness, crush your arrogance, whet your appetite for holiness, release your love, and fill you with hope."

"God, my questions remain, but I no longer want to ask them. I think I know a little bit more now of what it means to live them, to feel them, to embrace them in Your presence. I want to reread Proverbs more slowly, less defensively, with clearer expectations. I want to reflect on what it means to guard my heart [4:23], to resist temptation by realizing the cost of yielding [7:21–23], to believe that the prospect of the righteous is joy [10:28], to stop letting people know they annoy me [12:16], to realize I can laugh and ache at the same time without hypocrisy [14:13], to make my plans but surrender to Your purpose [19:21], not to demand justice but to wait for You to right all wrongs [20:22], to be content with good friends whether *important* people know me or not [25:6,7], not to try to cheer up a hurting person by acting cheerful [25:20], to keep my emotions under control even when I'm really ticked [29:11], and not to speak so quickly when people tell me what's going on in their lives [29:20]. I guess I have a lot to learn."

"I will continue the good work I have begun in your life. My plan is on track. But as you live more wisely, you will be inclined to regard a life well lived as an end in itself and to believe that making wise choices will reliably fill your soul with meaning and joy. It won't. Very few understand what life is really all about, what it is that constitutes the greatest good. I wrote My next letter to show you what the greatest good is not. Prepare to confront your loneliness, your emptiness, as you read on. It is the road to joy."

Love Letter Twenty-One: Ecclesiastes

THE WAY UP IS THE WAY DOWN

*G*od, reading through Your next love letter made me think of a quote from John Stuart Mill. He said somewhere that it's better to be Socrates dissatisfied than a pig satisfied. I've always agreed with Socrates that the unexamined life is not worth living. But in reflecting on what Solomon wrote in Ecclesiastes, I'm realizing that the examined life can be pretty tough to live. A satisfied pig seems a good way to go."

"Is that what you want, to cover up the emptiness of existence and to live with the illusion of satisfaction?"

"Sometimes, yes. If I could pull it off. But I can't. And it's Your fault. You went ahead and put eternity in my heart. I can't make myself settle for the shallow happiness and contrived excitement that too many churches and most of secular society provide. I wish I could. Even close family relationships and a fair amount of ministry success don't do it. I guess I agree with what William Barrett said: 'It's better to encounter one's existence in despair than never to encounter it at all.' But I do wonder if I have to feel so empty to receive the fullness You provide. Lots of popular preachers don't think so."

"There is no shortcut to a deep encounter with My Son. The beginning of the gospel is bad news, not only that you are a sinner but that your sin has left you empty and alone, desperate to feel fulfilled and connected, willing to do whatever provides an escape from boredom and futility. Until you stop running from real darkness into artificial light, until you hear the bad news that life is empty, that *you* are empty, you will not hear the good news My Son came to bring.

"I wrote Ecclesiastes through the mind and soul of the man who in all history was best equipped to find fullness of life without connecting deeply to Me. The failure to face the bad news that Solomon discovered, to ask the questions he could not answer, is responsible for the shallow church of today. Emptiness is covered by distraction. Loneliness is numbed with sociability. Futility is denied in activity. Premature and superficial satisfaction with the good things of life prevents My people from grasping the incredible news that My reality of joy, community, and meaning has invaded theirs."

"God, what are the questions Solomon asked but couldn't answer?"

"Solomon had the courage to ask why there is something rather than nothing, what is life all about, where is it headed, what is the ultimate good that, when discovered, wholly heals and fully satisfies. Many churches declare the truth that living for My glory answers those questions, but they repeat it glibly with all the depth of a sales clerk wishing you a good day as you exit the store."

"So what are You saying to me in Ecclesiastes? I know the right answer to Solomon's questions—it's what You just said: living for Your glory by depending entirely on You for my acceptance and satisfaction is the answer Jesus taught me to believe. And I do believe it. I believe Him. I believe You. But the truth of that answer hasn't reached me as deeply as I wish it would.

"For several months now, God, I've wondered if I'm clinically depressed. I have too many of the symptoms. I'm feeling emptier than ever before. And confused. More cynical too. Nothing really brings me deep joy. All day long I find myself asking, 'So what?' or 'Why bother?' I do what I have to do to get by, and I can still look forward to a good steak, but I'd prefer to do nothing. But that prospect bores me too."

"You are in the depths of the Ecclesiastes experience. It is the narrow road to life that most people avoid with distractions, sociability, and busyness. Hear what I am saying to all who have ears to hear. It is the message of My twenty-first love letter, a message that can only be heard in silence:

I lower you into the depths of despair to lift you into the heights of joy. The way up is the way down. There is no other way. You will not hear My song of love until you hear no other music."

"God, I feel like Your Son's disciples when they realized how hard His message was and saw lots of His followers begin looking around for another messiah."

"Then I will ask you the same question He asked them. Will you follow the crowd and go away? Or will you follow My Son on the narrow road to life?"

"Is the road really *this* narrow? Must I sink into the misery of emptiness before I can find my footing on the rock of hope? And how long will You leave me in this Ecclesiastes experience of Solomon before I hear Solomon's song?"

"If I answered your second question, you would depend on a timetable more than on Me. To your first question, I answer yes. Hear Me well:

- ❈ Until you fall into the dignity of despair where words about Me mean nothing to you and where service for Me seems futile;
- ❈ Until the wisdom that comes easily fails to stir you with hope;
- ❈ Until available pleasures, legitimate and illegitimate, moral and immoral, no longer satisfy or even bring more than temporary relief to your empty soul;
- ❈ Until whatever wealth you have accumulated, whatever possessions litter your life, whatever achievements decorate your résumé, until all of it leaves you with the realization that more will not fill the emptiness in your heart;

* Until time with friends doesn't energize you as it once did;
* Until sacrificial deeds of kindness that win the applause of many no longer have the power to help you feel worthwhile;
* Until the drama, passion, and activities of church become lifeless and dull;
* Until you have nowhere to turn for the satisfaction of your soul's desire, not to the Bible, not to prayer, not to music, not to friends, not to church;
* Until all this happens, *you will never dance to heaven's music as I designed you to dance.* You will not hear My song of love as clearly and beautifully as I sing it. You will not know that every moment of your life is a perfectly tuned note in the eternal harmony.

"That is what I'm saying to you in Ecclesiastes."

"God, I'm hearing You, I think, as never before, and I'm crying out to You from my heart: *may Your grace be sufficient for me!* Leave me in Ecclesiastes until I can hear the Song of Songs. When the narrow road crushes every hope that I've clung to for life, convince me that I can stay the course, that I am not justified in finding a bypath into a pleasant meadow, whether it's an entertaining church where smiles replace tears and excitement relieves boredom or whether it's sinful pleasures that obscure my need for hope beyond what I can see. God, lower me as deep into emptiness as is necessary to hear nothing but silence, to wait for You in the darkness of solitude. Let me hear the call of no seductive siren but only the voice of Your Son. And please, let me recognize His voice when He speaks."

"No voice is stronger. No voice is sweeter. No other voice can fill you with the hope of full and lasting satisfaction. You are ready to hear the voice of true love, not the counterfeit that disguises self-interest in the clothing of passion. My next letter sings the song of love. Listen and delight your soul with the music you've longed to hear from the moment you were conceived. Your taste buds have been awakened enough to delight yourself in a few bites of what soon will be a never-ending banquet."

Love Letter Twenty-Two:
Song of Songs

I WILL TEACH YOU HOW TO DANCE

*G*od, this is the first letter of Yours that's easy to recognize as a love letter. But for that very reason it even more disturbingly raises familiar questions. A Christian friend wrote me yesterday, a woman whom I know You love more than Solomon loved the woman he was singing to in this twenty-second letter. And that's the problem. It doesn't look like You're loving her well.

"In the past twelve months, she's been diagnosed with thyroid cancer, a computer glitch cancelled her life insurance (that mess got straightened out), migraines began, she needed a root canal and two crowns, a bad case of pneumonia developed into pulmonary edema, and an artery in her left eye closed off (likely due to her lupus) leaving her with partial but irreversible loss of vision. For the life of me, I can't see how people can honestly look around and still believe You're committed to everyone having the kind of life and the kind of feelings we all naturally want. Either they're wearing blinders, they think You're really well-meaning and nice but not all that strong, or they're hoping their preacher or the next latest book will tell them what they can do to pry open heaven's window so that all the blessings can spill out. Or worse, their lives are going well, and they think they've earned it.

"It's pretty clear to me. You're not committed to our happiness, at least not for now and certainly not on the basis of having all the blessings we want. If You were, You could be doing a better job."

"I AM committed to your happiness but only to your happiness in Me. There is no other kind, not now, not later. Only counterfeits."

"God, to so many people—and too often to me—that sounds like impractical, mystical, pie-in-the-sky theology. But this woman gets it, more than I do. I'm guessing she's read the Song of Songs. I'm sure she's heard what You're saying in that love letter or, at least, what I think You're saying. She knows You could reverse all her troubles today, and even though You don't, she's discovering the happiness of knowing You and hoping in You in the middle of her troubles.

"I was moved by how she finished her letter. She wrote, 'I do still believe there is a God—that I am His and He is mine—that He is on the throne—and that He groans with me and that He longs even more than I do for the day when evil will be crushed and tears and suffering will be done away with and everything will be made right.'

"I think she heard what You're saying in Solomon's song. Am I right?"

"What I am saying to you and to My suffering daughter and to all who want to hear Me is this:

I love you. I delight in you. I will do whatever it takes for you to enter into the exquisite, life-defining pleasure of the communion My Son and I enjoy. I invite you into the feast of love."

"But God, couldn't she enjoy the appetizers that are available now with a little less suffering? Wouldn't the kind of love the king had for his bride in Solomon's song want to relieve her troubles, not just hug her while she endures them?"

"With everything in Me, I want to relieve my daughter's troubles, to make her happy. But I want to relieve her troubles and bring her happiness by filling her heart with Me. All other relief is temporary. All other happiness is an illusion.

"I wrote My last five love letters to people like My Israelite children. From the first seventeen letters, you learned this: so many who claim to follow Me declare their devotion to Me but look for happiness wherever they can more easily find it. What they call worship amounts to pious, passionate, and sometimes frantic efforts to secure My cooperation, an intense expression of trust in My willingness to satisfy their desires, not in communion with Me but with blessings from Me.

"In these five letters you rightly call wisdom letters, I am arousing the desire I put in every human heart to experience satisfaction in an undeserved relationship of love. To arouse desire without providing hope is cruel. To feel desire without hope of satisfaction is hell. Dante's words written over the door into Satan's world were apt: 'Abandon hope, all ye who enter here.' But desire with hope is sweet. It is the abundant life . . . for now. Desire with satisfaction that excites more desire, which is then fully satisfied the moment it is felt—that's the party. That's the banquet. That's heaven.

"I want you to nibble on the appetizers now. But to do so requires wisdom. Hear My wisdom in these five letters:

❀ *The wisdom of repentance.* Identify and repent of the sin of demanding satisfaction, then looking for it from a source you can control. Crucify your flesh. My word in Job.

❀ *The wisdom of worship.* Relate authentically with Me. Hurt and celebrate, lament and praise, weep and laugh. Be all that you are without pretense, in My Presence. My word in Psalms.

❀ *The wisdom of discernment.* Ask Me to show you both the broad and narrow roads, in every moment of life. Trust that My Spirit has given you the desire to walk the narrow road, through life to *life*. Take one step at a time. My word in Proverbs.

❀ *The wisdom of emptiness.* Face the futility of life. Feel it. Sink into its depths. Then seize the opportunity your emptiness provides to release the power of hope. Hope only in Me. My word in Ecclesiastes.

"And now the peak after the valley, the dawn after the long night. The Song of Songs after the cry of despair. In this letter, I offer *the wisdom of communion.* I know the afflicted woman of whom you speak.

She is Mine, and I am hers. I have won her heart and am now claiming its every corner, crushing every lingering hope of satisfaction apart from Me. In moments of communion, she tastes Me. When those moments fade, she hurts, deeply. But even then she yearns for more, not less, than relief from her suffering. She legitimately yearns for happiness, for relief from her suffering, but she is learning to yearn for Me, for the deeper, fuller, more lasting enjoyment of Me. She is sustained by hope in Me, that I AM with her now and will make everything right forever. She is walking the narrow road. She is living the abundant life of aroused desire with sweet hope. The abundant life of satisfied desire comes later."

"God, when Your servant John heard Your wisdom 'on the Lord's Day' (Revelation 1:10 NKJV), when he ate Your words while imprisoned on Patmos, he tasted in his mouth the sweetness of Your plan but felt its pain in his stomach [Revelation 10:8–11]. Both Jeremiah and Ezekiel felt the agony Your plan requires, but when they ate Your words of wisdom, those words became 'the joy and rejoicing of my heart' (Jeremiah 15:16 NKJV); they tasted like honey on their tongues [Ezekiel 3:2–3]. As I hear You reveal the wisdom of communion in this love letter, I can taste the sweetness of Your love even while my stomach cramps as I realize what Your holiness requires. Just one question though. Is this letter about Your Son, or is He background to a romantic story of a rich king bringing a poor woman to his banquet?"

"My Son is background to no one. This letter celebrates love, passionate love, romantic love, sensual love. Because music is the language of love, the king in this letter celebrates the love between himself and his bride in lyric idylls, in musical pictures, not rational description. I created your brain with two halves, one to know My *truth*, the other to know My *way* and to desire the *life* to which My way leads. Read this letter with the half that sings, that yearns, that enjoys, that hopes, that can be aroused by the prospects of the feast.

"The human writer of the letter did not have My Son in mind as he recorded this song. I did. I always do. Read Solomon's song as a rich expression of love between an ancient king and his bride. But as you read, let your heart (and your right brain) soar into the joy of the love between My Son and Me, into the wonder of My Son's love for you, and into the hope of your communion with Us in that love. My troubled daughter is finding rest for her soul in that hope. That's My plan for all My children. It's My plan for you."

"God, there is so much of Your reality I have yet to experience. Will I ever learn to dance in *this* life? I know I will in the next. Can I even hear Your music with the noise of this world blaring so loud in my ears? Can I taste the honey with my mouth so full of the pleasures of junk food?"

"I raised up prophets to quiet the noise and to reveal what a diet of junk food is doing to your soul. Listen to what I am saying through them, and then you will be ready to hear what I am saying to you through My Son."

PART FOUR

A Word to the Foolish: Isaiah Through Malachi

A friend whose life on every front has fallen apart told me, "I'm trying to believe God still loves me, but it's hard. I'm having to rethink everything I've understood about love." After reading the first twenty-two of God's sixty-six love letters, I'm feeling the same way.

It's becoming clearer to me how easily I assume that if someone loves me, they'll be sensitive to what I want the most and will provide it if they can. And they'll care about what troubles me the most. My wants they will satisfy. My problems they'll fix—if they love me and if they can.

Well, God is good. We all know that. And because He's good, He loves us. "Jesus loves me, this I know." I've been singing that song since I was a kid. And He's powerful. One of the first big words I learned about God in Sunday school was *omnipotent*. God can do anything. I've sung that little chorus, too, a thousand times: "God can do anything, anything, anything. God can do anything but fail."

Add it up. It's not advanced math. One plus one equals two. A God who loves me and can do anything adds up to a wonderful life for me. It follows, as surely as bliss follows every wedding, that God's story of love tells the story of blessings for me.

Or does it? Maybe my understanding of love is in need of radical revision. It's dawning on this getting-old man now in his sixties that I might be thinking about love more like a three-year-old than like a mature

God-follower. Without giving it much thought, I assume that someone with the resources to love me well would satisfy the deepest desires of which I'm aware and would solve whatever problems I perceive as standing in the way of my satisfaction.

But suppose for some reason that I'm unaware of what I really do want the most, what I was wired by my Creator to enjoy. Suppose I'm like a child who sees candy in the bowl and broccoli on her plate and, quite innocently, reaches for the candy. If she gives it a thought, she expects her mother will smile and push the candy within reach of her outstretched arm.

Add to the fable the child's diabetes, a problem she neither recognizes nor understands but a problem that consumes her mother's attention. As the mother pulls the candy bowl out of the child's reach, then points to the broccoli and gently but firmly orders: "Eat!" I can hear the three-year-old's confused whimpering, "Mommy, I don't like broccoli. Why can't I have the candy? Don't you love me?"

I've heard the same puzzled complaint rising in me as I read story after biblical story where God pulled candy out of Israel's reach and piled their plate with vegetables. The twenty-two love letters we've read so far are wearyingly full of judgment; problems made worse, not better; unsatisfied desires; cruel enemies from which God provides seemingly random protection; cycles of heartache followed by blessings followed by more heartache; and hard-to-follow principles for living. To be sure, a fair number of world-class miracles are thrown in—the exodus from Egypt and a dry highway through two rivers, to name a couple—but God's goodness and power didn't provide the life I would have wanted had I been an Israelite in those early days of their history. This is a *love* story?

If you read these twenty-two letters with the maturity of a diabetic child who doesn't know she's sick and can't understand why her mom won't let her eat candy, you might hear something like this:

- Genesis: *from paradise to desert, from Disney World to the ghetto.*
- Exodus: *the tantalizing hope of paradise restored.*
- Leviticus: *rules for returning to paradise, enough rules to choke a legalist.*
- Numbers: *a family trip to Disney World, where only two out of a couple hundred thousand family members get there.*

- Deuteronomy: *a long lecture from an old man that nobody listens to, about what to do and what not to do in paradise.*
- Joshua: *seven years in Disney World but with crawling snakes and prowling tigers. More fear than fun. More death than delight.*
- Judges: *complaining kids and an inconsistent parent, a dad who indulges for a while then punishes. Makes no sense.*
- Ruth: *an oasis of love in a desert of tragedy. Just one oasis?*
- 1 Samuel: *rebellion in the ranks that leads to weak, corrupt government.*
- 2 Samuel: *finally, a good leader; a good life!*
- 1 Kings: *civil war; everything falls apart.*
- 2 Kings: *the bad guys lose; then the good guys lose too.*
- 1 Chronicles: *revisionist history; the glass is half-full.*
- 2 Chronicles: *more revisionism; hope stirs.*
- Ezra: *the return to Disney World after a tornado has ripped through it. This is the Promised Land?*
- Nehemiah: *rebuilding a few rides, feeling entitled to more, having fun however you can.*
- Esther: *disaster averted; making life work away from home.*
- Job: *a life that doesn't work because of God!*
- Psalms: *honest talking to God: happy songs, bitter complaints, desperate tears, vengeful anger, future hope.*
- Proverbs: *a thousand thoughts; how to make the best of things.*
- Ecclesiastes: *God to earth: "Don't you see? Are you so blind? Your best life now leaves you empty."*
- Song of Songs: *a glimpse of beauty in an ugly world.*

If I stick with my usual understanding of love, that's how God's story reads to me so far. Seventeen letters recount a dismal, depressing history, a roller-coaster ride through life that ends in a crash. Five more letters speak honestly about real struggles, then tease us with hints of a loving God who is at work behind the scenes to bring His story—and mine—to a happy conclusion.

So where does that leave you? It leaves me sitting in the dark, lost in the woods, squinting my eyes as I look east, desperately wanting to catch a glimpse of the sunrise I can't stop hoping is on its way. God is love, and He is all-powerful. I know that. I believe that. But what's He doing? What does real love look like? I'm puzzled, wondering, open to rethinking my ideas about love.

And now: *here come the prophets!* I've heard of them, but I haven't heard much from them. If you've read the letters so far, you're familiar with judges and priests and leaders and Levites. But *prophets*?

God seems to shift gears right here, maybe to change the way we think about love. It's time to hear from Him through prophets, sixteen of them who wrote what they spoke, the "writing prophets." Sixteen prophets, seventeen more love letters. (Jeremiah wrote two of them.) They're getting us ready to hear God speak to us through His Son. How will they do that? Who are they? Why now?

Prophets. Special servants who were given eyes to see what most people in every culture and generation don't see. Seers (literally, see-ers) who were compelled by an inner fire to tell others what they saw. And it landed them in trouble. Their message from the holy God of love was not what people who believed in a nice God of love expected.

Because prophets could see into the heart and mind of God, they could also see into the hearts and minds of people. They knew that people had been created by God to enjoy God Himself, by trusting Him completely in any situation. But like me—and I suspect like you—too many of the ancient Israelites saw things differently. They were in touch with only their compelling yearnings for a better life of blessings now, available on demand. Feeling their thirst for God would have put them out of control, so they admitted to consciousness only those desires for which they thought they could, perhaps through God, arrange satisfaction. And they faced only those longings whose satisfaction could be fully enjoyed in this life. The pleasures of sex, food, pride, and power come to mind.

Prophets knew that the kind of happiness everyone was created to enjoy, the kind of happiness God has gone to great trouble to provide, depends on holiness, on a consuming desire for God that's stronger than our desire for anything else that might be on our wish list.

And that insight let prophets see the real problem with people: *no one was holy*. Everyone wanted to use God more than honor Him. People felt entitled to the blessings they wanted, and that spirit of entitlement swallowed up whatever humility of surrender might have been alive within them.

So when people heard the prophets shout "Judgment!" their response was "For what?" They wanted the prophets to stop talking about the Holy One, about the need for holiness to precede happiness. They reasoned, "We're only trying to satisfy our desires so we can feel good about ourselves and our lives and not so lonely, less empty, happier. What's wrong with that? Tell us about the Loving One who will respond to those desires, the desires we can feel pressing for satisfaction. We want to hear about love that will solve the problems blocking the path to the happiness we're after. That's the God we want to hear about, the God we want to worship, the God who loves us the way we want to be loved."

I understand their sentiments. Lying in a cancer ward or worried about a troubled child or mourning a loved one's death or feeling alone and insecure—all of which I've experienced—tends to take the focus off holiness and put it on solutions. Especially when life is tough, love is assumed to mean someone else's cooperation with our agenda to feel satisfied, full, happy, complete. No wonder prophets were so unpopular then and still are today.

But they did promise solutions. They aroused hope. First, purifying judgment, brokenness, holiness. Then joy, beauty, the relationships we've always wanted. Prophets revealed a God whose love would win the day, a God who could—and should—be trusted, a God who right now is preparing a world-class banquet and has promised to bring everyone on the guest list to the party and to pay the enormous admission price Himself, a God who is restoring His Disney World to a level of magnificence that Walt never envisioned.

Judgment and purity. Brokenness and hope. Repentance and trust. Holiness then happiness. Waking up to feel our real desire and to face our real problems. Eyes opened to see God's life as the life we were made for, the life we've always wanted, the life we're willing to suffer the loss of everything else to receive, to live, to enjoy.

This is what the next seventeen love letters are all about, written by God to us through sixteen God-obsessed men who "boiled over" (one Hebrew word for *prophet* has that connotation) with what they had seen: dreadful terrors and unimaginable beauty. They spoke, and they wrote to change our understanding of love to what it needs to be if we're to know that God really does love us, no matter what we're going through. He's doing us good, right now. He loves us enough to satisfy our real desires, the deepest ones we may not see. And He's powerful enough to remove every block to holiness so we can be happy, like Him.

First, judgment for unholiness. Then hope, the beauty of holiness revealed. It's time to hear the prophets. We'll be tempted to close our ears. Maybe to stone the prophets. But it's a better idea to listen. Through them, God is telling a love story, a really good one.

Love Letter Twenty-Three: Isaiah

PREPARE TO BE SLAPPED, THEN HUGGED

God, I've just read through Your twenty-third love letter. I noticed that, except for Psalms, it's been divided into more chapters than all the other letters You wrote to me. And I noticed something else. Isaiah has been arranged into sixty-six chapters, and they follow the same pattern as Your sixty-six letters.

"Here's what I see. For thirty-nine chapters in Isaiah, You tell more about what's wrong with Your people than anything else. I've got to tell You, if I received a sixty-six-page love letter from Rachael where she detailed all my faults in the first thirty-nine pages, I'd expect to be reading her terms for divorce in the next twenty-seven. The message You deliver in Isaiah's first thirty-nine chapters—and You repeat it over and over—is that You're holy, and I'm not. It does sound like You're getting ready to tell me we're through. And it makes me want to find someone less perfect or maybe less fussy who'd be more likely to put up with me.

"But then You surprise me. You spend the last twenty-seven chapters talking mostly about our wonderful future together and how much You want me to join You in looking forward to it and how someone You simply call 'Your Servant' will make it all happen. God, I feel slapped, then hugged—slapped hard, then hugged tight. It catches me off guard. Courtships usually begin by identifying what one person finds attractive in another, then pursuing the other for long-term relationship. You are so different. Maybe that's what You mean when You say You're holy. And maybe it's just a literary accident, but as I already mentioned, You follow the same pattern in Your sixty-six love letters: thirty-nine slaps, then twenty-seven hugs. That's holy love, I guess."

"Nothing I do is an accident, and nothing I allow is a coincidence. I want you to notice something else. It will further define holy love. My last word in Isaiah is a hard slap [Isaiah 66:24]. I promise that all who rebel against Me will become contemptibly, disgustingly selfish. Read, too, My last word in Malachi [4:6]. I threaten to come to My people to curse them.

"But when I close My last love letter, I give the final word to My Son. Read Revelation 22:20–21. With joy that only My Spirit and I can fully feel, My Son announces, 'I am coming soon.' And My people know He is coming to bring life, not a curse. 'Yes, Lord Jesus. Come. Come soon,' they say. Then the apostle John, with eyes fixed on the unseen world of beauty, looks at the people he has pastored for so many years, sees all their pain and fear and failure, and with the power of well-tested faith whispers, 'Until He comes, His grace is with us, even in exile, in all our suffering. We may cry in heartache, but we live in hope.'

"From unholy misery—exposed and condemned—to holy joy, freely given and promised forever: *that is the story of My love*. Without My Son, the story would end after thirty-nine angry chapters in Isaiah. The comfort in chapter 40 would not be provided. The curse threatened in Malachi would be carried out. But—enter My Son. Behold beauty that you can see nowhere else. He was slapped that you might be hugged. I slapped Him—I can barely say those words— so that I can hug you, so that I can release My love for you as I've always poured love into My Son. Yes, a thunderous slap deserved by you, delivered by Me to One who merited My embrace, now no more judgment on those worthy of being abandoned, nothing now but an eternal hug. That is the story of Isaiah, the story I tell in all My sixty-six love letters, the hidden story of My love."

"God, it is hidden. It's hard to see. But why? Why don't we get it? Why don't I get it? Why do so many of us feel more slapped then hugged? Just yesterday, I put my arm around a friend whose life is a painful, confusing mess. My words felt limp, but I said them anyway because they're true. 'I want you to know how much Jesus loves you and that I love you too.' She looked at me as if I were a doctor offering aspirin to a patient with kidney stones and said, 'Well, I wish He'd show His love a little more. I feel more loved by you than by Him.'

"Another friend thinks Your love is all about the spiritual highs he sometimes experiences when he sobs over how empty he feels. But these 'divine encounters' with Your love don't seem to be freeing him to better love his difficult wife. He backs away from her so he can experience Your love without interruption. *God, what are we missing? What do we not understand about Your love?*"

"My love makes people holy. Only those who know they are unholy, who hate their unholiness more than their pain and emptiness, experience the transforming power of My love. Only holy people live well. Only holy people love."

"God, that goes counter to almost everything we believe. You're saying that love means nothing until we admit how unlovable we are. Most people who teach on these things say that our big problem is insecurity and the solution is to be hugged, not slapped. You just said that only *holy* people live well. Most everyone I know believes that only *loved* people, people affirmed as valuable rather than being judged as unholy, live well and are able to love. Is that wrong?"

"You cannot detach holiness from love. Love is reduced to mere sentiment when people fail to see their unholiness. And mere sentiment changes no one. It has no power to transform unholy people into people who love. This is what I'm saying in My twenty-third love letter, to all who have ears to hear:

No matter what is happening to you, your worst problem is in you. And that problem is not how badly you feel, it is how poorly you love. Your failure to love Me above all else and to love others at any cost to yourself defines your unholiness. When you recognize your unholiness and own it without excuse, your ears will be opened to hear My words of comfort and hope. And those words will set you on the narrow road to relating with holy love. There is no other kind."

"God, show me how You're saying that in Isaiah."

"Keep three words in mind as you read Isaiah: *judgment, comfort,* and *hope.* And realize, as my servant Paul said in Colossians 1:5, that faith to believe I am good in any circumstance and love that pays any price to bless another both spring from hope. Without My judgment, My comfort means nothing. Without comfort, there is no hope. And without hope, faith yields to doubt and cynicism, and love suffocates in the pain of living.

❀ *Judgment.* In the first thirty-nine chapters of Isaiah, hear Me pronounce the severest judgment on your desire for anything more than Me, on your refusal to trust Me when life gets rough.
❀ *Comfort.* Then hear Me provide comfort to My judged people, comfort that can be received only by those who are deeply troubled by how worthy they are of judgment; people who know their desires for more than Me are treasonous. Notice that the comfort I provide, described in chapters 40 to 55, is not the comfort of empathy or affirmation. It is the comfort of forgiveness rooted in My holy love and of healing available only through My power, the comfort and healing I provide for people ruined by their self-centeredness. The effect of My comfort is to direct your eyes away from your emptiness, not in denial but in hope of eternal fullness, which then releases you to demand nothing from anyone and give everything to everyone. Like My Son.
❀ *Hope.* My final eleven chapters, 56 to 66, point to hope. I do not cure your unholiness by overlooking or understanding it. To overlook it would be to miss the spot on the x-ray that will

destroy you. To understand it in light of what you've suffered would be to excuse it. I do not heal your selfishness by affirming your value. I solve your deepest problem with My self-sacrificing, reconciling embrace that forgives all that is unholy within you. Read Isaiah 53. My beauty is revealed in My Son whom, without My Spirit opening your eyes, you see as unattractive, someone to be despised, set aside. My Son reveals the beauty of holy love, a love that absorbs everything evil in another with no thought of protecting oneself from the pain that evil can inflict. Through the beauty of holy love, I am transforming your life into sheer joy; I am forming you into sheer delight. Read those words of hope in Isaiah 65:17–19."

"God, this is so radical. *You* are so radical. But I still don't get it, not deeply enough to make me as radical as Your Son. I'm still trying to avoid Your slap and enjoy Your hug."

"Your failure to 'get it' troubles you. Others' failure to 'get it' troubles you. That's good. Untroubled people have closed ears. Only troubled people hear My story of love. Jeremiah was a deeply troubled prophet who discovered that My love was in his heart, like a fire that would not die. Read My next letter. It will help you enter a little more deeply into My story of love."

Love Letter Twenty-Four:
Jeremiah

THERE IS WATER IN THE WELL

*G*od, I'm puzzled. Why am I so drawn to Jeremiah? Ever since I began thinking seriously about life, really since my late teens, Jeremiah has been my favorite biblical character. And yet just about everything that could go wrong in his life went wrong. His personal life was miserable, his ministry a total failure. Next to his, my life has been—and still is—a walk in the park. So why have I read this letter of Yours more than any of the others? Am I some sort of spiritual sadist? Or do I somehow think that if I read about the mess in his life and learn lessons vicariously through his suffering, then I'll be spared such extreme misery? I think my fascination with Jeremiah comes from something else, something deeper, but I don't know what it is. And I don't know what You're saying to me through his story."

"What do you fear the most?"

"May I ask why You're raising that question?"

"You'll understand when I respond to your answer."

"What do I fear the most? Well, I don't think it's dying. I came close with my cancer, but I felt calm either way. But—and this is strange—when my doctor told me a month ago that I was prediabetic, I was unnerved. The threat of a long-term illness that I'd have to manage hit something deep."

"What did it hit?"

"Something deep; that much I know. Maybe some basic fear that nothing works. I exercise regularly, eat sensibly, and keep my weight pretty close to target. I should be healthy. This diabetes scare feels like an unveiling of something I know but try hard not to face, that nothing is guaranteed to work as it should.

"But my fear goes deeper than that, beneath a pouty 'nothing works' to a terrified panic that, if I looked at life the way it really is, I'd realize that nothing matters. More than once, I've stood paralyzed at the foot of my bed in the middle of the night unable to come up with one good reason why I should move, why I should do anything. I've even had dreams where my life was a calloused hand dipped into a huge bucket of water. While it was there, some displacement was measurable. The hand made a difference. But when it was removed, the ripple lasted a few seconds, and then there was no evidence the hand was ever there, no evidence that my few years on earth amounted to anything.

"Sometimes I feel as if I'm desperately trying to keep on believing what I once knew was true, to return to a system of thought, to embrace a worldview, to be overwhelmed by an experience that would give me at least some place to rest, to know that following You was ultimately satisfying. God, I'm scared to death that something could happen that would lead to my giving up on You, that I'll finish poorly, stripped of energizing hope, and incapable of loving anyone. If that happens, I'll dissolve into nothing. God, that terrifies me. I don't want a faith that could be destroyed."

"Now you're ready to hear what I'm saying to you in My twenty-fourth love letter. It's this:

I make no promise to protect you from suffering in this world. I do promise the power to believe in My goodness when bad things happen, the power to hope with confidence that a good plan is unfolding when nothing visible supports that hope, and the power to reveal the goodness of My love no matter how distraught

or empty you feel, even to those who contribute to your distress and emptiness. That is the abundance I promise until you arrive at My party."

"God, do You ever say anything that fits our culture? For most people, faith means that You'll make our lives turn out well. We hope in the confidence that if we get it right, You'll give us what we want, like good health if we eat right and exercise. And love is about *being* loved, feeling good about who we are and loving the people, You included, who give us those good feelings.

"I'm seeing a collision of two kingdoms: the way You've set up life in this world and the way everyone wants life to be. I just read a review of what's right now the number-one best-selling book in America, *The Secret*. God, if I'm hearing You right, this book is worse than garbage. The contributors write stuff like this: 'The universe is supporting me in everything I do. The universe meets my needs immediately.' Change 'the universe' to 'God' and what this book teaches is what so many Christians believe. But You sent Jeremiah to tell the Jews precisely the opposite, that You would actively thwart their self-centered plans and destroy them if they didn't repent.

"But that's not the secret we want to hear. This awful book says that we 'deserve all good things life has to offer' and that wishing will make it so. And sometimes we believe that, even Christians. We really don't think we deserve hell, and we do believe that praying should bring into our lives all the good things we want and feel entitled to, like a diabetes-free life. The blind blasphemers who wrote this devilish drivel hype their book by promising to introduce people to 'the magnificence of You,' capital Y. Not You, God, but me, magnificent Me! God, this way of thinking has infected the church. I feel the collision of kingdoms most acutely when I sing some 'worship' music in church and hear sermons about how to get You to bless us.

"God, show me how You communicate Your culture-opposing message in this twenty-fourth love letter. I want to hear through Jeremiah's misery that I can be a man of faith, hope, and love even if nothing goes right in my life."

"Read My twenty-fourth letter knowing this: *no one hears My good news without trivializing its goodness unless they first hear My bad news without soft-*

ening its badness. You do not deserve the good things of life. I created you to enjoy them, but you do not deserve them. Kierkegaard, my nineteenth-century Jeremiah, had it right. He referred to the books of the Bible as love letters from Me to all who would hear, but he also called them 'a handbook for those who are to be sacrificed.' He confronted the culture of his day, as Jeremiah confronted his, with these words: 'Not until a person has become so wretched that his only wish, his only consolation, is to die—not until then does Christianity begin.' As I tell you this, Jeremiah is standing by My side, smiling with joy. He just said amen.

"Kierkegaard confronted the Danish church with the same message Jeremiah brought to Jerusalem. And the Danes liked it no more than the Jews. The Danes ridiculed Kierkegaard when they heard him say, 'It's precisely our consciousness of sin that can lead us nearer to God.' Without an ongoing consciousness of sin, any sense of nearness to Me is counterfeit. But with consciousness of sin, the fire of purifying holiness will sustain your faith in My goodness, your hope of a better day, and your love for Me and for this God-forsaking world. These truths run through My twenty-fourth letter:

❀ When King Josiah discovered the book of My law and realized how far short he and his people had fallen, he led Judah in the greatest Passover ever celebrated in Israel [2 Chronicles 35:1, 18]. But My people worshiped in pretense [Jeremiah 3:10]. Their praise was unholy noise in My ears [Jeremiah 7:1–8]. Their trust was a disguised spirit of entitlement; they presumed I would keep them from suffering; their religion provided them with the illusion of safety [Jeremiah 7:9–11]. *My people had no consciousness of sin.*

❀ Prophets who claimed to speak for Me preached the false gospel of indulgent love, blessing without holiness, no consequence for sin [Jeremiah 28]. And My people loved that lie then, and they love it now [Jeremiah 5:30–31].

❀ Three times I instructed Jeremiah to no longer pray for the people he and I both loved [Jeremiah 7:16; 11:14; 14:11]. He needed to know that holy love tears down before it builds up. Sin *will* be punished [Jeremiah 1:10]. He did not know then (he does now) that My plan was to bruise My Son so I could heal My people.

🌼 Read carefully the record of Jeremiah's struggles. Six times he put his inner distress into words [Jeremiah 11:18–23; 12:1–4; 15:10–21; 17:12–18; 18:18–23; 20:7–18]. He felt your fear. At one point, I seemed to him like a dried-up well, no longer a source of life-giving water. That was the one time I told him to repent. I rescued Jeremiah—and I will rescue you—from your worst fear, which is *not* your fear of suffering. Jeremiah suffered and so will you. I rescued him from faithless unbelief, from hopeless despair, and from unloving self-obsession. And now My Son has made it possible for you to live a life of abundant though severely tested *faith*, abundant though seriously challenged *hope*, and abundant though painfully sacrificial *love*. That is the good news I bring from Me to you in this letter."

"God, I believe, help my unbelief. I hope, help my hopelessness. I love, help my lack of love. Will reading Your next letter provide the help I need? I don't know if my faith in Your goodness or my hope in Your plan or my power to love when I'm miserable will survive reading Lamentations. I'm ready to see Your Son."

"Not yet. Only when the night is darkest is the Morning Star visible. Read on. True Christianity begins in desolation. Your faith will not fail. Your hope will not dim. Your love will not die. Let Jeremiah continue as your guide on the path to My Son. For you, perhaps your favorite guide."

Love Letter Twenty-Five: Lamentations

PAINFUL THIRST CREATES JOYFUL HOPE

*O*f all Your letters so far, God, this one raises the most difficult questions for me. Leviticus felt tedious, Judges was frustrating, but Lamentations is excruciating. And terrifying. The suffering You imposed on people You claimed to love is so far removed from anything I've seen or experienced that I have to ask: *what was so wrong in Your people that made You treat them so severely?* It seems cruel, more like what a mad dictator would do to citizens plotting a coup than how a loving God should treat misbehaving children. What possible value was there in such extreme suffering, suffering that You brought on?"

"You will recognize its value when you understand the sin that deserved it."

"God, are You more just than compassionate?"

"My justice serves the deeper purposes of My love. Always."

"Well, like I said in our conversation over Your last letter, I'm scared to death, given how You treat Your people, that enough bad things could happen to me that I'd lose sight of Your compassion. And I'm afraid that then I could scrap my faith in You as someone I want to know and serve, and instead live for whatever pleasure or relief I could find. Or maybe I'd just crawl into a dark corner and be miserable, feeling sorry for myself and terribly misunderstood. Anyone who claims to have no similar fears is assuming Your love guarantees a reasonable limit on catastrophes. And that's living in a fool's paradise."

"You will feel the warmth of My compassion only to the degree that you taste the terror of My wrath. Only when you acknowledge the justice of My anger will you marvel at and be transformed by the wonder of My grace. That's My plan. Lamentations will move it forward."

"God, right now I'm sitting on my deck surrounded by blooming flowers, cool air, and chirping birds. Suffering seems far away and entirely unnecessary. Am *I* resting in a fool's paradise?"

"I am whispering My love to you in your pleasures as a mother quietly sings over the child in her arms. But I want you to grow up."

"God, I'm not a baby who's known only the pain of a momentary empty stomach and a full diaper. My faith has already survived a plane crash that killed my only brother, a life-threatening bout with cancer, a half-dozen heartbreaking agonies in our family, and the unexpected, confusing deterioration of several long-term friendships. But I admit, I've suffered nothing remotely comparable to what You brought on Your people when Babylon laid siege to Jerusalem, carted off thousands of Jews into exile, slaughtered thousands more, then utterly destroyed the city, including Solomon's temple.

"In Your last letter, You went against nearly every preacher in America today when You promised to make Your people *unhappy* [Jeremiah 7:34]. And now in Lamentations, You're keeping Your word. The descendants of Your good friend Abraham were regarded as 'scum and refuse among the nations' (3:45). 'Young and old lie together in the dust of the streets . . . you have slaughtered them without pity' (2:21). And young mothers were eating 'their offspring, the children they have cared for' (2:20).

"Cannibalism, murder, humiliation. God, what were You thinking?

And You tell me that all this happened because of Your *fierce anger*, a phrase You use four times in Lamentations [1:12; 2:3,6; 4:11] and at least eight times in Jeremiah when You warned that these catastrophes were coming [4:8, 26; 12:13; 25:37–38; 44:6; 49:37; 51:45]. How could any of Your people back then cuddle up to You as a loving Father? And if You're the same today as yesterday, how am I to rest in Your mercies, to enjoy Your unfailing compassions that I'm supposed to believe are new every morning [3:22–23]?

"God, it just occurred to me. I can't remember ever hearing a sermon series on this letter. It just doesn't fit our culture's understanding of Christianity. A majority of Americans today say they believe in You and want to know You. *But who do they think You are?* And I wonder who all these years I've thought You were? I've never preached through the five laments that make up Lamentations either. I've sung about Your great faithfulness a thousand times, usually with images of enjoying my deck or playing with my grandchildren filling my mind. But that's ripping those two verses about Your compassion and faithfulness out of their horrible context [3:22–23]. Maybe I'm like most churchgoers today, spiritually flabby, narcissistically naïve, a good-enough Christian who's bought into the 'God-is-here-to-bless-me-with-a-good-life' gospel more than I've realized."

"In this moment, I am no longer whispering in your pleasures. My Spirit is now speaking through your conscience. Your mind is focusing more on where you are wrong than where you are scared, more on the evil in your heart than the fear in your stomach."

"I guess that's supposed to encourage me. Well, at least one thing's for sure. No rational person could read this twenty-fifth letter of Yours and still support Freud's theory that belief in You is a wish-fulfilling fantasy. No one, idealizing the Father they wanted, would make up the God You reveal Yourself to be in this letter. No one in their right mind wants a *holy* God of wrath. We'd all prefer an indulgent grandfather who wants all the children to have a good time. That's how C. S. Lewis put it. I think he's right. And that's the American God."

"Lewis is right. And that is the American God. But you're wrong to believe that no one in his right mind would wish Me to exist as I AM. It is only the wrong-minded who prefer a foolishly kind grandfather who takes his children to Disney World when they need to be in a hospital. People in their right minds are drawn to Me in every circumstance as their only source of true meaning, joyful belonging, and renewing rest. But everyone enters this world in their wrong mind. Unless I shout to them in suffering, everyone stays deceived."

"God, what are You shouting to me in this letter? I've left my deck. I'm in Your Word. I want to hear You."

"If you have ears to hear, you will hear this:

Every moment of suffering represents a strident but merciful call to repent. And every moment of suffering presents a painful opportunity to hope.

"Read how My prophet responded to suffering. 'The visions of your prophets'—he was referring to false prophets—'did not expose your sin' (2:14). And then when all that he had hoped from Me was gone, a different, truer hope was aroused when he called My character to mind, when he returned to his right mind [3:17–18, 21]."

"God, I'm so rarely in my right mind. Shout to me. Let me hear Your call to repent and hope."

"Learn the message of Lamentations: *something good happens in suffering that cannot happen in pleasure*. A fork in the road is reached. A choice point becomes clear that you cannot see from your deck. You have fallen into a ditch, from which only I can rescue you. It is a ditch of deceit. You deny that there are desires in your heart that the good things of life can never satisfy. And you do not recognize the ugliness in your soul, the arrogant passion that leads you to judge others more harshly than yourself.

"You foolishly continue to believe what Adam and Eve passed on to you, the wrong-minded and proud idea that you should be able to define what is good and bad for you and then live, with My cooperation, to gain the good and avoid the bad. Suffering lifts your denial of both desire and arrogance and opens your eyes to see that you are lying helpless in a ditch of your own making. When every good thing in life is either removed or exposed as unsatisfying, you discover your craving for the best thing in life, relationship with Me . . . on My terms. And then you recognize your inexcusable and hideous arrogance that thinks I exist to give you what you believe is good, a proud arrogance that assumes you have the wisdom needed to discern what is good for your soul and what is lethal. That arrogance is responsible for every divorce (in at least one spouse), every sexual addiction, every judgmental word, every hidden insecurity, every controlling tendency, every self-preoccupied fear—everything that is unholy.

"Perhaps now you better understand the sin that led Me to drive My people into exile. My actions were just. And My justice served My purposes of love. I was shouting to My people: *Do not live to arrange for your own satisfaction. Confess the evil of your arrogance. Repent of your self-provision. Trust Me, in every moment of suffering. I do not mean you harm. My plan for you is the prosperity of enjoying Me, of dancing at My party. You cannot dance in the ditch of denial.*"

"God, lift my denial. Let me see the ditch in which I so often live. Let me look up and see Your fiercest anger poured out on Your Son so that I could know Your mercy, Your compassions that are fresh every time I look up from the ditch. God, I know You've been quoting words written by Lewis: 'God whispers to us in our pleasures, speaks to us in our conscience, but shouts to us in our pain; it is His megaphone to a deaf world.' Please, let me hear Your gentle voice of love whispering beneath Your paralyzing shouts. But don't stop shouting. I'm still pretty deaf."

"I am faithful to My purposes of love. Read on."

Love Letter Twenty-Six: Ezekiel

FACE YOUR EVIL, THEN SEE MY GLORY

*G*od, why is it so hard for me to see what's really going on in my heart, stuff that You see so clearly? You see both the deep longings in my heart that the good things in this life can never satisfy and the determined arrogance that thinks those good things should satisfy, and that thinks I'm entitled to the satisfaction. I know the desire for You and the arrogance in me are both there, but I don't feel my desire for You strongly enough to seek You above every other good thing. And, more often than not, I think it's quite reasonable to assume that I should have the good things of life and to make it my priority to get them.

"But my blindness is so subtle. Just last night at dinner with good friends, godly friends who love You, we spent most of the evening talking about how troubled we are by the arrogant blindness of others. During that conversation, I felt superior, an innocent victim of another's sin. And I enjoyed the feeling. It satisfied a desire within me, certainly not my desire for You, but my desire to feel good about me. I sensed something going on in me that was wrong, but I was too caught up in the pleasure of the moment to pay much attention.

"How did Jonathan Edwards put it? 'Nothing puts a Christian so much out of the devil's reach than humility.' That night the devil could reach me rather easily. I think he had his arm around me. God, why don't I see my desire for You and my tendency to settle for something else more clearly, at least clearly enough to relate differently with friends over dinner? I bring this up because after reading Ezekiel, I think You're saying something in this letter that might improve my spiritual eyesight."

"Blindness to your own inner world gives you a false confidence that you are seeing clearly into another's faults. You can only discern another's failures accurately and with holy love when you first discern and more severely judge your own. Without Spirit-revealed self-awareness, what you assume is righteous discernment of another's wrongs is in fact proud judgment, which you are not qualified to exercise."

"But God, that's my point. I *was* judging people last night at dinner. I know that. I could see their faults much more easily than I could see my own. I wanted to see their faults. I enjoyed it. But why? What's wrong with me?"

"You are far enough along on the path to humility—though you have a long way to go—to hear what I'm saying to you in this twenty-sixth love letter:

Only when you are so grieved by the raw evil of your ongoing self-obsession that My glory overwhelms you with desire to love like My Son will you deeply change. Only then will the incomparable beauty of His character become visible in the way you relate."

"God, I am so sick of myself. I'm irritable, proud, impatient, and judgmental. And I disguise it as wise discernment so well that my wickedness sometimes passes for godliness, at least to my jaded conscience. God, I'm crying to You from the ditch, the ditch of deceit into which I've fallen. I want to feel my desire for You more passionately than I feel all other desires. I want to see where I'm so wrong that only a plea for mercy spills out of my mouth. Show me what You're saying to me in Ezekiel, what I need to hear."

"Remember the history you've already learned. Babylon invaded Judah in several stages. More than a decade before Nebuchadnezzar finally sacked Jerusalem and destroyed the temple, ten thousand of

My people, along with the young priest Ezekiel (then twenty years of age), were carried off into exile. They all expected to return to Jerusalem soon, never dreaming that I would allow the Holy City to lie desolate. They knew neither Me nor themselves.

"After five years in captivity, I revealed myself to Ezekiel in the first of three visions [Ezekiel 1–2], transforming him from priest into prophet. He saw My glory, a magnificence that exceeded Solomon's as the heavens exceed a grain of sand. Ezekiel became more aware of My glory than of the depressing condition of exile. He was now fit to speak for Me to My people.

"The people in exile recognized his calling as a prophet and, many months later, before Jerusalem fell, approached Ezekiel to hear what I would say to them, still expecting that I would tell them to pack their bags and go home to a good life in Jerusalem. They did not know that I AM the Lord, uncompromisingly holy and, therefore, just in punishing sin.

"While the leaders of My exiled people were waiting for Ezekiel to speak, I took control of his entire being and, in a second vision [Ezekiel 8], carried him back to Jerusalem's temple and showed him what was happening in the place designed for My people to meet Me and to know Me. What was happening in the temple is a picture of what is going on in every human heart, including yours.

"In the place I created for worship, I opened My young prophet's eyes to see four things that I will now open your eyes to see, four abominations that cannot exist in the presence of My glory.

"First, by the north gate, the main entrance through which Judah's king would come to the temple to worship, stood the idol of jealousy. That same idol is in your heart. It is your desire to feel loved, to enjoy good relationships, to be affirmed, to see yourself as worthy of respect and entitled to a pleasant life. These desires become your idol of jealousy when they rule your life.

"Second, on the walls of the temple were engravings of reptiles, insects, wolves. And the leaders of My people were gazing on these life-taking creatures *with appreciation*. When you, in the secret place of your heart, want something more than My pleasure, the power of your flesh is turned loose in the way you relate. The serpent of self-interest, the insect of self-obsession, the wolf of self-protection sink their poison into your conversations with friends. That is what happened last night.

"Third, again by the north gate, women were mourning the death of Tammuz, the Babylonian god of fertility, the god who promised the good life of blessings. When you value anything above Me, when self-interest rules your life, you feel only your desires for what is available in this world: good health, warm relationships, fulfilling work; and you assume it is My job and delight to satisfy those desires. There is a Tammuz in your heart. And you mourn his death—perhaps the failure of your spouse to love you well or the failure of your ministry to affirm your gifts and calling or the failure of family or friends to appreciate you—more than you mourn distance from Me. You do not know that I AM the Lord, the source of the life you were created to enjoy.

"Fourth, in the very center of the temple where communion with Me is available, the priests of My people turned their backs to Me and worshiped the sun, the reliable source of an immediate experience of warmth. It is that sort of spirituality that is still sought today. My servant Paul warned My followers in Colossae never to shift from the hope of the gospel, the hope of joy in suffering now and of joy later, in a perfect world forever [Colossians 1:23]. My people in exile exchanged true hope for false hope. You do the same thing every time you turn from Me to enjoy the smug satisfaction of superiority, every time you say in your heart, 'I am not like others, and my sense of being more together than another makes me feel good about myself.'

"Your sin is deep, your wickedness vile. Serpents from hell crawl through your soul. Their poison fills your words. I showed Ezekiel all of this, and now I am showing you, in this second vision described in chapter 8."

"God, I can say nothing. Like Job, I put my hand over my mouth."

"Your hand has been over your eyes. It belongs over your mouth. You can *say* nothing. Now *see* something. See My glory, this time not in holy wrath but now in merciful love, in My plan to free you to dance with Me. But My mercy is severe. My love stops at nothing to bring in My kingdom, to renew My people, to draw My servants into radical dependence on Me as their first thing. On the same day I used Nebuchadnezzar to destroy the temple where such vile abominations were going on, I took the life of the woman Ezekiel loved, his wife [Ezekiel 24]. And I instructed him not to cry. Through his strange behavior in the middle of grief, I was teaching My people that only in hopelessness will the mouths of the arrogant be closed. And only then will the glory, the sheer beauty, of My plan become visible.

"Seventy times in this letter I explain that I do all that I do for one purpose: *that My people will know that I AM the Lord.* To know Me in My holiness is to know yourself in your sinfulness. To know Me in My love is to experience life, to know that a party is coming. To know Me: *that's My plan.*

"In the third vision I gave Ezekiel (beginning in chapter 40), I revealed a rebuilt temple, restored under terms of a new covenant I made with My people. It was My plan all along to create a new heart in My people, a heart that would value Me as their greatest good, no more idol of jealousy; that would desire to love as I love, no more slithering serpents of self-obsession; that would drink only from My well of living water, no more Tammuz wells that dry up; that would find deep joy in communion with Me, no more turning from Me toward opportunities for cheap, immediate, temporary satisfaction of lesser desires [Ezekiel 36].

"It was—and is—My plan to bring the dry bones of My selfish people to life [Ezekiel 37], to create a community over which I could write the words that close this twenty-sixth letter: 'The LORD is There' (Ezekiel 48:35 NKJV)."

"I see it, God. I see it. I see Your glory. And I think I'm catching a clearer glimpse of my desire for You and of the ditch from which I can only plead for mercy. But I need a solid foundation to stand on, a place from which I can see Your glory again and again. I know I'll participate in self-talk again."

"You will see the foundation you want in My next letter. Keep reading. You're getting closer to the answer to your deepest questions."

Love Letter Twenty-Seven: Daniel

Your Life Is Off Course; My Plan Is Not

*G*od, what am I supposed to do when I read a letter of Yours and hear nothing? The stories in Daniel are all familiar to me since Sunday school days, about a fiery furnace and a lions' den and a disembodied hand spoiling a fun party by pronouncing doom on its host. But what's the point?

"And I've been confused for a long time about all the visions and cryptic timetables that are supposed to make the future clear but, instead, have led to sharp disagreement among scholars. I've read and reread this twenty-seventh letter a dozen times, and I've studied two recent commentaries by serious Bible students, all in this last week. And I've prayed, literally on my knees, begging You to let me hear what You're saying to me in all these stories and visions. So far, nothing. I'm tempted to skip ahead to Hosea, but I know You wrote this letter to me for a purpose. But I'm not hearing You. What am I supposed to do?"

"What's been happening in you this past week as you've been reading My letter?"

"I've wanted to close my Bible, grab the TV remote, and watch an *Andy Griffith* rerun. I don't like living in a world where I feel that I'm supposed to figure out what's going to happen tomorrow and how I should be living today. But that's how reading Daniel makes me feel. I want a simple, pleasant, uncomplicated life. I'd love to escape to Mayberry where Aunt Bee bakes pies and Barney arrests jaywalkers and Sheriff Taylor, after another shuffling day, sits on his porch with Opie's pretty schoolteacher and strums his guitar. The only thing I'd have to worry about in Mayberry is where in the lake the fish will be biting on my day off."

"Read My closing words to you in this letter."

"I already have, a dozen times. But since You're telling me to read them again, I will. 'But you, go your way till the end; for you shall rest, and will arise to your inheritance at the end of the days' (Daniel 12:13 NKJV).

"Something's coming to mind, I have no idea why. Just yesterday, good friends sent me five books by or about G. K. Chesterton. This morning in one of them I read that Chesterton always carried a sword concealed in his walking stick. I loved his answer when someone asked him why: 'I like things to come to a point.' I do too. Maybe I've been expecting You to bring everything You've said so far to a point in this letter. Scholars do call Daniel apocalyptic, so I assume it's a letter in which You unveil what was previously hidden. I think that's been my frustration. I think You're wanting me to see the point of all You've been saying in the first twenty-six letters. And I do feel something sharp pressing in on me as I read Daniel, something I sense is really important, but I can't put words to it."

"When You feel the sharpness of a point you cannot describe, what do you find yourself wanting the most? What do you think Mayberry could do for you?"

"As You ask that question, one desire rises within me: I want to laugh. I want to feel the sharpness of how everything comes together in Your Son until it draws blood and makes me giddy, alive with the thrill of dangerous adventure, full of passion as I enter the real battle and dream of victory. God, I want to look at Your Son and burst into song no matter what's irritating or scaring me at the moment; I want to feel like a little child tossed high in the air by a laughing, strong father who loves to see terrified delight in his child's face. I want to laugh like that."

"When I toss My children into the air, terror comes before delight. Put yourself in the place of My people in Daniel's day. They felt thrown into the air with no safety net beneath them. They couldn't see their God ready to catch them. For years, My people had misinterpreted My promises just as so many of My followers do today. They lived on the foundation of hope that David's throne would never be vacant, that Messiah would come, sit on the throne, and restore Israel to worldwide prominence and unparalleled prosperity. They never imagined the Holy City would be destroyed or that the Holy Temple, the place of My Presence, would ever be violated. My people laughed until their hopes were shattered, exposed as false. Then they despaired, struggling to know Me as I AM as they lived their lives in exile.

"Jerusalem lay in ruins. They had no king. Heathens had entered the Holy of Holies and lived to bring home the sacred treasures they stole. And the theology of My people, all their expectations, crumbled. What was I doing? What kind of God were they serving? What could they count on in the future?

"The greatest danger My people face today is prosperity, blessings that reinforce the false hope that nothing serious will ever go wrong in their lives if they just keep believing, expecting, trusting, and smiling. My people in Daniel's day were wrestling with hard questions that the prosperous church of today never asks. Your desire for Mayberry, for a rest you will never find in this world, is good. It means you are no longer living on a foundation of false hope.

"When you read Daniel, remember the people to whom I was then speaking, a disillusioned people in exile, wanting to discover who I AM and what I'm up to as they were living in a non-Mayberry world. This is what I said to them and what I'm now saying to you:

When every expectation of how your life should turn out is shattered; when I seem to you like an indifferent, cold sovereign, a promise-breaker, a useless God, an abandoning parent, rejoice! You are ready for the unveiling, to meet Me as I AM."

"God, I didn't hear that in this letter. I'm not sure I'm hearing it now. Please. Guide me through all the stories and visions until I hear that message in a way that builds a solid foundation of true hope beneath my feet."

"Daniel *labored* to hear My words and to understand what I was saying. He prayed all night for wisdom [2:17–19]; he was greatly confused for a season [4:19]; his mind was disturbed, his spirit troubled, as he wondered what I was saying [7:15–16, 28]; he spent hours trying to make sense of My words [8:15]; when I spoke, he fell down in terror [8:17]; his efforts to understand left him exhausted and ill [8:27]; as he pored over Scripture, he pled for understanding, in fasting and sackcloth [9:3]; when understanding came, he fell into depression [10:12]; he felt weak, his face turned pale, and he was helpless before Me when he heard Me speak [10:8]; My words left him overcome with anguish, barely able to breathe [10:16,17]; when he heard My final word to him, he did not understand its meaning, and I did not enlighten him [12:8–12].

"Like so many of My followers today, you want sound-bite theology, wisdom without struggle, formulas without mystery. Wrestle with My twenty-seventh letter until you hear these truths:

- ❈ In chapter 1: you must draw a line that reflects your unwillingness to compromise with culture.
- ❈ In chapter 2: depend on My wisdom as you face life's mysteries.
- ❈ In chapter 3: risk everything you cherish to obey Me.
- ❈ In chapter 4: realize that no one is beyond the reach of My holy love, not even the one who has hurt you the most.
- ❈ In chapter 5: I decide when the line of no return has been crossed. Never come near that line. Never scorn what is sacred.
- ❈ In chapter 6: know that your enemies can never thwart My plan for your life.
- ❈ In chapter 7: as culture becomes hopelessly evil, you will remain hopefully alive.
- ❈ In chapter 8: you do not live in Mayberry. Never act as if you do.

❀ In chapter 9: only deep awareness of sin in you empties your heart to receive deep wisdom about life from Me.

❀ In chapter 10: when you realize what lies ahead, you will faint with fear. Be strong!

❀ In chapter 11: I see the future with greater clarity than you see the past. I am in control. The story ends well. The point will make you laugh.

❀ In chapter 12: in difficult times, the foundation of true hope will empower you to shine with the brightness of the heavens.

"As for you, go your way. Your way is My way. Never despair. Your soul will experience pain that will feel like death. But hope in this: the worst turmoil opens the door to the richest gift. No matter how deep the ditch into which you fall, I will raise you up, into unspeakable joy. That is the point of this letter."

"God, I know I will not feel the point until I see Your Son. *Let me see Him!*"

"I have written twelve more letters with the sword concealed in My walking stick. Read on. At the right time, I will pull out My sword and pierce your heart. You will die laughing."

Love Letter Twenty-Eight: Hosea

LOVE IS DEEPER THAN HATE

*G*od, I've been reading Your love letters for one reason: I want to hear Your voice. But now, after reading the first two verses of this next letter, I'm not so sure I really do. The first words Hosea heard You say to him were 'marry a whore.' That's not my idea of a wonderful plan for anybody's life. If that was a marriage made in heaven, for Hosea it must have felt like a marriage made in hell. After listening in to what You said to Hosea, I'm a little hesitant to ask what You're saying to me in this letter."

"Every word I have ever said to you—and will ever say—represents an invitation to know My heart of love and to enter My community of love. You were designed for nothing less."

"And God, I want nothing more. Or maybe I do. I'm afraid that if experiencing Your love meant giving up my faithful, loving wife for a prostitute, I might have some trouble (or maybe none at all) figuring out which I really wanted. No one today seems to think You'd ever require such a thing of anybody. But that's pretty close to what You required of Hosea. Why did You do that? How was arranging a bad marriage for a good man an invitation to know Your heart?"

"No one understands the nature of true love without feeling the agony of betrayal and the hatred it releases. Only then will the true nature of love reveal itself beneath the hurt and anger. Real love, the only kind capable of building enduringly rich relationships among fallen people, draws its passion from the character of the one who loves, not the one loved. If you want to hear My voice, and you do, then listen to Me say these words to you in this letter:

You will be irresistibly drawn to My love and able to give it to others when you discover in your own experience that the love I have planted in your heart can never be destroyed by rejection, betrayal, criticism, or any other form of unlove you receive. True love reveals itself as the strongest of all passions when your impulse to hate those who hurt you is fully felt."

"God, You're from another world. No one loves like that."

"My Son came to your world to make possible that kind of love. When I told Hosea to bring back to his home the woman who had thrown the sharpest daggers into his heart, he caught sight of the kind of love I pour out on My adulterous people. And he was enabled to speak to My people from a heart like Mine, broken, angry, yet still loving. When the sword pierced My Son's side, the life of love began to spread like a good infection into everyone who bowed before the cross."

"God, when I take the story of Hosea seriously and realize You actually arranged for a godly man in a godless culture to have a miserable home life and when I understand that You experience profound pain every day in Your marriage and still love Your bride, I can see how shallow my love for You and everyone else really is. When someone hurts me, my immediate and natural goal is to protect myself from getting hurt again. And when I get mad at someone, I so easily express it in order to get them to see my point with no thought of looking deep within my heart to see the sacrificing love You've put there and to make sure they feel that love.

"But You're not like that. You're different. I think that's what You mean when You say You're holy. Even with Your people in Hosea's day, selfish people who were enjoying Your blessings during an evil king's reign and who, therefore, figured that You were pleased with them, You made known Your hurt without protecting Yourself from more, and You expressed Your fierce anger without failing to declare Your even fiercer love. That's how I want to relate. And I do a little. But not very much."

"As you read My twenty-eighth letter, visualize yourself sitting in My Presence as I invite you to see deeply into My character. Hear these words:

"Your sin breaks My heart. You have the power to cause Me deep pain. I suffer more than every abused spouse, every abandoned child, every heartbroken parent, every betrayed friend in the history of time. Hosea's pain was as one drop in the ocean of pain I feel every day.

"I respond to hurt with fury, with righteous anger, with holy hatred. Aristotle was wrong when he defined anger as the desire for retaliation. That is unholy anger, perverted hatred. Lactantius, a father to My people in the third century, got it right. Anger, he said, is 'a motion of the soul rousing itself to curb sin.' I look at My people, and I know this is not the way things are supposed to be, the way you were created to relate with Me. I began to hate My people when they turned from Me and toward another for the satisfaction they desired. My soul roused itself to curb their sins. They viewed Me as a lustful man views a woman. He uses her then discards her. He never loves her; he loves only the temporary pleasure she provides and seeks that pleasure wherever he can find it. My people knew nothing of the sheer delight of knowing Me in a relationship of true love. Read about that in Hosea 9:15.

"In My terrible hurt and boiling anger, I wanted to abandon My people. I wanted to abandon you, to throw you away into hell and return to the pleasures of heaven. But a deeper, stronger, more compelling emotion arose within Me. I can't stop wanting you to be with Me, and I will have you at My party, at any cost that I must pay. I love you with a love stronger than My desire to quickly end My pain, a love more powerful than the hatred My holiness requires Me to feel. It was that kind of love I provided Hosea the opportunity to illustrate to My people. I want you to love like that, to feel the pain when someone hurts you, to embrace the anger that condemns their wickedness and is roused to curb their sin, and then to identify the most dangerous and divine emotion of all, a love that cannot give them up [Hosea 11:8–9].

"To enjoy My love and to pour it into others, you must repent. Many will say that you must first be healed of the wounds suffered at the hands of others. But requiring relief from your pain is wailing on your bed. I want you to repent, to *cry from your heart*, identifying how you've hurt Me and incited My anger, and to give up all hope of finding satisfaction for your soul from anyone or anything but Me. Read again what I wrote in Hosea 7:13–14. Then read the first three verses of chapter 6, where My people thought they were repenting but in fact were only wailing. Then turn to chapter 14. It is there, in verses 1 through 3, that I provide a model for true repentance, for crying from your heart as you lay in the ditch of your sin. True repentance of real sin lets you experience the real joy of true love. Whatever else you hear Me say or see Me do in the next eleven letters, remember this: in the exact center of My infinite being, beneath all the hurt you cause Me and all the anger I feel toward you lies an ocean of infinite love. I invite you to come for a swim. Every word I say is part of that invitation."

"God, I *want* to accept Your invitation. I *long* to swim in Your love. But I'm still not sure how to dive in."

"Those you call the minor prophets (Hosea is the first) will more clearly reveal the depths of the ditch into which you have fallen and the heights of love I want you to enjoy. Do not miss the message they bring. There are many in the church today who see the ditches as a shallow gulley from which, with a little effort, they can lift themselves to walk through life on solid ground. They are wrong. Only from the depths of the ditch can you see the power of My love."

Love Letter Twenty-Nine:
Joel

Wake Up to Desire, Lose Hope in Yourself, and Pray Right for Life

*G*od, when things go wrong in my life, I tend to ask three questions: Why is this happening? What can I do about it? And how can I persuade You to make things better? As I think about what I'm asking, it's obvious that all three questions come out of my terrified demand to be in control. Trusting You is way too risky. And my questions reflect my stubbornly deep conviction that the good life is more about things going well than knowing You well.

"But that's the message that draws big crowds, and it's the message I sometimes wish You were preaching: if I just trust You enough and stay positive, everything will work out the way I want. I remember when the locusts You describe in this next letter were eating up my family. I went for a long walk at midnight and (I know You remember this too) I screamed at You for an hour, 'Just tell me what to do, and I'll do it. I'll do anything You say if it will put my family back together again.' After reading Joel, it's clear You want me to pray differently and ask different questions when disaster strikes. Am I right?"

"Your questions and your prayers are religious, not godly. They come out of your efforts to reach Me for your purposes. They need to come out of your submission to My efforts to reach you for My purposes."

"That's not easy, God, for me today or for Your people back in Joel's day. They had returned to the Promised Land after a long exile in Babylon. The temple was rebuilt. Their economy was moving again. They were struggling to rebuild their lives, and then, right when things were looking up, a huge invasion of locusts destroyed everything, like an epidemic of AIDS spreading across Africa or a tsunami drowning an entire country. And You wanted Your people to make sure their children and grandchildren and great-grandchildren would hear about how awful things were and would never forget it [1:3]. Why was that so important to You? How was this catastrophe part of Your efforts to reach Your people for Your purposes? And You told them to never let the message die out. *What message?* What are You saying to me in this twenty-ninth letter that will help me see it as a love letter?"

"A wife should always wear her wedding ring, as should her husband. Wherever she goes, whomever she's with, whatever she's doing, she is to remember her husband and the vows she has made to him. In every moment and detail of her life, she is to live as his treasure, valuing his love above all other wonders, never violating her highest calling to further his purposes in all she does. And her husband must never give himself to another. He is to find his richest delight in seeing his wife come fully alive in all her beauty and talents and opportunities, and his purposes must never suppress but always release her to be all that she is and can become. I am that husband. But you are not that wife. My message to you in this letter, what I want you to hear, is this:

Let every difficulty, big or little, reveal whether you are My faithful or My adulterous wife. Repent as necessary and surrender more fully to My plan. My plan is to make you fully alive with joy, meaning, and love."

"As always, God, I need Your help. How are You saying that in this letter, and what exactly *are* You saying?"

"In every other prophetic letter, I describe the sins of My people that require repentance. In this letter, I make no specific charges of wrongdoing, no indictment of idolatry or injustice or selfishness. Instead, I speak uniquely to three groups:

❀ To the alcoholic, I say: *wake up!* And when you do, you will weep. Stop numbing yourself with wine to the hard reality that your best life now leaves you longing for what you cannot have. Weep as a woman whose fiancé dies the day before her wedding [1:5–8].

❀ To the farmer, I say: *lose hope!* Your hope is in your crops. Your joy is in your blessings. Because a good crop has become your greatest good, your trust in Me has become complacent expectation. Lose all hope in this life in order to gain hope in My plan [1:11–12].

❀ To the spiritual leader, I say: *pray right!* In humility, as people entitled to no good thing; in surrender, to Me as the provider of every good thing; in trust, believing in My plan to give you every good thing; in humility, surrender, and trust, lead My people in holy prayer: no demand, absolute surrender, fervent trust [1:13–15].

"I wanted My people then, and I *want you today*, to quietly realize and humbly accept that life will never work as it should until My day, the day of the Lord. In that day, and not until, I will make everything right. I told My people in Joel's day to look forward to another day, when My Spirit would fall on every man, woman, and child who turns to Me in humble, abandoning trust, and He would empower them to bring My kingdom to earth. *That day has come.* My church is established. It is My Son's bride, My Spirit's temple. My kingdom is near, already present though not yet fully visible. The music has begun. The rainbow shines in the darkest sky, promising that every locust will be destroyed, that every crop will be bountiful. That is the message of Joel, the message I want every generation to hear until the final day comes and the eternal party begins."

"God, it's becoming embarrassingly clear—the questions I ask when things go wrong are really awful. I can see that now. When my life gets all messed

LOVE LETTER TWENTY-NINE: JOEL

up, when things go wrong, I don't want to complain, feel frantic, and angrily ask why this is happening to me. I don't want to make it my highest priority to get everything straightened out and to devote my deepest energy to knowing what I can do to make that happen. And I don't want to be so arrogantly foolish as to think there's something I can do that obligates You to cooperate with my plans. I can see how that attitude is religious, not godly.

"God, tell me if I'm hearing You or not. Here's what I want to learn to say when things go wrong and I come to You, scared to death, mad, frustrated, and feeling entitled to things going better. I want to ask Your forgiveness for my proud, unbroken, demanding spirit. I want to ask Your forgiveness for my stubbornly independent, unsurrendered spirit. I want to ask forgiveness for my desperate, untrusting spirit. I want to honor You as a good wife honors a great husband. I want to rest in Your provision as a child rests in her father's arms, even when those arms become instruments of hard-to-follow instruction or painfully stern discipline. And I want to pray that Your will be done, not mine, until my will becomes Yours, and I am trusting that Your will is better than mine even when it doesn't look like it. No more false comfort in wine. No more false hope in good crops. No more false prayer that values blessings from You above relationship with You."

"Your words are good. But you will speak them with neither consistency nor passion until you are plunged deeper into conviction and raised higher in hope. Read on. A vision of My Son is on the horizon."

Love Letter Thirty:
Amos

REAL WORSHIP PRODUCES REAL CHANGE

*I*f I just went to church and didn't read my Bible, I wouldn't ask so many questions. But reading this next letter brought questions to mind I wish had never come. Like these: What kind of God *are* You? And what on earth are You *doing*? You come across in Amos more like a wild animal than a compassionate lover. I'm beginning to understand why, after all these years of claiming to know You, I sometimes am drawn so near to atheism. Believing that You don't exist can seem safer than facing who You really are."

"With the savagery of a lion, I roar against everything in you that violates My being and opposes My plan."

"God, You're providing me no comfort."

"I comfort only the broken. I stand against the proud. The unrepentant I will destroy. The plumb line is dropped [7:7–9]. Your crookedness is exposed. You and everyone else are ripe for judgment [8:1–3]."

"God, what crookedness? What are You saying?"

"When you remain blind to your guilt, you seek Me (if you seek Me at all) for your purposes. And you call it church. But your gatherings are a club of self-seekers. I despise your religious gatherings. I cannot stand your assemblies [5:21]. You are not meeting Me; you are not even meeting yourselves though the excitement and camaraderie you generate delude you into thinking you are. The famine of truth that I send will reveal your emptiness, how starved and emaciated you really are. You are subsisting on spiritual cotton candy, thinking it is food."

"God, I'm not enjoying listening to You. I've heard You say this before, but it's becoming clearer: You really are not committed at all to making my life work the way I want it to. And yet You call Yourself good. I want to believe You. And I think I could if You would just answer one question: *what are You good for?*"

"I swear by My holiness [4:2]; like a fierce lion I oppose your desire for every good thing you value above Me. And I swear by all that I AM [6:8]; like a father who disciplines his child because he cannot bear to lose him, I will pay whatever price I must to bring you home."

"God, which are You—a lion or a father? You're confusing me. What are You saying to me in this letter that I'm having trouble hearing?"

"If you want to hear what I am saying and not what you assume I'm saying, you will hear this:

Worship that leaves unchanged the way you relate to Me and to others is false worship. I will not cooperate with any pursuit of spiritual maturity that leaves unrecognized and undisturbed your hidden energy of self-protection and self-enhancement.

"Read Amos and tremble. You are conscious only of your unsatisfied desires in the presence of My seeming indifference. Like worshipers dancing around Baal's altar on Mount Carmel [1 Kings 18:26], you sing and shout in your churches, thinking you will persuade Me to favor you with the blessings you want. Read Amos and tremble but with the consciousness of your relational sin in the presence of My relational purity. How I relate is the plumb line, the standard by which you will be judged. I will destroy every society, including what you call the church, that organizes itself around the goal of self-pleasing. I will build My kingdom, a community of broken, joyful people centered in My glory and dancing at My party. *That is the church!"*

"God, am I not supposed to want things to go well for me, to do what I can to make better my life and the lives of those I love? Am I not supposed to ask you for good health, godly children, a happy marriage, a decent income, or safe travel when I go on vacation?"

"It's not what you want that is wrong. It's what you want the most. When you want your life to go well more than you want to know and please Me, you relate to Me and to others in ways that violate My nature. And that is sin, relational sin. Relational sin destroys relationships and eliminates the source of identity and joy. In the first three chapters of this letter, I expose the character of relational sin, what My soul hates.

"Relational sin . . .

- ❀ *treats people as things to be used for personal advantage.* That was the sin of Damascus [1:3–5].
- ❀ *values financial gain for oneself over the well-being of others.* That was the sin of Gaza [1:6–8].
- ❀ *regards one's word as breakable when self-interest is served.* That was the sin of Tyre [1:9–10].
- ❀ *sees nothing wrong with nourishing hatred against people who hurt you deeply.* That was the sin of Edom [1:11–12].
- ❀ *justifies harming others to increase personal satisfaction.* That was the sin of Ammon [1:13–15].
- ❀ *presumes vengeance is a legitimate personal right.* That was the sin of Moab [2:1–3].
- ❀ *disregards the absolutes I reveal as the standard for all relating.* That was the sin of Judah [2:4–5].

❀ *pursues satisfaction by following a plan for life that is self-serving and not*
God-glorifying. That, along with all the others, was the sin of
Israel [2:6–3:2].

"And My people do not see it! Without deep consciousness of
relational sin, My people then and now feel falsely complacent in My
Presence, unaware and, therefore, untroubled by how far short their
style of relating falls below Mine [6:1]. Through Amos, I told My
people to stop worshiping Me at Bethel, Beersheba, and Gilgal [5:4–
6]. It wasn't worship at all.

"I met Jacob at Bethel [Genesis 28:16], and at a second meeting,
I changed his name from Jacob (one who grasps for himself) to Israel
(one who struggles with Me). My people assumed they would meet
Me at Bethel without any thought of being changed by Me. They
saw nothing in the way they were relating that desperately needed
changing.

"At Beersheba, I pledged that I would be with Abraham [Genesis
21:22–23] and Isaac [Genesis 26:23–24] and Jacob [Genesis 46:1–4].
In each case, My companionship was promised in order to achieve
My purposes. But My people in the days of Amos assumed My companionship was guaranteed even as they pursued their own self-serving
purposes.

"And Gilgal was the site where My people first camped in the
Promised Land and ate its food after forty years of manna. It was there
every male was circumcised to symbolize My power to preserve those
I love without the comforts of Egypt [Joshua 5:2–9]. But My people
whom I was addressing through Amos were like so many of My followers today. They believed life with Me meant a pleasant life of blessings
in this world rather than the good life of relating like My Son did when
He lived in this world without even a place to rest His head.

"Their religion never exposed and judged their relational sin.
That's why I told them—and I tell you—to stop practicing detestably
complacent religion at Bethel, Beersheba, and Gilgal.

"But you must read this letter to the end. In the final five verses,
I announce My plan to restore true worship and with it the

satisfaction of every human desire. Without My Son, I could promise no such thing. With My Son, I can promise nothing less."

"God, the famine of Your Word that You predicted [8:11–14] is here. Postmodern Christianity denies truth, at least truth that is knowable with certainty. It recognizes no plumb line reflecting Your character and, therefore, obscures relational sin. And popular Christianity leaves people satisfied with surface morality designed to secure Your favor and thus diminishes our felt need for grace. As I see it, the church's relativistic version of truth and its weakened dependence on grace has freed us to live a self-pleasing life with no inclination to tremble at all. God, where is truth? Where is grace?"

"He's coming. Keep reading."

Love Letter Thirty-One: Obadiah

CELEBRATE! I WILL DEFEAT EVIL

*G*od, why Obadiah? It seems You're taking a pretty big risk here. This letter is about severe family tensions going on for a long time between Esau and his descendants, the Edomites, and Jacob and his descendants, Israel. As I read it, You finally decide to step in (I never quite understand Your timing); You take sides with Israel and promise to punish Edom for treating Israel so badly.

"Here's the risk. If I were an Israelite living right after Babylon had burned down my house, killed half my friends, and carted me off to exile, I'd be really ticked at Edom for gloating over all my troubles and trying to make them worse, especially because they were my relatives. And then, if I read Your letter telling me Edom was going to go down, I think I'd do my own gloating. Is that what You intended?"

"Read My last two sentences in this thirty-first love letter."

"Okay. Here they are: 'Deliverers will go up on Mount Zion to govern the mountains of Esau. And the kingdom will be the LORD's.'"

"What do you see as you read those words?"

"What I've seen before, that You're very different from me. When someone mistreats me, my sense of justice kicks in, and I want wrongs to be righted so I can get on comfortably with my life. Or I just say 'whatever' and move ahead but with simmering irritation.

"But You're different. Both Your sense of justice and Your principle of divine retribution—'as you have done, it shall be done to you' (Obadiah 1:15 NKJV)—are always aimed at a higher goal than getting on with life or making things a little better. You're always moving toward Your plan to replace the kingdom of self-centered relating with the kingdom of God-obsessed relating. The last verses in this letter indicate that when Edom goes down, Israel will not gloat over their punishment but will rule from Your headquarters with Your passion and virtue. Is that what You wanted me to see?"

"Yes, but so much more. Remember, Obadiah follows Amos. I judge My people (in Amos) before I judge Edom (in Obadiah). My judgment always begins in My house [1 Peter 4:17], and what I judge in outsiders I judge first in My family. Hear My point: In Hebrew, *Edom* is a form of *Adam*. And Esau's name became Edom [Genesis 25:30] when he preferred the natural advantages of this world (a good meal of red stew) over the spiritual advantages of My plan (his birthright). Esau's nature is in you. It is your flesh. You are as guilty as Esau. You live like a child of Adam. You allow your desire for a life that works now to rule your choices, and you violate life in My kingdom.

"When your spouse mistreats you, a child hurts you, a friend betrays you, a colleague responds unfairly to you, your sense of justice blinds you to your own relational sin that is equally worthy of judgment."

"So what You're saying to me in this letter is . . . ?"

"I am saying this:

Never exact vengeance on another. Only one who is not worthy of judgment himself can administer just retribution without sinning himself. Vengeance is My prerogative, not yours. My vengeance is always rooted in redemptive desire. I kill to resurrect."

"All that is in this letter?"

"Study history. Esau was wronged by Jacob. But Esau was wrong to hold a grudge against Jacob [Genesis 27:41]. Forgiveness builds community. Getting even destroys it. I never get even. To do so would mean I was morally below another who was wrong. I am always above.

"Esau's grudge spread like a virulent infection. His descendants would not permit Israel (under Moses) to pass through their territory en route to the Promised Land [Numbers 20:14–18]. Edom's rage, like your simmering irritation, burned quietly for years until it spilled over like hot lava in their enjoyment of Israel's distress. I never enjoy another's distress even when I cause it. Judgment is always My strange work, My alien task [Isaiah 28:21]. I take no pleasure in the death of the wicked [Ezekiel 18:23].

"Edom got even with Israel. I did not get even with Edom. Getting even destroys community. Always. I stand against everything that stands against community. And pride, the energy behind getting even, heads the list. Edom was proudly sitting secure (so they thought) in their mountain kingdom, protected by rugged cliffs and strong warriors, counseled by men of great wisdom [Obadiah 3–4, 9–10]. In their pride, they never examined their hearts. The appeal of revenge made evil look good, and it directed their lives. Nothing blocks My plan to bring you to My party more than the conceit of presumed independence, which gives rise to an attitude of entitled vengeance.

"Take heart. My message to you in this letter includes the guarantee that I can and I will tear down every obstacle to building My kingdom, where My people will live in line with My plan and with My character. I will bring to a dismal end everything Edom-like in you as surely as I brought Edom to its dismal end. My Son has the authority to build His church; and no power, not even the gates of hell, will overcome it [Matthew 16:18]."

"God, I think I'm getting it. Vengeance in my hands, which amounts to getting even, obstructs Your plan. Vengeance in Your hands, which removes obstacles to community, furthers it. I'm tracking with You."

"You're tracking less than you think. I intend to allow things to come into your life, as they have before, that will seem inconsistent with My good plan for you. Little things, small irritations, and big things such as health concerns and relational fractures. As before, you will still hesitate to trust Me. Read My next letter to understand what I mean."

Love Letter Thirty-Two:
Jonah

YIELD TO MY PLAN; I WILL NOT YIELD TO YOURS

*G*od, I'm rereading all Your love letters as a man who has just left the ranks of the middle-aged, as a man who's claimed to be a follower of Yours for more than fifty years. I say 'claimed' because I'm beginning to wonder if I've ever really known You. And worse, I'm wondering if I've ever wanted to or desire to even now. If I could, I sometimes think I'd rather keep believing You're the God I wish You were, the God who as a younger man I thought You were. That would cause less trouble than seeing You as the God that I'm coming to realize You are.

"I can relate to what C. S. Lewis worried most about after his wife died. He didn't worry, nor do I, that he was in much danger of 'ceasing to believe' in Your existence. The real danger he faced was, as he put it, 'of coming to believe such dreadful things' about You. And then he added this clincher that I wish I didn't understand: 'The conclusion I dread is not *So there's no God after all* but *So this is what God's really like. Deceive yourself no longer.*'

"Wasn't that Jonah's problem? Didn't that dreaded conclusion smack him in the face when You ordered him to give Israel's worst enemy a chance to repent and be blessed? Didn't he see something about You that made no sense to him, that could mess up his life, something that repelled him? He couldn't believe You didn't exist, but he wanted to get as far away from You as he could. That sounds like the psalmist who said, 'I remembered you, O God, and I groaned' (Psalm 77:3). I sometimes feel like that."

"You are growing up. You can no longer celebrate My love the way a little boy celebrates the care he receives from a good mother, from a tender woman who provides her child with a nutritious meal and a sweet dessert and then, after an hour of play and reading, tucks him into a warm, comfortable bed with the promise of another fun day tomorrow.

"Part of growing up, of seeing Me as I am, tempts My followers to run from Me, to establish a safe distance from the distinctly unsafe and inexplicably disagreeable ways I sometimes involve Myself in the lives of those I love. If atheism proves impossible (and it is, except to arrogant fools), a sort of functional deism will seem attractive. Don't think about Me too much. Distract yourself with the good things of life that you can enjoy and deal with only the hard things of life you can do something about.

"But deism will prove impossible too. You cannot escape My Presence. As Amos said, 'Though they dig down to the depths of the grave, from there my hand will take them' (9:2). The psalmist understood what Jonah did not: 'Where can I go from Your Spirit? Where can I flee from your presence' (Psalm 139:7). You are growing up. Your days of naïve worship and shallow but exciting intimacy are over. It is always difficult for a child to become an adult, to draw close to Me as I AM."

"God, I'm really a bit surprised that Jonah was the only one of Your servants whose story You tell who actually fled from Your presence. Again, I resonate with Lewis as he describes his experience of growing up: 'Go to Him when your need is desperate, when all other help is vain, and what do you find? A door slammed shut in your face, and a sound of bolting and double-bolting on the inside. After that, silence. You may as well turn away.' That's what Jonah did. During her long years of sacrificial service, even Mother Teresa felt Your absence more than Your presence. She didn't turn away, but I'll bet it was tough for her not to.

"As I understand his story, Jonah came to You, like Lewis, in desperate need. He longed for his people to be protected from Assyria, the evil empire of that day. That seems a reasonable, legitimate desire. But You were not only silent to his need, You actively acted against it by commanding him to give Nineveh, Assyria's capital city, a chance to prosper and remain strong.

"God, sometimes You don't seem to be on the side of Your people against those who oppose Your standards: abortionists, advocates of gay marriage, pedophiles, terrorists, and power-hungry, crooked politicians. Why don't You more powerfully advance the cause of Your church? I sometimes wonder if the bigger problem is not my fleeing Your presence but You fleeing mine. I know lots of people who are fighting social evils that You don't seem to be helping very much."

"Be still! I flee from your impulses when they are wrong, never from your presence. What you assume are My purposes are often yours, fashioned by and pursued with pride and self-righteousness and disdain for people I love. As you read My thirty-second letter, hear this:

You reduce Me to a God who is supposed to submit to your understanding of what matters most. You do not discern the lethal self-interest behind the purposes for which you seek divine approval. You are wrong to demand My cooperation with your understanding of life. Because I love you and because My plans for you are good, I demand your cooperation with Mine. There is no other way to enjoy My Presence."

"God, show me exactly where Jonah was wrong. I think I might be making the same mistake."

"You are. Listen well. I first called Jonah to predict prosperity for My people even while a wicked king ruled [2 Kings 14:23–27]. When My call matched his desires, Jonah was happy to be My prophet. But when I called him to a mission that was countercultural, an offense to his people and an embarrassment to his reputation, he ran away. Jonah's ability to rationalize disobedience was as stubborn as yours. He deemed it legitimate to compromise his calling in order to preserve his blessings. Not even imminent death in a watery grave or seventy-two hours in the stomach of a fish brought him to his senses.

He obeyed Me, grudgingly, but still convinced I should be the kind of God who looked after him and his people as he thought best. No prophet was more successful in his ministry nor more offended by his success. The Ninevites repented. I forgave them. And Jonah got mad. Israel's enemy was not destroyed.

"Following My call always requires that you die to your self-interested and self-righteously moralistic understanding of life. The death is slow and agonizing, so painful that physical death might at times seem preferable. I relieved Jonah's misery by providing shade from the hot desert sun, and I did so to expose his shallow self-centeredness. He actually felt happy in the shade while still wishing that people I cared for would die.

"I left Jonah with the same question I now ask you: when your life hits a bump that I could smooth but don't, will you continue to think I should surrender My wisdom to yours and do what you think best?"

"God, I am Jonah. When life hassles me, I reflexively think You should make things better. I've been thinking like that for fifty years. Will I ever change?"

"Through the prophet Micah, I make known what I *require* that you fail to do, what I *reveal* that you do not see, and how I *redeem* what you cannot change. I will make you holy. And I will do it through My Son. Soon you will love Him as I do, when you see His love for Me and for you. Nothing less will change what needs changing in your heart. Read on."

Love Letter Thirty-Three: Micah

You Are Guilty! You Are Pardoned!

*G*od, sometimes I wonder if I'm going to have to give up Christianity in order to follow Christ. So much of what I hear from pulpits (especially on television) and so much of what I read in Christian books seems to ignore, even flatly contradict, what I've been understanding from Your letters. Are You really wanting the hard things You've said in letters such as Hosea, Amos, and now Micah to be said to Your people today?

"As I read this thirty-third love letter, I picture You getting up in front of the church I preached in last weekend—a good church full of people who have trusted Your Son to forgive them, people who really get into worship, people who stay happily busy doing good things in Your name—and I wonder: would You greet those people the way You greeted the people in Micah's day? Here's what You said then: 'Listen, people—all of you. The Master, God, takes the witness stand against you' (Micah 1:2 MSG).

"The folks I preached to last Sunday would have been shocked to hear words like that. I would have been too. You were treating the Jews back then like a bunch of defendants guilty of capital crimes. You gathered them in a courtroom and began the trial with no defense attorney and with You as prosecutor, judge, and jury. Would You do the same thing today in a church full of excited Jesus-followers?"

"Tell Me what you see in My people today as they gather, sometimes in huge crowds, to worship Me and to hear what I'm saying."

"I see mostly friendly people who are glad to be in church, who get stirred by rhythmic music and drawn to passionate preaching, who come away thinking of You as a good God, a God of love who is for them and who longs to bless them with joy, purpose, and the good things of life."

"Do you see brokenness before a holy God? Do you see lament over their struggle with emptiness and failure? Do you see repentance from ways of relating that deserve severe punishment?"

"Not much."

"Then My message in Micah's day is as necessary now as then."

"But, God, we live on the *other* side of Calvary. We're already forgiven. So many believe that You've revealed Yourself now as a loving God, as a God whose anger has been spent, as Lord of a community of people who can now be affirmed and valued and released into mission. You've got to help me here. What were You saying in this thirty-third letter to Your people then that You want me to hear today?"

"I wrote this letter when Judah and Israel were prosperous, strong nations, when, just as today, My people thought that My plan was to keep them prosperous and strong as long as they included Me in their lives. It was true then, it was true after Calvary during Paul's time, and it is still true in churches now: *My people gather to hear preachers say what they want to hear* [2 Timothy 4:3–4].

"They listened in the temple then and in too many churches now to hypocritical liars disguised as shepherds and teachers, spiritual leaders with dead consciences who claim to represent Me but instead turn from ego-offending truth to offer what markets well [1 Timothy 6:5]. And there are some who pride themselves on their courage to deliver a self-chosen unpopular message, who deceive themselves into believing they are principled martyrs on behalf of truth that few want to hear, but who, in fact, are self-serving narcissists boldly stirring up division with controversial teachings that confuse My people and satisfy the teacher's need to be noticed. Still others feel a call to larger fields of ministry that is more a call from their flesh than My Spirit.

"Huge crowds gather to hear pleasant-sounding lies [Jeremiah 5:31] while the pharisaical few enjoy taking bold stands on issues that divide churches into insiders and outsiders, the enlightened and the still blind. Listen to what I said to My people in Micah's day. I say it to you now.

"If someone shows up behind a pulpit (or in front of a television camera) with a good smile and glib tongue and tells attractive lies every time he speaks, if a spiritual personality preaches sermons that tell you how you can get anything you want from Me—more money, better health, bigger ministry, happier family, improved self-esteem, a more satisfying experience of My Presence—people will flock to his church and make his books a bestseller [Micah 2:11].

"That is the message I spoke through Micah, and it is the message I am speaking today. But few are listening. If you have ears to hear, hear this as you read My thirty-third letter:

Like My unbroken and, therefore, unrepentant people in Samaria and Jerusalem in the days of Micah, you will remain brain-dead, so caught up in proud thinking that you will not permit truth to humble you. And you will stay soul-dead, so calloused by your demand for satisfaction that you will fail to accept emptiness as the path to knowing Me. You are without hope. Unless I AM a God who pardons sin, who in mercy and compassion hurls your self-centeredness into the depths of the sea, you are doomed [Micah 7:16–20]."

"God, with only a few exceptions, that is *not* the message I'm hearing in today's churches. And I don't think it would go over too well or draw crowds."

"When Micah delivered this message to My people, the rulers, priests, and prophets ordered him to be quiet. They charged him with heresy, with preaching a message that a God of affirming love would never deliver. They were wrong.

"Three times in this letter, I tell you to listen [1:2; 3:1; 6:1]. Each time, I deliver a message of doom followed by a message of hope. The message of doom brings Me no joy. And those who faithfully speak this message speak it through tears [Micah 1:8; 7:1]. But those whose self-satisfied complacency dulls their hearing continue to believe their hope lies in religious excitement and activity [Micah 6:6–7].

"But the hope of doomed people lies in One who comes out of Bethlehem [Micah 5:2–5]. Even in Micah's day, My delight was in My Son. With sheer joy, I hinted at My plan. My plan is on course. It was then. It is now. I called My people then, and I call My people now to find both Me and themselves in the rest of brokenness, in the quiet trust of repentance [Isaiah 30:15]. Only then will they hear My message of hope. Only then will they treat others fairly at whatever cost to self-interest. Only then will they long to forgive others as I've forgiven them. Only then will they learn to walk humbly and wisely through every circumstance of life guided by what they have come to know of who I AM. Only then will they regard all their favor-currying activity as detestable and pointless [Micah 6:6–8]. That is what I am saying to you in this thirty-third love letter."

"God, give me the strength to stand against my religious culture and with tears and hope to stand for Your truth. I want to follow Your Son into the life of Your family."

"You will need strength beyond what you imagine. My enemy is reducing My message of doom into a slap on the wrist. He has cheapened My message of hope into mere affirmation of your value. And he does much of his work from behind pulpits. You must trust Me to conquer My enemy and to carry out My plan even, *especially*, when you see no evidence to support your trust. My next letter is designed to strengthen you to stand against ear-tickling false teachers and to stand in the power of pride-offending truth that leads to life. You're hearing My word in Micah. Now hear Me in Nahum."

Love Letter Thirty-Four: Nahum

YOUR RELATIONSHIPS WILL WORK; I WILL SEE TO IT

*G*od, I'm not at all clear what You're saying to me in this next letter. I know all three chapters are about Your plan to destroy Nineveh—the capital of Assyria—whose citizens, one hundred years earlier, had repented of their cruel ways under Jonah's preaching. And You make it clear that Your people should celebrate the news that Nineveh would be wiped out. That makes sense since Assyria was still a strong nation and a constant threat to Judah. It does, though, seem like quite a reversal. You didn't like it at all when Jonah wanted to see Nineveh destroyed. But now through Nahum You announce Your plan to destroy Nineveh, and You tell Your people to throw a party.

"God, I don't know what You're wanting me to hear You say in this letter. It's interesting history, I guess. But You said that Your message to me in Nahum would strengthen me to stand firm for truth in the truth-compromising culture of today's Christianity. I'm not seeing how this letter is supposed to do that. Frankly, I'm rather bored by this bit of ancient history."

"What has been happening in your life and in your soul as you've been reading My thirty-fourth love letter?"

"I'm hassled and weary. This past week, two letters arrived from two people with whom I've been associated in ministry. Both letters made me mad, I think, legitimately, and I've been obsessing over whether to respond gently with concessions or to let them know what I think of their arrogant position and not give an inch. I hate these hassles. They never let up. It's always something. Now I've got to deal with these guys' unfairness and my desire to stick it to them. I'm weary. I just want to live, to get to know You better, to love and enjoy my family, to engage in conversations that matter with thoughtful friends, and to sneak in a little golf. I'd like to feel rested in my soul and eager to seize life's opportunities. Instead I feel hassled, pressured, and tired."

"I see your weariness. I know your struggle. *Nahum* is a name that means "compassion." Read this letter to know My compassion, to feel My comfort."

"You've completely lost me. How is reading about Your angry determination to destroy a city thousands of years ago supposed to help me rest in the middle of my hassles and feel energized to fight for what I believe?"

"Listen to what I'm saying to you in this letter:

I swear by My holy love: I will defeat every enemy who gets in the way of the satisfaction you desire, the rest you crave, the enjoyment you long to experience in relationships."

"God, it's not happening. Hassles are not letting up. The older I get, the more difficult life becomes. Are You telling me that Your promise to destroy Nineveh somehow includes a promise to give me a hassle-free life?"

"No, not yet. In this world, I promise you trouble. But I have overcome this world [John 16:33]. It no longer has the power to destroy the joy of hope, the rest that comes from knowing Me and longing to relate like Me in every circumstance. The day is coming when no one will relate out of pride, self-interest, and fear. This letter is My call for you to celebrate now what I will do later and to let your hope release My love into you and through you to others.

"Through Nahum, I reveal Myself as the divine warrior who has the necessary resolve and resources to rid My world of sin and restore its beauty [Nahum 1:2–6]. When I look at Nineveh, I remember Nimrod, a man who thought he had the strength to resist Mine. He built Nineveh, and ever since, that great city has stood as an altar to self-worship [Genesis 10:8–12]. I pledged to make an end of Nineveh [Nahum 1:8], and I will. No descendants energized by a relational style that opposes My style of self-giving will be allowed to crash My party [Nahum 1:14].

❀ I announced Nineveh's destruction while it still enjoyed great power. I announced My plan to give you rest while hassles still plague you every day.

❀ I see Nineveh in the two men who hassled you with their letters. I see Nineveh in you. Sacrificing love has not yet displaced self-serving demands in them or in you. Look up! I am sending One with good news; the peace of no hassles is on His way. Celebrate My plan now by relating in the middle of your hassles in a manner that reflects Me and shows your confidence in My plan [Nahum 1:5]."

"God, I hear You. But it's not getting through. I'm still ticked about those letters, and I still feel like giving up on most of what's happening in churches today. Nothing's working right."

"As My servant Martin Luther once wrote, 'You have not yet considered the weightiness of sin.' The self-serving energy behind those letters, ruling so often in the church and actively present in you, is a far greater offense to Me than to you. Only when you see the source of your hassles as a greater insult to Me than to you will you rest in My plan to deal with it. Let Me give you a preview of how I deal with sin. Listen again to Luther. He spoke of the call I placed on My Son, a call He willingly accepted.

Our most merciful Father . . . sent his only Son into the world, and laid upon him all the sins of all men, saying, Be thou Peter, that denier; Paul, that persecutor, blasphemer, and cruel oppressor; that sinner which did eat the apple in paradise; that thief hanged upon the cross—briefly, be thou the person which hath committed the sins of all men; see therefore that thou pay and satisfy for them. Now cometh the law, and saith: I find him a sinner, one that hath taken upon him the sins of all men, and I see no sins but in him: therefore let him die upon the cross . . . By this means the whole world is purged . . . God would see nothing else in the whole world, if it did believe, but a mere cleansing and righteousness.

"I destroyed Nineveh by killing all its citizens. I destroyed the energy of Nineveh that is in every citizen of this world by killing My Son. My plan is to remove the weeds of hassles and the thorns of suffering, and to let you live forever with no self-serving energy in a world better than Eden. That is the truth. Believe it, live it, and preach it to people still ruled by the energy of Nineveh, that evil passion to make life work for them at any cost to others."

"God, I know I'll still struggle with letters that upset me and with my impulse to straighten out people who write letters like that. I'll still struggle with churches that value affirmation more than brokenness because they fail to see the Nineveh that remains in all of us. But I want to struggle well. This thirty-fourth letter strengthens that desire."

"Except for My Son, no person has ever struggled perfectly. But no one has struggled better in a world filled with hassles that bewildered and bothered him than Habakkuk. I tell his story in My next letter."

Love Letter Thirty-Five: Habakkuk

WHEN NOTHING WORKS, WAIT! MY PLAN IS GOOD

*G*od, reading this next letter of Yours makes me realize how little I understand or appreciate the way You operate. Never have I experienced such a consuming desire for more in my relationship with You and never have I felt less of what I so badly want.

"I just read that John Newton, one of Your sincere and notable followers, cried out for a deeper, more thrilling knowledge of You. He expected a compelling vision of Your glory but experienced only a bewildering sense of Your absence, for a long time. I can relate. I want to know You so well that I sing with joy and speak with power, but more often than not I struggle with doubt and feel empty, alone, unconvinced and unconvincing as I speak.

"I'm not quite sure what to do with this, but I woke up this morning with my frustrated desire to know You strangely awakened and alive with hope. And I went to bed last night, rehearsing in my mind all that I knew of Your thirty-fifth letter to me. Is there a connection between my nighttime thoughts and my morning hope? I'm almost afraid to ask; I've been disappointed so many times, but, God, are You speaking to me through Habakkuk?"

"Of course. I am always speaking. But you are not always listening."

"God, I'm not sure why, but I think I'm listening now. What are You saying to me? I must know!"

"Your desperation is good. It is the work of My Spirit in you. People hear Me speak clearly when they are honest enough to face their confusion with how I respond to their prayers. Read My thirty-fifth letter of love and hear Me say this:

Never ignore your struggle with how I do things. Ask every question that rises in your heart as you live in this world. But prepare yourself to struggle even more with My response. You must stumble in confusion before you dance with joy."

"God, Your words tease me with hope. I'm feeling right now what Jeremiah felt when he experienced You as a God who seduces but doesn't deliver [Jeremiah 20:7]. You enticed him with the promise of water, but when he came to You thirsty, he found only a dried-up well [Jeremiah 15:16–18]. And he got frustrated with You. It was then You told him to repent, to never let his struggle with how he experienced You or with how You operate keep him from waiting for You to deliver what You promised [Jeremiah 15:19–21].

"God, show me how Habakkuk's story can help me wait with confidence. I want to know You better. Let me hear You speak to that desire in this letter."

"Like you, Habakkuk saw problems in the church of his day, problems that I opened his eyes to see and then did nothing about. Through My letters so far, I have opened your eyes to see what bothers you and appalls Me in today's Christianity:

- ❀ surface worship that provides excitement but no power to change;
- ❀ recognition-hungry spiritual leaders who remain blind to their insecurity-driven ministry and, therefore, are unable to call people to true brokenness;
- ❀ cheapening views of the cross that reduce My Son's death to an affirmation of people's value and a call to similarly affirm others;
- ❀ a postmodern revision of Christianity into a kingdom-building story told on a foundation of either truth-denying uncertainty

or unknowable truth—resulting in a religion of moral flexibility that weakens the demands of holiness;

❀ a pride-enhancing emphasis on size, activity, and celebrity that corrupts church into a merely inspiring event and moves it away from a supernatural opportunity to know Me, and to know oneself and others with a painful realism that drives My people to ever-deepening dependence and trust.

"Habakkuk prayed for brokenness in his people and revival through My Spirit. He saw neither.

"Now hear Me well as I unfold the dialogue I entered into with My frustrated servant. It's the dialogue I long to have with you. I permitted Habakkuk to continue in the mystery of My silence until he was worn out. Only when false hope is abandoned will My strange but true hope be embraced [Habakkuk 1:2–4].

"I shattered his false hope by revealing My plan for Babylon, a nation more evil than Judah, to rise up and discipline My people. And I made it clear it would all happen under My direction [1:5–11]. I want you and all My people to know that nothing catches Me off guard—not even Adolf Hitler or Osama bin Laden. Nothing has happened or ever will happen that I am not using for My purposes.

"But what I allow seems to contradict My holy and pure character. I required Habakkuk, as I require you, to live in the tension between the evil that prospers, whether in the church or in secular society, and My plan to restore the beauty of My character in this world. It is that tension that shifted Habakkuk's focus away from frustration with what he saw in the world toward the mystery of how I execute My plan [2:1]. With that shift, Habakkuk was silenced and I spoke.

"It was then I revealed My plan that everyone must wait to see unfold [2:2]. People respond in one of only two ways to My require-ment to wait. Either they refuse to wait and instead try to manage life according to their desires; or they live by faith in My character, con-fessing their own selfish ways and yielding to My plan and to My timetable to get them to My party [2:4].

"Know this: those who live by faith will struggle in ways that those who live to make their lives work will never know. It is that struggle, to believe despite desperate pain and confusion that a good plan is unfolding, that will open your eyes to see Me more clearly. Is that what you want? Will you pay the price?

"The price is this: you will tremble in agony as you live in a sinful, self-prioritizing world as a sinful, self-prioritizing person, knowing that no sin will go unpunished even though, for a time, I will appear to be doing nothing [3:16].

"You will learn to wait in emptiness and frustrated desire for My plan of love to reveal itself [3:17]. With confidence in Me and hope in My plan, you will not only feel the pain of living in the valley but also see My glory from the mountaintop of faith [3:18]. Only those who struggle in confusion and wait in hope will be strengthened to struggle well and to wait with confidence.

"That is My message to you in this thirty-fifth love letter. Struggle well! Wait in hope!"

"God, I still worry that You're awakening my desire to know You only to frustrate me, that I'll run to the well and find no water, again. Please! Lift me to the heights. Let me skip with confidence over all the cliffs of confusion. Let me see Your glory. That's my prayer. I will wait in silence for Your answer. But, God, waiting is hard!"

"Today is the day of evil. But My day is coming. Dawn is breaking. Read about it in My next letter."

Love Letter Thirty-Six: Zephaniah

Do Not Settle for Cosmetic Change; That Is Not My Plan

Another letter about judgment? God, how many times do You have to remind me that You punish sins before I'm ready to see Your Son and appreciate grace? More threats of doom with hints of hope sprinkled in—it seems like overkill. And I've got three more letters of doom to read before You reveal Your Son. What's Your point? What are You saying to me in this letter that I haven't yet heard in the others?"

"Sincere spiritual leadership can produce only the appearance of revival, never its reality. Stirring music and passionate preaching, though good, have no power in themselves to change what is wrong in My people. Only death destroys evil. Only death opens the door to resurrection, to a new way to live. Without My Spirit's work, your exciting religious gatherings do little that excites My heart. I want you to see beneath appearances to the problem that only My Son can solve."

"God, I've just read Your thirty-sixth letter five times. I studied the comments of scholars. And I've spent hours reflecting on all that I understood You to be saying through Zephaniah. But I never heard You say *that*."

"Listen carefully. My message to you is woven into a story. Zephaniah was the great-great-grandson of godly Hezekiah, and he was cousin to Josiah, the king who brought revival to My people after a long time of being ruled by two thoroughly ungodly kings, Amon for only two years and Manasseh before him for fifty-five. Remember your history. I changed the heart of Manasseh—one of the most evil kings ever to occupy David's throne—but only through severe judgment after five decades of wicked rule. In his final years, Manasseh honored Me and instructed the Israelites to follow Me. *But My people did not listen!* (Read the story in 2 Chronicles 33, especially verses 15 through 17.) The lesson of history was not lost on the discerning Zephaniah. He understood that judgment, nothing less, brings new life. And he realized that no leader, no matter how broken, humble, and repentant, has the power to change what needs changing in the human heart.

"Zephaniah learned that lesson. Josiah did not. When Josiah became king at age eight, he was, of course, spiritually yet unformed. At age sixteen, he began to meaningfully seek Me as his grandfather Manasseh did in his old age. Soon after Josiah's twenty-sixth birthday, My book of instructions, hidden for many years, was found. Josiah read it and realized how far short My people had fallen below My standards. Like the religious moralists of today, he determined not only to follow My commands, which was good, but also required the citizens of Judah to pledge obedience to Me, which was naïve [2 Chronicles 34].

"Josiah behaved much like you when, as a young father, you thought that setting high standards for your two sons and enforcing them would lead to their becoming godly young men. As they listened to your devotions and attended youth group, you assumed their hearts were right. When Josiah saw his subjects following My rules and celebrating their God in huge gatherings, he, like you, assumed that the *appearance* of godliness evidenced the *reality* of godliness. It was at that same time that My prophet Jeremiah saw what looked like a mighty work of My Spirit and heard Me say, 'Judah did not return to me with all her heart, but only in pretense' (Jeremiah 3:10).

"Zephaniah understood, too, that the revival led by his godly cousin Josiah was only skin-deep. It was then he began to speak to Judah. What would have led most spiritual leaders to affirm My work in people's hearts led Zephaniah to pronounce judgment."

"God, I hear the history, and I think I hear its point. But can You tell me in a couple of sentences what You want me to hear in this letter that I haven't clearly heard before?"

"Hear this:

Surface change is often mistaken for deep change. When the medication of exciting worship and inspiring preaching relieves the symptoms of sin, the need for the surgery of brokenness is no longer recognized.

"If you greet My Son believing that instruction, discipline, and inspiration are enough to keep you on track, You will see Him as merely a religious cheerleader, not the holy Savior you desperately need."

"God, show me where You're saying that in this letter."

"My people were satisfied with how they were following Me. They assumed I was satisfied as well. I was not. I began My message to them by promising to 'sweep away' everything I saw (Zephaniah 1:2), to stretch out My hand against everyone who thought they could both worship Me and live for themselves [1:4–6], to bring down all those who thought they could continue to enjoy the good life of blessings without seeking Me with humble, broken hearts [1:13–18; 2:1–3].

"The great day of the Lord that My people looked forward to as a day of even greater blessing instead promised severe judgment before blessing. My people did not see in themselves the evil that no spiritual director who affirms or spiritual gathering that excites or spiritual leader who exhorts can change. I want you, like Jeremiah and Zephaniah, to look under the appearance of spiritual celebration to see the reality of spiritual pride that often lurks beneath. It must be destroyed.

"Then I want you to wait for Me, to wait for Me to pour out My death-dealing judgment on every self-centered urge that I discern beneath your religious veneer [3:8]. Settle for nothing less. Only crucifixion is sufficient to deal with the self-protective, self-obsessed passion within you that spoils relationship, that destroys true community and eliminates the possibility of its restoration.

"The judgment I pour out will 'purify the lips of the peoples, that all of them may call on' My name in unity (3:9), as a community of God-worshiping, God-obsessed people. When the tower of Babel was built [Genesis 11], reflecting the people's determination to unite together to secure a good life without Me at the center (as so many governments do today), I destroyed the possibility of mutual understanding and cooperation by forcing them to speak in words that emerged from their self-obsessed agendas. They could not hear each other because they didn't want to. They wanted only to make their point and pursue their personal goals. In this letter, I promise to reverse the curse of Babel, to gather My people around Me and to teach them a common language of worship and waiting, the language of My kingdom, not theirs.

"Only when surface revival where hearts remain unchanged is replaced by deep renewal, only when the judgment of death destroys the power of selfishness and opens the door to the resurrected power of love, only then will My plan become visible.

"My thirty-sixth letter begins with My promise to sweep away everything [1:2] and ends with My ironclad promise to bring My people home, to change their hearts so that I can look on them with delight, to pour into them the life of My Son [3:18–20]. *What a day that will be!*"

"God, is my life more appearance than reality? The passion to use You for my immediate satisfaction still competes in my soul with my longing for You to use me for Your pleasure. The bad guy wins far too often. God, I'm weary of the battle. *Let me see Jesus! Bring on that day!*"

"Soon. Very soon. For now, you must wait, and you must struggle. The glory that will not only fill your soul and expel everything dark but will also cover the entire earth and restore its beauty is worth the agonizing wait. Do not be controlled by fear or discouragement. That is the message of My next letter. Read and rejoice in hope."

Love Letter Thirty-Seven:
Haggai

I HAVE THE POWER; YOU WILL BE HOLY

*G*od, there's one small point I'd like to bring up from this thirty-seventh letter before we dive into more important matters. Through Haggai, You refer to Yourself as the *Lord Almighty* fourteen times. That's a lot in this short letter, the shortest of Your first thirty-nine except Obadiah. Why? I know it's a minor point, but is there something I should be hearing You say when You use that name for Yourself?"

"How I *refer* to Myself is how I *reveal* Myself. Better translated the LORD *of hosts*, I call Myself by this name nearly three hundred times in My first thirty-nine letters but never in the first eight. I introduced Myself by this name for the first time in 1 Samuel when I wrote, 'This man [Elkanah] went up from his town to worship and sacrifice to the LORD *of hosts* at Shiloh, where Hophni and Phineas . . . were priests' (1 Samuel 1:3). Then Hannah, in deep distress, prayed to Me by this name: 'O LORD *of hosts*, if you will only look upon your servant's misery' (1 Samuel 1:11). By this name, in the presence of godless spiritual leaders, such as Hophni and Phineas, and in the middle of human misery, like Hannah's, I reveal Myself as the God with the power needed to win the war against sin and sorrow no matter how vile the sin or deep the sorrow. When you know Me by this name, when you hope in all that this name reveals about Me, you will hear the message of Haggai. You will live, not to build your house but to build my temple."

"God, I didn't see it. The small point I've raised is not so small."

"No, it's not. You will not learn what I'm saying to you in this letter until you realize that the *Lord of hosts* is a strong tower to which you can run for safety in any circumstance, no matter how discouraging your circumstances may be [Proverbs 18:10]."

"Tell me more about this name."

"David blessed the people in the name of the *Lord of hosts* after he returned the ark to Jerusalem [2 Samuel 6:18]. Until that time, My Presence (represented in the ark) had been housed in a mere tent. When David wanted to build a temple more suited to My glory, I told him two things: one, a mobile tent aptly symbolized My desire to be with My people as they stumbled through life [2 Samuel 7:5–7]; and two, My temple would bring peace; therefore, I would permit only a man of peace to build it. David did not qualify. His son did [2 Samuel 22:5–10].

"David humbly and gladly but dimly caught My point. My plan was (and is) to bring peace to the whole world through My Son, a descendant of David, and through My people, the temple of My Presence. As the *Lord of hosts*, I will build My temple. David recognized the day would come when all men would say, 'The LORD *of hosts* is over Israel' (2 Samuel 7:26; emphasis added). Remember, too, it was when Isaiah saw My glory in the temple that he heard My angels cry out 'Holy, holy, holy is the LORD *of hosts*' (Isaiah 6:1–3; emphasis added). To your eyes it will appear that I am losing the fight against all that is wrong in this world. I AM not! I AM the *Lord of hosts*, the commander of heaven's armies, and I am building My temple through you.

"From the beginning, My plan was (and still is) to reveal My Presence and My power and My purpose *in the temple*. Imagine My delight when I heard My Son say, referring to Himself, that 'one greater than the temple is here' (Matthew 12:6). Imagine My infinite sorrow and joy as I listened to My Son on another occasion declare, 'Destroy this temple, and I will raise it again in three days' (John

2:19). Imagine the release of My power after the temple of My Son's body was destroyed then raised again and I breathed into Peter these post-Pentecost words: 'As you come to him, the living Stone—rejected by men, chosen by God and precious to him—you also, like living stones, are being built into a spiritual house' (1 Peter 2:4–5). My Son is the 'chief cornerstone' (Ephesians 2:20), 'a precious cornerstone for a sure foundation' (Isaiah 28:16), the 'cornerstone that comes from Judah' (Zechariah 10:4). And 'you yourselves are God's temple . . . God's temple is sacred, and you are that temple' (1 Corinthians 3:16, 17); your body is now the temple where My Spirit lives [1 Corinthians 6:19]; and I now live and walk among you as the *Lord of hosts* because you are now 'the temple of the living God' (2 Corinthians 6:16–17).

"I have been critical of Israel. I am critical of My church. But I, the *Lord of hosts*, have the power to build a beautiful temple. I love My people. I love My church. You must love her too. She is My temple. *Build it!*

"Haggai did not realize it, but all of that was in My mind when I spoke through him as the *Lord of hosts* and told My people to build my temple. My mind is always on My Son. My heart is always consumed by Him and by My people, the church through whom I am revealing Myself to the world."

"God, I'm overwhelmed. What I thought was a small point is a doorway into a universe of truth. I don't pretend to understand all You have just said, but what I do understand leaves me speechless."

"With your mouth now closed and your ears open, hear what I'm saying to you in this thirty-seventh love letter:

No matter how discouraged you feel, no matter how little evidence you see of My power, no matter how off course My plan appears to be or how unlikely of fulfillment My promise seems to be, no matter how dark your night or empty your soul, build My temple. I, the Lord of hosts, am speaking."

"God, what does it mean for me to build Your temple?"

"Whatever you do for My sake that involves the sacrifice of self-interest, whatever you do to reveal Me to others when you feel least able to do so, whatever you do that pleases Me at any cost to yourself, that is building My temple."

"God, show me how You're saying that in this letter."

"Remember your history. Solomon's temple was destroyed in 587 BC, ten years after Nebuchadnezzar, king of Babylon, carried many of My people to exile in his country. For years, they felt like the dry bones Ezekiel saw in the valley [Ezekiel 37]. It was difficult for them to even dream that the day would come when they could return to Jerusalem and rebuild both the Holy City and the Holy Temple.

"That day came in 538 BC. My people immediately went to work. Within two years, the temple's foundation was in place. The young people danced with joy while the old folks wept in despair [Ezra 3:10–13]. The old folks had seen Solomon's temple and realized that what they were building would never come close to the splendor of the original. Discouragement from the older men and the shallow enthusiasm of the younger folks and opposition from neighbors who didn't want to see Jerusalem prosper combined forces and the 'work on the house of God in Jerusalem came to a standstill' for sixteen years (Ezra 4:24). The same thing happens today when you see what church is and compare it against what it should be and withdraw in disgust or discouragement.

"It was then I raised up Haggai, himself an old man, to speak in My name as Lord of hosts with one message: *build My temple!* Over the space of four short months, Haggai delivered four messages:

1. *Do not let discouragement or opposition get you off course* [1:1–15]. When it seems that nothing good is happening, it is easy to live for whatever good things you can provide for yourself and to lose interest in My plan. Before you build your house, *build My temple!*

2. *Know that what seems insignificant today will be revealed as significant tomorrow* [2:1–10]. My people got to work with Zerubbabel the governor, Joshua the priest, and Haggai the old prophet working side-by-side with his younger colleague, Zechariah, all pitching in [Ezra 5:1–2]. I knew they would be sustained only by hope, by the promise of results they would not see in their lifetimes. So I gave Haggai this second message. Read it carefully. It was fun to write. Present suffering is worth future glory. My church will triumph, so *build My temple!*

3. *Evil is more contagious than goodness* [2:10–19]. Defilement from wrong priorities weakens the passion to obey and blocks the blessing I long to bring into your soul. But the holy resolve to obey spreads only by My Spirit. Even in darkness, I will supply the power to advance My plan. Evil will lose. Goodness will win. *Build My temple!*

4. *I will fulfill My plan through the Man of My choosing* [2:20–23]. Not every descendant of David is My choice. Jehoiachin, king of Judah and grandfather of Zerubbabel, was not My choice. I removed the seal of My power, symbolized by the signet ring, from his finger [Jeremiah 22:24–30]. But I placed that same ring on Zerubbabel's finger to declare that the Man of My choosing is coming to occupy David's throne, to bring forgiveness and peace. Do not lose hope. My Son is coming. *Build My temple!"*

"God, I have no greater desire. Empower me to build Your temple, to *be* Your temple, until Jesus comes."

"Your words are good. Your desire is real. But I must reach deeper yet into your heart. You need to see what is happening in the heavenlies, where no human eye unaided by My Spirit can see. In My next letter, I pull back the curtain covering the earth to reveal what is happening in the invisible but real world. The Lord of hosts is building the temple. Read on."

Love Letter Thirty-Eight: Zechariah

BELIEVE WHAT YOU CANNOT SEE

*G*od, I'm trying to think what it would be like if I were a Jew working hard to build the temple after getting charged up by Haggai with promises of great days ahead. I think I might get discouraged with slow progress and meager resources, and I'd probably be wondering how soon I'd see all the blessings I was told were coming. It would be hard not to get weary in well doing.

"I spoke with a good friend last night, a young widow who feels empty, no sense of Your comforting presence and no real enjoyment of anything in her life. But she's building the temple. She's staying faithful to You and doing what she can to encourage others. And yet she's not sure what to hope for. Is she going to feel better? Are You going to visit her with an encounter that will fill her with joy—*before* she gets to heaven?

"I wonder the same thing. Right now, I'm so tired I just want to lie down. I don't feel excited about reading this next letter. But I'm committed to doing what needs doing. I want to spend more time with my grandkids and play golf with my wife, but I've got a lot of stones I need to haul to the temple. Right now, I feel no passion, just obligation. And I really don't know what to hope for. It's hard to keep going.

"I know You told Zechariah to start speaking to the Jews a couple of months after Haggai got them working on the temple. Were they feeling what I'm feeling, perhaps as empty and frustrated as my bereaved friend? If so—and I think they were—I'd really like to hear what You said to them in this thirty-eighth letter."

"Yes, My people needed encouragement to continue. When the woman you know as Mother Teresa built the temple by bringing Me to unloved souls and unloved souls to Me, for more than fifty years she, too, was desperate for a sense of My Presence. She once asked her spiritual director to pray 'that it may please God to lift this darkness from my soul for only a few days.' I left it in place for many years. Only in darkness could she learn to say 'my agony of desolation is so great and at the same time the longing for the Absent One so deep, that the only prayer which I can still say is— . . . Jesus, I trust in Thee. I will satiate Thy thirst for souls.'"

"God, You're not encouraging me. Did You leave the Jews desperate for a sense of Your presence that never came? Will the widowed woman feel empty till she dies? What is going to keep me going or my friend whose adult child is breaking his heart with no change in sight? What are You saying in Zechariah, to Your people, to my friends, to me?"

"As you read My thirty-eighth love letter, hear this:

If you could see right now what is happening in the unseen world, you would be filled with hope. You must trust Me for whatever tastes of glory I choose to provide in this life as you continue to build the temple. You have become a prisoner of hope."

"God, You wrote that 'faith is being sure of what we hope for and certain of what we do not see' (Hebrews 11:1). And You added that faith like that is what some of Your people in Old Testament days were commended for [v. 2] and that if we hope for what we do not yet have, we wait for it patiently [Romans 8:25]. But here's my question: *does hope feel good?*"

"The hope I provide anchors a weary, empty, troubled soul in My plan. Beneath difficult feelings, hope encourages by giving you reason to persevere with the joy of anticipation. *Happiness* depends on present blessing, which I do not guarantee. *Joy* depends on future hope, which I do guarantee."

"God, show me how You gave hope to the temple builders in Zechariah's day, and show me how You give that same hope to me today."

"Do not expect to feel good. You may. You may not. My work of hope reaches into the center of your soul to strengthen your character and deepen your resolve in any circumstance of life.

"My first message in this love letter is, 'Return to Me' [Zechariah 1:1–6]. What sustained My daughter Teresa through fifty years of darkness was her longing for relationship with Me. Many people work hard in My cause without ever discovering their insatiable thirst for Me, the thirst Mother Teresa felt so strongly.

"When My people were humbled by My call to repent of finding fulfillment as the reason for temple building and instead to work for love of Me, I then opened Zechariah's eyes to see into the unseen world and to tell My people what he saw. Notice My people did not receive the visions. They heard Zechariah's report and were responsible to believe his words as My word to them. I ask the same of you. I do not promise that you will receive visions. You may. You may not. Believe what you're told by Me in these letters.

"The eight visions (chapters 1 through 6) were apocalyptic— that is, they revealed what could best be seen in symbol form. Each of these eight visions unveiled what the natural eye could never see:

1. *My Army Waits* [1:7–17]. My troops are armed and ready to restore beauty to My earth. My Son eagerly awaits My command [1:12]. He knows My anger will yield to mercy. *Live in hope!*
2. *My Army Prepares* [1:18–21]. Four horns visible to My prophet symbolize the powers of the world intent on thwarting My plan. Four blacksmiths represent My power to destroy the four horns. Zechariah saw the blacksmiths prepare to throw the horns down. *Live in hope!*
3. *My Protected City* [2:1–12]. Zechariah saw a man surveying Jerusalem, anticipating the protective wall around the city he thought would be needed. I sent an angel to tell the man to put away his measuring

tools and be glad. I will Myself be a wall of fire around My city. Nothing will happen to you or any of My followers that has the power to destroy My plan. And My plan for you is good. *Live in hope!*

4. *My Cleansed People* [3:1–10]. Fathers with rebellious children wonder how they failed. Widows worry that greater faith might have kept their husbands alive. Satan encourages an obsessive and superstitious look at your failure. I see all your failure, all your filth, and I bathe you until you become a sweet fragrance. Learn the lesson of Joshua. *Live in hope!*

5. *My Resources Provided* [4:1–14]. Pressing on in darkness is difficult. In Isaiah, I told you to never light your own fires [Isaiah 50:10–11]. In this vision, I promise adequate resources in community (the two olive trees pouring oil into the lamp) to sustain hope. *Live in that hope!*

6. *My Holiness Prevails* [5:1–4]. The grotesquely large book of judgment, written on both sides like the original tablets of law [Exodus 32:15], will find everyone who has not turned to Me for mercy and destroy them. Only forgiven and cleansed people will want to dance at My party. You are among them. *Live in hope!*

7. *My People Purified* [5:5–11]. Though you are forgiven and cleansed, your inclination toward self-interest remains. I will remove it from you, lock it in a container, and carry it away, as far as the east is from the west. One day you will dance well. *Live in hope!*

8. *My Spirit Rests* [6:1–15]. My waiting and prepared army will conquer the world. All will be well. My Spirit will rest, His work done. Nothing will be left but joy and happiness. *Live in hope!*

"The legalist in you will want to mourn what was painful in the past and what is still painful today. Like the delegation from Bethel [7:2–3], you will want to focus more on healing past wounds and filling present emptiness than living in hope. Do not obsess over yesterday's troubles or today's problems. Read My word to the people from Bethel in Zechariah 7–8, and take heed.

"Then read My last six chapters of this letter, slowly. And hear this as you read: I give advance notice that My Son would come, that He would be hated and killed, that what His killers meant for evil I meant for good, that I would then open the eyes of those I invite to the party to realize what they did in killing My Son, that I would meet them in their brokenness with a cleansing fountain, that I would then set My Son on the throne of this world and everything would be as it should be. The party will begin. *Live in hope!*"

"God, for a few seconds, I catch a glimpse of what You're doing, and I'm filled with hope. But the glimpse so quickly fades. I get cranky, disillusioned, unaware of hope. I want Your Spirit to open my eyes more widely, more often."

"I am one letter away from introducing My Son to you. You will see Him clearly to the degree you clearly see your need of Him, not for the blessings of a good life now but for the forgiveness that guarantees you your best life forever. My last letter reveals what you do not want to see and leaves you broken, desperate for what only My Son can provide. My plan is that you see Him as your supreme treasure and live as a prisoner of hope until the party begins.

"Six months before I brought her home, my persevering daughter you called Mother Teresa, who lived as My prisoner of hope for so long, experienced an even deeper darkness of unbearable physical and spiritual pain. She whispered to a friend, 'Jesus is asking too much.' But what I asked was needed to release her soul into nearly perfect union with My Son. In her weakest moment, she reached for a pencil and scribbled three words: 'I want Jesus.'

"My word in Zechariah will lead you to that single desire as you come to believe what I said. My word in Malachi will prepare you to welcome My Son as life itself. Read on. We're almost there!"

Love Letter Thirty-Nine: Malachi

SOON YOU WILL SEE:
THE LIGHT OF THE WORLD IS COMING!

*Y*ou have been listening well as I have been speaking to you in these first thirty-eight love letters. In this last one before I introduce My Son, I want to speak clearly and directly. Listen now as you've never listened before. There are a few things you must know before you will understand what I want to say to you in this thirty-ninth letter.

"Malachi was My last prophet to speak My words before My Son became a human infant. His message carries unique importance.

"By the time he spoke, My people had been living with a rebuilt temple in Jerusalem for nearly one hundred years. Once the temple was built, they thought that My promises of prosperity should have been fulfilled. My people were disappointed and disillusioned. They weren't convinced I could be trusted.

"A few years earlier, I had sent Ezra back from Babylon to teach them that, though disappointed, they were still responsible to keep My law. They repented. I was pleased.

"I next brought Nehemiah to Jerusalem to rebuild the wall around the city. My people responded and, despite fierce opposition, the wall was completed in fifty-two days. Then Nehemiah returned to Babylon as he had promised to do, stayed there awhile, and when he came back to Jerusalem, he was surprised and enraged to find My people indifferent to My law, sloppy in worship, arrogantly assuming their religious practices entitled them to My blessings, and hardened to everything but their comfort.

"It was then I called Malachi to deliver My last word before My Son arrived, four hundred years after this letter was penned. After centuries of faithfully loving My people, I found them blind to their deplorable condition. Through Malachi, I brought seven charges against them and endured seven inexcusably calloused responses.

"Review these charges and responses, and then you will be ready to hear My word to you in this thirty-ninth letter:

❀ **Charge 1:** I have loved you. You refuse to love Me in return.
❀ **Response 1:** How have You loved us? You could love us better [1:2].

❀ **Charge 2:** You show contempt for My name.
❀ **Response 2:** What are You talking about? [1:6].

❀ **Charge 3:** Your worship of Me is deficient.
❀ **Response 3:** We think it's fine [1:7].

❀ **Charge 4:** You weary Me.
❀ **Response 4:** We think You should be pleased with us [2:17].

❀ **Charge 5:** You have turned from Me. Turn toward Me.
❀ **Response 5:** We're facing You. What's Your problem? [3:6–7].

❀ **Charge 6:** You've robbed Me.
❀ **Response 6:** We've done no such thing [3:8].

❀ **Charge 7:** You've said harsh things against Me.
❀ **Response 7:** Nothing You haven't deserved. C'mon. Treat us better. We're Your kids, Your favorites [3:13–14].

"But among those hardened, blind people, I found My remnant. A small group got together to wait in hope, trusting Me to be carrying out a good plan even when things were bad [3:16]. I want all My people to live together as prisoners of hope, encouraging each other with My word until My party begins. To demand the good life now will result in the misery of apathy to the good life of knowing Me well. With that thought, I finish My thirty-ninth letter. Now, let Me hear from you."

"God, You said I've been listening well. Right now, even as You were speaking, I was feeling distracted. After reading thirty-eight letters, I should be in a better place. But I'm not. I just got word that the six-year-old daughter of good friends is developing unusual anxieties. Just this morning they asked us to pray. So I did. But as I was talking to You about their concerns, I had my Bible open to this thirty-ninth letter and, forgive me, but I found myself thinking, *Why am I wasting my time reading Malachi when I could be using my psychologist's mind to figure out what's going on in that little girl and how I could help?*

"I'm sitting in a coffee shop right now, reading this letter for the umpteenth time, with three books by scholars explaining what Malachi is all about scattered around me, and I'm feeling irritable, cheated, bored, and useless. It didn't help when two guys in biking outfits just came in and I overheard them talking about where they plan to ride today. I'll bet neither of them has a clue what You're saying in Malachi, and they look happy. I do have a clue, and I'm cranky. God, to tell You the truth, I'd much rather be riding a bike than reading this letter. But my Bible's still open, and I'm still here. So what are You saying to me in Malachi?"

"What I said to My people then, I am now saying to you: I have loved you."

"And my response—again forgive me—is just like theirs. I don't feel loved (Charge 1). Am I supposed to? I'd probably be in a better mood to worship You if I hiked in the mountains today. A woman just came in to the coffee shop and told a friend about the hike she took yesterday in the Colorado mountains and how excited she is to be heading out again today. I think I'd be more aware of Your love if I were standing on top of a mountain, looking over an endless stretch of yellow aspens. But You told Your people who were living in far worse conditions than a coffee shop that You loved them. What did You mean?"

"Hear what I'm saying to you in this thirty-ninth letter:

I have loved you in a way that people who live for no higher purpose than to enjoy this life do not realize. I love them, too, but they do not see it. I have chosen you to be part of My plan to restore this earth to its full beauty and My people to their full beauty. I have chosen you to invite folks who merely ride bikes to soar like eagles into My Presence, to invite hikers who are hungry for adventure and excitement to feast their eyes on My glory. Your calling is to reveal My love."

"But God, like Mother Teresa, I'm calling people to what I experience so little. I limp more than I soar. And I see more darkness than glory."

"You show contempt for My name when you treat Me as though I were a vending machine stocked with sweets that temporarily satisfy (Charge 2). I wish the doors to your church were shut and locked so that I wouldn't have to endure the self-serving noise you call worship (Charge 3). Where is the hope, or the lament that discovers hope?

"You weary Me with your idea that people enjoying the pleasant life of prosperity and peace are the real winners while saints like My son Paul and My daughter Teresa, who sacrificed good things now for better things later, are the losers. Arrogance! Nonsense! (Charge 4).

"Every moment spent in seizing pleasure is a moment with your back to Me. Return! Return to Me, not for the blessings of life that bring pleasure but for the blessing of My Presence that sustains hope (Charge 5). Every time you look at a calendar to see when you can schedule an activity designed for your fulfillment, you rob Me. Every time you use whatever is in your wallet to purchase satisfaction, you steal from Me. Enjoy every pleasure I provide, but never live for every pleasure you can experience. Sheer foolishness! (Charge 6).

"And worse, you spend time with friends who share your disillusioned and cynical feelings and you actually entertain the thought that serving Me is futile. Blasphemy! (Charge 7)."

"God, I am guilty on all seven counts."

"I have loved you. I love you still. Beneath your darkness, disillusionment, and doubts, you long to know Me, to serve Me, to honor My name, to wait for Me as My prisoner of hope. That delights Me. You are My treasure.

"Listen now to My last word before you see My Son: Turn toward yourself, live for satisfaction and fullness now, and you will lose yourself. Turn toward Me, sacrifice your pleasure for Mine, and you will find Me and yourself, purpose now and joy forever."

"God, something is stirring. I don't feel it, but I sense it, like the seasoned sailor who can smell land before he sees it. I think I'm catching a whiff of heaven. And I want to spray that fragrance into the heart of an anxious little girl and into her parents and into all who settle for the small pleasures of hiking and biking."

"You are ready. It is time to meet My Son."

PART FIVE

The Hero Takes Center Stage: Matthew Through John

We want every love story to have a happy ending. Too many don't. God's does. It just takes a long time to get there. And for good reason. Our understanding of love is so twisted that it takes a lot of work, centuries worth, to straighten it out.

Think about it. Somehow we've gotten the idea that if God loves us, He wouldn't let hurricanes ravage New Orleans or tornadoes devastate Myanmar or earthquakes kill thousands in China, not if He could help it. Every time I hear about the latest natural disaster or yesterday's terrorist bombing or someone's parental heartbreak or a good friend's diagnosis of level 4 leukemia, a voice inside me that I can't quite muffle whispers, "God, I know You're good, but tell me again: What are You good for?"

Maybe the demonic twist in our understanding of love boils down to this: because God is love, the abundant life that Jesus promised us means an abundance of blessings now, you know, all the good things of life that make us happy.

Where did we get that idea? Certainly not from the Old Testament. And (I peeked ahead) not from the New Testament either.

Jesus made it clear that life, real life—the life He died to give us— centers not on nice homes, happy families, and good health in a safe world with a booming economy but rather on knowing Jesus' Father as our Father—in good times and bad—and relating to His Father and everyone else the way Jesus does—in good times and bad. I think that's what it means to be holy. Holiness does not consist of doing good things and not doing bad things. Holiness is wrapped up in relating well, deeply, with love.

And if that's holiness, if that's what life is really all about, then:

The abundant life Jesus came to give us is (at least for now) an abundance not of material blessings but an abundance of knowing God as our supreme treasure and relating to Him and to others lovingly, no matter what assortment of blessings and hardships come our way or what variety of feelings—joy, emptiness, peace, terror—we're experiencing.

I've just reread everything I've written so far, all my dialogues with God about what He's trying to get across to me in His first thirty-nine love letters. And I've come to a rather inelegant conclusion: the Old Testament is a set-up for the New. Let me put it less inelegantly: *if we miss the message of His first thirty-nine letters, we'll miss the message of His last twenty-seven.* Or worse, we'll pervert it and think we've got it. We'll make it fit into our hellishly twisted definition of love and never be captured by the real story of love that could take our breath away, that could humble us enough to change us from self-obsessed lovers of short term well-being to God-obsessed lovers of others at any temporary cost to ourselves.

The crimson thread running through the entire Old Testament, from Genesis through Malachi; the message that I hear God delivering in thirty-nine unique ways to anyone with open ears is this:

"What most needs changing is not your circumstances. Blessings in the short term are dangerous to your long-term joy. If I used My power to make your life work in ways that you found easily and quickly satisfying, you would become even less aware than you already are of what I designed you to enjoy and more stubborn in your pursuit of everything else.

"You are on the road to eternal misery. I cannot sit back and do nothing. I love you too much. The only cure that works will at times seem worse than the disease. Your naïve self-centeredness can only be transformed in suffering, yours in measure and Mine without measure.

"But know this: no suffering that you will endure in this life is worthy to be compared with the joy that awaits you in the next. *Live in hope!* True hope breeds joy and empowers love. My love story has a terrific ending that never ends."

Let me run through a quick and spotty review of the story as God has told it so far to get us ready to hear Him tell the rest of the story. It gets good. Be patient.

In Genesis, I hear God pouring out His love to all of us as He sings the opening line of His love song: "I have a terrific plan. It's why I made you. You're invited to My party of perfect relationship in a perfect world. And I mean to get you there."

In that same letter, God goes on to say that we've made a big mess of things. We've thrown a huge monkey wrench into His plans that of course He fully anticipated (and actually planned for), but a monkey wrench nonetheless that He has to deal with. We've made a seriously wrong turn and are now heading away from the eternal dance and toward relational failure, loneliness, and hatred-filled frustration. We're more concerned to get what we want now than to trust God to give us what we need now and what we most want forever. And, thanks to devilish deception, we think our approach to life is Christian. Our moral compass has gotten so out of whack that we actually think we're moving in a good direction. His party, His kingdom of relational intimacy and satisfying togetherness and joy-filled meaning, is now hopelessly beyond our reach. We're heading away from it. We've got to turn around. *But we don't want to!* We don't even see that we need to.

From Genesis on, I feel God's burning anger aimed at everything that keeps us moving in the wrong direction. Something is terribly wrong inside us that must be severely dealt with before we'll even entertain the idea of turning around. And something must change in us before we'll be able to enjoy the party God is planning for us and to move toward it with any real consistency. We're unholy. We've separated ourselves *from* God. We need to be made holy. We need to separate ourselves *for* God.

In Leviticus, God makes it clear that "holiness must precede true happiness" and that making us holy, getting us to turn toward Him so that we relate well, is hard work. But it must be done. I hear Him saying in Joshua that we actually must "learn to hate our sin, what's wrong in us, more than we hate our suffering, all the wrong that's done to us." That's a tall order, a rough assignment.

And the learning curve is slow. Who do you know who would rather sin less than suffer less? Not many, I would guess. Why not? Sin is lodged so deeply inside us that we assume it's just who we are, that it's no big deal; and we actually believe the unholy road of self-interest will take us where we most want to go. That's what I hear God telling me in Judges, that I have a big problem, a deep and stubborn one.

And we'll never get entirely rid of that deeply lodged unholy thinking until the next life. Until we're perfectly holy we'll never be perfectly happy. It follows that we must expect to experience "emptiness now, with the promise of fullness forever." God makes that clear in 1 Chronicles.

But we don't like that. We insist on our "right to immediate happiness." And since pursuing holiness doesn't provide the present experience of full happiness that we crave, we pursue our objectives by a different road. But we still want to see ourselves as good, God-fearing folk. So to maintain the illusion that we're still wanting and following God, we think of Him as a vending machine for blessings rather than a burning fire who makes us holy. We worship the God we create, and we do it with gusto.

In Ezekiel, I learn that "until we recognize the evil of demanding anything from God, of treating Him like a vending machine whose job it is to slide out the candy, we will not understand how His presence can bring hope and joy and release from self-centeredness."

But we stay blind. We continue on the broad road of expecting God to make our lives work. We get religious to secure His favor and call it worship. We don't hear God telling us in Amos that real worship produces real change, from self-obsessed religion to God-centered relating.

At this point in the story, it becomes clear that if I'm really chasing after God, if I'm worshiping the real God as a lifestyle, my unholy and ugly spirit of entitlement will be slowly dislodged from its controlling place in my heart. I will sense the stirrings of a faith that allows me to wait in darkness with the peace of knowing the light of God's love will one day shine brightly enough for my dim eyes to see.

Even as life remains dark and foreboding, even as I face the ugliness within me that shakes my fist at God as I tell Him to make me happier, I realize I can still "celebrate in the confidence that everything ugly will one day be destroyed." I hear that in Obadiah.

And from Jonah I learn that in measure now, while God's ways continue to defy my self-obsessed expectations of Him, my unholy demand that God cooperate with my agendas can "yield more deeply to God's plan." It will be tough going. I'm plenty stubborn. But God won't give up on me. I like that, I think.

When life makes no sense, when what God is visibly doing is more frustrating than fulfilling, He wants me to live by faith. Even when God seems absent or, worse, indifferent; or worse still, utterly unfair by my standards of justice, for example, when a two-year-old grandson dies in his grandmother's arms or a husband commits suicide or a colleague is indifferent to my needs, He "wants me to wait, to feel life deeply but not to lash out in despairing frustration or angry rebellion but rather to still believe that His plan is good and on track." That's what I hear God say in Habakkuk. He's always loving me no matter how it looks.

This is very tough going. His plan to get me ready for the party by making me holy involves a lot of internal struggle. It triggers a fierce battle inside my psyche. I want to be happy now. God wants to make me holy now and promises happiness later. He tells me in Zephaniah that He is *not* committed to making me happy now with the blessings of life. *Cosmetic surgery is not His plan.* I'm starting to believe Him. But I don't always like what I'm starting to believe.

Haggai follows up by reassuring me that *God has the power to make me holy*, to perform successful open heart surgery, to actually stir a passion within me that wants to bring Him pleasure, a holy passion that can successfully compete with my already strong but unholy passion that wants to persuade Him to bring me pleasure now, on my terms.

Of course, I won't always understand or appreciate how the Master Surgeon is doing His work. So God tells me in Zechariah to *believe what I cannot see*, that a good plan is unfolding in the middle of bad times, painful times. The love story is continuing.

I want to see. But I'm so blind. For the life of me, I struggle to see the sheer goodness of His plan that is always flowing from the pure love in His heart. But I can't see it! In Malachi, God's thirty-ninth love letter, He exposes my blindness and tells me to wait hopefully in the dark until the "Light of the world comes." If I will trust Him, "the sun of righteousness will rise with healing in its wings" (Malachi 4:29), and I will start dancing, leaping with joy like "calves released from the stall" (Malachi 4:26).

After dialoguing with God through His first thirty-nine love letters and trying to hear what He's saying, I feel hopeful *and* discouraged, expectant *and* impatient, warmed by God's love *and* beaten down by His wrath. *The battle is on!* I know I'm a mess. I know there's a life-and-death struggle going on deep in my inner being that I'd prefer to ignore. I know there's an energy flowing through me that wants God, if at all, only on my terms.

And I know that that despicable energy seeps out every time I relate with someone, every time I make a decision about anything, every time I drive my car. I want to be happy, to feel a certain way about myself and my life, and I think you and God and life—and other drivers—should cooperate. I want this world to feel more like home than it does.

But I also want to know God, to follow Him, to be His servant, His friend. I want to dance with Him as well as I can now and look forward to dancing up a wonderfully happy and joyful storm forever.

My opposing wants collide. God's first thirty-nine letters have convinced me that the dark side will win unless He does something unimaginable.

They've also convinced me that this world I'm trying to decorate to feel like home is a rat-infested hovel that I can never fix up to my liking. I can do a little but only God can turn this dump into a mansion. And He will. He promised to make all things new—me, you, everything on earth, even the earth itself, and the heavens. All things!

For now, I see myself lying on the floor of this falling-down shack, filthy, emaciated, shivering, too weak to stand up. Had I not read God's first thirty-nine letters, I might still see myself living in a rather comfortable house as a rather decent person who, if I "trust" God, can live more decently and comfortably.

No longer. God has awakened me to the realization that this world as it is now is not my home and I am not who I nor He wants me to be. I'm not even close. All I can do as I lie helplessly on the floor is cry out for mercy. If no mercy comes, I'm a goner, destined to live forever in the misery of my own making, never loving anyone more than myself, always insisting that this world in its present condition make me happy or trying to change it for my sake, to make my life more comfortable and fulfilling.

But now, as I open the first of His last twenty-seven letters, discouragement yields to hope, impatience gives way to expectancy, and life rises out of my beaten-down self. I find myself singing words to an old gospel chorus: *something good is about to happen*.

As I open my Bible to Matthew, the rotting door to my shack opens. I hear the rusty hinges creak in glad surrender to a strong hand. I look up. It's the divine doctor. *He makes house calls!* It's the divine Savior. *He's heard my cry for mercy!* It's the divine Lord. *He's come to take over, to build His kingdom in me, in my friends, in the world!*

I've never seen Him before but I recognize Him, as if we're meeting again for the first time. We've already been introduced to each other by God, in His first thirty-nine letters. But the introduction is over. It's time to embrace.

Hope stirs within me, not yet for a better world with less suffering and more blessings, not even for a better community of friends, but for a better me. I've always somehow known I was born to dance, with Him, in holy rhythm. Maybe now I will.

He moves toward me, slowly, purposefully. I'm still on the floor, in the ditch of my own self-centeredness. But He keeps coming, moving toward me the way I've always imagined Mother Teresa moving toward a leper. With a smile. With hope. Eyes filled with love.

He kneels down next to me. His knees sink deep into the mud, mud I've created. The wonder of the incarnation overwhelms me.

He gently rests His right hand on my forehead. He looks me directly in the eye, with a strange mixture of holy fire and quiet love coming out of His eyes. His lips move. He's about to speak. I'm glad now that I've carefully read God's first thirty-nine love letters, even though at the time they didn't always feel like love letters. Somehow I realize in this moment that every word in all those letters, no exceptions, has prepared me to hear what God's Son is about to say.

Let's listen. He's come, with good news that we're finally ready to hear.

Love Letter Forty: Matthew

JESUS TAKES OVER

*G*od, I've just read Your fortieth love letter. After reading the first thirty-nine, I think You're asking me to change my mind about almost everything I've believed. Am I right?"

"Yes."

"And I think that in order to do that I need to remember what You've said to me in Your first thirty-nine letters. Otherwise, I'd pick out a few sentences I like and build an understanding of the Christian life that appeals to me and feels good but will keep me believing things You want me to stop believing. Am I right about that too?"

"Yes."

"And one more thing. You want me to see that every letter in the Old Testament is a love letter that is part of the one story of love You're telling. Otherwise, I'll think Your letters in the New Testament are telling a new story that's different from the one You've been telling in the Old, one that better fits with my wrong understanding of love and confirms it. Is that also right?"

"Yes."

"But that troubles me. Most of Your people today have no idea what You're saying to us in 1 Chronicles or Obadiah or Zephaniah. And they often don't see their ignorance as a problem. Does that mean Your church is in danger of making up a story and thinking they heard it from You?"

"The danger is real. What you fear is happening."

"God, I don't see how that danger can be overcome. It's hard to grasp how Old Testament history has anything to do with what's going on in our lives today. Like everyone else who says they believe in You, I want to know You now, to know You as You are today and to see how I'm supposed to follow You through whatever life is throwing at me right now. I want to know You, to find strength to live well in today's world, to get practical help. None of Your followers wants a history lesson about Your people centuries ago."

"I don't teach history. I *am* history. I *am* yesterday. I *am* today. I *am* tomorrow. Nothing I say is irrelevant. I tell one story, not two. I have one plan: to bring all My people to the Great Dance, to lead them on the narrow road that moves through suffering to unimaginable joy.

"You risk misunderstanding the continuity of My plan when you think of My first thirty-nine letters as the 'Old' Testament. I never used that term. It was coined during the days of My servant Origen, during the second and third centuries. The evil one has since seized the opportunity to get My people thinking that *Old* means out of date, that the Old Testament offers little more than occasionally interesting history sprinkled with a few inspiring stories for children and several compelling illustrations of New Testament truths for adults to ponder."

"God, that seems to be how many of Your followers today are thinking. The Old Testament seems old not only because it was written long before the New Testament but also, and more so, because what You said then can feel as relevant to me today as a 1950s medical text would to a modern physician or a Smith-Corona typewriter to Bill Gates.

"And God, it's worse than that. Many of Your followers today believe that the Old Testament makes You look like an angry God of wrath, a disagreeable God we can forget about and replace with the loving God You've revealed Yourself to be in the New Testament. I'm not sure how to counter that line of thinking. You do come across in many of those first thirty-nine letters as really angry with Your people for sinning so much."

"I relate in love. I always have. I always will. My anger was directed then and is directed now at everything that stands in the way of My purpose of love. You must never set aside or regard as outdated anything I reveal. My later letters *continue;* they do not dismiss the loving story I began to tell in My earlier ones."

"God, help me bridge the gap. Malachi leaves me hanging. I finish reading that thirty-ninth letter not certain if another flood is coming or if You're going to make everything good again. Show me how You pick up the story again after four hundred years of no additional chapters."

"John the Baptist. Zechariah. Mary. Simeon. Anna. These five choice servants of Mine bridge the gap. They continue the story of My relentless and holy love for My relentlessly and inexcusably sinful people."

"How? I don't see it."

"I filled John the Baptist from birth with My Spirit [Luke 1:15]. I allowed no risk of miscommunication. The message I gave him to say was too important. My people were blinded by their self-centered understanding of what should come next in the story. They thought I should send the Messiah to *bless* them. John knew the Messiah would come to *change* them, to restore their souls before I restored their blessings.

"John told people to repent, to change their expectations, to realize that I would empower them to dance to My music while hell's noise still blared. I revealed My plan to John, that My Son would come as a Lamb who would forgive their sins before He would roar as a Lion and take over the world. That plan was clear in My first thirty-nine letters to all with eyes to see.

"John's father, Zechariah, also bridged the gap. He doubted that I had the power to bring life out of death, to move My plan forward against impossible odds. When I told Zechariah that in their old age he and Elizabeth would give birth to a son who would prepare people for the next chapter in My story, his faith faltered. No one advances My story without faith. I, therefore, blessed him by removing his ability to speak for the nine months of his wife's pregnancy. Silence is an opportunity for faith to grow.

"When I released him to speak, I filled him with My Spirit. With the promises of My earlier letters singing in his heart, Zechariah praised Me for continuing the story, for keeping My promise to David [Luke 1:68–71], to Abraham [Luke 1:72–74], and to Zechariah himself [Luke 1:78–79]. When he realized the long-promised 'rising sun' was about to appear (a reference to what he had read in Malachi 4:2), Zechariah declared My goodness. He knew the story was continuing.

"And My surrendered Mary, how I love her. When before his birth John leaped in Elizabeth's womb in recognition that he was in the presence of the woman through whom the Messiah would come, Mary couldn't contain her excitement. She magnified Me as the powerful, holy, and merciful God who would have My way in the world I had created, whose plan despite all appearances was on course. Mary joyfully linked the two parts of My story even as the second part was miraculously unfolding in her body.

"Simeon, too, bridged the Old and the New. After decades of meditating on verses such as Isaiah 49:6, that righteous man knew that one day I would bring comfort not only to My long distressed people but also to the whole world. I was delighted to promise this Old Testament saint that before he died, with his own eyes, he would see the beginning of the New. When Simeon saw God in diapers (yes, the incarnation is that incredible), he celebrated the plan being revealed in a child, knowing (and telling Mary) that the plan involved pain. Not everyone would welcome her Son. And Mary's heart would be pierced with sorrow before she would dance with joy [Luke 2:25–35].

"And the elderly but forever beautiful Anna, My first prophetess in the second part of My story, like Miriam [Exodus 15:20], Deborah

[Judges 4:4], and Huldah [2 Kings 22:14] in the first part. Anna was specially favored as a prophetess through whom I would shine light on My plan. I arranged for Anna to be present when Simeon spoke to Mary. I so enjoyed that moment. Anna's husband had died eighty-four years earlier after only seven years of a happy marriage. For all those lonely years, this sorrowing widow had waited in My Presence, waiting in confident hope that her long night would yield to a dazzling dawn. When she heard Simeon speak to Mary, she knew the dawn had come. She turned to Me in joyful thanks, then turned to those around her to declare that the child in Mary's arms would bring redemption to My people [Luke 2:36–38]. Anna died a happy woman. She's much happier now.

"As you now listen to Me in Matthew, keep these five people in mind. I'm especially fond of each one. Together, they will help you know that the story I tell is one great story of love. From Genesis through Malachi and now from Matthew to Revelation, I never change. I always love. I can do nothing less. *I AM* love.

"Know this: no one can pass over My first thirty-nine love letters and expect to accurately grasp and profoundly delight in the story I continue in the last twenty-seven. I want you to be caught up in the eternal story that began before time began, that develops in Genesis through Malachi, continues in Matthew through Revelation, and will continue forever when time ends.

"My Son is here. The King has come. My kingdom is near. Repent! That was John's message. My Son confirmed it. *Change your mind about everything*. Only then will you hear the good news My Son brings, news so good that even John couldn't quite fit it into his head. Only then will you be able to dance to My music in a world where hell's noise is easier to hear and where it can sound like music. Only then will you hear the music of heaven that will one day be the only sound heard across the world, the day when everyone who loves My Son as I do will dance forever at My party."

"God, I'm having a hard time hearing what You're saying to me in Matthew. Your Son isn't bringing the good news I expected."

"Tell Me about your conversation yesterday afternoon with your troubled friend."

"What's that got to do with . . . I'm sorry. I should know better. Well, he's been in a tough marriage for years. I think he's reached the end of his rope. He came into marriage an empty man. He's never felt deeply wanted by anyone. And now, years later, he's facing how unwanted he feels by his wife."

"What has he been giving to his wife?"

"Everything but his heart. He's been guarding that since he was a kid. To give her his heart, to love her with no strings attached, would be too big a risk. She might reject him."

"Your friend is still ruled by fear, not broken by failure. He has not come to the end of his rope. When he does, there will be less stubborn self-protection in his motives and more room for the Spirit of My Son to take over. My Son made that exact point in His first sermon: 'You're blessed when you're at the end of your rope. With less of you there is more of God and his rule' (Matthew 5:3 MSG). You will hear My voice in Matthew more clearly when you pay close attention to what's happening in people's lives, including your own. I always say what you and your friend—and everyone else— most need to hear. See where you are. Then you will hear My truth.

"Listen closely. This is what I'm saying in My fortieth letter:

My Son's mission was to change your life, to bring you into My kingdom of love by forgiving your self-worshiping rebellion that keeps you falling short of My way of relating and by empowering you to bring My kingdom near to others by the radically changed way you can now relate. He never intended to keep you visibly good and pleasantly happy until heaven. He came to reveal My nature for your sake and to change your nature for Mine."

"God, I think that's why I'm having a hard time with this letter. What You've just said is not the gospel I was taught. As an eight-year-old staring into a huge bonfire at boys' camp, I was told I'd better get saved, or I'd burn in hell forever. So I whispered a prayer. I asked Jesus to forgive me and take me to heaven when I died. And I promised I'd try hard to be good until then. And if I was good or, at least, pretty good, I assumed I'd be happy and blessed. I've since learned there's a whole lot more to Christianity than I knew then and maybe a lot less. But isn't what I understood as a child pretty much the center of the gospel?"

"My Spirit began Our good work in you when you were eight. In that moment by the campfire you were saved from hell and destined for heaven. But what you understood then—that living well would keep your life going well until you got to heaven—had no power to change you to deal with your worst relational problem, and it added moralistic pressure to your life that blocked the freedom I want you to enjoy. And it obscured your mission, what I've left you in this world to do. That message—get saved, live well, enjoy My blessings, then go to heaven—is not what I'm saying to you in Matthew."

"That's what troubles me. The very first words out of Your Son's mouth recorded by Matthew were 'Repent, for the kingdom of heaven is at hand' (4:17 NKJV). I would have expected Him to begin with something like I heard at boys' camp."

"My Spirit used what you heard then to bring you into the kingdom. But now you must hear what Matthew heard. His message—what I am saying to you through his writings—will point you to the center of the good news. It will empower your friend to stop grasping for what he mistakenly thinks will meet his needs and instead to give his wife what I have already placed in his heart. The kingdom is near to your friend."

"I think I know where I'm stuck. You talk of the center of the good news. I'm not sure what that is. I feel a little like John the Baptist sitting in jail waiting to be executed, wondering what the good news of Jesus is for him. What does it mean to say the kingdom of heaven is near? If the party's already underway, I don't see it. What difference has Your Son made? Oncologists are still busy. Divorce lawyers have plenty of clients. John the Baptist was killed. And I still have bad headaches even though lots of friends are praying that the headaches will go away. Maybe I should know better, but somewhere down deep, I guess, I've always thought the good news was that heaven is coming up, that I'd dance then. And for now, I'm supposed to hang in there through hard times and live the way You want me to. And I've assumed I could expect a fair number of blessings to be thrown in—maybe an abundance if I have enough faith—like a pain-free head."

"Open your ears to hear Me speak:

The center of the good news is that you can know My Son and by My Spirit enter into the relationship My Son and I enjoy. That news has the power to transform you and your friend from grasping for life for your sake to losing your life for My sake. Any time with prioritized energy you do anything designed to fill your emptiness or to protect yourself from more rejection you are serving the wrong kingdom. But you are now empowered to serve My kingdom, to relate as We relate within the Trinity. That's the dance, the dance you can enjoy in measure now and will fully enjoy forever when My Son returns and heaven's kingdom fills the earth. That's the good news."

"God, it feels too hard, too remote. That news might feel good if I could do what You say."

"Read Matthew 12:28. Right now!"

"Okay. That's where Your Son says, 'If I drive out demons by the Spirit of God, then the kingdom has come upon you.' I don't get it. What did He mean? Why did You want me to read that verse now?"

"When Adam turned from Me, the devil took over. All his descendants live now in a kingdom where grasping for satisfaction seems justified by the very real pain of emptiness. That kingdom is led by Satan [Luke 4:6]. To this day he continues to deceive people like your friend into believing that protecting his empty heart and grasping after whatever fullness seems available is warranted [Hebrews 2:14].

"I sent My Son to destroy the devil's work [1 John 3:8–9]. And He did. He has taken over. You ask what difference He has made. *There is now a community of people who, though their souls may feel empty, are filled with My Spirit, a people whose lifestyle is giving from trusted fullness rather than grasping for demanded fullness.* They are My people. I am their God. They are My Son's church, His bride and body, and the power of hell cannot destroy them. They are the army I have raised up and equipped to represent Me and to advance My purposes in this world.

"My Spirit is forming these people to be like Jesus, 'who did not consider equality with God something to be grasped but made himself nothing' (Philippians 2:6). If My Spirit can change Matthew from a tax collector who lived only for his own advantage into a follower of My Son, then He can change your friend from an empty grasper into a much-loved giver."

"How does that happen? How did it happen for Matthew?"

"He met My Son. He realized that everything My prophets prophesied about the coming Messiah had come true in My Son: born of a virgin [Isaiah 7:14], born in Bethlehem [Micah 5:2], returned from Egypt [Hosea 11:1], announced by a voice in the wilderness [Isaiah 40:3], and ministered in Galilee [Isaiah 9:1–2].

"But more than fulfilled prophecy, Matthew saw that I was keeping My promise to get My people to My party when he understood I was bringing My party to earth. My Son made clear what it meant to dance in rhythm with heaven's kingdom when He preached the sermon on the mount [Matthew 5–7]. He demonstrated His defeat of Satan and His superior power over illness, nature, sin, and death in ten miracles that Matthew recorded [Matthew 8–10]—there were many more. And then after dealing with authority over all who opposed Him [Matthew 11–18], He left Galilee for Judea heading toward Jerusalem to die. He rode into the city on a donkey as predicted by Zechariah [9:9]. He endured betrayal by a friend as described in Psalm 41:9 and then suffered the unspeakable agonies detailed in Psalm 22—agonies that only sinners and all sinners should rightly endure.

"Above all, Matthew saw that the Father-Son relationship that My Son and I enjoyed in heaven was now offered to people on earth [11:27]. He realized My Son came not merely to get people into heaven but to get heaven's kingdom—the way We relate within the Trinity—into people.

"And He can do it. My Son has taken over. He is the head over every power and principality [Colossians 2:10]. Matthew heard My Son's invitation to all whose lifestyle of grasping had left them tired, burnt out, disillusioned, and empty [Matthew 11:28–30 MSG], and he responded. He would resonate with the hymn 'Heaven came down and glory filled my soul.' Matthew learned the unforced rhythms of grace, from grasping for life as a Roman tax collector to giving life to others as a follower of My Son. That's the dance. The kingdom is near. The party has begun."

"God, I want to dance. I hear the good news, that I have been forgiven for my sins and infused with the life of Your Son, that no matter how I feel or what goes wrong, I can live to give and not to grasp. I can bring a taste of heaven to earth, knowing that one day heaven's love will rule over every heart on earth, and I'll be there dancing at Your fully revealed party. God, I believe all of that, but I still fall short."

"Listen to My Son's final words on earth: 'All authority in heaven and earth has been given to me [and taken away from the devil]. Therefore go and make disciples of all nations, baptizing them in the name of the Father and of the Son and of the Holy Spirit, and teaching them to obey everything I have commanded you. And surely I am with you always, even to the very end of the age' (Matthew 28:18–20)."

"God, since the devil's power has been stripped and since I have been born again out of this world's kingdom into heaven's, that means the real battle now is within me, between my own urge to grasp after whatever seems necessary and the desire to give, to love others like Jesus does—a desire Your Spirit has put in me. That gives a whole new meaning to spiritual warfare. I must still resist the devil and not conform myself to this world, but the real battle is going on in me, between my flesh and spirit. I want to win that battle."

"You have heard My message to you in Matthew. There is so much more to hear, more than you can imagine or think. My Son has taken over. He has defeated the devil and overcome the world. Read on. Your friend will learn to love. So will you."

Love Letter Forty-One: Mark

JESUS WILL TAKE YOU BACK THEN FORWARD

*G*od, I'm not sure why, but as I'm reading through Your forty-first letter, I'm feeling very small. To actually speak with the Creator of the universe through letters You've written to me is a staggering privilege. It would be right to fall flat on my face and to be overwhelmed by even one word from Your mouth. And yet You speak many words. Even more staggering, You invite me to stand in Your presence and to make known my confusion, to actually wrestle with You as Jacob did.

"I guess this strikes me now because in Mark, I'm reading about Your Son, not as King (though He is the King of kings) but as a servant who, after creating everything for Himself, came here to suffer because of the mess we've made. I'm so familiar with the story that I tend to take it for granted, even to read the story as historical fiction rather than, in C. S. Lewis's words, as a 'true myth, a myth that actually happened.' Forgive me!

"But—may this be true—I think I'm hearing a little of what You're saying. In Matthew, I heard words that made me more clearly aware of two things. First, You want to get heaven into me, to get me living more like Your Son so I can begin enjoying heaven's party now. And the more I do live like Him, the more Your kingdom is taking over my life and positioning itself to spread into others. Second, the real battle I'm fighting is going on inside me. As You bring Your kingdom into me, the devil and the world system oppose every move You make, but my worst enemy is my own self-centeredness, the spirit within me that thinks it's my right for life to go the way I want it to. Did I hear You correctly?"

"Yes."

"Well, God, I know You know this, but the battle isn't going so well at the moment. I'm in a down mood. Discouraged. Empty. Frustrated. Worried. Passionless. But I'm still passionate about me. My desire for my life to run smoothly and for me to feel good seems stronger right now than my desire to serve You with all the suffering that might be involved."

"It's time to hear Me speak in My forty-first letter."

"I've already read it, more than once. All I see is Your Son healing people in ways He's not doing today and then, after dying and rising from the dead, telling me to preach good news to everyone. I'm getting that the good news, the gospel, is not centered in the promise that someday You'll get us out of this troubled world by fixing it up although that is true. And the good news does *not* include a promise that You'll pave an easy, comfortable road for Your followers to walk on through all the troubles of life. The good news of the kingdom that Your Son came to bring centers on the truth that somehow—but not completely—Your kingdom is here now. Kingdom life is available now. We can live under the authority and with the power of our King, now, every day. We can serve Your purposes as we serve people—as Jesus did—until we arrive in the world where every human desire is satisfied, stretched, then satisfied again, and on like that forever.

"But God, that news isn't grabbing me. It isn't reaching deep. I can think of news that would sound much better to me, that would excite me more. I hate to say it, but the promise of a good life now, a good life of an intimate marriage, children healthy and happy, meaningful friendships that include lots of fun, no threat of cancer, plenty of money, a fulfilling career that makes this world a better place—if that were the abundant life Your Son came to bring, I could get pretty excited and preach it to anyone who'd listen. I think that message would draw big crowds. That would be easily recognized as really good news. What am I missing?"

"You've read My words *through* Mark. You've not read My life *in* Mark."

"You've lost me. I have no idea what You're talking about."

"I chose Mark just as I chose Matthew, Luke, and John, to present a portrait of My Son that the others could never paint as well. Four portraits. One Person. I want you to see My Son in all His beauty. He's irresistible!

"Like you, Mark was used to comfort. Raised in a large home where My followers were always welcomed by Mark's mother, Mary, he—again like you—mixed personal comfort with spiritual reality. My servant Peter, who was Mark's spiritual father [1 Peter 5:13], showed up at Mark's door after My angel freed him from a Roman prison where he was awaiting execution [Acts 12:1–19]. Mark was stirred.

"When he was later invited to join Barnabas and Paul on their first mission trip, Mark (sometimes called John) was eager to serve. But he was not yet prepared to put his comfort into second place and give first place to kingdom service. Spreading My good news always meets with opposition. Mark listened as Paul confronted an occultist by calling him a 'child of the devil,' then striking him blind, and then leading Sergio Paulus—a city official in Paphos—to faith in My Son.

"After a one-hundred-mile voyage to Perga, their next mission target, Mark was having second thoughts. He was beginning to see clearly that the excitement of ministry included conflict and hardship and danger. Before Paul and Barnabas began preaching in Perga, Mark sailed back to Jerusalem to his comfortable home and pleasant life [Acts 13:1–13].

"You are right now where Mark was, feeling the squeeze of the narrow road I have called you to walk. Paul resisted the suggestion of Barnabas to include Mark on a later mission trip [Acts 15:36–40]. No one who refuses to press on through the battle between looking out for oneself and service for Me, between comfort and suffering, is much use to My purposes."

"God, meeting You in Your Word is not always pleasant. I feel exposed."

"That's My intent. Your desire to experience Me when life gets rough has become a demand. Demand nothing. Surrender everything. Those are My terms. Like you, Mark failed. Like you, Mark wrongly believed that the good news of following Me into kingdom living included the good news of a life blessed with a certain level of comfort and freedom from hassle.

"But My Son brought him back and moved him forward. During the next decade, after he repented of choosing comfort over service and suffering, Mark traveled with Peter, who couldn't stop talking about his time with My Son. (It was from Peter's report that Mark wrote this letter, capturing all the excitement in Peter's voice as he told Mark story after story that matched Peter's active spirit.) Mark more fully realized that My Son lived a life of selfless servanthood that led to undeserved suffering. He realized what kingdom living meant.

"Mark was transformed. Years after his failure and Paul's rejection of him, Mark was welcomed by Paul to be with him in prison [Colossians 4:10–11]. And just before his execution, Paul wanted Mark with him again [2 Timothy 4:11]. Mark yielded his desire for comfort to the privilege of servanthood and suffering. He planted the first church in Egypt and for his faithfulness was dragged through the streets, thrown into a dungeon, then burned to death."

"God, after hearing You tell Mark's story, I've just reread this letter. It's taken on a whole new meaning. Please, tell me clearly, what do You want me to hear from You as I read Your forty-first letter?"

"Hear this:

Because of My Son, no failure of yours can block My plan for your life. But you must see My Son so clearly, so up close and personally, that you realize He is worthy of your losing everything you value in life in order to know Him, to serve Him. The more clearly you see Christ, the more willing you will be to suffer any loss for His sake. Kingdom living consists of radical servanthood (the end of entitlement to personal comfort) and self-denying suffering with the hope of joy forever."

"Guide me. I want to read this letter again. Show me how You're getting that message across in Mark."

"There are many brushstrokes in Mark that paint the portrait of My Son as the suffering servant. Here are a few.

"Mark often repeats My Son's instructions to keep His identity a secret, of course, for good reason. He came not to satisfy the expectations for a pleasant, much blessed life held by so many. He came to serve and to suffer, 'to give his life as a ransom for many' (Mark 10:45). He did not come the first time to visibly assert His authority over all the world. He'll do that when He comes again.

"The Greek word *euthios*, meaning 'immediately' or 'right away,' occurs forty-two times in this letter, more than in My other twenty-six New Testament letters combined. My Son came to serve, and service involves readiness to follow My Spirit's promptings. To be formed like My Son does not mean indolence disguised as contemplative rest. It rather means internal rest that releases servant activity.

"Notice the shift at Mark 8:31: '*then* he began to teach them that the Son of Man'—His favorite term for Himself in Mark—'must suffer . . . and be killed . . . and after three days rise again.' Until that verse, I emphasized My Son's *service*. After that verse, I traced His journey toward *suffering*.

"Peter missed the point. He instructed My Son—can you imagine?—to stop talking about the cross [Mark 8:32–33]. You, too, are prone to miss the point: there is no gospel without the cross, there is no obedience without servanthood, and there is no spiritual formation without suffering.

"In Mark, I provided no genealogy of My Son, no birth narrative, no Christmas story with singing angels and worshiping shepherds. Learn the lesson: the King of kings and Lord of lords, Creator of everything, came as a humble servant, the ultimate Somebody disguised as a mere nobody. Consider that in your understanding of spiritual formation.

"This letter focuses on My Son's deeds more than His words. All the good He did on earth is essential to 'the gospel about Jesus Christ, the Son of God' (Mark 1:1). At His death, even a Roman soldier was compelled to confess, 'Surely this man was the Son of God' (15:39)."

"God, I can't comprehend it—Your eternal Son, the serving and suffering Son of Man. I feel humbled and very small. I think You've just led me one step further on the narrow road. God, help me keep moving."

"I will. It's My plan. Your spirit of entitlement to the blessings of life dies hard. Your battle continues. Mark finished well. You can too. Keep reading."

Love Letter Forty-Two:
Luke

LET JESUS LEAD THE WAY

*F*ather, I want to be more like Jesus. I know I have a long way to go. You just told me that the battle in my heart would continue. Can You tell me in terms I can understand what the battle is, what's going on in me that's blocking my progress in becoming like Your Son?"

"Your heart is divided."

"Divided? What do you mean?"

"You want a better life now. You're discouraged by how tired you feel and by the promises you wish I'd made but know I haven't—promises for good health, a good economy, and good relationships. You've become cynical toward what you see in today's church and with Christians who report an intimacy with Me that you rarely feel."

"You're right, God, of course. I do struggle with all of that. I don't know how to stop. And I sometimes get really irritated and worried by how empty I feel, by how unmotivated I often am even as I do good things."

"You said you want to be more like My Son. You seem to most want more energy, an upbeat attitude, a fulfilling sense of personal significance, to be someone who seizes all the good opportunities for felt happiness and welcomed impact that life offers. Does that describe My Son when He lived on earth? In your heart, at least in the part you've so far accessed, you rarely find a desire stronger than your wish to be satisfied with life's blessings, to feel *both* confident in My goodness that they'll continue *and* excited about life's opportunities. Your desire for spiritual formation lies on top of those self-focused desires like an attractive veneer. It needs to lie beneath as the controlling foundation of your life."

"I'm not sure I follow. Am I wrong to want more energy, to feel alive and passionate and freely unpressured?"

"If you desire nothing else more strongly, yes. Listen closely. You are in a good place. You are standing at a crossroads that not many reach, a crossroads where the choice between absolute surrender and lukewarm Christianity (which isn't Christianity at all) is clear. You must now determine which you want more: *apparent* maturity that wins recognition from others and numbs the anguish of feeling desires that nothing in this world can satisfy—a way to live that never enters the deep battle going on in every redeemed soul—or *perfect* maturity that puts you in touch with desires that will remain unsatisfied till the next life, that engage you in an internal battle that depletes your resources and leaves you exhausted—sometimes feeling that your worst nightmare has come true: that you're worth nothing and that you *are* nothing—a battle that leaves you entirely dependent on Me for the courage and strength to continue.

"The road to perfect maturity will make you vulnerable to severe temptations that those who settle for apparent maturity will feel less strongly. And it will stir doubts about My reality that you could avoid by choosing the easier path. But if you want to be formed like My Son, this is the road you must choose, the one less traveled."

"You're right. I am divided. I want perfect maturity, and at times more strongly, I want the kind of comfortable Christianity that enjoys the trappings of apparent maturity. And those two desires cannot coexist with equal strength. One must yield to the other. I gather it's no coincidence that I'm becoming aware of my divided heart and my attraction to something less than true spiritual formation while I've been reading Your forty-second love letter."

"It is no coincidence. There are no coincidences in the lives of My children."

"Then tell me: what am I faintly hearing in Luke that You want me to hear more clearly?"

"In Matthew, I introduced My Son to you as your King. He told you how citizens of My kingdom are to live. In Mark, you met My Son as your humble Servant, a man who made no demands for Himself. His complete lack of a spirit of entitlement called you to recognize and hate yours.

"And now in Luke I take things a step further. Hear this as you read My forty-second letter:

My Son is the perfect Person I had in mind for all people to be. He is the perfect Person whose image you will become. The more clearly you see perfect maturity in Him, the more you'll be drawn to that goal, the less divided you'll be, and the more willing you'll become to persevere through anything in order to be formed like My Son."

"Father, I need to see Him. I want to want to be like Him more than anything else. I'm not there."

"You just addressed Me as Father for the second time. In our previous forty-one conversations, you've always called Me *God*. Why are you now calling Me *Father?*"

"I don't know."

"Yes, you do. Look deep into your heart. You really do long to know Me as your Father, to serve Me and enjoy Me as My Son did perfectly during His thirty-three years on earth. Read this letter to access your desire to be like My Son, the only human being who with full meaning called Me Father. Meditate on all that I say until that desire is stronger than all others."

"Show me what I'm to see."

"I chose Luke to present My Son as the perfect Person because Luke was a Greek. He was caught up in the central aim of Greek philosophy, to understand what perfection would look like in a human being. When he began collecting all the accounts of My Son's life, Luke realized he was seeing a kind of virtue that no philosopher could imagine. And as he traveled with Paul, Luke heard Paul speak passionately about the man Jesus, and he felt compelled (My doing!) to write to his Greek mentor Theophilus to describe the perfect Person he had found.

"If you miss everything in this letter but one thing, don't miss this: My Son *wished forward*. Seven times I had Luke record that He prayed, using the word *proseuchomai*, which means 'to wish forward.' That is the core of human maturity in this life. My Son had no greater desire than to carry out His part in My plan. That is the center of spiritual formation, not more energy, not feeling more upbeat, but a clear awareness of the deepest truly *human* desire, a desire that releases resolve, an unflinching determination to follow the lead of My Son in bringing heaven's kingdom to earth, a longing to love.

"The first time I recorded that He wished forward was at His baptism. As He was praying [Luke 3:21], My Spirit descended on Him, and I declared My pleasure in Him. He was surrendering Himself fully to the calling I had placed on His life. A perfectly mature person has confidence in the goodness of My plan and knows no greater desire than to move it ahead. Get a vision of what defined My Son as a human being. (Reflect on the other six times Luke mentions that Jesus wished forward: Luke 5:16; 6:12; 9:18; 9:29; 11:1; 22:41.)

"Notice, too, that seven times I record that My Son's wishing forward meant going to Jerusalem to die [Luke 9:51; 13:22; 17:11; 18:31; 19:11, 28, 37]. Perfect maturity counts the cost and keeps moving.

"And on the way to Jerusalem, knowing He was about to suffer unbearable agony, My Son did good to others by teaching, healing, and rebuking. I recorded more than two dozen incidents in Luke that I did not record in Matthew, Mark, or John, each one revealing what a perfect Person looks like even when He is facing terrible pain. Read the parables that fell from His lips, such as the parables of the Good Samaritan [10:25–37] and the Prodigal Son [15:11–32]; notice My Son's reply to James and John when they wanted to call down fire on the Samaritans [9:51–56] and how He handled Zacchaeus [19:1–10] on His way to die for the sins of James and John and the Samaritans and Zacchaeus. Then you will see that perfect maturity feels deeply and loves generously even when life is hard. That's what it means to become like My Son. Still interested?"

"More than ever. But it seems impossible."

"That's why only in Luke do I include my Son's specific promise of the Holy Spirit before He returned to heaven [Luke 24:49]. He pointedly told His followers to wait until the Spirit came and 'clothed them with power from on high.' Hear this: you can become *apparently* mature without My Spirit's power. Human effort is sufficient. But I find no pleasure in what it produces. Peace will come to earth only when I find pleasure in all its inhabitants [Luke 2:14]. And that will not happen until everyone is *perfectly* mature, formed exactly like My Son. Movement toward that desire requires the power of My Spirit, to divide and expose the two roads within you [Luke 12:51] and lead you to wish forward on the right one—the narrow one—to follow in My Son's footsteps."

"Father, is it possible? I'm not sure I believe it is."

"That's why I wrote My next letter. Keep reading. You are about to discover that the deepest desire in your heart is not for blessings. Your deepest *need* is to be loved with forgiving and empowering grace. Your deepest *desire* is to love."

Love Letter Forty-Three:
John

HEAVEN'S REALITY HAS MOVED INTO YOURS

$\mathcal{F}$ather, what You say seems so often out of my reach."

"What I want for you is always out of your reach. That's why I had to send My Son and then My Spirit to bring real life within your reach."

"But that's the problem. It's the way You define real life that makes me feel hopeless. If I'm seeing what You're saying in this forty-third letter, then nearly everyone I know, beginning with me, has bought into a less radical understanding of what it means to really live than Your Son taught, an understanding that's more easily lived than Yours. The way I naturally think about living a full life seems so much more reasonable, more human, more doable—go to church, work hard, be good, pray, read the Bible every day, and trust You for whatever blessings I really want.

"I just read a letter from a pastor in Zimbabwe whose people face real danger every day from the ruthless dictator who runs their country. Church members get beat up if they express anything but full support for the monster who heads up their national government. The pastor felt that You led him to preach a series on Habakkuk, focusing on the two questions that the prophet's circumstances forced him to ask: Lord, how long will I call and You will not hear? How long will I cry and You will not save? [Habakkuk 1:2]. For his people, the pastor rephrased those questions this way: 'Lord, do You hear? Why are You doing nothing?' If I were a follower of Yours living in Zimbabwe, I'd be asking those questions, too, thinking that what it means to really live should involve at least a little less suffering, a little more justice.

"And so many husbands and wives that I know personally seem to think that to be alive in a marriage means that their spouses must treat them with some reasonable standard of kindness. A good friend of mine has felt empty in his marriage for years. Just recently he got in touch with how unwanted and demeaned and controlled he's felt, and now he's been begging You for enough of an experience of Your presence to help him hang in there without blowing up or taking off. I'd think asking to feel a little more alive, a little happier and more settled, would be a reasonable request. But so far, nothing. If I felt as miserable as he does or as rejected as his wife now feels, I'd have a hard time hearing what I think You're saying in this fourth gospel."

"There are not four gospels. My servant Origen was right: there is one fourfold gospel. My forty-third love letter completes (for now) the portrait I am painting of My Son, a portrait that makes it clear what it means to be fully alive as a human being."

"Maybe I'm hearing something more extreme than You're saying, but I think You'd tell the Zimbabwe pastor that even if their suffering gets worse, he and his people can live the abundant life of loving their enemies, standing against corruption, and trusting You in prayer. And I think You'd tell every hurting spouse that to really live would mean to do whatever it takes to advance Your kingdom, to give You pleasure, and to be an opportunity for the Spirit to do His work in the most disappointing husband or frustrating wife. You'd tell them that living the real life Jesus lived is *that* radical and, now that Your Spirit has come, within their reach. Am I right?"

"Yes."

"Then You've got to help me. I can live what I call the Christian life in a country where I won't get beat up for believing in Your Son and in a marriage to a woman I really like being married to. I'm not sure I could do it in Zimbabwe or with a spouse like some I've seen."

"You're seeing real life the way a beginning art student would see Rembrandt's *Return of the Prodigal* if she glanced at it on her way to a cup of coffee in the Hermitage Museum's café. There's more to see, much more."

"Father, show me what You're saying to me in this forty-third letter."

"No single artist could capture the beauty of life as it was meant to be lived. I commissioned four specially chosen artists—each selected for his temperament and because of his circumstances—to paint four portraits of the only Person who ever fully lived. Together they sketched a beauty that is not in the eye of the beholder but is in the person of My Son, a beauty that a thousand portraits could never capture, a glory that though dimly visible now will one day fill the heavens and the earth. You will catch a glimpse of the compelling beauty of His life if you linger before each portrait as a preview of heaven's soon coming attraction:

※ My Son, the *Sovereign King* of a kingdom long promised, whose citizens are instructed by the King Himself to live in a way that makes no sense to citizens of this world's kingdom. Matthew, the tax collector turned saint, painted that picture.

※ My Son, the *Suffering Servant*, who by His unexpected example led His followers to sacrifice every comfort that gets in the way of serving others. Mark, the man who once failed to serve when things got rough, highlighted that facet of My Son's beauty.

※ My Son, the *Perfect Person*, whose brothers and sisters are learning to wish forward as He did, the only Person whose ruling passion was never to suffer less or feel good but was always to advance My plan to get My people to the party. I enjoyed watching Him live as I've enjoyed watching no one else. The Greek physician Luke, who longed to see the human ideal and who found Him in My Son, sketched the perfection he saw.

※ My Son, the *Divine Life* itself. Now John, the dreamer, the poet, a man to whom I revealed the deepest truth about My Son, a truth that no one without My Spirit's prompting could imagine—I chose this man to present the One who fully revealed what it means to live as I live, who revealed My heart, My nature, My love.

"See this as you see My Son in the forty-third letter:

In the world you now inhabit, communion with Me is not defined by an experience of Me. Nor does it depend on blessings from Me. To really live is to release My Son's life through yours, in any circumstance, no matter what you feel; to relate as He related, giving when no one gives back, loving when no one returns love, forgiving when no one deserves forgiveness, suffering in the place of those who should suffer.

"*Understand this*: to commune with Me in this life is to live like My Son with His life alive in you. *Believe this*: communion with Me leads to an eternal experience of Me and unimaginable blessings from Me, tastes of both now—as My Spirit chooses—and the banquet later when you see My Son."

"God, I can't do it. If I don't feel Your presence now, I won't be able to live like Your Son. And if too many things go wrong in my life, I think I'll just crumble."

"Don't look at your inability. Look at My Son's ability. As you read John, pause before a portrait Rembrandt could never paint. Notice that no miracle Jesus ever performed served His well-being, that no teaching He ever presented was designed to win popularity, and that in no conversation in which He ever engaged did He maneuver things to His advantage but always to Mine. As you gaze at My Son's portrait, let Me point out only four brushstrokes from My hand through John's. There are many more, so many more that the whole world could not contain the paintings needed to depict every one.

"First, My Son is the only human being who was with Me *before*

He was born. He came to reveal all that He knew of Me that you could absorb or imagine. He came to 'exegete' Me—that's the word in John 1:18 translated 'made him known.' It means to make visible what could be seen in no other way. *See My Son.*

"Second, My Son revealed what He had personally *seen* and *heard* in the unseen and unheard world from which He came [John 3:32]. He had *seen* perfect community from the inside, Three Persons living life as it was meant to be lived. And He had *heard* the plan We same Three Persons had made to throw a party for forgiven sinners whom My Spirit would teach to dance, to really live—people who would become fully alive with the exact life that My Son revealed in everything He said and did.

"Third, My Son confronted and contradicted every lesser understanding of what it means to really live, every understanding that centrally defines life as less suffering and more happiness. Real life, the life that My Son and I and Our Spirit have always and will forever enjoy is the joy of loving. We *give* to each other. You bear Our image. Your deepest *desire* is to love as We love. Your deepest *need* is to be loved. I love you. Your need is met. You are now free to do what you most want to do, what I created you to do, to live life to the full, to love, to love Me and others as My Son did during His time on earth and still does.

"Fourth, many who were at first drawn to My Son turned away when they realized what He was saying. Like so many today, they heard His teachings as 'hard' (in John 6:60, the word *hard* is a translation of *skleros*: offensive, not merely difficult or obscure). To love with nails in your hands and to love those who put them there captures the essence of what it means to really live. My forty-third love letter makes that clear."

"Father, I'm like Your Son's early disciples who believed what He said but as soon as He disappeared from sight went fishing [John 20:2–3]. I want to live a life I'm good at, a life that lets me protect myself from avoidable pain and feel good in available pleasures. But You want me to live a life I can't live!"

"In My next letter, you will see what happens when My followers not only understand what it means to really live but also are empowered to live that way. When My followers became a Spirit-filled community, they became the church! Know this: *heaven's reality has invaded yours*. Prepare to live a *new way*. Real life, the surprising route to joy, is within reach."

PART SIX

Clumsy People Take Dance Lessons: Acts Through Jude

*G*od's story centers on creating a new kind of community, a group of people (a very large group) who dance together in the rhythm of the Trinity and, therefore, relate with tastes of the delight that the Three Persons of the Godhead have always and always will enjoy.

But changing the way we relate starts a battle. I'm naturally self-obsessed. I'm committed to my well-being at any cost to others. God is naturally others-obsessed. He's committed to our well-being at any cost to Himself.

The miracle of the cross of Christ has provided forgiveness for how selfish I am and placed in me a new heart, a new desire to love like Jesus. But my old desire to look after myself is still present. I still tend to dance to the rhythm of my fall into selfishness.

So the dance lessons—what theologians call *sanctification* and what many call *spiritual formation*—don't always go so well. The next twenty-two love letters tell the story of clumsy people taking dance lessons. But take heart. The Spirit is a first-rate teacher. He *will* teach willing hearts how to dance.

Love Letter Forty-Four:
Acts

*F*ather, my first reaction to reading this letter was discouragement. Maybe I'm an idealistic cynic, but if Stephen or Peter or Paul could see what so many of us modern Jesus-followers are calling Christianity, if they visited what so often passes for church today, I think they'd fall flat on their faces and weep.

"And it occurred to me, too, that if Ananias and Sapphira—the couple You killed—were to talk to us now, they'd tell us that if our churches were as Spirit-filled as the one they were part of, a whole lot of us, including some pastors and elders—and maybe me—would drop dead during what we call worship.

"Reading Acts is opening my eyes to see how phony we've become and how unaware we are of our phoniness. We've become a community of pretenders who've made such a habit of presenting ourselves to each other as more spiritually alive than we are that we actually believe our own posturing. We're like people with cancer who ignore our symptoms and play golf, pretending that we're healthy. But I know I can't throw stones at anybody else. The house I'm living in has too many glass walls and rests on too sandy a foundation.

"Father, what You described in this letter about how Your early followers lived sent me into a tailspin. And that made me mad at You. I don't understand why You let those believers see such obvious demonstrations of Your power that I've never seen. You sent an angel to get Peter out of prison before the authorities could kill him, and You had the iron gate leading to the city open like the automatic doors at a hotel so Peter could return to his friends [Acts 12:1–10].

"I've never seen city gates miraculously open or lame people jump or dead women like Dorcas come back to life [Acts 9:32–42]. What's supposed to get me living with the faith and zeal of those early Christians who saw stuff like that? I hear about similar miracles in China and South America, but all I see in America are the counterfeits that televangelists parade to get people to open their wallets. Why don't You publicly rebuke them? You inspired Peter to severely rebuke Simon the sorcerer who professed to believe You but only wanted spiritual power to make more money [Acts 8:9–24].

"The way things are today in so many churches seems so far beneath what went on in the church You described in Acts that I felt a wave of futility smothering the life out of me. I mean, why bother? My urge to live comfortably, to give up on the hope of living supernaturally, got really strong as I read this letter. The tension between hope for what could be and the reality of what I see in me and all around me paralyzed my heart. I got really depressed, then mad. I want to be revived. I want to see Your people revived to live the kind of life Your Son lived, the kind of life those early Christians lived—imperfectly, I know, but a lot better than how I see Your people, including me, living today.

"I want to be able to say what Paul said and mean it: 'I consider my life worth nothing to me, if only I may finish the race to complete the task the Lord Jesus has given me—the task of testifying to the gospel of God's grace' (Acts 20:24). But I still consider my life worth something to me. God, I'm having a hard time knowing what it's going to take for me to live the radical life You want me to live.

"Look, I know I'm talking like a spiritual idiot. I ought to shut up and listen. But can I say one more thing?"

"I permitted Job to speak at length before I responded. I will do the same for you. Continue."

"Well, that's not very reassuring. I remember my dad telling me the best thing Job ever did was to stop talking. I just looked up the verse: 'The words of Job are ended' (Job 31:40). Maybe I should stop right here. "

"Continue. The words you are about to say will open your heart to hear what is in My heart to say to you through this letter."

"Okay. After all my ranting, I'm beginning to feel the stirrings of hope. As I've been reading Acts, I've also been reading a book my wife gave me for my sixty-fourth birthday. It's a biography of J. R. R. Tolkien that includes a letter C. S. Lewis wrote to a friend after he, Lewis, became a theist but before he became a Christian. These words got to me. He expressed confusion about 'how the life and death of Someone Else (whoever he was) two thousand years ago could help us here and now—except in so far as his *example* could help us.'

"I read that, and it hit me deeply; it isn't only the *example* of Your Son's life that inspires us, it's the *death* of Your Son that puts us right with You and gives us His *life* to energize how we live. And Your Spirit put that life in us at Pentecost. Father, I believe that. Lewis came to believe it too. Help my unbelief.

"I read, too, that Tolkien, at age twenty-one, was reading an obscure Anglo-Saxon religious poem about the 'brightest of angels above the middle-earth sent to men' and years later wrote: 'I felt a curious thrill as if something had stirred in me, half wakened from sleep.' As I read Tolkien's words, I could feel something similar welling up in me as I read through Your forty-fourth letter again. I think You had him read that poem to prepare him to write the *Lord of the Rings* series.

"And when Tolkien was only nineteen, he bought a picture postcard during a summer trip to Switzerland, a picture of a painting called *The Mountain Spirit* by German artist Josef Madlener. It showed an old man with a long white beard wearing a wide-brimmed round hat and a long cloak, talking to a white fawn that is nuzzling the old man's upturned hand. Tolkien kept that postcard and years later wrote on the paper in which he kept it wrapped: Origen of Gandolf.

"I'm not sure why, but reading those stories brought something out of me that both relieved my sense of futility and dissipated the anger I felt as

I read Acts. I had a strange and compelling sense that You're still at work in people's lives, in my life, in ways I don't notice."

"Discouragement. Futility. Anger. And now hope. It's time to listen. You can now hear what I'm saying to you in My forty-fourth letter:

What My Son began through His birth, life, death, resurrection, and ascension—the center of history—He now continues through what My Spirit birthed at Pentecost: the church. From then until My Son returns to take over the earth, every member of the church is empowered to tell the full message of their new life in Christ.

"I sent My angel to release the apostles from jail for one purpose: to 'stand in the temple courts and tell the people the full message of this new life' (Acts 5:19–20) and to do so through a community that lives the new way. You are not alive in this world in order to experience Me or to enjoy the blessings of a comfortable life. If that were My purpose, I'd have brought you into My Presence in heaven the moment you were forgiven and adopted into My family.

"Your purpose till you die is to reveal a *new attitude toward suffering* and a *new agenda in prayer* that flows out of your *new purpose in life* that makes sense only if you claim your *new hope of resurrection*. As I tell you this, both Lewis and Tolkien are laughing and nodding in vigorous agreement."

"Father, that's a lot. Show me how You're saying all that in this letter."

"It's all through the record I provided through Luke of the early church. Notice a few examples.

"When My Son's followers first faced opposition, they prayed, not for protection from suffering but for boldness in testifying [Acts 4:29–30]. They were so devoted to their new purpose [4:18–20], so confident in their new hope [4:12], so dependent on their new power [1:8], and so willing to suffer in their new mission [20:22–23] that they became a holy community, set apart to live their passion to dance with Me and to invite others to the party.

"That level of Spirit-fullness could not coexist with pretense. When Peter discerned pretense in Ananias, he spoke against it, and Ananias—and soon after, his equally duplicitous wife, Sapphira—fell dead. In a holy church, unholiness will be exposed and dealt with. People love to join entertaining churches today. In the early church, 'no one dared join' their fellowship (5:13) without embracing what it means to radically follow My Son.

"You are right to be discouraged with what your culture so often calls Christianity. You are wrong to give in to futility. My Son's work has only begun. My plan is on track. My Spirit is working. *Never give up on the church!*

"You are right to notice that My power is no longer commonly revealed in obvious miracles. You are wrong to think My power is no longer on display. My servant Martin Luther observed that since the early days after Pentecost, My demonstration of power is 'left-handed': it appears weak to the natural eye. But to eyes opened by My Spirit, My power is more evident than ever in your desire for Me that no agony of soul or fall into sin can destroy.

"You are now free from slavery to the demands of self: for recognition, for life to go as you want, for good health and prosperity, for freedom from emptiness, and for the experience of fullness. You are now free to live for one purpose, and it is toward that one purpose that the wishing-forward life within you wells up as you read of how I worked in Lewis and Tolkien. You are free to advance the only plan whose promise of joy will be kept. You are free to tell people the full message of this new life, even as Stephen did by his death, as Paul did by his difficult missionary journeys and imprisonment, and as Agabus did through the two prophecies I gave him then recorded [11:27–29; 21:10–11]. *You are now free to really live!*"

"Father, thank You. And thank You, too, for giving me a prophetic word through my sister in Christ who lifts me into Your presence every day. You sent it as I was stumbling through Your forty-fourth letter. She wrote these words from You to me through her: 'Put on your sandals. Walk steadily. Look not to the right or left. Acts is waiting for you. It is no wonder they didn't even call it Christianity. Oh, my Lord, forgive us.'"

"You are hearing My word to you in Acts. You must now trust truth, not your experience or your blessings. I most fully revealed the truth you must hear and know and believe to the servant I chose to most greatly suffer. My next letter lays the foundation of truth on which you must build your life. Read it carefully. Your fruitfulness depends on it."

Love Letter Forty-Five:
Romans

THINK HARD AND, AT THE SAME TIME,
LET YOUR IMAGINATION SOAR

*F*ather, I'm feeling a strong premonition that this conversation will lead me into unfamiliar territory. I'm sensing that this is Your chewiest letter yet. As I've been thinking about how to get a handle on what I'm hearing in Your forty-fifth letter, the thought hit me: *I'm trying to reduce what You're saying to ideas I can understand and, more importantly, to ideas I can manage.* The clarity of that disturbing realization seemed to release a pure longing I've never before felt so powerfully, a desire to ride Your reasonable words into a reality that reason can't reach.

"But that longing immediately bumped into a wall. I recognized a defensive attitude in me about what I claim to believe, about my position on Christian things, an attitude that betrays an obvious void I prefer to ignore. But it's there. It's a void of uncertainty and confusion, terror really, that I try to fill with fixed ideas about what You're saying. And these are ideas I don't want anyone to challenge. When someone does, I attack when I can and retreat into pouty isolation when I can't.

"Father, that's pathetic. But it scares me. I wonder if I'm really listening to You as I read Your letters. Or am I listening for what I think You should be saying and then hearing myself when I think I'm hearing You?"

"It's fun to watch My children grow up. It's happening to you. Like so many others, though, you still tend to approach My letters the way a chess player comes to his game board. G. K. Chesterton—My Spirit grew him up to real stature—was quite right when he observed that people who play chess with My truth try to get the heavens into their heads, and it's their heads that crack. (I recall hearing you complain of rather frequent headaches.) Poets, on the other hand, fill their heads with truths that lift their imaginations into the heavens. They are the grown-ups who hear the music of truth and dance like children."

"Father, I want to dance. But don't You want me to *think* my way through Your letters, especially this one? I've been taught that of all Your letters, Romans is the most rational and orderly presentation of what You most want us to know. I've assumed You expected me to take a seat in Your class-room, adjust my thinking cap, and take lots of notes when You lecture Your way through this letter. Was I wrong?"

"Well, do you want to learn facts you can organize into a system of truth that will let you feel smug in the belief that you're right? Or do you want to discover truth that sings? Do you suppose Coleridge put aside his poetic imagination when he read this letter, which he once referred to as 'the most profound work in existence'? Was Garrett Green on to something when he wrote that proclaiming My truth 'can be thought of as singing the scriptural melody so that others may also learn to hear and enjoy it and to join in the singing'? And why do you think My intellectually brilliant servant Godet read My forty-fifth letter with the image in his mind of entering 'the cathedral of the Christian faith'?"

"My premonition was right. I *am* entering unfamiliar territory."

"It's time for you to pass through the corridors where truth is carefully outlined on the walls, where those who fail to realize that the corridor is but a hallway leading to a far better place do nothing but take notes. They mistake the truth that is living water for the dry dust of mere facts. These parched souls endlessly analyze the composition of the water I've provided but never seem to realize it was meant for drinking.

"Move through the corridor. Study the outlines on the wall. Yes, take notes. Organize your thinking into clear doctrine. Truth matters. Doctrine matters. Orthodoxy matters. But keep moving, not *beyond* truth but *into* truth. The corridor opens onto fields where flowers bloom and birds sing. If you listen, you can catch the scent and hear the music while you're still in the corridor. Let the fragrance and the melody awaken your desire to drink from cool springs and stir your longing to swim in refreshing lakes. Let your time in the corridor achieve its purpose, to increase your capacity to drink more and to strengthen you to swim further, further away from shore, in sight of home."

"Father, this is new territory, but it feels strangely familiar."

"Of course. It's where I created you to live, in a land better than Eden. Now, tell Me what you underlined earlier this morning when you read that letter written to a friend by C. S. Lewis in 1926. I had a good time watching you wonder if it was I who arranged for your wife yesterday to buy the book in which that letter is recorded and for you this morning—more than eighty years after Lewis wrote it—to read it before we began this conversation. It was."

"I'm silenced."

"Good. Now read what you underlined. The shades on the windows of your soul are about to lift."

"Well, his words are a little over my head, but they did wake up something in my heart. As I understand it, Lewis was responding to a friend who had recently bought into a religion—something called Anthroposophy—whose founder rightly believed in a reality beyond reason but wrongly (at least in Lewis's view) tried to capture that reality with reason. Here's some of what stood out to me in the letter:

> About powers other than reason—I would be sorry if you mistook my position. No one is more convinced than I that reason is utterly inadequate to

the richness and spirituality of real things . . . Nor do I doubt the presence . . . of faculties embryonic or atrophied, that lie in an indefinite margin around the little finite bit of focus which is intelligence—faculties anticipating or remembering the possession of huge tracts of reality that slip through the meshes of the intellect.

"I assume Lewis is referring here to the faculty of desire or, perhaps, to the faculty of imagination that envisions desire's satisfaction. I hear him calling me to a beauty I can taste but can never fully describe. Then he nailed me with this comment: 'My skepticism begins when people offer me explicit accounts of the super-intelligible and in doing so use all the categories of the intellect.'

"Bringing truth from the heavens into the small space of my head and thinking I have it all or, at least, far more than I do—God, that's me. What foolishness. What arrogance. Chess playing. It's what I do. People like me, Lewis writes, allow 'their intellects to fasten on those hints that come from the fringe, and squeezing them, has made a hint (that was full of truth) into a mere false hard statement.'

"Father, is that why I so often feel more organized in my thinking than joyful in my heart, more thoughtful and proud than free and humble?"

"There is no refreshment in describing water. Test its purity before you drink it; make sure it's not Kool-Aid—that's what can and must be done in the corridor. But then drink it. You may never understand *how* water refreshes you, but that it *does*, you will not doubt."

"Father, with Lewis I'm 'inclined to believe that we must be content to feel the highest truth in our bones.' But too often my soul feels like a valley of dry bones. Father, make them live, with truth."

"You are now ready to hear, with your mind and heart, what I'm saying to you in this letter:

I have found a way to supply the power you lack, the power you need, to become the person you most long to be, the person you most truly are, the person I alone can make you: a worshiper of Me in any circumstance; a lover like My Son who desired forgiveness for His murderers; a dancer who hears heaven's music on earth and moves freely in rhythm with My Spirit in a worshiping, loving, dancing community of friends who feel indebted to reveal My Son to the world by the way they relate and through the creative expression of whatever gifts they possess and opportunities they find.

"Think hard. And at the same time, let your imagination soar. As you study in the corridor, notice the desires that awaken in your heart, then follow them into the field alive with wildflowers—and dance. Here is what I'm telling you in this letter:

"You have broken the law of love. You love no one more than yourself. I have given you over to the path you've chosen, to using community for your sake. That path leads to eternal loneliness and to terrible tastes of it now. I created you to give yourself in community for My sake and for the joy and well-being of others and, in so doing, to discover and rejoice with gratitude in your solid identity and value. But you have rebelled against love itself, against Me. You must now be silenced before Me, able to ask only one question: 'How can I, a lost and guilty sinner, stand before a just and holy God?' (Romans 1:18–3:20).

"When you sincerely ask that question, when you realize how poorly you love and how badly you long to be loved with a love you don't deserve and can never earn, you will hear the answer: I have found one way, the only way, to love you as if you have always loved Me and to empower you to realize your destiny—to actually love Me and all those around you, even those who fail and hurt and disappoint you terribly. You can now stand before Me with no fear and live like Me and for Me. Your name is now on the invitation list for the party, written in indelible ink [1:16–17; 3:21–8:39].

"Be clear on the *one way* that makes it all possible. It is the gospel. My Son died in your place as a 'sacrifice of atonement' (3:25), a sacrifice that fully exhausted My holy wrath against you as a sinner who rightfully deserves to be forever banished from My Presence. His death frees Me now—without compromising My holiness or weakening My hatred of sin—to welcome you into My family, to bring you to the divine party, ready, eagerly willing, and miraculously able to join the Trinitarian dance. Apart from what My Son accomplished in His death and resurrection, you are worthy to be paralyzed forever in the misery of eternal loneliness, unable to receive love and unable to love. But by believing in the value of what He did (and of what I did through Him as I explained in 2 Corinthians 5:19), you are now qualified, *as qualified as My Son because you are now in Him*, to enter and enjoy the party of love, to receive love and to love in return. Study these mind-expanding truths in the corridor.

"But to sing these truths, to learn them in the corridor and celebrate them in the meadow, you must recognize your lingering inclination to think you've arrived, to believe that you have lived in such a way that obligates Me to bless you. Brokenness and dependence must define your journey. There is a battle raging inside you. You stand with confidence before Me now and will one day dance at My party because of My Son—because of nothing and no one else [Romans 9–11].

"Right now, you have everything you need to live a *new way*, the way you long to live, the way I designed you to live. You can stop living the *old way* of pride, self-dependence, and manipulation, of trying to do whatever you think might persuade Me to satisfy you with less than My Son [Romans 12–15].

"And do not read the last chapter of this letter as a mere appendix. The melody of heaven can be heard in every verse. Eleven times I moved Paul to focus every relationship, every life, where it belongs: on My Son. Notice: *in the Lord* (verse 2), *in Christ Jesus* (verse 3), *to Christ* (verse 5), *in Christ* (verse 7), *in the Lord* (verse 8), *in Christ* (verse 9), *in Christ* (verse 10), *in the Lord* (verse 11), *in the Lord* (twice in verse 12), and *in the Lord* (verse 13). I have a good time watching My children depend on and live in and enjoy My Son. There's no one like Him. But soon the earth will be filled with people in whom the character of My Son is fully formed and the life of My Son is passionately released. And you'll be one of them.

"But understand this: many people, including too many of My followers, continue to relate with others for their own purposes. They use people like ticks use dogs. When My enemy seems to be winning in the world or in the church or in your life, don't be troubled. Hear the music of verse 20: 'The God of peace will soon crush Satan under your feet.' Think hard about all that I tell you. And let your imagination soar. I have a plan. It's a good one. You can only imagine how good. You, the beloved, are becoming a lover."

"Father, I picture myself riding the bus of Your truth into pleasures that only my imagination can begin to grasp. Hints of those pleasures are all around me. And this conversation has lifted the shades that have covered the windows, at least a little. I see new territory.

"But I have to go on living with people on the bus who, like me, either pull the shades back down or don't look out the windows. I fail and hurt and disappoint them and they fail and hurt and disappoint me. How can I keep the beauty of Your truth alive in both my mind and imagination when what I see around me and in me is often so ugly, so frightening, so maddening?"

"I'm a romantic. I have a plan. But I'm also a realist. The plan unfolds slowly and not without what seems to you to be irreparable glitches. But know this: nothing takes Me by surprise, and nothing can stand for long in the way of My plan. You are right to ask how you can stay connected to the hope of beauty when so little of what I have planned is visible in you and in this world and in the community of My followers. I take up your question in My next letter. Keep reading."

Love Letter Forty-Six: 1 Corinthians

I Never Give Up on My People; My Plan Will Succeed

*F*ather, I've been avoiding talking to You about this letter for three months. It's not an easy read. I didn't understand everything You told me in Romans, but what I did understand really encouraged me. I more clearly saw the plot of Your story, and I felt confident it was a good plot and on a good track. Everything seemed under control.

"But now, after reading 1 Corinthians, I'm not feeling what I want to feel. And I'm not believing what I wish were more firmly settled in my mind."

"How do you want to feel? What do you want to believe?"

"I want to feel hopeful, so hopeful that I'm full of energy to do whatever You tell me to do and confident that I'm part of a plan that's working. I want to believe, to be firmly persuaded, that You're doing good things in the middle of whatever life throws at me. But here's what's happening: I can believe that the *end* of the story You're telling is good. But it's sometimes a stretch to believe that how You're *getting* me there is good."

"Tell Me how My forty-sixth love letter is taking away the feelings you want to experience and eroding your confidence in the goodness of My unfolding story."

"Father, sometimes I feel like an imposter, a fraud. I talk to others about who You are and what You're doing with an air of conviction that I'm not always experiencing. Sometimes—I hate to admit this—it seems that atheism explains what I see happening in this world better than Christianity. So many apparently pointless tragedies. So many unanswered prayers. So many people excited about experiences of You that so often to me seem contrived.

"But becoming an atheist isn't my real fear. I could say the same words I've mentioned before, words that C. S. Lewis wrote when his wife died: 'I don't think I'm in much danger of ceasing to believe in God. The real danger is of coming to believe such dreadful things about Him. The conclusion I dread is not *So there's no God after all*, but *So this is what God's really like*.' Reading this letter somehow triggered deep struggles with faith that I try to ignore but can't deny are still there."

"How?"

"After reading forty-five of Your letters, You've convinced me that You've not promised to protect me in this life from things that scare the daylights out of me or to provide me with what I think I need to trust You. But what You have promised is to change me, to make me enough like Your Son that I'll be able to love You and love others no matter what goes on in me or in my life, no matter what I struggle with or how many bad things happen to me.

"But when I read 1 Corinthians, I realize that the apostle Paul, the greatest Christian in the history of the church, pastored the church in Corinth for eighteen months, and not much happened. And that makes me lose confidence in Your guarantee that I'll change. I mean, if Paul couldn't get through to the Corinthians, who's going to get through to me? Maybe I'll remain so spiritually unformed that something *could* happen that would destroy my faith.

"I know the Christians there came out of a worse background than I did. I know Corinth was a pagan culture, a terrible place to raise a family. I know a thousand prostitutes in the temple of Aphrodite, the goddess of pleasure, serviced her worshipers every day. I know that Julius Caesar resettled Corinth in 44 BC, a hundred years after a predecessor had destroyed it and a hundred-plus years before Paul brought the gospel to it. And I know the system of patronage Caesar set up to prosper the city encouraged both manipulative grabs for power and indulgent surrender to passions in order to feel immediate pleasure. So I know the Corinthians who became Christians came into the church with a lot of baggage that directly contradicted everything they heard Paul tell them.

"But I've got baggage too. Isn't the whole point of Your story that the gospel of Your Son has the power to transform people no matter how messed up they are, to transform me, to transform anyone who believes in Your Son? I just spent time with a leading Christian, a man revered by many, who has no idea how he comes across. People who work with him feel his arrogance, his petty and demanding attitude. He's in his sixties, and he hasn't changed in relational ways that count. I'm in my sixties, and You know how many ways I have yet to change. After more than fifty years as a Christian, I thought I'd be so much different than I am, so much more patient and caring and self-controlled. And the Corinthians didn't change, at least not much. Isn't that why Paul felt so troubled when he wrote this letter? Isn't that why he lost confidence in the power of the story he was telling to effect deep change?"

"Paul was troubled, but he never lost confidence in Me or in the power of My story. Haven't you read My letter?"

"A dozen times."

"Then you know that Paul continued to tell My story of love to quarrelsome, arrogant, and selfish people. He knew they were still living according to the saying that Corinthians loved to repeat: 'All things are lawful for me' (6:12; 10:23 NKJV). Four times Paul mentioned that phrase in this letter. Although My people in Corinth were living more like Corinthians than Christians, Paul continued to call them to a new way to live. He never gave up on them. Neither did I. I never give up on My children.

"Every word in this letter highlights the plot of My story, My call to community, My vision of others-centered relating, and My plan for your spiritual formation—My power to place within you the desire to love and to release that love in the worst of circumstances, in the most hopeless of conditions, and in the most painful of relationships.

"Let Me briefly overview what Paul was saying to the still immature Corinthian Christians, what I am now saying to you as you struggle with your confidence in Me:

❁ Turn away from haughtiness, the wisdom of this world, and a spirit of entitlement that blocks love and causes division (chapters 1 through 4). Thanks to My Son and My Spirit, you can do better.

❁ Deal decisively with blatant sin (chapter 5); resolve differences within the church community, not through the legal system; deny yourself the pleasures of sex outside marriage (chapter 6); let love for Me drive your decision to marry or to remain single, and if you marry, let love for Me and for your spouse control your sexual activity (chapter 7); and exercise your freedom, not to get your own way but for the common good (chapter 8).

❁ Spiritual leadership is an opportunity to serve, not to gain recognition. Joy depends on giving, not getting. The legitimacy of leadership is measured by sacrifice (chapter 9).

❁ Steer clear of every form of idolatry, blatant or subtle (chapter 10).

❁ I long to enjoy My people's worship, to delight in their unselfish exercise of the gifts My Spirit has given them (chapters 11 through 12); to take pleasure in seeing My community, My way of relating, mirrored in their relationships (chapter 13); and to be honored in their genuine commitment to encourage each other without displaying themselves (chapter 14).

"Was Paul, was I, uttering idealistic gas, wishing that short people would grow tall? If it served My purpose, I'd make that happen. Or did Paul have confidence that the Corinthian Christians were, in fact, capable of living tall, of loving well, and that eventually, because they were Mine, they would?

"Notice that the climax of this letter is *resurrection!* Without hope that what begins in this life will be brought to completion in the next, Paul would have had no confidence in My story. Without resurrection, belief that a good story is unfolding now is impossible. So is love [15:19]."

"Father, will You tell this doubting, frustrated, scared, and empty believer in You what You want me to hear You saying in this forty-sixth letter?"

"Hear this:

The change I bring about comes slowly. The more you attempt to hold on to your confidence in the goodness of the story I am telling while at the same time acknowledging all that is bewildering and maddening and shatteringly disappointing in this life, the more you will be confronted with the ongoing moment of decision, to trust or not to trust. Only in dark nights will hope burn bright enough to sustain your faith and release your love."

"Father, this is *hard!*"

"Let what you *see* drive you to the precipice of unbelief. Let what you *feel* bring you to the brink of despair. If I exist, if I am good, if My story is loving and My plan on course, My Spirit will speak into the deep place in your heart that only terrifying doubt renders accessible. And in that place, He will anchor you in hope."

"Father, I need the certainty of hope to sustain me now."

"I know. Keep reading."

Love Letter Forty-Seven: 2 Corinthians

You Will Be Immersed in Tears
yet Filled with Deep Joy

God, I just reread Your previous letter to get ready for this one. One sentence really grabbed me: 'Go after a life of love as if your life depended on it—because it does' (1 Corinthians 14:1 MSG). Father, I fall short of Your standard of love in every other sentence I speak, in nearly every thought I think, and in most choices I make every day. Everything is so about me. And yet You've written me all these love letters because Your plan for me is to actually live a life of love, of love as You define it. Am I right?"

"Yes."

"Then I really want to know how Your plan works. Can we back up a minute before we talk through this next letter? I want to make sure I'm following You so far."

"Of course."

"One thing that I got out of Your first thirty-nine letters, maybe the main thing, was the idea of *relational* sin. Every time I don't love You or anyone else perfectly, I'm relationally sinning. I don't need to have an affair or kill someone or lose my temper to violate real love. I finished the Old

Testament pretty convinced that I break Your moral law every day and that I deserve to be judged by You, condemned to existing forever neither being loved nor loving. But it also became clear that You have a plan not only to forgive me and get our wrong relationship righted but also to form me into a person who really does love. I know there's so much more for me to see in all those thirty-nine letters, but that's the gist of what You were saying to me, isn't it?"

"Yes."

"And then I began reading and talking with You about the next twenty-seven love letters. In the first four, You painted a fourfold portrait of Your Son so I could catch a glimpse of what You're really like and of the plan You've come up with to bring Your way of doing things into this messed-up world through people like me. That stirred something in me.

"In Acts, You let me see what a community of people looks like—people who not only live the new way of love that Your Spirit makes possible but also accept the mission of moving into their culture to make known 'the full message of this new life' (Acts 5:20). That got me even more excited about being a part of a missional community of love.

"I think You wrote Your next letter to keep me from thriving on shallow excitement. You don't want me to be zealous for You and Your mission with a zeal that's 'not according to knowledge' (Romans 10:2 NKJV). So You wrote Romans to ground me in the truth of Your story, truth that invites me to let my imagination soar with all that could happen in churches across the world if Your story were understood, then lived out and told out by Your people.

"And then came 1 Corinthians. Reading it felt like a thud, a slap of realism in my naïve face. It made me realize that there is an incredible story to be told, but there's also a bloody battle to be fought, both with others but more within myself. Your followers in Corinth heard Your story from the most convinced Christian of all time, and they believed it. But they still behaved more like citizens of their self-satisfied culture than like citizens of Your self-denying kingdom of love.

"So now I'm ready to read Your forty-seventh letter. In the forty-sixth one, I heard what You said, that change is slow. But my question now is—not only how do I live Your story of slow change in me but also how do I find the energy to keep telling that story when so little of the slow change is visible in others? I don't want to be so hungry for the excitement of seeing visible growth that I settle for the kind of shallow change in me and in others that great music and passionate preaching can create.

"I know Paul was after real change, the kind of spiritual formation that puts people in touch with their desires to love and supplies the power to release those desires at any cost to themselves. And I know, too, that Paul didn't have it all together. He wasn't living the new life perfectly, but for some reason he didn't feel like a fraud—the way I sometimes feel—and he never tired of telling people that a new way to live was available.

"And even when the Corinthian Christians kept living more like Corinthians than Christians, even when they turned against Paul; and even when he went through a near-death experience and debilitating sickness and personal heartache, Paul kept right on living Your story as best he could and telling Your story as well as he could, and he lived and told it really well. *How did he do that?* I think I'd have felt so annoyed, so futile, that I'd have told the Corinthians to shape up, then moved on to more rewarding ministry.

"But Paul somehow managed to be 'immersed in tears and yet always filled with deep joy' (2 Corinthians 6:10 MSG). How did that happen?"

"I planted real hope deep in Paul's heart, the kind of hope that I wired him to long for more than any other kind. 'With this kind of hope to excite us,' Paul wrote, 'nothing holds us back' (2 Corinthians 3:12 MSG)."

"Father, what is that kind of hope? *Plant it in me!*"

"If you were discussing with C. S. Lewis what that kind of hope is and if you wondered out loud how you could become fertile soil in which My Spirit could plant that hope, you would have heard him reply in these words that he once wrote: 'Christianity tells people to repent and promises them forgiveness. It therefore has nothing (as far as I know) to say to people who do not know that they have anything to repent of and who do not feel that they need forgiveness. It is after you have realized that there is a real Moral Law, and a Power behind that law, and that you have broken that law and put yourself wrong with that Power—it is after all this, and not a moment sooner, that Christianity begins to talk.'

"My Spirit is telling My story to your psychological culture, a culture that actually believes woundedness—how others treat you— is a more serious problem than selfishness—how you treat others. Wounded people need healing, so the culture says, and a nicer group of people to hang out with. But according to the story I'm telling, selfish people need forgiveness, and they need the power to love those by whom they have been most wounded.

"Paul knew that whatever wounds were inflicted on him, either in childhood or during his years of service to Me, were not his worst problem. When My Son first spoke directly to Paul, He said nothing comforting; He exposed Paul's sin. He brought into the light Paul's self-serving determination to ignore his conscience and to feel superior, powerful, and important, all in My name [Acts 26:14].

"As soon as Paul opened himself to My Son, as soon—and not a moment sooner—as Paul realized he had been living *against* Me and not *for* Me, he heard these words from My Son: 'Now get up and stand on your feet. I have appeared to you to appoint you as a servant and as a witness of what you have seen of me and what I will show you' (Acts 26:16). At that moment, Paul was saved and sent.

"What had Paul seen of My Son? He saw that he deserved to be hated by My sin-hating Son but instead was loved by My sin-bearing Son, that through forgiveness he was brought into a close relationship with Me, then commissioned to tell My story to everyone he met, especially to non-Jews. Paul couldn't get over it. Forgiven for violating love? Brought into relationship with the One he had most offended? Empowered to love others the way he had been loved? Guaranteed a never-ending existence of sheer delight in a perfect world?

"Listen to his words: 'We've been given a glimpse of the real thing, our true home, our resurrection bodies. The Spirit of God whets our appetite by giving us a taste of what's ahead. He puts a little of heaven in our hearts so that we will never settle for less' (2 Corinthians 5:4–5 MSG). Paul couldn't bear the thought of anyone settling for less than the power to live the new way of radical love, to walk the narrow road of self-denial to real life in community. That was the heaven My Spirit put into Paul's heart. It's the heaven He's put into yours.

"Understand this: no one who fails to see their selfishness as their absolutely worst problem, no one who continues to believe that their feelings of emptiness and pain and loneliness deserve priority attention from a grandfather-like God who simply wants all His little ones to feel good, will ever know the kind of hope that energized and sustained Paul through all his disappointments and discouragement. He was wonderfully encouraged when the Corinthians responded well to his earlier instructions and rebukes, but his unwavering hope remained in Me."

"Father, I need to hear You tell me exactly what Paul knew that kept him faithful to his calling and would keep me faithful to mine."

"Hear this. Paul knew what I will now tell you:

Live for your relational comfort, and your joy will be shallow and temporary. It will not free you to love. Live to know the truth of My story of forgiving love, and you will be deeply unsettled by how profoundly you need forgiveness. You will then suffer the slow death of your entitled demand that you be treated well. But you will discover, slowly but surely, the power of My ongoing forgiveness and Presence to change you into a person who loves.

"Living to love is difficult. In this life, I promise you no comfort but My Presence (sometimes unfelt), My power to love (often unclaimed), and My promised hope (typically undervalued) of a never-ending existence of experiencing My perfect love in a perfect world where everyone loves perfectly. It was that kind of comfort and hope that excited Paul so that nothing could hold him back."

"Father, I'm still inclined, strongly at times, to chase after immediate comfort more than truth."

"What I have to say to you does not begin in comfort. In the long run, it provides unimaginable comfort. But the inclination to twist My story into a tale of relief and recovery rather than redemption and restoration is strong in everyone. Know this: the corruption within you, evidenced in your ongoing failure to love that needs ongoing forgiveness, can be and will be used by My Spirit to draw you closer to Me. You'll understand better what I mean when we talk through My next letter."

Love Letter Forty-Eight: Galatians

DO NOT MISUNDERSTAND FREEDOM;
YOUR FRUITFULNESS DEPENDS ON IT!

*G*od, one verse in Your next letter has frustrated me since I first heard it years ago in Sunday school. In Galatians 5:16, You tell me that if I 'live by the Spirit,' I won't 'gratify the desires of the sinful nature.' I've been fighting a win-lose battle with temptation ever since I tried not to look at Ricky Murphy's spelling test answers in fourth grade.

"I lost that battle and am losing lots of others, right up until now. If that verse hides the secret of how not to indulge sinful desires, I've not yet found it.

"Father, I *want* to know You better. I *want* to live like Your Son. I *want* to follow Your Spirit's lead. But I'm still losing my battle against temptation too often and too easily. What am I supposed to do when a favorite desire hits me with addictive force? At that moment, I lose all sense of freedom to do what's right.

"It's as if I'm innocently floating along in the freshwater stream of a good Christian life, doing nothing visibly or consciously wrong; and then without warning I find myself hurtling down a fast-moving river of delicious temptation, heading straight for the falls of misery. I feel no power to reverse direction, no will strong enough to paddle over to my nice Christian way of doing things. And worse, *at that moment I don't want to.* Flying over the falls seems more exciting than dangerous, more necessary than wrong. The thrill blinds me to the risk. And whatever love is within me dries up. I don't care about anyone or anything else, including You. The only sense I have as I think about You is a guilty anger.

"Standing in Your grace seems more resistible than falling into my selfishness. It feels as if a compulsive force within me takes over my mind with lies, my heart with self-serving affections, and my will with unrelenting strength. Yielding becomes inevitable. And—I hate to admit this—part of me yields gladly with a smug sense of freedom. Father, what's happening to me?"

"It's what's happening *in* you that matters, not what's happening *to* you. My Son has set you free to make choices that will release you from your compulsions. Only when you see deeply enough into your heart to recognize the corruption beneath the compulsions will you discover freedom. Pray like David: 'Search me, O God . . . see if there is any offensive way in me' (Psalm 139:23, 24 MSG). There is. You need to see it. Not many do."

"Father, I'll pray that prayer for the rest of our conversation. I want to hear what You're saying to me in Galatians. I read somewhere that Martin Luther considered this Your best letter of all sixty-six. He went so far as to say, 'The letter to the Galatians is my epistle. To it I am as it were in wedlock. It is my Katherine.'

"I'm wondering if Luther was so drawn to this letter because he knew how unfree most Christians are to love well. I remember he once wrote that living the Christian life is like a drunk riding a horse. We keep falling off one side or the other, either into legalism, which chokes the freedom to love, or into license, which perverts freedom into guilt-free selfishness.

"I relate. I can feel myself one day trying to live right so You'll give me what I want, then the next day doing whatever feels good in the moment. Whether I'm living right or doing wrong, I can feel myself struggling with a relentless urge to relieve a vague but unbearable sense of incompleteness, to fill a void within me that demands fullness. When that urge becomes compelling, I lose all capacity to care about anything until the unbearable feeling of incompleteness is relieved and the dark void filled, at least for a moment.

"When living as I should doesn't persuade You to satisfy me as I want, in some deep place within me I feel resentfully justified in doing whatever it takes to feel better. But it never works, not for long. I do experience a kind of satisfaction that nothing else provides, but soon after I feel more incomplete and emptier than before, more addicted to experiencing that temporary satisfaction again.

"But here's my problem. When the opportunity presents itself to repeat whatever activity felt so good before, *I don't see the activity as wrong*. Whether it's a single woman addicted to feeling wanted by a man; a respected professional who requires sexual pleasure to fill the void his success can't touch; or whether it's people like me who just want to feel less bored, more complete, even as we do our best to follow You, we're all in the same boat, and as G. K. Chesterton once quipped, we're all seasick together. We're all looking for relief from a strange unnamed misery that You don't relieve. We want to feel alive. It's hard to see that as wrong."

"Your god is your stomach. You assume every strong desire in you needs to be satisfied now in this life. You, therefore, are caught up in thinking about your desires and the satisfaction you long to feel and could be experiencing right now. Look ahead to Philippians, My fiftieth love letter, and read 3:19. It tells you exactly what I just said.

"You are on the verge of discovering as if for the first time a compelling and holy desire in your depths that will expose every other desire as less, every other satisfaction as unworthy to be compared with the satisfying joy of loving others with divine power. But that discovery will only be made as you more clearly see the demand that keeps you in bondage to lesser desires and unworthy satisfactions.

"Your preoccupation with satisfaction when it feels most necessary is the corruption beneath your compulsions. Your expectation of feeling everything you want to feel in this fallen world renders you vulnerable to false teachers who, in the name of My Son, offer you a strategy that promises to let you feel as complete now as you will feel forever in heaven. And like My followers in the province of Galatia, you're drawn to their perversion of My story. And your freedom to love no matter how you feel is replaced by slavery to a compulsive need to feel whole, to feel good about yourself before you feel able to love another.

"Listen well. I will now lay out for you what I am saying in My forty-eighth letter:

❀ You have trusted My Son to forgive you and give you life. You are a Christian.

❀ As you live the Christian life, free from condemnation for past, present, and future sins and free at any moment and in any circumstance to love, you become aware of deep longings in your heart that remain unsatisfied despite your best efforts at faith and obedience.

❀ The pain of those unmet longings becomes within you a void, an empty space, a lonely feeling of incompleteness. The desire for relief from that pain seems more compelling than your desire to love. And the disappointments you've suffered in your relationships have created wounds that beg so strongly for relief that nothing seems more necessary to your well-being.

❀ Consistent with the message of your culture, your resolve shifts from loving others to healing your wounds, to feeling complete as a loved and significant person. The corruption lying dormant within you since conception, the spirit of entitlement, now roars into death-dealing life.

❀ You become convinced that your wounds must be healed, your void must be filled, *before* you can love. That conviction is the devil's lie disguised as My Spirit's empathic tenderness.

❀ With that conviction ruling within you, you live your life in the flesh, in the corruption of demanding satisfaction, and you become addicted to the experience of satisfaction, whether through food, sex, ministry, close relationships, worship times, meaningful work, or happy family life.

❀ You resonate with the message of false teachers who insist that you should be able to feel now what you want to feel, who lay out a plan to get on better terms with Me than My Son has already provided, terms that they tell you will provide the sense of completion you so long to enjoy.

❀ You then fall off one side of the horse into a modern form of the Galatian heresy, one that teaches that you can do something to get on better terms with Me, that My Son's death and resurrection was a good foundation for stronger efforts to do everything right. That's legalism. It's living by the old way of the written code [Romans 7:6]. If living well brings a pleasant experience and enjoyable blessings, you feel a self-satisfaction that you mistake for worship. And the more self-satisfied you become with My apparent response to your desire for the good life, the more superficial and less sacrificial your love becomes.

❀ Now hear Me well. I saved you so that you could believe in Me even when I seem absent and unresponsive (faith); to wait in confidence that My plan is on course for an unimaginably happy ending (hope); and to relate to Me in humble, nondemanding worship and to others with a wise and priority concern for their well-being (love). When you fail to nourish your soul with faith, hope, and love, when instead you live for the feeling of completeness you desire, you become obsessed with the empty loneliness within you that I don't quickly relieve.

❀ And now you fall off the other side of the horse. You exchange legalism for license. The void within you (*which My Spirit longs to transform into the hope of glory*) degenerates into a powerful force that tempts you to do whatever relieves your pain, heals your wounds, and restores the experience of completion that you can't stop wanting. You now live by the flesh and lose your freedom to resist its demands.

❀ The inevitable result is a deeper suffering than unmet longings. *You now suffer from the inability to love.* Your freedom to live for your own experience of completeness destroys your freedom to love, to care about anyone more than yourself."

"Father, You're describing me in repulsive detail. What am I to do? I want to live by Your Spirit so I am able to resist the demands of my sinful nature. How do I do it?"

"Listen to My good friend John Owen, the Puritan pastor who, like Luther, understood that true freedom develops in fierce battle, who heard what I wrote to you in this letter, that 'doing things for God is the opposite of entering into what God does for you' (2:11 MSG). Owen knew that I have saved you from self-centeredness and freed you to love. The battle is on.

"Listen to his words:

The Christian may be like a ship tossed in a storm. Nobody on board may be aware that the ship is making any headway at all. Yet it is sailing on at great speed. Great winds and storms help fruit-bearing trees. So also do corruptions and temptations help the fruitfulness of grace and holiness . . . corruptions and temptations develop the fruit of humility, self-abasement and mourning in a deeper search for the grace by which holiness grows strong. But only later will there be visible fruits of increased holiness.

"Now hear Me:

Gospel freedom means to neither indulge your whims nor keep My rules. Whim-indulgers and rule-keepers are slaves to the corruption within them that demands a kind of satisfaction My Son will not provide for you in this life. My Son has set you free to love, to believe I am good and that the good story I am telling is unfolding under His control. Faith in Me and hope for tomorrow frees you to love today. And loving with divine power releases a kind of joy into your soul that nothing else can bring."

"God, I think I'm hearing You. Trying hard to follow all Your rules creates both pride and pressure that sets the stage for addictively wanting the relief that addictions provide, an illusory but strangely satisfying relief that feels necessary and, therefore, justified. That's 'the great winds and storms' that Owen spoke of, the corruptions and temptations that are inevitable. You're not freeing me to keep on sinning so You can keep on forgiving, but You do want me to live in the freedom of knowing that You will keep on forgiving when I keep on sinning.

"I'm not free to do everything right—I can't. And I'm not free to do whatever makes me feel complete—that's wrong. But I am free to love. And exercising that freedom releases joy that provides power to resist the appeal of lesser but still strongly appealing satisfactions. Am I hearing You?"

"Yes! I'm delighted! My Spirit is the love that My Son and I have for each other and for the world. To live by My Spirit means to love others no matter how painfully you're hurting or how badly you fail. *Focus more on loving others than resisting temptation.* The fruits of holiness, the fruit of My Spirit, will become visible in increased power over compulsive sin and more freedom to love.

"Let the corruption within you become an occasion for humility and self-abasement that will release your desire to move toward others for their sakes. Make every effort not to sin less but to love more. Whatever sin continues not only will be forgiven but also will become an opportunity to celebrate the grace that supplies the power to love again, which in turn will supply the power to resist temptation as you realize that yielding to it gets in the way of what you most want to do, to love as I love. You are free not to do everything right and not to do whatever pleases you in the moment. *You are free to love.*"

"Father, I can only imagine what a community of free people would look like and the power they would have to change the world."

"That community is My Son's bride, His body, My Spirit's building. It is the church. And it's beautiful. Read about it in My next letter."

Love Letter Forty-Nine: Ephesians

THE POWER TO DESCEND WILL LIFT YOU UP

*G*od, one thing is clear from reading Your forty-ninth letter: turn Paul loose to talk about what excites him rather than to straighten people out, and he jumps all over the opportunity.

"After dealing with all the problems in Corinth and Galatia, he's now writing to a church he pastored for three years then left on wonderfully warm terms [Acts 20:17–38]. And I gather he intended that this letter be read by other churches near Ephesus, all of which he had heard were doing pretty well—no major problems with what they were believing or how they were living.

"I think this is Paul's most warmly passionate letter yet, and it's all about the church, about how privileged and powerful it is. But I've got to be honest, Father; You're talking through Paul about a reality I can imagine, what a real church could be, but it's a reality I can't clearly or completely see. I get a glimpse here and there, but nothing close to what Paul envisions.

"And he was in jail when he wrote this letter, under house arrest and chained to a Roman guard. Are You trying to tell me something, that a bright vision of what church could be becomes clearest when I'm living in a dark night of tough circumstances? Strange, but I'm drawn to that thought.

"When I look around at churches today, the vision You describe in this letter sounds more like a fairy tale than a real possibility. I know I'm a hopeless cynic, but . . ."

"You're not a cynic. You are cynical, but you're not hopeless. See more clearly what's wrong in you than in the churches you're familiar with, experience the power to descend into the deep darkness of corruption in your own soul, and you'll discover the power to 'grasp how wide and long and high and deep' (Ephesians 3:17–19) is My Son's love. Grasp that love, and you'll grasp My vision for His church, and you'll know it's reachable, not completely but meaningfully.

"Paul saw what he was resurrected *from* and what he was resurrected *to*. My resurrection power so stunned him that he knew I am able to do immeasurably more in the church of resurrected people than its most visionary leaders, including Paul, could imagine [Ephesians 3:20]."

"Maybe I don't realize how far I'd fallen when You saved me."

"You don't. If I had not gotten hold of you, you'd right now be buying into Satan's lies and thinking you were wise. You'd be following the ways of this world, expecting to find life. And you'd be irresistibly attracted to Satan's lies and to the world's ways [Ephesians 2:1–3]."

"But Father, I'm *still* attracted to his lies, and I'm *still* drawn to pleasures that You tell me will leave me miserable. I'm *still* not living as a man who's been freed to love. The bad stuff in me is *still* tossing me around like a ship in a storm. Will the sailing ever get smooth?"

"Smoother, yes. Smooth, no, not until you're home. The power you need to see who you are *without* My Son is the same power that will let you see who you are *in* My Son. That vision of who you are in My Son will lift you into the vision I have for My Son's church, the vision that protected Paul from yielding to cynicism and discouraged futility."

"As I listen to You, Father, one word comes to mind: *help!*"

"Listen to words written a century ago by a man who learned to sail quite smoothly through this world until, when he was forty-three, I called him home to completely smooth sailing forever. When Oswald Chambers wrote these words, I had you and many others in mind. Read them slowly: 'What is needed today is not a new gospel, but live men and woman who can restate the Gospel of the Son of God in terms that will reach the heart of our problems.'"

"Father, I want to be that man."

"Then you must decide. Do you want from My Son what He longs to give? Do you want to believe I'm good no matter what happens in your life, to trust My plan no matter how off course it appears, to love well when you feel no love within you?

"Or are your desires too weak? Do you want merely to lead a relatively satisfying life in the midst of reliably pleasant circumstances as a reasonably good person? If that's what you want, the gospel of My Son has nothing for you. If you want what only My Son can provide, you will learn to celebrate the good news He came to bring.

"Hear what I'm saying in this letter. Hear the gospel that will lift your vision for the church—and for yourself—to new heights:

❀ You are now, with countless others, My Son's body. Live to complete Him.
❀ You are now, with countless others, My Son's building. Live to reveal Him.
❀ You are now, with countless others, My Son's bride. Live to delight Him."

"God, show me how You're saying that in this letter and how I can grasp it. The sun's peeking over the horizon, but I'm not yet feeling its warmth."

"I weave six messages to you in Ephesians that will bring the warmth of light into your heart.

"First, I have blessed you with blessings far superior to all the blessings you naturally want to enjoy [1:3]. Until you regard earthly blessings as second things and see spiritual blessings as first things, you'll remain immature, self-centered, and powerless to resist temptation. You'll continue living in a chilly dawn.

"Second, without My Son, you are utterly incapable of real love. Without My Son, all the virtue and goodness and kindness so applauded in this world is energized by desire for less than what My Son provides. Without My Son, no one can do anything out of gratitude to Him for providing not only forgiveness but also relationship with Me and the power to truly love [2:1–3; 4:17–19].

"Third, you are now part of My Son's body, more literally than you imagine. When you respond to the leadership of your Head, you *complete* Him. He is now present in this world through His body, through communities of people who trust My Spirit to understand and follow His lead. Relating to others under His direction brings My Son the joy of a completeness He cannot enjoy when you relate in the rhythm of your own self-centered impulses. *Live under His authority. Complete Him* [1:22–23].

"Fourth, you are also a stone, a living stone in the building He calls His home [1 Peter 2:5]. You are joined together with all My Son's followers—Jew, Gentile, man, woman, black, white, rich, poor—as a community of people who light up your world by the way you relate to one another: without prejudice, with humility, without cutting comments, with mutual respect and sacrificial love. *Live in His light. Reveal Him* [2:19–23; 4:1–6].

"Fifth, you are now My Son's bride. He loves you infinitely more than you think possible. You are now washed clean of all corruption by His blood, made beautiful by His life. When your wife receives your imperfect love, you celebrate. Imagine My Son's delight when you surrender to His perfect love. *Live to receive His love. Delight Him* [5:22–23].

"And finally, expect opposition. My enemy will stand against you at every turn. You are no match for him. But My Spirit is in you. My enemy is no match for Him.

❊ *Wear the belt of truth.* What My Spirit tells you will help you oppose your opposer.

❀ *Put on the breastplate of righteousness.* Resolve to fight every trace of self-centeredness within you.

❀ *Identify the peace the gospel provides.* I will never condemn you; you are at peace with Me. You can rest as I rest; My peace is in you. Think of that peace as a pair of shoes you can wear to keep running the race in the face of all opposition.

❀ *Hold on to the shield of faith.* Know that I am who I AM, that My plan is on course, that you are My child, and that one day you will be fully formed like My Son.

❀ *Keep the helmet of salvation on your head.* Keep hope alive. No matter what happens, no matter how you fail, all shall be well and (as Julian of Norwich heard Me say) all manner of things shall be well.

❀ *Never stop reading My letters.* My word is My Spirit's sword. Use it to fight evil, first in you, then around you.

❀ *Learn to pray.* Pray in My Spirit, on all occasions, with all kinds of prayers and requests, for everyone you know, especially those who suffer for My sake [6:1–18]."

"Father, as I hear You, I feel almost released to say what Pascal once said: 'The Gospel to me is simply irresistible. Being the man I am, full of lust and pride and envy and malice and hatred and false good . . . to me, the Gospel of the grace of God, the Redemption of Christ and the resurrection and sanctification of the Holy Ghost, that Gospel is to me simply irresistible. And I cannot understand why it is not equally irresistible to every mortal man born of woman.'

"Father, take me *further up and further in.* I want to lose myself in Your vision for the church."

"You are on your way. I am pleased. There is no real happiness out-side of My plan. In My next letter, I celebrate the joy you can know when you live to complete My Son, to reveal Him to the world, to delight Him with your response to His love. Keep reading."

Love Letter Fifty: Philippians

GIVE ME EVERYTHING, AND YOU WILL LOSE NOTHING

Father, is it possible? Am I hearing You right? Are You saying in Philippians that I could actually *experience* resurrection power to recognize and then resist the temptation to do something bad that feels irresistibly good?

"I so easily depend on things going well in my life for whatever joy I feel. And when they don't, when sometimes even for no apparent reason I feel empty and miserable, I'm compulsively drawn to whatever will provide me a mere moment of pleasure.

"Is Your message in this fiftieth letter that I could know a different kind of joy that is not circumstance-dependent, a richer, lasting, more deeply internal kind that would provide the power to resist temptation? What I think I'm hearing sounds not only radical but undoable, that if I somehow stop depending on whatever I think I need to feel good that I'll discover the better pleasure of knowing Your Son and that I'll understand what Puritan Thomas Chalmers meant when he spoke of 'the expulsive power of a new affection.' Does the joy of knowing Your Son actually *feel* good? Or is it more a faith conviction than a felt experience? Pleasures from other sources somehow seem more real.

"And here's the big question. Is it just a fanciful metaphor or could I really pour Your Son's literal life out of my soul into someone else's when I see so much insecurity and defensiveness and self-protection and resentment and arrogant selfishness in mine? Is that possible? Is any of this possible?"

"My power transforms the possible into the actual—it's My plan."

"Father, I believe You. At least I'm trying to. And I think You're helping my unbelief. For a week now I've been reading and studying and reflecting on Philippians, and it's been doing some good things in me."

"Put those good things into words. I delight to hear what My Spirit's been up to. I already know, of course; but it's fun to hear you say it."

"Well, here's a list:

- *The battle You've called me to enter, the one going on in me, seems a lot clearer now.* It's Your will against mine. My willingness versus my willfulness. How did C. S. Lewis put it? Either I say to You, 'Your will be done,' or You'll say to me, '*Your* will be done.'
- *The stakes have never looked greater.* Paul was happy in a prison. I can be miserable in a hot tub. I'm seeing that my will carries me down the broad road to the lonely death of self-obsession. Yours squeezes me onto the narrow road to life, to real joy (I hope) in a community of God-obsessed, soul-connected, self-giving people, a community something like Yours.
- *The vision has never reached higher.* The possibilities, which earlier seemed uncompellingly spiritual, now feel staggering. After reading Ephesians, I see that Your dream is for me to *complete* Your Son—I still don't really get that; to *reveal* what He's like by the way I relate—that challenges and invigorates me; and to *delight* His heart—the idea that I could be an ingredient in the divine happiness (another Lewisism) stuns me. And more, it excites me. What a privilege!
- *The enemy has never felt stronger.* The more I'm drawn to these possibilities, the more I feel a strangely attractive urge to sabotage the process. Sometimes I get so discouraged and frustrated, so empty and down, that I don't give a rip whether I complete anything but my dreams or reveal anything other than my needs or delight anyone but myself.

- *But deep inside I've never been more attracted to the possibility of becoming a meaningfully mature Christian, a little Christ.* I want what Your Son wants for me, more now than ever. I'm catching a glimpse of my destiny, of Your plan for me to dance at Your party, starting now, and I'm stirred. *I'm believing it's possible!*

"All that's been happening. But I know myself. I've had to endure living with me for more than sixty years. I'm hot now. I could be cold tomorrow and lukewarm next week. Father, I want to hear whatever You're saying to me in this letter. And I want to know what to do with it."

"Did you just hear yourself?"

"What?"

"You said you want to know what to do with what I'm about to say. Your desire to manage My message is a problem. Before you ask what you can do with what I tell you—the question breeds both pressure and pride—I want you to sit with My words. Let them lift you into the realm of unmanageable mystery, of impossible possibilities. Then listen both with a humble mind that desperately trusts that nothing is impossible with Me and with an open heart, a willingness to hope for what you can never pull off on your own.

"Here's My message to you in this letter:

The joy I offer grows in the soil of emptiness and brokenness. In My Spirit's hands, your felt emptiness will become a consuming thirst to know My Son. Your agonizing brokenness over the ongoing corruption in your soul will transform into overwhelming gratitude for My Son's forgiveness. It is empty and broken people who at the same time are thirsty and grateful who discover the power to live in ways they never thought possible."

"I'm following about 10 percent of what You've just said. If all that's in Philippians, I don't see it. Can You unpack it for my simple mind? I really want to get it. No, that's not right. I want to see what You're saying clearly enough to rest in it, to rest in You."

"Another problem stands in the way: you feel more often empty than broken. Be open to My Spirit. He intends to use your emptiness to reveal the corruption of your proud demand for fullness. That demand justifies your refusal to love others until you feel loved yourself. When your emptiness reveals your spirit of entitlement, that void will become a space within you that longs for My Son on His terms. And brokenness over your demand for satisfaction on your terms will slowly be changed into liberating gratitude for what you will see more clearly as amazing grace."

"I'm humbled. I'm listening."

"Then know this as you read My letter. Paul's life was not easy. Shortly after he met My Son, he was shown 'how much he must suffer' for Our cause (Acts 9:16). Suffering is always difficult. Paul suffered physically, and his consuming desire for genuine converts to become wise and passionate disciples was often frustrated.

"He wrote Philippians as well as Ephesians, Colossians, and Philemon from prison, under house arrest in Rome for the *crime* of preaching the good news of My plan. Like My Son, though to an infinitely lesser degree, Paul was a man of sorrows [Philippians 2:27].

"And yet he sang in prison, first in Philippians ten years before he wrote this letter [Acts 16:25] and again during his two years of house arrest in Rome. Philippians is a love letter to his closest friends wrapped up in a song of joy. Never assume, as many do, that the sorrows of this life, even the severest ones, are incompatible with the joy I give.

"The pain of suffering in this world, the emptiness of unmet longings, became in Paul a resolute thirst both to see what I was doing in the unseen world [2 Corinthians 4:18] and to anticipate life in the next world [Philippians 1:23]. And more. Paul's awareness that he had once been the worst of all sinners [1 Timothy 1:15] and that he had not yet become all that he longed to be [Philippians 3:12] produced a consuming gratitude for the grace of My Son, whom he came to see as his supreme treasure, his fellow-sufferer, his sufficient power, and his certain hope [Philippians 3:7–11].

"From a heart relentlessly thirsty and filled with gratitude, Paul sang four messages of joy to the Christians at Philippi. My Spirit is singing them now to you. If you hear the music, you *will* be able to pour the literal life of My Son into the hearts of others. My fiftieth letter is helpfully divided into four chapters, each one a verse in the song of joy that I want you to hear and learn to sing.

❀ Chapter 1: *To live is Christ* [1:21]. In any circumstance—in jail or at home, in a divorce court or at a happy anniversary party, in a hospital or on a golf course—you can complete, reveal, and delight My Son by loving well. That *is* the joy you're wanting.

❀ Chapter 2: *The attitude that ruled in My Son can fill your mind and direct your will* [2:5–11]. He emptied Himself of His holy right to display His eternal magnificence. You can empty yourself of demanding and parading success, of seeking and winning recognition, of requiring and depending on good treatment from others—you can empty yourself in order to advance My plan, to honor My Son, and through My Spirit to bring Us pleasure.

❀ Chapter 3: *The desire to know My Son can trump all other desires* [3:10]. Like Paul, you can 'dump in the trash' every past achievement and present satisfaction, counting them as 'dog dung' (3:7–8 MSG) in comparison with the joy available in knowing My Son.

❀ Chapter 4: *My power is sufficient to resurrect you from the death of a terror-driven, entitlement-justified, self-protective style of relating to the life of a grace-released, humility-empowered, self-giving style of relating* [4:13]. That's a new way to live. It's a divine way to love. It's more than a possibility. It's your destiny. I've already begun that good work in you. And I will carry it through to completion [1:6].

"These four messages reveal the secret of contentment. To be content does not mean to *feel* content but rather to know that in My Son you have everything you need to live in rhythm with My Spirit in any circumstance of life [4:12–13]. In emptiness and brokenness changed by My Spirit into thirst and gratitude, you are able to complete, reveal, and delight My Son. Nothing you do brings Me more pleasure and you more joy—joy that exists deep within you as a sustaining reality."

"Father, I entered this conversation seeing my battle, recognizing the stakes involved, glimpsing Your vision for me, feeling the strength of my enemy, and awed by the hope of experiencing resurrection power. I leave this conversation with one truth burning in my soul: *it's all about Jesus*—Your plan, my life, every circumstance. It's all about Him.

"And I think I'm believing, perhaps more than ever, that if I give up everything but Him, I gain everything. I lose nothing."

"Do you recall the words your earthly father once said to you? Looking at his Bible sitting opened on his lap, he shook his head in quiet wonder and said, 'God is so in love with His Son that He wrote a whole book about Him.' You didn't understand it then, but you're seeing it now: from the first word in Genesis to the last word in Revelation, all sixty-six love letters are about My Son, your Savior, your Lord. He is My greatest delight and your supreme treasure. I want you to know why that's true—as fully as you can now understand. That's what I want to talk with you about in My next letter."

Love Letter Fifty-One: Colossians

Do Not Expect Today What I Have Promised for Tomorrow: Live in Hope!

*F*ather, I'm struggling with boredom. Nothing excites me. I feel no deep passion for anything, including—I hate to say it—You, Your Son, or Your plan.

"I felt so alive after we talked about Philippians. What You said in that letter got me believing that I was on my way to becoming the man of God I long to be: self-controlled, quietly settled on the inside, full of the kind of joy Paul felt even in prison, and gratefully eager to do what You told me in Ephesians that I could do: *complete* Your Son as His body on earth, *reveal* His incredible love to everyone I meet, and *delight* His heart with my delight in Him. All that filled me with hope.

"But it didn't last. Right now, I feel disengaged and disconnected from You, myself, and others. It's as if nothing really matters. I'm just plain bored. I hate it.

"I've lived long enough to know that when nothing legitimate fills me with satisfaction, I become dangerously open to illegitimate excitement, to the temporary but satisfying pleasures of sin. Father, I don't know why I'm feeling so bored. But a strange thought keeps floating through my mind. I think it might be coming from Your Spirit. Is there some sense in which boredom, maybe a certain kind, is a good thing? Maybe a necessary part of my journey into Your plan?

"That thought got stirred by what I think You've been saying to me especially in the last couple of letters and now more clearly in this one. I think You've been telling me that if I admit to how bored I am; if I face the fact that I don't always have now what I really wish I had, like feelings of excitement and passion; if I accept the idea that You won't provide in this life the level of continuous satisfaction that I want and that, sometimes—for no discernible reason—You allow blessings I do enjoy to be withdrawn; and if I make no effort to numb the ache I feel or fill the void inside me that screams for fullness; then Your Son and what He accomplished on the cross will mean more to me than ever before. I think You're telling me that Your Spirit will then seize the opportunity provided by my boredom to let me rest in a holy thirst for what's lacking in this life but promised in the next—for what I can taste now but will fully enjoy then. I know those are long, clumsy sentences, but am I close?"

"I love My Spirit. He's opening your eyes to see the least understood ingredient in the gospel. What you're now seeing needs to sink deep into your heart and mind. It will help to think about the words Dick Lucas, a faithful pastor to my people in Britain, wrote as he immersed himself in My fifty-first love letter. Listen: 'The Christian's present taste of reality in fellowship with God and his people is but an anticipation of the substantial realities which are reserved for the future, "laid up" in heaven for us. Therefore we are not to think of ourselves as largely enjoying the fruits of Christ's victory now, with heaven as some glorious consummation, a kind of finishing touch. Rather we are to recognize that heaven holds most of the great things won for us by Christ, and that our present experience is no more than a precious foretaste of what is to come.'"

"Father, was C. S. Lewis saying the same thing in *Surprised by Joy*? In his experience, longings for what this world can never provide released a 'sweet desire' for what he knew You'd provide at the eternal party. And that sweet desire actually became his joy."

"Remember what I told you in 1 Corinthians 15:19, that 'if in this life only' you have hope in My Son, then 'you are to be pitied more than all men.' Along with Lewis, Lucas was exactly right when he wrote that 'the greatest gift of Christ in the present is hope for the future.'"

"But Father, so many in the revived spiritual formation movement are teaching that a fully satisfying intimacy of union with You is available now, a level of intimacy that will make boredom a faint memory."

"What I now am telling you in Colossians flies squarely in the face of what many of My followers are teaching. It was the same in Colossae, where the spirit of the age influenced the theology of the church. My people there were in danger of placing their hope in experiences that I've never promised in this life. It was that danger that I used in prompting Paul to write this letter. Pay careful attention to what I'm now saying to you through his words:

Place no hope in the experience of satisfaction now. If you do, you are shifting away from the hope held out in the gospel of My Son. You will then disfigure the Christian life into a search for a fullness of felt spiritual reality and complete freedom from evil's power that together promise to provide the life you've always wanted in this world.

"That is *not* the Christian life. To believe that it is blurs and discounts what My Son accomplished in His death and resurrection."

"Father, what You're telling me is radical, counter-church-cultural, and, frankly, not immediately appealing."

"It will not prove appealing until you recognize the future you'd be facing had My Son not died."

"So You're saying that I'm to live now with desires You won't satisfy fully until I die. And You're saying, if I'm reading Colossians 1:5 correctly, that my fruitfulness as a Christian in this life depends on hope, on fully wanting what I will not fully enjoy until I get to heaven. Father, this is hard teaching."

"But it's *good*. Right now, My Son is in you as your *hope* of glory, not as your opportunity to *experience* glory now. That hope, when grasped, will fill you with gratitude for forgiveness. Only then will you realize that what My Son offers you now, what He is doing in you now, is far greater than the satisfying, trouble-free, always fulfilling life that you think would be best, the life that too many counselors, pastors, spiritual warfare warriors, spiritual directors, and Christian friends tell you is available now."

"So am I right, Father? Was the strange thought I earlier mentioned on track? Is the boredom I'm feeling more an opportunity to aim my hope in the right direction than an emotional or spiritual problem to fix?"

"Even as you teach against it—and you have for some years now—you have been influenced by the Colossian heresy more than you realize. Taught by spiritual leaders in the Colossian church, its message has great appeal. 'You want? God gives! Yes, you're forgiven. But you want so much more. Forgiveness is a vital beginning. What Christ provides through the cross is good, even necessary. But following Him on a difficult journey through life is for beginners in the faith. We have special knowledge, special understanding, special methods that can guide you into a new level of spiritual experience.'

"These false teachers continued. 'Are you bored? Do you not experience the fullness of life you desire? Are you still struggling against the powers of evil? We know the road to the spiritual satisfaction you were created to enjoy, to the freedom from struggle that will bring you great joy. But it's not for the common Christian, the one who goes no further than a class in basic Christianity. What we offer is for the followers of Christ who are ready for the advanced course.'

"Their teaching is as appealing as it is appalling. Its error is subtle. You *do* long for a completely satisfying experience of union with Me. And My Son died to give you that experience, forever, in His visible presence. His fullness, the exact fullness of deity, is in you, now! My Son is in you. You are in My Son. As a result you are now in relationship with Me, an entirely new relationship that only My Son's crucifixion made possible.

"Consider the relationship with Me that you now possess: once alienated, now beloved; once enemies, now friends; once separated, now reconciled; once under wrath, now forgiven; once dead in self-ishness, now alive in selflessness. Fully seen and fully wanted by an inflexibly holy God who in Christ has given you the gift of absolute, secure righteousness. That's what you have now. Believe it. Trust it. Enjoy it. With that relationship securely fixed, with divine impulses now prompting your heart, you are free to live the new way of My Spirit. You are alive, even when you feel bored.

"The false teachers in the Colossian church spoke of power, the power to *feel* the fullness of the relationship that is now yours, the power to *enjoy* the freedom of final victory over the world, the flesh, and the devil. But all that comes later. For now, I give you, according to My glorious might, the power, not to experience the satisfaction you want or the relief from struggle you desire but the power to *endure* difficult circumstances and to be *patient* with difficult people [1:11]. With that power, you can continue to believe My plan is on course and to advance My plan by loving others while you wait in hope for satisfaction beyond what you can now imagine."

"Father, I have been influenced, more than I thought, by the spirit of my age and Paul's—the spirit that tells me to claim my rights, to live for my satis-faction, and to enjoy the freedom I want from struggle, such as my current struggle with boredom. I've never seen quite so clearly how hope for the next life is essential to faithful living in this one, bored or not.

"With Your Son in me as my *hope* of glory, I can see how my boredom now could become a passionate thirst for what's coming and how that hope-filled thirst would release a glad resolve to trust You and love well until Your Son returns and the full party begins."

"What you're seeing is good. It will fill you with longing for the Second Coming of My Son. Read on. The best is yet to come. I discuss the best in My next two letters."

Love Letter Fifty-Two: 1 Thessalonians

Turn! Serve! Wait!

A good question recently put to me by a friend disturbed me, I think because I didn't like my answer. He asked what impact I've felt so far from spending so much time reading Your love letters and trying to hear what You've been telling me in each one. I told him I felt frustrated. I expected more would be happening in me.

"In an article I wrote ten years ago, I said then that I worried I was way behind where I should have been in my spiritual growth by that point in my life. I felt like a teenager still stuck in second grade. Now in my sixties and after nearly three years of immersing myself in fifty-one of Your letters, I feel like a grown-up sitting at a tiny table in nursery school with other spiritual beginners. I'm frustrated, Father. And more than a little self-condemning. What am I missing? What am I not hearing? What am I doing wrong?

"The more I see where I could be, given the possibilities You've opened up for me, the more I see how stuck I am. It's discouraging. I thought by now I'd be gliding easily through lingering remnants of doubt, indecision, struggle, fear, and temptation on my way to a deeper and more consistent experience of You. I guess I expected to be pretty well done with dark nights and more caught up in the joy of bright mornings. But I'm not. I was a little encouraged, however, and somewhat surprised, when I read that, according to John of the Cross, the dark night is not something that happens to spiritual beginners."

"Where you are is good. Only when you see yourself as far behind are you moving ahead."

"But I'm frustrated. And I can't yet see how that's taking me anywhere good. Frustrated is not where I want to be. Father, I've just read through Your next letter. And all I hear is You telling me to hang in there and wait, that Your Son is coming back and everything will then be as it should be. Until He returns, I'm to keep trusting You and serving Your purposes even while I stay frustrated. Is that what You're saying in 1 Thessalonians?

"I know I could be wrong, but it sure seems that way. One student of Your letters—I think it was Leon Morris—said that in all Your last twenty-seven letters, no topic is mentioned more frequently than the Second Coming. And another scholar observed that some allusion to Your Son's return comes, on average, once in every thirteen verses, from Matthew right through to Revelation. That's a lot!

"And I just noticed that You end all five chapters in this letter with a focus on that day [1:10; 2:19; 3:13; 4:13–18; 5:23]. So here's my question: Am I supposed to sit in nursery school for the rest of my life hearing stories about the Second Coming while I continue to suck my spiritual thumb?"

"You continue to misunderstand maturity. You're expecting richer experiences of nearness to Me. But in this life I more often provide a deepened thirst for Me, a thirst that strengthens you to more consistently turn away from immediately compelling satisfactions, a thirst that keeps you engaged with My purposes in this disappointing world, a thirst that surfaces your desire for what nothing in this life can provide. *That's* maturity."

"So the more frustrated I feel with myself and life, the more thirsty I'll become for You? And that's maturity? Father, what are You saying to me in this letter? You are always so counterintuitive."

"Only in unplanned, unarranged, unwelcomed, unmanageable, and thoroughly unenjoyable dark nights will My plan for your maturity unfold. Listen to what an offbeat follower of Mine, Tim Farrington, wrote in *A Hell of Mercy*: 'You will be graced with the disaster your soul requires to find its way home.' John of the Cross put it this way: 'No matter how much an individual does through his own efforts, he cannot actively purify himself enough to be disposed in the least degree for the divine union of the perfection of love.'

"You are in a good place. You're losing confidence in your own resources for steering your way through life. That loss of confidence, that dying to self, what you feel as frustration, is opening your ears to hear what I'm saying in this fifty-second love letter. It is this:

Your frustration with everything else, including yourself, makes it possible to turn in deeper dependence to Me. Your weariness requires the strength of supernatural love to continue serving Me. Your haunting sense of futility shuts you up to a kind of endurance that can be sustained only with hope in My Son's return.

"My followers in Thessalonica were less than a year old in their Christian life when, through Paul, I wrote this letter to them. Their nursery-school faith was more mature than the faith of many Christians today who think they're in college. Their *work of faith* kept them turning away from idols toward Me. Their *labor of love* kept them serving Me, the living and true God, despite severe opposition. And their *endurance of hope* kept them waiting for My Son's return to rescue them from the coming wrath. Everything I've just said I wrote in chapter one, verses three, nine, and ten.

"That's college-level maturity practiced by My children in nursery school. Now look at your own life. You turn to Me, not fully, but meaningfully. You serve Me—sometimes yielding to fatigue—but never for long. And you're waiting for My Son's return, not always passionately but with an anchoring hope that never fully disappears. I'm pleased."

"But I struggle so much. I fail so often. And I experience Your presence so little."

"Listen to My servant John Owen. He said things that you rarely hear from today's pulpits or in today's books. Owen wrote: 'Later in the Christian life . . . God sees that the exercise of humility, godly sorrow, fear, diligent warring with temptations and all things that strike at the very root of faith and love, are now needed.'"

"So he's saying that *more* mature Christians wrestle with things that make them feel *less* mature?"

"Of course. What did you think My Son was talking about when He said that you'll only find your life when you lose it?

"Listen to more from Owen: 'Older, more experienced Christians often have greater troubles, temptations, and difficulties in the world. God has new work for them to do. He now plans that all the graces they have be used in new and harder ways. They may not find their spiritual desires to be as strong as before or have such delight in spiritual duties as they had before. Because of this, they feel that grace has dried up in them. They do not know where they are or what they are. But in spite of all this, the real work of sanctification is still thriving in them, and the Holy Spirit is still working effectively in them. God is faithful. Therefore, let us cling to our hope without wavering.'"

"Father, if a pastor preached that sermon today, his church would shrink. If a modern author put that message in a book, it wouldn't sell. I hear You telling me that feeling further behind may in fact be evidence that I'm really moving further ahead. I get that in Owen. But how are You saying that in this fifty-second letter?"

"I led Paul to write this letter while he was interim pastor in Corinth. He arrived there a battle-weary man. In three cities, he had been forced to leave because of hateful and violent opposition: Philippi, where he was beaten and jailed [Acts 16:19–40]; Thessalonica, where after only a month of evangelizing and discipling his converts he had to cut short his ministry because of severe threats [Acts 17:1–9]; and Berea, where good people were open to Paul's message, but his enemies followed him from Thessalonica to drive him out of Berea [Acts 17:10–15].

"And then, just before coming to Corinth, he had preached in the high-culture city of Athens, where intellectuals ridiculed Paul for believing that dead people could be resurrected into a new world when My Son came back [Acts 17:32]. By the time he limped into Corinth, he came 'in weakness and fear, and with much trembling' (1 Corinthians 2:3).

"Add to all that a deep concern that his short season of teaching the new Christians in Thessalonica might not prove enough to keep them turning, serving, and waiting in the face of the severe trials he knew they were enduring. Paul was beside himself with worry. Would they fall away from the faith? Had his brief time with them been a waste [3:5]?

"But Paul, though physically and spiritually exhausted and knocked down with debilitating concerns, kept his soul turned toward Me. *He was a man of faith.* He continued to serve Me in the face of frustrating opposition. *He was a man of love.* And the secret of his endurance lay in his confidence that My Son would return to make every wrong right for sinful people like him and that he would see My Son face to face, that he would *know* Him in all His glory. *Paul was a man of hope.*

"And when he heard from Timothy that his friends in Thessalonica were still turned toward Me and serving Me and waiting for My Son's appearing, Paul was ecstatic. They were less than year-old Christians, too young even for nursery school, yet they were displaying college-level maturity. It was on receipt of that news that I prompted Paul to write to them, encouraging them for their maturity and instructing them further in what even deeper maturity would involve. He cleared up their concerns about whether members of the church who died before My Son returned would miss out on anything [4:13–18].

"So, yes. You're in a good place. I know you're frustrated. I know you fail. I know you struggle with doubt. But you're still turning to Me in faith. You're still serving Me in love. And you're still waiting in hope for My Son to return. I teach advanced courses to My followers who know they're in nursery school."

"But Father, I still feel the pull of idolatry. I want satisfaction now. I still feel the weight of fatigue. Some days I want to quit. And I still don't like waiting. It's hard to endure everything that goes on in this world with hope for the next. I want things to be good now.

"I think I'd trust You more fully and serve You more willingly and wait for your Son more patiently if what You're saying to me in this letter were reaching more deeply into my heart and mind. Then maybe I'd better see how frustration is a necessary part of becoming mature."

"What you say is true. And it's why I wrote My next letter."

Love Letter Fifty-Three: 2 Thessalonians

LET *THEN* INTERPRET *NOW*

As I read through this next letter, I was struck by how little I think about what You talk about the most, the Second Coming of Your Son. My life in this world feels more important and certainly more in need of attention than my life in the next. Apparently, a pretty good number of Your followers feel the same way. What we hear in church is mostly about how we can get You to make things better for us now and how we can experience Your presence more fully. I can't remember when I last heard a sermon concerned with what's going to happen when Your Son returns. Come to think of it, I haven't preached one either, not for a long time.

"When Your Son's return is mentioned from pulpits or in books, it usually has to do with Your missional purpose to change the world. I'm hearing a new emphasis these days on kingdom theology, on every Christian's responsibility to get involved in our communities, to do all we can now to bring heaven's kingdom to earth until Jesus arrives to finish the job. Without that focus, the Second Coming doesn't seem to have much market appeal unless the horrors of being left behind when He comes to take His true believers out of this world are graphically depicted in a series of novels.

"In these last two letters, I'm hearing You talk more about a *relational hope* in Your Son's coming than about a world-changing *missional agenda*. Am I right?"

"You're moving on the right track. Let Me take you further. My children in Thessalonica, young in the faith and taught well but briefly, were worried that loved ones who had died would miss out on something when My Son returned. In My first letter to them, I put their fears to rest by assuring them that the Second Coming would include a great reunion with every Christian loved one present, alive and well—friends and relatives they had already buried in death. I told them that My Son would raise them in life, and together they would *meet* My Son and be *with* Him from them on—no more death, no more separation, happy relationships forever [1 Thessalonians 4:13–18]."

"Father, the prospect of a family reunion where all of us gather around Jesus grabs my heart, but the change-the-world agenda is grabbing all the headlines."

"You used to think more about meeting My Son than you do now. What happened?"

"Your question stirs up old memories. I can remember a dozen times, maybe more, when my dad literally trembled with excitement as he talked about actually seeing Jesus. He loved the hymn that no one sings anymore, 'Face to Face with Christ my Savior.'

"But the church I was raised in seemed more interested in the correct sequence of events at the Second Coming than in meeting Your Son. First, the rapture; then a seven-year wedding party for everyone who was raptured into the air, during which all the left-behind Christ-deniers endure seven years of misery; then a thousand years of peace when Your Son descends from the party to take over the government on earth, a millennium that ends when Satan and all his minions (I love that word) lose their final battle and get thrown into fire while all us Christians go to heaven.

"That whole scenario fascinated me, like Flash Gordon movies used to. It sometimes kept me up at night. Was I really a Christian? Would I be left behind? But even when I was pretty sure I wouldn't be—I got saved twenty-eight times before I turned thirteen—Your Son's return never drew me with the kind of relational passion I felt when I dreamed of marrying

Rachael and spending my life with her. The Second Coming felt more *programmed* than *alive*. It certainly wasn't romantic.

"And then in my twenties, I met other serious Christians who believed the system I had been taught did in fact resemble a Flash Gordon movie more than good theology. For nearly a decade, I struggled to decide if I was premillennialist, amillennialist, or postmillennialist. It was a confusing and dry ten years. But during that time, my studies in psychology and my work as a therapist and, more recently, my shift into spiritual direction got some new juices flowing.

"I began worrying less about how everything would turn out later and thinking more about how messed up we all are now. And I wanted to understand the mess and know how to deal with it today, according to Your wisdom. So I did my best to become a *biblical* counselor. But I couldn't see how developing a good theology of the Second Coming would contribute much to helping me understand and relate effectively to people with today's problems. I'm not sure I see it any more clearly now."

"Every letter I've written is vital to your calling. And My fifty-third letter holds special importance. Listen carefully to what I'm saying to you in 2 Thessalonians:

You will never think clearly about what's happening now and how I want you to live today until you're thinking clearly about what will happen when My Son returns."

"Father, tell me You're not dragging me back into the millennial debate. If You are, I'll come because I trust You. But I'll come with more than a little kicking and screaming."

"What you anticipated in marriage and have now been enjoying for more than forty years is only a small taste of what you will experience when My love story reaches its climax. My Son will restore the world to a splendor Eden never knew. And He will bring you to the party I planned before the world began. No, I'm not concerned right now with your millennial position. Above every concern with the details,

I want you to know that My Son's mission is relational. Lose sight of that and your present reality will be unbearable. I created you for a kind of joy, an unmitigated sheer delight, that you cannot now experience. If you don't live *now* with *then* in view, you will move through life with a self-focused demand to have things go your way, to find relief from a misery you cannot escape.

"But it is true that you live today in reality's shadowlands, where the experience of misery is often painfully real. Without hope in My Son, the best you can offer to hurting people is distraction, anesthesia, meaningless pleasures, and more effective strategies for getting their own way."

"Father, I'm listening. You have my attention."

"In this letter, I reveal a powerful hope that frees you from self-centeredness, from demanding anything now, a hope that strengthens you to endure everything I allow and empowers you to walk the narrow road of love, no matter how you are treated. And that road is one, the only one, that leads to the joy and wholeness and rest you will experience when My Son returns, not before. As I now tell you the content of your hope, remember I am not merely teaching a system of thought; I am issuing an invitation to My party with your name engraved in gold. Listen.

"My Son's return will be one Great Event in two parts: the Great Gathering and the Great Judgment. Do not confuse them.

"The Great Gathering is the supreme relational event of all time, the beginning of the party, together forever.

"The Great Judgment is a terrible *isolating* event. My servant Joel was the first to identify it as the 'day of the LORD' (Joel 2:31 NKJV). Those whose felt entitlement to blessings blinded them to their need of forgiveness will be punished with 'everlasting destruction' (2 Thessalonians 1:9 NKJV). They will experience what they never anticipated, the misery of reality without Me, the reality of isolation from which Freud refused escape. Over the doorway into hell, Dante correctly envisioned this greeting: 'Abandon hope, all ye who enter here.' Isolation—the unending absence of everything I created people to enjoy, of everything I provided in My Son—that is the destiny so many have chosen. I take no pleasure in their choice.

"The Great Gathering and the Great Judgment are future events; they are part of My story, not a science fiction novel. They *will* happen. The Thessalonian Christians, however, made a terrible mistake. They believed the Great Judgment, in its beginning stage, had already taken place and that sin no longer had the power to ruin lives, and because the Great Gathering was now imminent, working today in order to eat tomorrow was no longer necessary [3:6–15]. Rather than living responsibly as they waited for My Son's return, they sat around drooling over the banquet they thought was sure to come soon. But passive anticipation has never been part of My plan. I wanted them—and I want you—to live responsibly in your own lives and missionally in the world.

"And worse, believing that sin was on its way out and joy on its way in, they assumed that all the pleasures of My party were now available. The call to suffer for My Son's name was no longer in effect. The need to wait for undiluted pleasure was over. Joy was the order of the day, joy without suffering or responsibility.

"*That same error is being made today.* The truth of sin's defeat at the cross is now thought to be the full experience of its defeat. As a result, too often the embraced mission of the church is now to bring the joys of heaven to earth with less focus on the offer of forgiveness. Sin is no longer the priority concern. Spreading love that cares only about relieving suffering is now the call. The gospel of a toothless love, which fails to center on the forgiving grace that alone makes possible a perfect life later, is now in vogue. It is a false gospel that focuses on a better life now.

"The day of the Lord had not begun when I wrote this letter. It has not yet begun today. The mystery of lawlessness continues to have its way [2:7], held back only for a little longer until the moral structure of society completely breaks down (it's happening now) and the church that claims to know Me becomes nauseatingly lukewarm (that's happening too). Then the devil will reveal his man, the man of lawlessness who with impressive displays of power will persuade many that he is the messiah who can restore society to its entitled comfort [2:3, 9–11].

"My church's legitimate effort to bring heaven's kingdom to earth will hit a wall, an insurmountable obstacle. It is then the day of Great Judgment will come. With a single breath, My Son will blow away His counterfeit. Our missional purpose from eternity past will then be realized.

"With the hope that evil will be destroyed, wait eagerly and actively for the day of the Great Gathering. It could happen at any moment. On that day and not before, all My Son's relational longings—and yours—will be fully and forever satisfied.

"With all this in mind, interpret what happens now—the evil you see, the suffering you endure, the goodness and blessings you enjoy—in light of what will happen then.

"Celebrate and preach the good news of forgiveness to all who accept it, a forgiveness that centers you on the cross and fills you with hope for My Son's return, a supremely relational event. Spread the good news of My kingdom. This world will be changed and all My children will be with My Son forever. He is coming again!"

"Father, I've just been drinking from the proverbial fire hose. I'm soaked, but I'm still thirsty. I want to drink so much more."

"To clearly hear what I'm saying, to anticipate *then* in a way that directs how you live *now*, you must listen to Me in community. Talk together, think together, and learn as you live together with other followers of Mine who are also eager to hear Me. In My next three letters, what many call the pastoral letters, I lay out My plan for how My people can relate together in ways that let them drink more deeply of My life-giving water and pour it into others more generously. My story continues. It's a relational story. All love stories are."

Love Letter Fifty-Four: 1 Timothy

GUARD THE TRUTH; IT IS YOUR LIFELINE TO REAL CHURCH

*F*ather, can I count on anything in this world going right? Last night I couldn't sleep. Everything that scares me flew into my mind like bullets from an assassin's rifle. About one in the morning, I gave up any hope of sleep and from then till six I must have repeated the Jesus Prayer a thousand times. Between brief moments of dozing, over and over I begged Your Son, 'Jesus, Son of David, have mercy on me, a sinner.'"

"Did He?"

"Huh?"

"Did My Son answer your prayer?"

"I'm not sure what His answer would look like."

"Read three portions from two of My other letters before we discuss 1 Timothy. Read 2 Timothy 3:1–5; Hebrews 13:14; and Hebrews 10:36–39, in that order."

"Will I like what's there?"

"Not right away."

"Well, the example of my dad helps me to believe that Your words are life whether they feel like life or not. So here goes. In the first passage, You tell me to anticipate 'terrible times,' that some Christian folks I'll meet will be miserable to live with, 'abusive . . . unforgiving . . . brutal . . . treacherous,' and that some church leaders will look spiritual but know nothing of the power to actually live spiritually (2 Timothy 3:1–5). Can we stop here for a moment? I'm not sure I get that."

"Every heresy is a perversion of truth. Paul taught the Colossians that all My followers were raised with My Son in His resurrection [Colossians 2:12]. What he meant, of course, was that My people are fully forgiven, guaranteed an eternal place in My family, and spiritually empowered to live in this world in a way that meaningfully but imperfectly reveals heaven's reality of love.

"But because they had neither recognized nor rejected the evil energy within them—it's in you too—that feels entitled to life going well, a few leaders in the Ephesian church twisted Paul's words into a lie. Hymenaeus and Philetus taught that a special kind of spiritual resurrection had already taken place [2 Timothy 2:17–18], a resurrection that provided people who knew this *special truth* with the full blessings of salvation now: no more need to battle the already defeated fleshly urges within them or to wait for the complete joys of heaven until they got there.

"With that lie in their minds, they became preoccupied with their own spirituality and could talk of little else than their ecstatic experiences of My Presence. And they encouraged others to join them in the elite ranks of the fully enlightened. These leaders had the appearance of godliness but knew nothing of the power of godliness, the power to persevere in love though still plagued with vile motives lodged deeply in their souls and though still living in a difficult and painfully disappointing world."

"Father, I know Christians who think like that today."

"I don't want you to think that way. Read the next two passages."

"Okay. In the next one, You tell me that in this world, I 'do not have an enduring city' and that I am to live in this one waiting 'for the city that is to come' (Hebrews 13:14). So I have no guarantee that anything in this world will go right. And then in the third passage, You emphasize the 'need to persevere' through all the things that trouble me because 'in just a very little while' Your Son will return. And then You express confidence in me that I will not be among 'those who shrink back and are destroyed' (Hebrews 10:36–39). I'm not sure I share Your confidence.

"I waver. You tell me to *hold fast* without wavering to the hope that I tell others is real [Hebrews 10:23]. You tell me to *hold on* to the truth I believe until Your Son returns [Revelation 2:25]. But I'm more like Timothy than Paul. I'm not always certain I have anything worthwhile to say [2 Timothy 1:6]. Even when I know I'm serving You, I can feel hesitant, even scared, uncertain whether anything good is happening [1 Corinthians 16:10]. And like Timothy, I'm easily discouraged [2 Timothy 1:8] and lots of things physically wrong with my body wear me out [1 Timothy 5:23]."

"Did My Son show you mercy?"

"Father, I know the answer is yes. But I'm not sure what it means for Him to show mercy in the context we're talking about—in a difficult life lived by a weak man. But I want to know. Am I ready to hear what You're saying to me in this letter?"

"You are. My Spirit *is* working. He is such a delight. And My Son is showing you mercy. He always does. Listen well.

You are called to guard My truth. If in this uncertain world you risk everything on what you know to be true, you will finish well. You will impact others. You will strengthen My church. You will fight the good fight. All this will happen but only if you risk everything on My Son's return.

"You are empowered by the knowledge of His return to guard My truth with your life in this world. That is mercy provided by My Son.

For many people today, My truth has been watered down into principles for making this life more comfortable and satisfying, either circumstantially or spiritually. Churches that make it their mission to teach people how to relieve stress, avoid difficulties, enjoy tension-free relationships, and feel spiritual promote a form of godliness that has no power to keep still-sinful people loving well in this still-disappointing world.

"Even with My Son's mercy-filled grace, you know that you are still prone to wander off the narrow road onto the broad road of living to protect yourself from pain and to satisfy yourself with comfort. And you know that spiritual leaders will sometimes encourage you to walk that broad road, and you will be tempted to listen. Churches led by such leaders lose their capacity to recognize truth, they fail to discern and honor the unique privileges of men and women, they don't identify who among them are qualified to guide the church into godliness, and they live for worldly advantages, such as money, without seeing their self-serving greed."

"Is all this in I Timothy?"

"One verse, 1 Timothy 3:15, ties everything together. I want you to know how to conduct yourself in My household, to honor Me as your Father. I want you to realize that when My people gather together, they are 'the church of the living God, the pillar and foundation of truth.' I want you to accept My call—along with all My followers who listen to My voice—to become *the guardian of the mystery of godliness*, the truth with power to expose and defeat the mystery of lawlessness we discussed in our previous conversation.

"You are not yet spiritually resurrected into a sinless existence, into a struggle-free life where things always go well, into the full joy you will know when you see My Son. Until then, guard the truth that has the power to keep you turned toward Me, persevering in love and waiting in hope—the truth that makes possible a new way to live as an imperfect person in an imperfect world.

"That truth is expressed in a song My people used to sing

[1 Timothy 3:16]. It's all about My Son. You would do well to sing it today, every day. It goes like this:

❀ *He appeared in a body.* My Son became human to reveal what human means.

❀ *He was vindicated by the Spirit.* As a person, My Son lived in the supernatural realm.

❀ *He was seen by angels.* What holy angels longed to look into [1 Peter 1:12] centered on My Son's birth, life, death, and resurrection.

❀ *He was preached among the nations.* The good news of forgiveness spread to all people.

❀ *He was believed on in the world.* The truth overcame Satan, penetrated hearts, and changed lives.

❀ *He was taken up in glory.* My Son, still human, always God, is now with Me, waiting My command to return. He's eager!

"Do not sing this song as religious rhetoric. Guard it as life-giving truth. If you do, My Spirit will provide the wisdom to conduct yourself well in My household, in My church. It's all in this letter: how to recognize error; to pray; to honor the uniqueness of men and women; to select spiritual leaders; to minister to widows, leaders, and slaves; to handle money; to fight for the truth like a soldier in battle [1:18]; and to run toward truth like an athlete in a race [6:12].

"After enduring whatever troubles life may bring, if you have faithfully guarded the truth, you will leave this world with the enjoyment of anticipation. Charles Simeon, after steady opposition from the church he faithfully pastored in Britain for nearly fifty years, was asked on his deathbed in October 1836 what he was thinking. Having faithfully guarded the truth of his sinfulness and My Son's grace for so many years, he replied, 'I don't think now. I am *enjoying.*'"

"Father, I long to finish well. I want to endure whatever comes my way with my mind set on truth. I want to enjoy the hope You give me. Can I? Will I?"

"My Son has answered your prayer for mercy, the same way He answered Paul. He empowered a man who suffered greatly to live faithfully and to face death confidently. You can read about it in My next letter."

Love Letter Fifty-Five:
2 Timothy

A SOON-TO-DIE SAINT
LOOKS BACK AT LIFE—AND AHEAD TO *LIFE!*

*W*ell, one thing is clear from reading this fifty-fifth letter: Paul was no triumphalist. He wouldn't buy into the popular message delivered from lots of pulpits today. I can't read any of the letters You wrote through Paul, especially this one, and come away thinking the Christian message is a quick and satisfying solution to all life's problems. I come away instead wondering again if You've promised protection from anything bad. And You're telling me again—this time even more directly—that following Your Son is no picnic.

"Paul seemed to have no illusion that walking the narrow road would carry him around difficulties. I gather he believed that You would use Your power to protect him *through* hardships *for* Your purposes [Philippians 2:23–24] and that You would rescue him from every attack of evil, not by shielding him from its impact but by bringing him safely home into Your presence to dance at Your party [2 Timothy 4:16–18].

"Father, that is *so* different from the kind of thinking that energizes so many of our prayers. Too often I pray counting on You for successful surgery, a more peaceful emotional life, visibly impactful ministry—whatever I think I need to feel happily mature. But You tell me to count on You for enough strength to stay faithful to Your purposes no matter what happens and—through either my death or Your Son's return—to count on You to get me to Your party. Once again, what I hear You saying is not what I often hear today's Christian leaders saying or, at least, emphasizing.

"Father, this is really an astonishing letter. Here's Paul, chained in a desolate, hard-to-find Roman dungeon [1:16–17] after years of beatings, imprisonments, hateful opposition, vicious slander, at least one shipwreck, days without food or drink, clothed in rags, feelings of unbearable pressure, and many sleepless nights [1 Corinthians 4:11–13; 2 Corinthians 1:8–10; 6:3–5]. And now he's waiting to be murdered by Rome for the crime of telling people Your story.

"For Paul to even entertain triumphalism, to think for a moment that You promised Your faithful followers a comfortable life and a pleasant retirement, would require psychotic-level denial. Maybe that's our problem today. Things generally go well for us, at least well enough to assume that they should continue to go well—no permanent stock market downturns, no cancer diagnoses, no drug-abusing kids. It takes only a little denial to believe that our spirit of entitlement is compatible with or even the outcome of our trust in You.

"If Paul took the pulpit in one of our churches today, I can't imagine he'd leave any doubt that we're out of line when we expect (or worse, insist) that our lives move along smoothly. He begins this letter to a young pastor by encouraging him to get over his fears and join in 'suffering for the gospel' (1:6–8). From a jail cell, he's exhorting Timothy to tell the same story that earned Paul a death sentence, to live the same life that ruined any chance Paul had for an easy existence. Like no other, this letter forever destroys the illusion that You call us to struggle-free maturity.

"Father, I read 2 Timothy, and I feel inspired. I long to surrender more fully, to be willing to suffer in any way that telling Your story and living Your life requires, to speak as an old man to my children and grandchildren the way Paul spoke to Timothy, and to have joyful confidence in what will happen to me after I die.

"But then I check the stock market, I hear my doctor urgently schedule extensive blood work, I receive another critical letter, I impatiently struggle with debilitating fatigue when there's so much to do, and the battle heats up—the battle between entitlement and surrender, frustration and contentment, terror and rest, irritability and patience. At the core, it feels like a battle between an obsession with my present comfort as the highest value and a commitment to Your present purposes as my greatest good.

"You've given me the extraordinary privilege of reading the last words written by perhaps the greatest Christian who ever lived. I want to hear, no, I *need* to hear, what You're saying to me in this letter."

"I am for you. My Son is with you. My Spirit is in you. Never forget that as you hear My instructions. My instructions are always an invitation to *life*:

Fight the good fight now. Enjoy the good life forever."

"Father, are You telling me to live a good life now that I can't enjoy until I'm dead?"

"For now, endurance and enjoyment are linked. Did My Son experience no joy while He lived on earth? Did Paul? The Ephesian Christians to whom Timothy was ministering believed the full joy of complete salvation was available to them in this life. It isn't. But don't make the opposite mistake. A sustaining joy is available now, a joy that Paul knew and My Son knew better.

"The life I want you to live now is a life both to endure and enjoy. At times, such strong endurance will be required that joy will seem a far-off hope, a lost experience. But without endurance, you will know little of the very real joy I provide. With endurance, a joy will develop that frees you to appreciate the pleasures of life's blessings without requiring from them a satisfaction they cannot provide. And that same joy, more deeply felt as a longing whose complete satisfaction is guaranteed, frees you to endure whatever hardships lie ahead without indulging your still-alive spirit of entitlement by justifying illegitimate relief."

"That last sentence flew right over my head. Help me see what You're saying in this letter."

"The eternal life I give you can be enjoyed now to the degree you endure the hardships of fighting the good fight. Through Paul's earlier letter to Timothy, I told you that godliness, a life lived consistently with My story, has 'value for all things, holding promise for *both the present life* and the life to come' (1 Timothy 4:8; emphasis added). As he looked back on his life with all its problems and as he looked ahead to his execution, Paul had no regrets. He had endured hardship 'like a good soldier of Christ Jesus' (2 Timothy 2:3) and invited Timothy to do the same.

"But he also invited Timothy while he lived in this world to 'take hold of the life that is truly life' (1 Timothy 6:19), to 'take hold of the eternal life' that was in him from the moment he was converted, by fighting 'the good fight of the faith' (1 Timothy 6:12). Looking back, Paul knew that enduring the bloody battle of the good fight for truth with the prospect of a certain and eternal victory brought joy."

"Father, if I'm accurately piecing together some of the history, Timothy had fought the battle for truth pretty well after receiving Paul's first letter; but false teaching was still spreading like gangrene in the Ephesus church and through other churches in Asia. Some Christians were still believing that some sort of spiritual resurrection had already taken place [2:17–18], that the need for endurance in the battle against sin was over and the time for full enjoyment had come.

"Wasn't Paul a little discouraged? Didn't he feel—like I too often feel—a wearying sense of futility, kind of a why-bother-I've-been-fighting-but-nothing's-happening attitude? And what was it like for Timothy to read this letter? He must have been feeling a little down too."

"Sit with Paul in his dungeon. He's old, his body is frail, he's feeling deserted by his friends [4:16], and he's lonely and tired, with no hope of seeing daylight again. He's been fighting the good fight for a long time. Listen as he speaks for the last time before he dies—words I am now speaking to you, words My Spirit will help you say to those behind you on the narrow road.

❀ 'I am not ashamed, because I know whom I have believed, and am convinced that he is able to guard what I have entrusted to him for that day' (1:12). The gospel will win. My plan is on course. The party is on. The day will come.

❀ 'If we died with him, we will also live with him; if we endure, we will also reign with him' (2:11–12). Die to your self-focused demands. Live in the truth of My love-filled design. Endure hardship. Enjoy the pleasure you bring Me now until the day I satisfy all your desires—and Mine—forever.

❀ 'There will be terrible times in the last days' (3:1); 'but as for you, continue in what you have learned and have become convinced of' (3:14). Guard the truth at any cost. The cost will be great, but the truth is greater, and the coming joy greater still. Learn My truth until you're convinced it's true.

❀ 'For I am already being poured out like a drink offering, and the time has come for my departure. I have fought the good fight, I have finished the race, I have kept the faith. Now there is in store for me the crown of righteousness . . . and not only to me, but also to all who have longed for his appearing' (4:6–8). My Old Testament people poured wine over all their offerings, every morning and every night, as a way of declaring their willingness to give themselves entirely to Me and My purposes [Numbers 15:1–12; 28:7–8]. Fight the fight, run the race, keep the faith. Endure and enjoy until you enjoy Me forever with nothing to endure."

"Father, whether my pension fund goes to zero, whether my blood tests reveal disease, whether my critics turn many against me, or whether my fatigue becomes debilitating, I want to finish well. I want to be able to say what C. S. Lewis said within weeks of his death: 'I've done what I was put on earth to do. I'm ready to go home.' I want my last words to be like his, and Paul's.

"But right now, I can declare my intentions better than I seem able to live them."

"Declare them as clearly as you can *in* community. Live them as well as you can *with* community. The truth must be heard and the life of truth must be seen *in the church* so that My truth and My life are heard and seen throughout the world. That's what I want you to hear in My next letter."

Love Letter Fifty-Six:
Titus

How You Relate Makes My Story Attractive—or Not

*Y*ou are now ready for My Spirit to reach deeper into what you long for, to lift you higher into a vision for what's possible, and to make clearer the kind of community you need in order to live into that vision. Paul was speaking for Me when he began My fifty-sixth letter by writing, 'My aim is to raise hopes by pointing to life without end' (Titus 1:2 MSG)."

"Father, I want to be ready, but . . ."

"You are ready. Prepared by our previous fifty-five conversations, you are now ready to more fully realize what it means to live well between the two epiphanies that define the story I am telling."

"*Epiphany* means 'appearing,' correct? So You're thinking I'm ready to see a little more clearly how You want me to live and how You know I want to live—whether I know it or not—between Your Son's first appearing and His second. Well, I do want to know what it means to live as Your follower. I'm just not sure I'll be able to live that way as consistently as I wish I could."

"When you grasp the significance of My Son's two comings, you'll understand how you can live in the power of His first coming and in the hope of His second coming. Grasping why He came once and why He'll come again will help you want to hear everything I am saying to You in this fifty-sixth letter.

"Though not with the authority of Paul, My servant George MacDonald in a book called *Lilith* was speaking for Me, My Son, and My Spirit when he wrote, 'We are often unable to tell people what they need to hear because they want to hear something else.'

"Without understanding the distinct purposes in the two epiphanies, too many of My professing followers expect Me to tell them how to live in a way that persuades others to treat them as they think they need to be treated and that coaxes Me to satisfy them with the good things available in this life. They naïvely (though not innocently) assume My Son came to make their lives on earth comfortable, to protect them from what they fear, and to fix whatever problems come their way until He returns a second time to indulge their entitled demands even more fully."

"Is what You want me to know about the two epiphanies in this letter?"

"Yes, in a classical but brief passage. Read Titus 2:11–14. When My Son first appeared in My devil-invaded and sin-filled world, He displayed none of the trappings of deity [Isaiah 53:2]. Except for the transfiguration, His essential glory as the Second Person of the Trinity was not made visible. He came the first time to reveal the *beauty of grace*, more specifically, the kind of relating that only My grace makes possible. Like so many others, your vision of how He has freed you to relate is too low.

"When He appears the second time with an army of angels, My Son will display for the world to see the *beauty of glory*, the sheer delight of the relational party the Three of Us have been enjoying since before time began [Matthew 16:27].

"The beauty of grace frees you to reveal that same beauty—never perfectly but substantially—in the way you relate, especially to people who hurt, disappoint, betray, or assault you. The yet-to-be-revealed beauty of glory—if you have the faith to wait in the light of hope—will sustain you in relating well with the certain prospect of dancing in a community where everyone moves in rhythm with perfect love, where you will never hurt again.

"As you read My fifty-sixth love letter, hear what you are now ready to hear:

You are living between two epiphanies. You have no higher calling in this life than to relate for one supreme purpose—to reveal the beauty of My grace until the beauty of My glory fills you with joy forever.

"And know this: My high calling, the vision I am about to set before you, corresponds perfectly to your deepest desire. And My community, to the degree it functions according to the design I make known in this letter, will release the power you need to live into My calling, to live the way you most want to live. Saunter with Me as we continue this conversation."

"What?"

"When pilgrims in the Middle Ages traveled to 'la Saint Terre,' to the Holy Land, they frequently stopped along the way to beg for the alms they needed to support their journey. They became known as saint-terrers, which over time was Anglicized into *saunterers*. Don't let your eagerness to mature create pressure to mature. You'll walk too fast. Saunter with Me as we continue our conversations, especially this one. Don't rush ahead looking for immediate relevance and quick insights to make you mature sooner than is possible.

"You know, of course, that I prompted Paul to write his second letter to Timothy several years *after* I led him to write his letter to Titus. But I've arranged My love letters in a sequence that encourages you to read 2 Timothy *before* you read Titus. Do you know why?"

"I haven't a clue."

"Let Me give you one reason. Saunter with Me. Trace what you know of Paul's life from his two years of house arrest in Rome to his final imprisonment and execution a few years later."

"But I want to hear what You're telling me in Titus. What's the relevance of . . . I'm sorry. Well, as I understand it, when he was released from house arrest in AD 62, Paul went right back to telling Your story, knowing it was against the law. His fourth and final missionary trip included a short visit with Titus to the pagan Mediterranean island of Crete. After seeing some of the islanders converted, he moved on but left Titus there to organize the new Christians into a church, a community with spiritual leaders who could help people live in a way that revealed something of the beauty of Your story.

"After a short stay in Colossae with Philemon, he revisited Ephesus, where almost a decade earlier he had pastored the church in that city for three years. When he saw that they were listening to dangerous teaching that perverted Your story, Paul asked Timothy to remain there and pastor them back into Your truth while he went on to Greece.

"From there, he wrote his first letter to Timothy and his single letter to Titus, coaching them both on how to carry out their different missions. When he later returned to Rome to encourage the Christians he had so richly taught in the letter he had much earlier written to them, he was promptly arrested, thrown into a dungeon, and eventually killed. While awaiting execution, he wrote his second letter to Timothy. And then Paul died. Did I get it right?"

"Close enough. Now let Me add one detail that will help you see why I wanted you to read 2 Timothy before Titus. Rome's judicial system required a preliminary hearing for the judge to hear charges against a prisoner and, if guilt was clear, to pronounce sentence. At that first hearing, what Rome called the *prima actio*, friends of the accused were permitted to advocate on his behalf.

"Now here's the detail you must not miss. *No one from the Roman church showed up at the prima actio to advocate for Paul* [2 Timothy 4:16]. His community failed him. But see what Paul did. Between the *prima actio* when he was abandoned and the *secunda actio*—the second trial when he was sentenced to death—Paul seized the painful opportunity of

failed friendship to reveal the beauty of grace in the strength of anticipating the beauty of glory. Paul focused not on the pain of being
failed but on the mission of making My story attractive by the way he
related.

"Rather than complaining about mistreatment—as so many do
by repeating grace-empty words such as, 'Well, I have to be honest
with you. You really hurt me. Now, how can we straighten things
out?' —My suffering servant forgave his friends and told My story
[2 Timothy 4:16–18]. And, thanks to My Spirit, that's how you want
to relate. It's a new way to relate, but it's the way you were redeemed
to relate. It's My vision for you. It was Paul's vision for the church
on Crete. Paul *lived* the vision in a Roman dungeon. That's 2 Timothy.
He *taught* the vision in Titus. That's the order: first *live* My story,
then *tell* it. First, 2 Timothy, then Titus."

"Father, is it possible? When someone hurts me, I naturally want to self-
righteously back away from them or tell them how I feel with the intent that
they'll treat me better. Can I really live that way with people as messed up
as I am?"

"I wrote My fifty-sixth letter to answer that question. I led Paul to
Crete in the confidence that even the most relationally dysfunctional
people can learn to live well between the two epiphanies. And the
Cretans were dysfunctional. Six centuries before Paul told them My
story, one of their revered poets, a man named Epimenides, described
his fellow Cretans as 'always lying, evil brutes, lazy gluttons' (Titus
1:12). In My churches today, too many of My followers, by hiding
their self-centered energy beneath a sociable veneer, see themselves
as not nearly so bad as awful people like the Cretans. I never intended
that My story be told to polish the veneer. So I brought My truth to a
society without a veneer in order to show, as My servant G. Campbell
Morgan put it, 'the true spiritual power of the church, and the possibility of the lowest exercising it.' For that purpose, 'the most difficult
soil was selected; the most difficult circumstances were employed.'

"When Paul wrote to Titus, he never intended for Titus to help the new converts in Crete to merely get along. Sociably pleasant Christianity is no Christianity at all. It aims too low. It fails to reveal the beauty of grace. From personal experience, Paul knew My story has the power to change a stupid and stubborn man duped by the appeal of living for himself into a sacrificial servant [3:3–7], to change even Paul and to change Cretans into people who make My story irresistibly attractive by the new way they relate.

"He told Titus what I'm now telling you: aim yourself and your friends toward becoming a community where:

❀ men and women who long to live well between the two epiphanies enjoy spiritual influence [1:6–9]

❀ My story is told in a way that stirs people's desire to always do good, to live and love well; that creates a vision of what revealing the beauty of grace actually looks like in tough relationships [1:9]

❀ teaching that makes self-preserving choices seem right or, at least, justified and necessary is exposed and rejected [1:9–16]

❀ the way you live reveals the beauty of grace-energized relating until the beauty of glory-filled community can be enjoyed forever [2:11–14; 3:3–7], where even the underprivileged live in a manner that makes My story attractive [2:10]

"If you experience even a taste of that kind of community as Paul did with Timothy and Titus, you'll be able, like Paul, when others fail you badly to reveal the beauty of grace even if you're a Cretan."

"Father, I've got to ask You again. Can I really live that way? My inclination to hang out with friends who treat me well and to avoid those who don't is strong. I'm just an ordinary Christian. I'm no Paul."

"In My next letter, I called an otherwise unknown man to live into a high vision that aroused his deepest desires, to reveal the beauty of My grace and the power of My story as he related to someone who had severely wronged him. He could do it. So can you. There are no ordinary Christians. Keep reading."

Love Letter Fifty-Seven: Philemon

REAL LIFE CHANGES EVERY RELATIONSHIP

*W*hen Martin Luther read this next letter of Yours, he called it 'a masterly, lovely example' of how You want us to relate to each other. If he were looking at my life, he could find too many examples of exactly the opposite.

"Father, just reading Philemon got me thinking about who has wronged me and how I have responded. I mean, here's Philemon, a good Christian man, a spiritual leader led to Your Son by Paul, and his slave Onesimus steals from him and then runs away to avoid punishment. When I tried to put myself in Philemon's shoes, my mind, way too easily, came up with the names of seven men who in my view have seriously wronged me. I'm not sure what Philemon felt, but I'm quite clear how I've felt and still feel.

"I have no ongoing relationship with any of these men, not even Christmas card contact. I've written them off. And I assume they've done the same with me and likely feel quite happy to keep our relationship in an antique dust bin. And I'm okay with that.

"Even though each of these guys is a Christian, when one of their names crosses my mind, when someone mentions any one of them, I feel a smoldering indifference. All I can think about is what they did to me, the pain they caused me, and the injustice I've suffered—about how wrong *they* are. And all I experience going on in me is a proudly restrained urge to get even—sometimes even the hope that You'll somehow make them pay for how they've mistreated me—and a self-righteous desire to just forget about them and move on with my ministry. Father, that's really awful!"

"You have no idea how your life brings Me great joy. Words cannot express the love for you that fills My heart. I am so glad you're Mine."

"Huh? I guess I didn't expect to hear You say that after what I just said. I know You're not telling me I'm right for scrubbing those guys' names off my list of friends. (Darn! An eighth name just popped into my head.) But in Your last letter, You did tell me to 'have nothing to do with' people who spread division (Titus 3:9–11), people who are useless to Your purposes because their understanding of Your story is warped and their motives for ministry are self-serving. Do all eight of these guys belong in that category? Is it okay for me to have nothing to do with any of them?"

"Your longing to know My story well makes the angels sing. They share your desire [1 Peter 1:12]. How I relate to people stuns them as it is beginning to stun you. I want you to know that every time you relate in love, every time you sacrifice self-interest for the sake of another, you are drawn deeper into the wonder of My story. Your appreciation for how I relate grows. Your grasp of My story increases [Philemon 6]."

"Forgive my impertinence; I know I'm wrong to say this, but I still don't know what to do with those eight men. You're not answering my question."

"I so easily could. I could tell you exactly where you're wrong. I could let you know exactly who falls into the category of warped and sinful men you are right to ignore. I could lay out exactly what I want you to do in every relationship at every moment, and I could command you to obey. I AM the Lord. But instead, I want you to think about how I relate to people who wrong Me. It's the greatest love story ever told. It frees you to love as I do. Thanks to My Son, the power with which I love is now in you. And thanks to My Spirit, the wisdom to know what love requires in every relationship is available to you.

"Like Onesimus with Philemon, you have stolen from Me My rightful claim to enjoy your obedience and love [Malachi 3:7–8], and you have run away from home. Like the prodigal son, you have left your properly and deeply offended Father, thinking you could escape My holy punishment and enjoy your illegitimate freedom. I would have been entirely just in abandoning you to yourself forever. But like Paul between Philemon and Onesimus [Philemon 18], My Son stood between My holy wrath and your hell-deserving sin and looking at Me with eyes full of love said, 'Charge his debt to Me.' I was wronged by you, and I have swallowed the injustice of your wrong into the ocean of My grace."

"Father, as I listen to what You're saying, I'm realizing how naturally I see myself more as the offended and self-righteous elder brother than as the offending prodigal, more like a wronged Philemon than a wrong Onesimus. I just came across something else Martin Luther wrote that puts it well: 'As Christ doth for us with God the Father, so doth St. Paul with Philemon for Onesimus. We are all God's Onesimi, to my thinking.'"

"You are now recognizing a delightful opportunity to become an even tastier ingredient in My happiness and in yours. Hear what I'm now saying to you in this fifty-seventh love letter:

Wronged people tell My story to those who wrong them only when they are overwhelmed by the story I tell to those who wrong Me and count themselves among the offenders.

"You've quoted Luther twice. When Alexander Smellie, a lesser-known but wonderfully wise servant of Mine, read Luther's response to Paul's letter to Philemon, he wrote, referring to all My followers: 'Fugitives, outcasts, who have stolen our Master's property and fled His house, aforetime unprofitable to Him. Ah, but God's Onesimi too because He welcomes us back, and then at last we begin to be profitable; not now slaves, but children beloved . . . You and I may well be glad to be God's Onesimi. For, when the name is ours, we come to our true self, to our proper home, and to our satisfying future.'

"And don't forget. The name *Onesimus* means 'profitable' or 'useful.' Speaking to Philemon, Paul, using an intentional play on his name, said this about Onesimus: 'Formerly he was useless to you, but now he has become useful both to you and to me' (v. 11). The real life that My story provides has the power to change every person and every relationship."

"Father, I just looked at my list of eight names again. And I prayed over each one. I know You were listening as I asked You to forgive me for nursing a grudge against them and to keep working in them to make each one more useful to Your plan. But I'm just not yet ready to ask You to use me to encourage them. I know this is terrible, but I can almost feel *spiritual enough* by even entertaining the possibility of praying that prayer, spiritual enough to then just get on with serving You as best I can."

"As you began this conversation with Me, you were thinking that I would rebuke you for how you're relating to these eight men. You expected Me to command you to ask My forgiveness for your sinful lack of love, to forgive each of them for wronging you, and to move toward them with kindness. You pictured Me with holy arms folded across My chest, waiting with a stern face to see what you'd do. Had I related to you in that way, at best, you'd have gone through the motions of love. And you'd have drawn no closer to Me.

"Instead, I have revealed My way of relating to you by telling the story of Onesimus, and reporting how Paul spoke to Philemon. I stand before you with holy arms of grace opened wide, inviting you to do what I know you most want to do and to do it as a free choice of love. You are forgiven for wrongs done against Me that are far greater than any wrongs done to you. And you are empowered and, therefore, free to relate to those who have wronged you as I have related and will forever relate to you.

"Philemon not only forgave Onesimus but also received him as a brother in the church that Philemon led in Colossae. And he did so as a free response to another brother, Paul, who believed in him and who reminded Philemon that through Paul's ministry I had forgiven him for sins against Me greater than the sins of Onesimus against him [v. 19]."

"Father, something good is stirring in me. I think it's my new heart beating a little stronger. I want to tell Your story in all my relationships . . . even with those eight men. But the battle is real. Help me!"

"Your flesh is strong. My Spirit is stronger. To experience His strength, you must drop all the trappings of religion, all dependence on the external good things you do that make you feel spiritual enough. And you must drop all the dynamics of religion, all the internal attitudes that make you think you can become all you were meant to be without radical ongoing dependence on My Son. My servant Eugene Peterson was quite correct when he wrote, 'Religion is the most dangerous energy source known to humankind.' Exchange religion for My Son. He's the *better way*. My next letter makes that clear."

Love Letter Fifty-Eight: Hebrews

BELIEVE! WAIT! LOVE! DO NOT QUIT ON MY SON!

*F*ather, I think our conversation about this next letter of Yours might be a little longer than some of the others and likely more confusing. This letter is a tough read, the toughest since Romans.

"Let me see if I have some patterns in place before we start. After the nine letters You wrote through Paul to various churches (Romans through 2 Thessalonians, what most refer to as the Church Epistles) and four letters to individuals, still through Paul (1 Timothy through Philemon, known as the Pastoral Epistles because Paul was pastoring pastors in the first three and, maybe, in the fourth as well), Hebrews now begins the last nine of Your sixty-six love letters (Hebrews through Revelation). I've heard them called the Hebrew Christian Epistles, but that seems to apply most clearly to Hebrews and James and, perhaps, to both letters of Peter. Since all of the last nine (except, maybe, 3 John?) were written not to churches or individuals but to general audiences—neither to Christians in specific local churches nor to specific individual Christians—I think it makes more sense to refer to them as the General Epistles.

"And every one of Your final twenty-seven letters has an almost obvious human author except this one although there is some debate about who wrote James. Are You going to tell me who actually wrote this fifty-eighth letter? It would be fun to clear up this centuries-old controversy."

"I'm glad you've reviewed the structure of My last twenty-two letters after the four Gospels and Acts. That will help you to keep My message in each of them more clearly in mind. But I'm less interested in telling you whom I used to write the words in Hebrews (though quite obviously I could) than in exploring their impact on you. Whomever I chose to compose this letter, the words and their message remain Mine. Hebrews is one more love letter from Me to you."

"Well, whomever You used to write it (I think it was Paul or maybe Apollos?), this letter is making me uncomfortable. Again, You're requiring me to redefine my natural understanding of love in order to read what You've written as love letters. This one is making me painfully aware of how tempted I am to do exactly what You warned these Hebrew Christians not to do; as You put it, not to *shrink back*, not to *throw away* their confidence that You're still telling a love story when life gets rough [10:35–38]. And for them, it got really rough: persecution, ridicule, assaults, all kinds of bad stuff.

"What I'm seeing is that every time I get really down or things go really bad, what I want the most is to feel better and for things to go better. And that priority amounts to losing confidence in Your story, to wanting to hear and believe a different version of the story You're telling. The urge is so strong—I want to write my own script, at least a chapter, even a paragraph, that's more to my liking. And that urge comes out in my prayers. I think You should go along with my suggested revisions to Your story. I know that's nonsense, but it can feel so legitimate.

"Father, that temptation is hard to resist. And yielding to it can be subtle. I can let someone know they hurt me for no better reason than trying to get them to treat me well. And right while I'm doing it, I can think that I'm relating well. It's yielding to that temptation in relationships that's so subtle. Thinking I need relief from feeling empty and looking at porn would be an obvious demand that I get what I want, an obvious shrinking back. But I struggle more with that same core temptation, not by looking at porn but in how I relate and by changing more to my liking how I think about You and how I understand the story You're telling.

"I'm seeing, too, that the appeal of the temptation to shrink back from Your story and telling my own involves the pleasure of defiance. *I don't like what You're doing in my life, so I'll take over. There! Take that!* Father, that's worse than pathetic. It's dangerous.

"The Hebrew Christians wanted to go back to their familiar and comforting Jewish rituals when things got tough. I shrink back by arranging for my own satisfaction—by eating too much comfort food, by insisting people get my point when I teach or am in a conversation, by doing whatever it takes to feel more significant and less empty, or by getting involved in a church that lets me stay content with my version of Your story. I could easily list a dozen other ways that I shrink back from telling Your story.

"The faith You want me to have is so much stronger and more securely anchored than the faith I see in myself. All those examples of faith You give in Hebrews 11 make mine seem especially weak, especially the one in verse 35. You referred there to unnamed people who were tortured but refused to secure their release by giving up on Your story. They were waiting to 'gain a better resurrection.'

"That one got to me. I checked it out and discovered that *tortured* is a translation of *tumpanizo*, which means 'beat to death.' Those followers of Yours were stretched out on a *tympanum*—a wheel-shaped rack—and while they were being pulled apart, their torturers beat them with a club or leather strap. Father, I lose confidence that Your story is good when my fax machine doesn't work, let alone when I'm stretched out on a rack and beaten. How did these Christians *not* shrink back?

"I know You want me to *believe*, to keep faith in Your soul-satisfying goodness when I'm in the middle of dream-shattering badness. I know You want me to *wait*, to hold on to the happy hope of the coming party when I so badly want happiness now. I know You want me to *love*, to love You when the doctor tells me I have cancer or my accountant tells me I'm broke and to be there for others when my own struggles seem overwhelming.

"Father, *it's not happening!* I know Your Son believed and waited and loved, but it's not happening in me, not nearly as much as I want. How can I keep from shrinking back? How can I not throw away confidence in Your story of love when I don't see what I think would be evidence of Your love? How can I resist the perverse pleasure of defying You and doing whatever I can to feel better, to live a more comfortable and fulfilling and satisfying life as my priority?"

"You might begin by listening to Martin Luther's advice. After hearing all you've just said, Luther would reply with the counsel he gave himself and his friends: 'If you would believe, you must crucify the question, How?' Like all Adam's descendants, you're a natural-born chess player at life. You want to know how to make your next move to win the blessings or the kind of maturity you want.

"Crucify the *how* question. Stop trying to figure out what you can do to develop stronger faith, brighter hope, richer love. Keep drinking the milk I've poured into your bottle. But come to My table as an adult prepared to eat meat [5:11–14]. I love you too much not to grow you up with solid food."

"Father, help me resist the temptation to shrink back into the familiar pleasure of easily digested milk. Serve me the meat that will deepen my faith, that will sustain me in hope, that will free me to love. What are You saying in this letter that You want me to hear, to eat?"

"There's so much. For now, hear this—and more, *chew* this:

In this moment My Son is serving you as your priest. The more you understand what I mean when I tell you that My Son is your priest 'in the order of Melchizedek,' the less inclined you will be to defiantly shrink back from the story I am telling.

"See Jesus, still incarnate as a human but no longer on earth, still the crucified One with nail-scarred hands and feet but no longer on the cross, still resurrected but no longer visible among you, and still ascended but no longer ascending through the devil-filled heavens. See Jesus where He is right now, where He is when you awake in a cold sweat at two in the morning, where He is when you're alone in a hotel room and tempted to watch what should never cross your eyes, where He is when you've been devastated by loss or rejection, where He is when your failure has brought you into the depths of despair.

"I want you to reflect on the words of a woman who in the fourteenth century saw Jesus as few ever do. She delivered meat that you're ready to chew. Do so now. Listen to Julian of Norwich: 'In the beholding of God we fall not, and in the beholding of ourselves we stand not; yet while we are in this life it is needful that we behold both at once. The higher beholding keepeth us in joy and in the true love of God; the lower beholding keepeth us in godly fear and self-abasement. Our good Lord would that we hold us much more in the beholding of Him, and yet not wholly leave the beholding of our-selves, until the time when we shall be brought up above, where we shall dwell with the Lord Jesus, according to our heart's desire, and be filled with joy without end, beholding Him as He is.'"

"Father, how are You saying that in Hebrews? How does thinking about Your Son's priesthood in the order of Melchizedek help me see Him? I'm not getting it."

"Those are a different kind of how-questions. They're inquiries into My words and My ways, not requests for a formula to make your life work. Questions that reflect your desire to know and follow Me are good. They are questions I will answer. First, understand that milk is My story told simply. Never stop drinking it. Meat is the same story explored deeply. Always keep chewing it. The meat I provide in this letter includes the truth of:

- ❀ the unique beauty of My Son's life and death that reveals who I am and how I relate, revealed to all who see My glory in the face of My Son [2 Corinthians 4:6; Hebrews 1:3].
- ❀ the superiority of My Son to the angels who were with Me when I revealed My character at Sinai in the giving of the Law [Deuteronomy 33:2; Hebrews 1]; the superiority of My Son to Moses, who received My law and pastored My people in a failed attempt to keep it [Hebrews 3]; the superiority of My Son to Joshua, who led My people into a rest they could not maintain [Hebrews 4:8]; and the superiority of My Son to Aaron, the priest whose shrinking back prevented him from enjoying free access into My Presence. Aaron was a priest because he came

from the tribe of Levi. My Son was a priest 'on the basis of the power of an indestructible life' (Hebrews 7:15–16)."

"Father, I'm already choking on the meat You're describing. I want to do more than study the menu. I want to digest the meal. But I'm not getting the Melchizedek thing."

"Let Me cut up the meat into small pieces. Read Genesis 14:18–20, the three-verse history of the man named Melchizedek. Then read Psalm 110:4, where David first grasped that My people needed a different kind of priest than Aaron. Here are bite-sized pieces of meat.

"Melchizedek, King of Righteousness, ruled over Salem, a name for Jerusalem that means peace. I provided no genealogy of this King of Righteousness and Peace and made no mention of his family background or his death. Why? I was painting a picture of the Priest to come who, unlike every other priest in the order of Aaron, was also King; the Man who, with neither beginning nor end, on the basis of His indestructible life would rule over My people as King and at the same time advocate for My people as Priest. No king in Israel could function as priest. No priest in Israel was ever king.

"*No leader of Israel, neither king nor priest, ever had free and continuous access into My Presence. And no follower of My Son today can ever present himself or herself before Me on the basis of a blameless life other than My Son's.*

"Melchizedek accepted tithes from Abraham, the father of faith, indicating his superiority over Abraham and establishing, in picture form, My Son, not Abraham, as the author and beginner of faith, the kind of faith you need in order to believe in Me and My story.

"*And by My Spirit, He gives that exact faith to you. It is now in you, always waiting to be nourished and released.*

"Aaron lost confidence in My story when, among other times, he became impatient with how long Moses remained on the mountain with Me [Exodus 32]. My Son never once shrank back into telling His own story; He never threw away His trust in Me even when stretched on the tympanum of the cross. He never sinned, even when in the garden of Gethsemane (a garden so unlike the garden where

Adam began telling his own story) He wept in agony over where My story would take Him. That was inexpressibly hard for Me to watch. But I was never more proud of My Son.

"And you are now in Him. You share His life. You lack nothing that is needed to keep pressing on in the worst of circumstances or the most painful emotions.

"He *suffered* death and He *tasted* death [2:9]. Aaron killed animals to cover sin. My Son decisively surrendered Himself to death to put away sin. No one took His life from Him [John 10:18]. He *willed* Himself to suffer death. And He yielded to My plan that He die an agonizing, slow death as the Passover lamb who was 'roasted over the fire' (Exodus 12:8–9). He tasted sin in all its loathsomeness and *never* shrank back or turned away from My story. I so love My Son.

"I now call you to suffer when telling My story requires it, to suffer not for your sins but to reveal My worth. My Spirit supplies the desire and the power to follow My Son's example.

"And now, as your Great High Priest—not like the sinful Aaron, who had limited access into My Presence, a man who died a normal death and remained in the grave, but like Melchizedek, who in picture form neither sinned nor died—My Son knows exactly what you're going through and what it takes not to shrink back. He feels the strength of your temptation to escape from your tympanum, to renounce My story and tell your own, to protect yourself from relational pain in any way that works, and to live the lukewarm good-enough Christian life that My Son and I thoroughly detest. And He has already given you the life you need to overcome that seemingly irresistible temptation.

"In ways you'll never understand, He knows how tough it can be to tell My story. When you're tempted to shrink back, He feels the temptation. When you yield, He forgives you. The pressure to perform is gone. The desire to obey, the same desire that was centered in My Son's heart during all His earthly life, and most keenly felt in Gethsemane and on Golgotha, is in you.

"Chew this meat slowly. Eat a fresh helping again and again. Soon you will be awed by the privilege, not of figuring out how to develop more faith and feel more hope and relate with more love but of coming to Me as you are and seeing Jesus welcoming you into My

Presence where you can now present yourself before Me with all that's ugly within you and not be destroyed; where you can know someone understands the temptation to shrink back, to throw away your confidence in My story; and where the indestructible life that is now in you as a gift can be aroused into believing, waiting, and loving. But the urge to shrink back remains strong. The battle is on. Get to know your Savior, your Lord, your King, *Your Priest in the order of Melchizedek*. The better you know Him, the more you will know the joy of ongoing repentance. Repentance puts you more closely in touch with Him and more fully releases His life through yours."

"Like I expected, this conversation was longer than most of our others, and more confusing. I didn't expect the meat to be so hard to chew. But the few bites I've been able to swallow tasted really good. Father, I want to see Jesus, to see Him high and lifted up and to see me, though forever undeserving, right there with Him. I want to tell Your story. Will I? I'm still so tempted to shrink back."

"Keep chewing. You'll know that the nourishment from this meat is generating strength to believe, wait, and love when the prospect of becoming a coheir with My Son energizes you to reveal My goodness by the way you relate during difficult times. That's the message of My next letter. It's another helping of rich meat. Chew on."

Love Letter Fifty-Nine:
James

SAVE YOUR SOUL BY LIVING WELL

*F*ather, I think I'm missing something. No surprise there. But as I read through Your fifty-ninth love letter, I think I'm missing something I really need to see from where I am right now on this journey of following You.

"It's likely neither here nor there, but I think You wrote this short letter through Your Son's half brother James, a son Mary and Joseph conceived in the usual way after Jesus was conceived in a once-only unusual way, the same James who provided strong leadership for the church in Jerusalem [Acts 15:13–21].

"As I read this letter, two things stood out that I found troubling. First, You seem to contradict Yourself. Through Paul You couldn't have made it clearer that no one gets into right relationship with You by being good [Galatians 3:11]. No one gets saved by good works. It's always by faith in who Your Son is and what He accomplished on the cross [Ephesians 2:8–9]. Paul built his entire understanding of Your plan on what You had earlier told Habakkuk, that 'the righteous will live by his faith' (Habakkuk 2:4). Here's what You said through Paul: 'For in the gospel a righteousness from God is revealed, a righteousness that is by faith from first to last' (Romans 1:17). All faith, no works required to merit salvation, no works involved. It's by grace I've been saved, through faith, not through the work of living well. You made that clear in previous letters.

"But now in this letter You inspire James to write, 'What good is it, my brothers, if a man claims to have faith but has no deeds? Can such faith save him?' (2:14). Clearly, I think, James is answering no. Wouldn't Paul say yes? A few verses later You say through James, 'faith by itself, if it is not accompanied by action, is dead' (2:17). And then with these next words You seem to even more blatantly contradict what You earlier said to Habakkuk and through Paul: 'As the body without the spirit is dead, so faith without works is dead' (2:26).

"I'm in pretty good company when I tell You I'm troubled by what You're saying in James. Didn't Martin Luther call this letter an 'epistle of straw'? He wasn't even convinced that this fifty-ninth letter was from You. So, yes, I'm confused. Which is it? Is salvation by faith without works? Or is it by faith plus works? Am I supposed to somehow blend Your message through Habakkuk and Paul with what You're now saying through James? If so, I don't know how.

"That's my first reaction. Here's the second. Your letter seems scattered. It leaves me feeling scattered. Your words in this letter strike me as a random collection of good tips on how to live well: *welcome troubles*—You're telling me to hang in there and pray until a hard life makes me mature [1:2–7]; *be quick to listen*—I'm to hear what You want me to do and remember to do it [1:19–27; 2:1–26]; *be slow to speak*—You want me to watch what I say, knowing that one careless or mean-spirited word out of my mouth can cause a world of hurt, and that real humility reveals itself in a few good words and a lot of good works [1:19; 3:1–17]; and *be slow to anger*—I'm supposed to confess that my relational failures can all be traced back to my self-righteous and angry demand that I get what I want out of life and from people, and I should stop laughing as if my soul is already healthy; I should rather start weeping over how much selfish energy remains in me and stop counting on tomorrow's opportunities to keep my life going smoothly [1:19; 4:1–17].

"And then You tack on some depressing advice for rich people to realize they'll one day be broke, and in the meantime, they should treat well those who work for them [5:1–6]. That's followed by a strong challenge to be patient when life gets hard [5:7–12], to pray when I'm struggling or sick [5:13–18], and to restore shrinking-back Christians to life on the narrow road [5:19–20].

"All of that's good, of course. But it seems so scattered. So, yes, I do feel confused by Your teaching on how to be saved, and I do feel scattered as I listen to Your directions on how to live well. Well, I've said a lot. So much for being slow to speak. I guess I wasn't being quick to listen, but I do want to listen now. What are You saying to me in this letter? What am I missing?"

"Quite a bit. Chew on these next words slowly. They are rich meat. By *faith* you are already saved from an eternity without Me. I said that before, and I meant it. I always mean what I say. And I'm telling you now that by *works* you can save your soul from a life that eternity will reveal was wasted. There's no contradiction at all. You are justified before Me by faith in My Son, not by living well. As My child, you will inherit a place in the kingdom, a seat at My table, a dance card for the party. That's My gift to you. It's guaranteed. But you can now be qualified to rule with My Son in the coming kingdom by living well before others in this world.

"When you were justified before Me by faith and guaranteed heaven as My gift, My Spirit made you alive to Me with the life of My Son. He *regenerated* you. He gave you a new heart, a new and potentially consuming desire to love Me and others at any cost to yourself. Justification *makes* you My child. Regeneration provides the power to *live* like My child. And because justification is always accompanied by regeneration, every justified person's way of relating will evidence the presence of divine life though that evidence may be visible only to Me. Remember Lot?

"You can *know* you are saved by your confidence in My Son, in what He accomplished on the cross: salvation by grace alone through faith alone. You can *enjoy* your salvation by your growing resemblance to My Son. And your motivation to live like Him, to resist the demands of your flesh and to freely indulge the desires of your new heart, does not rest on your hope of getting into heaven—your place is already secured by faith without works—but rather on your hope of deepening My delight in you, of advancing My purposes through you, and of enjoying the unique privileges of heaven reserved for the faithful.

"In this fifty-ninth letter, I guide you toward living the life of good works that qualifies you to rule as coheir with My Son."

"Father, I think I'm hearing something that I've missed. I've been bugged for years by the nagging thought that sloppy Christians and serious Christians alike end up together in the full bliss of heaven. That never seemed quite right to me. But now if I'm hearing You correctly, You're telling me that Christians who shrink back and don't consistently resolve to put away their selfish ways of relating, Christians whose love for You remains weakly expressed, will be saved from hell to enjoy the pleasures of heaven but only as those 'escaping through the flames' (1 Corinthians 3:15). And Christians who grow to love You deeply and are willing to pay the price of not giving in to discouragement and not demanding an easier life, these Christians will enjoy the same heaven, *but their joy will somehow be deeper*. Is that what You're saying?"

"Listen well:

When grasped, the prospect of living as a coheir with My Son, in both the already and the not-yet eternal kingdom, will energize you to press on, to reveal My character and My plan by the way you live and relate, and to love Me and others at any cost to you, whether you are joyfully encouraged or despairingly discouraged.

"I sprinkled hints pointing to that truth throughout My fifty-ninth letter. Here's one: 'Blessed is the man who perseveres under trial because when he has stood the test, he will receive the crown of life that God has promised to those who love him' (1:12). Is that verse telling you how to save your soul from eternal death or does it tell you how to save your soul from the death of a wasted life?"

"The latter?"

"Of course. Here's another: 'Has not God chosen those who are very poor in the eyes of the world to be rich in faith and to inherit the kingdom he promised to those who love him?' (2:5). Let Me unpack that one further.

"*Little* faith, if sincerely placed in My Son, guarantees your invitation to the party. You will live forever in My Presence. You will dance. But *rich* faith, the kind that perseveres through terrible hardships, wins you a share in the inheritance I give to My Son as King of kings, the eternal and supreme Ruler over His kingdom. Remember what I said through Paul as he was facing death from the Roman court: 'if you endure, you will reign' (2 Timothy 2:12).

"All My children are My heirs. But only My faithful children, those who press on in faithfulness to My Son through suffering, will be coheirs with My Son in His inheritance of glory. I made this clear in an earlier letter. Listen: 'Now if we are children, then we are heirs—heirs of God, and co-heirs with Christ if indeed we share in his sufferings in order that we may also share in his glory' (Romans 8:17).

"All My children will dance at My party and be blessed to the brim of their capacity for joy. Only My faithful children will join My Son in leading the dance. Faith alone will get you to the party. And yet, as one of My servants put it, 'While it's true that we're saved by faith alone, the faith that saves is never alone.' Justifying faith is always accompanied by regenerated life, and that life *will* reveal itself, though, perhaps, to My eyes only.

"But when your faith leads to a consuming desire to love Me and others at any cost, when your faith is accompanied by a consistent pattern of good works, your life in this world will not be wasted, and your life in the next world will be uniquely blessed. Grasp that truth, and you will discover the power to resist your favorite temptations and to keep walking the narrow road to life, to fill your life with good works.

"I want you to begin dancing now. In this letter, I lay out the basic steps for beginners. *Be quick to listen* to everything I say and keep listening no matter what happens. Never forget My words. Live them every day. *Be slow to speak;* realize that you have more to hear than to say. And *be slow to anger.* Anger on My behalf is good. Anger that rises from the cesspool of your demanding spirit is bad. Wait till you are confident that your anger is holy before you express it.

"I spoke clearly in James. Abraham was accepted into My family because he believed Me. But his willingness to sacrifice his son revealed rich faith that qualified him as a coheir with My Son [James 2:21–24]. And Rahab, though a prostitute, was welcomed into My family when she trusted Me enough to welcome Israel's spies into her house [Hebrews 11:31]. But she was counted worthy to lead the dance when she not only welcomed the enemies of her people but also, as mentioned only in James and not in Hebrews, 'sent them off' (James 2:25) to destroy the culture that supported her sinful way of life. And at great risk to herself, she refused to betray the Israelite spies after she had sent them off, trusting Me for the life I created her to enjoy. The rich faith that her good works reflected has made her worthy to be a coheir with My Son.

"I saved your soul from eternal separation from Me when you placed your faith in My Son. Now save your soul from a wasted life by listening to Me, by using your tongue to celebrate Me and advance My plan, and by expressing anger only when whatever offends you is offensive to Me. In so doing, you will save your soul from missing out on the unique joy of reigning with My Son in the glory of His well-deserved leadership, of taking part in leading the dance."

"Thank You. You've replaced my confusion with excited anticipation. And my feeling of scatteredness is now yielding to a sense of directedness toward dance steps I need to keep practicing. You've again shown me what I could not see without You. The prospect of leading the dance releases something good in me, an energy that competes with my desire to provide myself with illegitimate relief when I feel hurt or to arrange for counterfeit satisfaction when I feel empty. But, as always, I need more. I need to be overwhelmed by the wonder of Your grace. Only a deep appreciation of Your true grace can overpower my still-fleshly soul."

"You're now ready to read My next letter."

Love Letter Sixty:
1 Peter

Soon! In a Little While. Soon!

*F*ather, I'd like to quote back to You some confusing words from this next letter. Here's what I read in 1 Peter 3:19–20. After saying that Your Son died and was then made alive by the Spirit, You wrote that through Him (the Spirit?), He (Jesus?) 'also went and preached to the spirits in prison who disobeyed long ago when God waited patiently in the days of Noah while the ark was being built.'

"I'm aware that scholars hold different views on those two verses, but the one that makes the most sense to me suggests that through Noah, Your Son told the people who were alive in Noah's day that a flood, something they had never before seen, was about to happen, and soon! But they laughed it off and mocked the idea that things were not going to continue on pretty much as they always had. And here's something else. You called them 'spirits in prison' because . . ."

"Do you want Me to penetrate your soul with life-changing power, or would you prefer that I satisfy your curiosity with academic knowledge?"

"Can't You do both?"

"When you grasp My central message of love in this letter, I will then provide whatever knowledge about seemingly obscure particulars that you need in order to draw closer to Me. Let's begin our conversation in a different place. Tell Me what stirred in you as you read My sixtieth letter."

"Well, as I was reading 1 Peter, a troubling possibility of something bad that might happen appeared in my mind out of nowhere and triggered immediate panic. It felt like someone punched me somewhere deep and knocked the air out of my soul.

"You tell me in this letter (and in nearly every previous one) not to expect things to always go well, not until heaven. I get that. And in James, You told me to welcome unforeseen troubles when they come. I sort of get that too. But then You tell me to go a step beyond welcoming. In this letter, You want me to actually *rejoice* when bad things happen and even (I think You're saying this) to rejoice at the prospect of bad things that might yet happen [1:6] because in this life I'm participating in 'the sufferings of Christ' (4:12–13). That's something I don't get. And I don't do it, at least not very well and not consistently. I too often anticipate trouble with fear."

"Do you believe Me, unlike the scoffers in Noah's day?"

"I believe You more than ever but, apparently, not enough. Father, we've talked our way through fifty-nine of Your letters. And counting this one, we've only seven more to go. And (I know I've said this before, several times) I thought I'd be further ahead on my spiritual journey by now. But I'm reminded every day that I'm still a long way off from thinking and feeling and living like Your Son."

"You're troubled. So was My Son. In Gethsemane He was 'troubled and deeply distressed' (Mark 14:33 NKJV). His life was by no means always emotionally pleasant. And His death was horrible. The prospect of the cross unnerved Him."

"Yes, I know. But neither the prospect nor the experience of trouble generated a terror that pushed Him off course. Not once. Not for a second.

Mine do. Often. Father, how long? How long before I become the man I long to be, fully alive for Your glory?"

"Soon! In a little while. Soon!"

"In this letter, Father, You twice repeat that phrase, 'in a little while.' The first time [1:6], I hear You telling me that in a little while I'll be dancing at Your party and that everything that happens now, including every moment of suffering, is a dance lesson that's getting me ready for then. The second time [5:10], You seem to be assuring me that in a little while—*but sometime in this life before I go to heaven*—I'll be dancing through whatever life throws at me in rhythm with Your Spirit.

"I'm not sure why, but the promise that I'll be substantially spiritually formed before I die triggered something. I remembered what Meister Eckhart wrote centuries ago: 'God is at home. It is we who have gone out for a walk.'

"Father, that's what I do. You have me living in a world that I know is not my home, but I'm tempted every day to go for a walk into my culture and compromise myself just enough to feel like I belong here, to feel comfortable and at peace with my life in this world. I feel like a foreigner in my own surroundings, sometimes even in church, and I don't like it."

"You are a stranger, and so, too, were the original recipients of this letter. Through Peter, I wrote My sixtieth letter to Jewish Christians who had been forced to leave their homes. They were living as *strangers* [1:1], a word I chose to designate My followers as holy misfits in a neighborhood of people who rejected the radical message of My Son, people who felt happily at home in their godless culture. I am your home. And you can come home now. You can make your home in Me. You can meaningfully live in My Presence and substantially reveal now the love and peace and joy that will fill you forever. But you cannot experience Me in this life with the unmingled and unchallenged satisfaction you will know in the next."

"And that's why I feel stuck. I can't seem to get close enough to You to kick off my shoes and rest, and I can't compromise myself enough to go about having as good a time as possible in this world. Father, it's hard not to feel fully at home anywhere. I'd like to experience a little more at-homeness here even though I know this world is not my home and I'm just passing through. Is that so wrong?"

"I AM your home. I don't want you to go out for a walk away from Me."

"Okay, but when will I learn to rest fully enough in Your love and to hope firmly enough in Your plan to have the kind of faith that quiets my fears and helps me to fight the good fight and to keep walking the narrow road through a disappointing world toward a home I can't yet completely enjoy?"

"Soon! In a little while. Soon! Listen to what I'm saying to you in this sixtieth love letter:

I will never deceive you with false hope.

"What you're waiting for in the next life and the maturity you long to know in this life will come. No one who trusts in Me will be put to shame [2:6]."

"Father, I believe You. But waiting for a day is one thing. Waiting for a decade is another. And it's been a couple thousand years since You made that promise. It's so hard to wait an indefinite, long time for what I most want to experience, and while I'm waiting, it feels even harder not to focus on what I can get now. It's easier to feel at home in a world I can see than with a Person I've never seen."

"I closed My sixtieth love letter by telling My strangers then and now that 'I have written to you briefly, encouraging you and testifying that this is the true grace of God. Stand fast in it' (5:12).

"My grace will prove sufficient for you to wait well if you:

❀ prepare your mind for action [1:13],

❀ understand what I mean when I say that My Son's wounds have healed you [2:24], and

❀ expect that I will restore you [5:10]."

"Unpack that for me, Father. I'm listening. I want to wait well."

"Too many of My followers prepare their minds for comfort. I want you to prepare your mind for *action*. Live in the tragic gap between desire and reality, between what you want and what is now available. Buddha taught his followers not to *wait* in the gap but to *close* the gap by killing desire, by wanting nothing that lies beyond one's immediate reach. And too often My followers, professing Christians, live as practicing Buddhists.

"They deny those desires that nothing in this world can satisfy and embrace only those desires for which they have hope of satisfaction now, in this world, sooner than soon, in less than My little while. Following Me requires groaning, living as a stranger in a world that only can leave you disappointed. But know this: only in the felt and accepted tension of unmet longings will you prepare your mind, not for comfort but for action, for living as a stranger devoted to bringing My kingdom to earth. Only in tension will you depend enough on My Word and My Spirit to enter the battle whose victory is guaranteed.

"And I want you to *understand the healing I provide through My Son's wounds.* Despite the claims of feel-good preachers, I have not promised to heal sickness, poverty, unemployment, painful emotions, or relational problems . . . not until heaven. Those are all second things. I sometimes provide them in this world. I sometimes don't. Pray for them but never demand them. Don't expect Me to keep promises I have not made.

"Coming home to Me is the first thing. I will heal every obstacle to your finding your way home. Listen to My words: 'by his wounds you have been healed. For you were like sheep going astray, but now you have returned to the Shepherd and Overseer of your souls'

(2:24–25). I heal waywardness, not difficulties. I make the journey possible, not easy.

"In Matthew 13:15, I promise to heal (same word) the stubborn blindness that keeps you from finding your way home. In Luke 14:18, My Son promises to heal (same word) heaviness of soul that has the power to keep you from finding your way home. In Hebrews 12:13, I pledge My strength to heal (same word) your moral weakness that gets in the way of finding your way home.

"Understand that because My Son's wounds have healed you from everything that stands in the way of finding your way back home to Me, you can now *expect that I will restore you,* that I will mend your soul as I mended the fishing nets of James and John so that their nets could serve their intended purpose (in Mark 1:19, 'preparing their nets,' *preparing* is the same word translated *restore* in 1 Peter 5:10).

"Expect to be richly equipped to tell My story of love in any circumstance—as you face any experience or prospect of trouble during any season of dryness, discouragement, or despair. I will empower you to dance on the narrow road that leads to living life with My Son. I will make you firm enough in your faith to resist the temptation to go for a long walk into this world. And I will make you steadfast, centered on a foundation of hope that cannot crumble and released enough from self-centeredness to care about others more than yourself [5:10]. *I will never deceive you with false hope.*

"Tell My story of suffering love as a stranger living under human governments, including bad ones [2:13–17]; as a worker responsible to employers, even when they are unfair [2:18–20]; as a spouse in either a fulfilling or a difficult marriage [3:1–7]; as a participant in relationships of every kind [3:8–17]; and especially in your leadership role among My people, no matter how blind they seem to My truth [5:1–9].

"Soon, in a little while, you will dance through life in this world more rhythmically than you ever thought possible. *It's already happening, more than you realize!* And soon, in a little while, you will be dancing forever in perfect rhythm with heaven's music. *My Son will return.* I will never deceive you with false hope."

"Father, I want to walk toward You, not away from You. And I want to do so with Your people. But sometimes I feel like a stranger not only in this world but also in church. What's happening?"

"Through Paul, I earlier told you that in the last days, times would be terrible in the church [2 Timothy 3:1]. You are now living in those days. In My next five letters, I uncover the false teaching and fleshly living that will pass for Christianity among My followers before My Son returns. Read on, and beware. Stand firm in My true grace. Prepare your mind for action. Know that your inclination to walk away from Me has been healed by My Son's wounds. It no longer has controlling power. Expect to be restored. Wait well!"

Love Letter Sixty-One: 2 Peter

I Know How to Rescue My Children
from Their Worst Problem

"*F*ather, this may not be the best time to talk with You about Your next letter. Right now, I'm in the middle of . . . ."

"I know what you're going through. I know you're scared. And I know you're frustrated by how poorly you sometimes relate. I know, too, that you're sorely tempted to settle for easy relief from your fear and discouragement.

"But I also know the good My Spirit is working in you as you anxiously wait for the doctor's phone call, and I know the good He will continue to work in you whether the news brings added fear or sweet relief. And I want you to know that your relational failures discourage only your pride and, at the same time, deepen your dependence on Me for relational success. Know this too: your real temptation is to use your fear and failure to justify walking away from Me into pleasures you can arrange for yourself.

"I'm smiling as I say this: My timing is never off. Now is the perfect time to hear My message to you in My sixty-first love letter. My plan for your life is not at risk. *I know how to rescue My children from their worst problem, through all their difficulties* [2 Peter 2:9]. Trials and testing provide My Spirit with the opportunity to nourish and release the divine nature that is in you, the same nature that became dazzlingly visible in My Son when He ran into trouble [2 Peter 1:3–4; Luke 22:28]."

"Father, I am scared. And yes, I am discouraged. I hadn't thought of it, but I guess it is my pride that's wounded. I can't pull life off the way I want to. And I can feel the defiance behind my urge to do whatever it takes to feel better if only for a moment. So are You speaking to all that mess in this letter?"

"I presume you've read My words to you in 2 Peter 1:3–4?"

"A dozen times today."

"Read them again but this time as words from you to Me."

"Okay. 'Your divine power has given me everything I need for life and godliness through my knowledge of You who called me by Your own glory and goodness. Through these You have given me Your very great and precious promises so that through them I may participate in Your divine nature and escape the corruption in the world caused by evil desires.'

"Father, I think I am standing fast in Your grace, as You told me to do at the end of Your first letter through Peter [1 Peter 5:12]. At least I'm not giving up on it. But I'm not sure I'm doing so well with what You told me to do when You finished up this second letter, to *grow* in that grace [2 Peter 3:18].

"Just yesterday, for example, a good friend called to say he's leaving tomorrow with his wife for a month-long vacation in Europe. I immediately felt jealous and a little superior. Horrible thoughts like these, uninvited but welcomed, ran through my mind. While he'll be cruising through France and Italy, I'll be listening to You talk to me through more of Your love letters. I'm in fellowship with You. He's not!

"Father, that's pathetic. It's awful. I'm a natural-born judge, a self-appointed critic. Will I ever mature beyond such worldly self-pity and such a proud, critical spirit?"

"You will never, until heaven, mature beyond having to fight the battle against flesh-driven relational wickedness. But something else, something better, is in you, and it's lodged in a deeper place in your heart than where your natural self-centeredness lives. Listen to what I'm saying to you in this letter:

You now share in My nature. You have within you the power necessary to resist every natural impulse that stands in the way of loving others as I love you. Neither fear, failure, nor temptation is stronger than the divine power available to you that can keep you walking the narrow road to life."

"When You tell me that I 'may participate in the divine nature,' I know You don't mean that I can become the fourth member of the Trinity. So what do You mean?"

"My nature, what comes naturally to Me, is to live for the well-being of others at any cost to Myself. Your nature, what comes naturally to you, is to live for your own well-being at any cost to Me or to others. My nature, the holy inclination to love, is now in you. When you relate in the energy of that inclination, you are relating not naturally but supernaturally, above and in conflict with your natural inclination. Expect a battle.

"Because you are forgiven for all the evil your nature spews into the way you relate and because My Son bought you out of slavery to self-centeredness and freed you to live according to My nature, you are now able to 'look not to your own interests, but beyond them to the interests of others' (Philippians 2:4), just like My Son did when He lived on earth."

"Didn't You just misquote that verse? The copy I have of Your letter to the Philippians reads 'look not *only* to your own interests, but *also* to the interests of others.' Aren't You telling me it's okay to look after myself, to practice self-care as long as I'm also looking out for others?"

"The word *only* is not in the verse I wrote through Paul. I am calling you to trust Me with your interests as My Son trusted Me with His. I want you to look *beyond* what you can get out of relationships and *toward* what you can bring into them. When a leper asked My Son to heal him, My Son did not reply, 'What's in it for Me?' He never looked out for Himself."

"Father, that's not merely a new way to live; it's an *impossible* way to live. I can't escape from my desire to take care of myself."

"You cannot escape from the *desire* for your own happiness and well-being. And I don't want you to. But you can escape from the *demand* to arrange for your own happiness and well-being. You can do so by trusting Me with your life and devoting yourself to revealing My nature to others by how you relate.

"It's a narrow road that not many find [Matthew 7:13–14]. Remember what Paul said about Timothy and then about others: 'I have no one else like him, who takes a genuine interest in your welfare. For everyone else looks out for his own interests, not those of Jesus Christ' (Philippians 2:20–22).

"I chose Peter to bring this message to you because with two others he saw My Son in the full glory of His divine nature [Matthew 17:1–8]. The sheer brilliance of perfect love worked its way into Peter's soul until he was blind to everything less. It took some time, but he saw the light of a new way to live reaching into this dark world and into his own dark heart. And after Pentecost when My Spirit took over his desires, Peter lived for the day when he would relate like My Son in perfect love, and he longed for the morning star of My nature to rise in his heart and change him into the man I saved him to become—into the likeness of the Man he saw on the mount of transfiguration [2 Peter 1:19]."

"Father, like Isaiah, I'm seeing Your Son lifted up so high that I'm realizing even more how low I've fallen [Isaiah 6:1–6], and I'm feeling energized by a vision of how Your Spirit can lift me higher than I've ever dreamed possible. And I'm getting all that from the first chapter of this letter.

"But I'm puzzled. Why, after exciting me with such lofty possibilities and such incredible realities—I actually participate in Your nature—why do You then spend most of the next two chapters in such a scorching denunciation of false teachers? It doesn't seem to follow."

"As I write in this love letter, many of My people are 'nearsighted and blind' (1:9). They see only the possibility of socializing their self-centeredness into what they mistakenly regard as an acceptable way for My followers to live. I call them, and I call you to crucify your old way of relating, not to disguise it beneath a friendly Christian-looking veneer. But false teachers come along with stories they have made up that pervert My story into an opportunity to use Me for the satisfaction of their self-obsessed desires. If you buy into their lies, you will relate out of self-interest and see nothing wrong with it. You won't even realize you're relating from that energy. You will recognize no conflict between relating in a way that gains personal advantage and living as a follower of My Son."

"Father, what stories, what lies are these false teachers telling? What are they saying?"

"Two things. First, they 'deny the Sovereign Lord who bought them' (2:1). Rather than celebrating the freedom from the penalty and power of selfish relating that My Son purchased for them with His blood, they turn the cross into an example of love that justifies as Christian whatever lets them feel loved and happy. In so doing, they 'bring the way of truth,' the new way to live selflessly won by My Son's death, into disrepute (2:2).

"Understand this: when spiritual leaders nudge the cross of My Son into the outskirts of their thinking, when they stubbornly fail to realize that only through the cross are they both forgiven for their arrogant self-obsession and empowered to love sacrificially, then painful wounds will be seen as a greater problem than selfish relating.

When that happens, relating in a way that protects you from further wounding and enhances a sense of personal well-being seems not only necessary but moral. That's error #1.

"Error #2 is this: false teachers dismiss the promise of My Son's return as if it were a fiction, a promise with no implications for how they should live now [3:3–4]. This second error leads to a greater concern for making this life work well than for personal holiness. The hope of a better life now determines how they choose to live. It justifies self-centered choices. The hope for a better life later—the only hope that has power to sustain My followers in claiming the unique opportunity that suffering in this life brings to reveal My radically other-centered nature to a watching world—is largely ignored, treated with contempt.

"Listen to such false teaching, and you will not be rescued from your worst problem of *selfish* relating into *selfless* relating. But look by My Spirit and through My Word into the blazing light of My nature revealed fully in My Son, and you will be blinded to the urge to look after yourself. I know how to rescue My children from the corruption of their evil desires, from their demand that life work well for them now."

"As always, Father, You are right. It was a good time to talk with You about this letter."

"I want you to tell My story well, to reveal My nature by the way you relate in this fearful and discouraging world with all its temptations to walk away from Me into immediate relief. To do so, you must remain in fellowship with Me. In My next love letter, I tell you what that means. You're nearing the finish line. You're on your way home. Keep walking with Me and toward Me. Perfect joy is waiting."

Love Letter Sixty-Two: 1 John

I WANT YOU TO KNOW THE REAL TRUTH
ABOUT WHO YOU ARE

*F*ather, it happened *again* earlier this morning. Driving to my favorite coffee shop, I suddenly began talking out loud about Your love. Tears started rolling down my face, and I sang 'Jesus loves me, this I know,' over and over again. I couldn't stop crying, and I couldn't stop singing. *Father, what's happening to me?*"

"What have you been asking Me for these past few weeks?"

"I've wanted to know, to really *know* that You love me. I believe it, but I long to experience Your love in a way I never have."

"Don't quench My Spirit. Receive Him. He's offering you fellowship with Me and My Son."

"Father, that's what I want more than anything. But I don't get it—how can I feel so spiritually in tune one moment as I did this morning and so out of tune the next? Yesterday morning I woke up feeling flat, utterly indifferent to the story You're telling. My doctor called the afternoon before, two days ago. I had to face *again* how desperately and foolishly dependent I am on broken wells not leaking. His call made it clear, my broken wells *are* broken. They're guaranteed to leak no matter how hard I try to patch them up.

"I felt empty. The life I was holding on to drained out of me. And I felt irritable, inconvenienced. Some nasty procedures are in the cards. And some big plans are now in limbo. Mostly though, I felt shaken and sad, very sad. The possibilities are unpleasant, for me certainly but more for my wife and family.

"The next morning, I couldn't get You in sight. I was more aware of me and my plans than of You and Yours. The party we've been talking about as we worked our way through Your first sixty-one letters seemed a long way off, like it belonged to another world, a world I couldn't see.

"I was with a close friend when the doctor's call came. I got pretty emotional, more scared than anything else. When my friend asked what was going on in me, an unexpected word flew into my mind: *important*. In that moment, the word felt alive. *I* felt alive. I sensed something deeply good was about to happen, that something important was moving ahead in Your story. But the next morning, the sense of importance had faded.

"And then it came back, suddenly. I was driving to that same coffee shop, thinking about what You're saying in 1 John, that I could actually have fellowship with You; *koinonia* is the Greek word You used. I heard You telling me that we share things together. Something wonderful happened, almost exactly what happened again this morning. I began to cry. I heard myself shouting, 'I'm part of Your story!'

"And just like this morning, I couldn't stop crying. And I kept on shouting: 'How could someone like me have anything in common with Someone like You? How could a forgiven but still empty well-digger, a saved but still whiny comfort-seeker, a regenerate but still blessing-demander like me be part of a story like Yours? And how on earth—or in heaven for that matter—could it ever happen that Someone like You would want to make Your home in someone like me, then actually do it, and then like it?'

"Father, I've never felt more sinful and unworthy and, at the same time, more loved and alive. I was alive with awe and joy."

"I love watching My Spirit work. He's always up to something good."

"But Father, the joy has faded. I've just felt visited by Your Spirit two mornings in a row. But whatever happened then isn't happening now. And I'm left wondering who I am. Am I still the self-obsessed, whiny person I know myself to be? Or am I Your deeply loved, Spirit-filled child who, like Your Son, longs to stay close to You and to keep on telling Your story no matter what happens? Father, who am I? Where am I?"

"You're on the journey. You're My little child, walking the narrow road that My Son promised leads to life. You're about to learn what you've dimly known before, that when the narrow road gets especially narrow, My Spirit has a unique opportunity to do important work. You may laugh with joy. You may cry in hope.

"He worked deeply in My friend Dietrich Bonhoeffer when Dietrich was in a Nazi prison camp, awaiting a hangman's noose. In a poem called 'Who Am I?,' My faithful child recorded what happened when his narrow road became crushingly narrow. Dietrich felt himself to be 'struggling for breath, as though hands were compressing' his throat. 'Powerlessly trembling for friends at an infinite distance'—he would never marry or again see his fiancée. And he felt 'weary and empty at praying, at thinking, at making.'

"But even as he felt that way, Dietrich was seen by others as a man stepping from his 'cell's confinement, calmly, cheerfully, firmly, like a squire from his country home;' as a man who spoke to his captors 'freely and friendly and clearly' as though the guards were his 'to command;' as a man who bore 'the days of misfortune equably, smilingly, proudly, as one accustomed to win.'

"I wept as I listened to My suffering child agonize over the same questions you're now asking: 'Who am I? This or the other? Am I one person today and tomorrow another? Am I both at once? A hypocrite before others and before myself a contemptibly woebegone weakling?'

"But I listened with joy as My Spirit led Dietrich through the narrowness of confusion into the open country of certainty. He reached deep into Dietrich's heart as He is now reaching deep into yours. Under His influence, Dietrich wrote: 'Who am I? They mock me, these lonely questions of mine. Whoever I am, thou knowest, O God, I am Thine.'

"This is what I want you to hear as you read My sixty-second love letter:

You are Mine. The life that defines My Son now defines you. You are alive *in* Me. You are alive *to* Me. You are alive *with* Me. Inexpressible joy is yours for the asking . . . on My Spirit's time-table."

"Father, I tasted that joy the last two mornings in my car. But it was only a taste. Why are moments like that so elusive, so fleeting?"

"Never deny My Spirit's sovereignty. The divine wind of joy blows as He chooses. And never deny your responsibility. You *exist* in My light. You don't always *walk* in My light. To walk in My light requires that you pay more attention to your failure to love than to the pain you feel when others fail to love you. When the light of how My Son and I relate in perfect love reveals the dark stains in how you relate, confess your failure to Me, immediately. Agree with Me that how you're relating is awful, vile, despicable; that you hate it as I do. When you confess your sins, I will not only forgive the relational failures you see, but I will also clean up everything you have yet to see that keeps you feeling at a distance from Me [1 John 1:5–9]. If you understand relational sin, confession will become a daily exercise.

"The dance of love, the life of joy that My Son and My Spirit celebrate with Me has appeared to you. The way We love has been made visible in My Son. He became human to reveal what divine life looks like in a created being. And He died to forgive you for how far short you fall of perfect love and to share the life of perfect love with you. When He returned to Me, He sent Our Spirit to pour that life into you. *And that has happened* [1 John 1:1–4; 2:20, 27]. The tastes of Our love come as My Son decides. The power to love is always in you."

"Father, the way I relate still falls so far short of the way You relate. And yet I believe I have Your Son's life in me. It gets discouraging."

"Discouragement, when it drives you to Me in broken confession rather than away from Me in wounded pride, brings the realism of humility. You are never without sin. Whether you recognize it or not, there is never a moment when you relate as perfectly as My Son. One day you will. Until then, humility will free you to live in awe of My endless supply of grace. And the worship that awe inspires will release more of My Son's life to flow out of you into others, even into those who have hurt you though never as badly as you have hurt Me [1 John 1:10; 2:1–12].

"You are alive *in* Me, as a fully forgiven and fully loved *child* who can rest in his Father's arms. You are alive *to* Me, as a mature person, a wise *father* who knows who I am as an eternally happy community of Three Persons whose love has devised a foolproof plan to bring you to Our party. And you are alive *with* Me, as a *young man* who is loved enough and wise enough and, therefore, strong enough to overcome the evil one, to trust Me by never—at least, not for long— leaving the narrow road to life no matter how narrow it becomes [1 John 2:12–14].

"But you must be on your guard. There are teachers in the church today who resist the truth that the power to love comes only through My crucified Son [1 John 2:18–19; 4:1–6]. They focus more on what I have called you to do than on who I have created you to be and who you now are because of My Son. In John's day, a teacher named Cerinthus, whom John would have nothing to do with, taught wicked nonsense, that the divine Christ came on the human Jesus at His baptism but left Him when He went to the cross. The effect of such teaching is to deny that My divine life is now in you, that you are forgiven for loving poorly, and are now empowered to love well. The death of a mere man could never accomplish what I accomplished through the death of My fully divine and fully human Son.

"Reject such lies. Celebrate the cross. Know that My seed, My relational energy, is now in you. You're still quite capable of living like the devil. Adam's seed is still in you, the self-centered fleshly energy that continues to argue that living for your own well-being at the expense of others is justified and sometimes necessary.

"But you are *not* the devil's child. You are *not* a citizen of this world. You are *not* a slave to your flesh. *You are Mine!* You are loved as a child. You are wise as a father. You are strong as a youth."

"Father, what happened in the car these past two mornings? Did Your Spirit fall on me? Was I freshly baptized with Your Spirit?"

"My Spirit longs to drench you with the water of life, to fill you with gladness even when the narrowness of the narrow road is acutely felt. I want you to know truth with doctrinal accuracy but also, as My Puritan children put it, with *experimental* passion.

"Listen to John Owen, a brilliant thinker with a passionate heart, as he speaks of the joy you experienced those two mornings in your car: 'Of this joy there is no account to be given but that the Spirit worketh it when and how He will.' He had divine joy in mind, the kind with which My Spirit 'infuseth the soul, prevailing against all fears and sorrows, filling it with gladness . . . and sometimes with unspeakable raptures.'"

"Father, something important *is* happening. It's not that I felt joy. And it has nothing to do with whether I'm healthy or sick. I'm seeing more clearly than ever that there is a well that doesn't leak, that Your Spirit, the dance of perfect love, is in me. I can have fellowship with You. I can join the eternal dance, right now, no matter what happens. *I am Yours!* Therefore, I can love."

"You may lose sight of what you're now seeing. I don't want that to happen. I wrote My next letter to help you stay on the narrow road when it gets especially narrow and you feel empty and scared. Immerse yourself in truth. Remain open to the experimental knowledge of truth. You are alive in ways you have yet to realize. Keep reading."

Love Letter Sixty-Three: 2 John

WATCH OUT! THE DEEPEST TRUTH
IS THE MOST EASILY MISSED

*W*e're nearing the end of this round of conversations through My sixty-six love letters. You've learned a great deal. But you're in great danger. Hear My message in this letter:

Watch out that you do not lose what you have worked for, but that you may be rewarded fully. (v. 8)"

"Father, does what You're saying now have something to do with how alive and energized I felt when Your Spirit visited me those two mornings in my car? In all that I'm facing right now (and it could be rough), I sensed so clearly that something truly important was happening. Father, I felt Your presence. It was wonderful. *Important* doesn't adequately describe the experience.

"In those moments, I knew that I could remain faithful to You, no matter what life throws at me, as long as I feel Your presence with me."

"Will you remain faithful to Me when I withdraw My sense of presence from you? Will you remain fully faithful when the feeling of My Presence is fully absent? My Son did. Or do you assume that after all your years of faithful service to Me that it's now time for My Spirit to make your obedience easy? Do you think that from now on walking in truth will mean to be carried along on the narrow road with all opposition swept away by the excitement of walking with Me?"

"Your words expose me. I guess my spirit of entitlement is still alive. Yes, I have been thinking a deeper and more continuous level of spiritual passion is about due."

"It was no accident that yesterday your good friend sent you that quote from C. S. Lewis. You were struggling to hear Me speaking in 2 John. Deep truth is easily missed. Lewis was asking an important question that you were unwittingly asking, and he grasped the deep and difficult answer. Read his words again:

Does God then just forsake those who serve Him best? Well, He who served Him best of all said, near His tortured death, "Why hast Thou forsaken Me?"

When God becomes man, that Man, of all others, is least comforted by God, at His greatest need. There is a mystery here which, even if I had the power, I might not have the courage to explore. Meanwhile, little people like you and me, if our prayers are sometimes granted, beyond all hope and probability, had better not draw hasty conclusions to our own advantage. If we were stronger, we might be less tenderly treated. If we were braver, we might be sent, with far less help, to defend more desperate outposts in the great battle."

"Father, that's what I have done. I asked to feel Your presence more power-fully, and when You answered that prayer, I quickly assumed, to my own advantage, that finally from then on I'd skip happily and lightly with You on my way to the finish line.

"I think perhaps I'm understanding why that assumption came so eas-ily, so readily to mind. I'm tired of seeing myself as perpetually troubled. I'm sick of being so easily plunged into morbid apathy, so often consumed by cynical discouragement, so predictably feeling weary and empty when I most long for energy and fiery motivation. I see others, especially spiritual leaders whom I respect, who come across as so much more together than me, who appear to be fighting fewer battles than I do. I wanted to assume that now it was my turn to consistently feel spiritually alive, to feel full of passion and excitedly aware of Your presence. I was hoping Your Spirit would make all that happen."

"If He did, your ministry would suffer. You would have less to say to My followers, and there are many, who wonder why they feel so alone and distant from Me after praying so hard to feel otherwise. And you would have less power to speak into the hidden struggles of others, struggles that sometimes rage beneath the facade of togetherness and cheerful contentment that you often mistake for maturity.

"In this second letter through John, I tell you that My truth lives in you. What you *know* to be true (My focus in 1 John) is *alive* in you (My focus in 2 John), not always as passionate excitement but always as a strong and trustworthy anchor. When the storm rages, you can remain faithful, not thrown off course, even when you feel cold and wet and blown about by relentless winds. Anchoring truth, not giddy excitement, has the power to keep you others-centered when your own pain screams for relief as it kept My Son, fully devoted to My plan while He hung on the cross though He was fully in pain, aware only of My absence. John was speaking for Me when he said it gave him great joy to find some of My children walking in truth [v. 4]. You are among their number."

"Father, I need to know: *what truth are You talking about?*"

"Read 1 John 4:2."

"You say there that 'Every spirit that acknowledges that Jesus Christ has come in the flesh is from God.'"

"Now read 2 John 7."

"Father, aren't You making the same point twice in both verses? In 2 John 7, You're telling me to watch out for teachers who don't acknowledge 'Jesus Christ as coming in the flesh.' You're wanting me to trust only those teachers who make a big point out of the incarnation, that Your divine Son became fully human. And You're telling me that twice."

"You haven't noticed the change in verb tense. In 1 John I insist on the truth that My fully divine Son *came* into your world as fully man. In 2 John I say that as a fully divine, fully human person He *comes*. The truth of the incarnation, deity in humanity, is both an historical event (past tense) and a timeless reality (present tense). That truth is easily missed."

"I don't think I'm getting it. Why is all this so important?"

"After years of brilliant observation, Albert Einstein concluded, 'There does in fact, appear to be a plan.' There is. But until you know that the plan is Mine and until you realize that My plan centers on My Son, by My Spirit continuously pouring into you the kind of life He lived as a human being, you're missing deep truth. Your understanding of what is truly important is wrong. Your vision of what I'm doing is blurred. Your hope for what is possible now in this life is off base and limited.

"It isn't only that My Son *came*, that He was born in a stable as a helpless squealing infant. It's also that He *comes*. With the life that He lived for thirty-three years, *He comes into you today*. Think about that life: obscure for thirty years; popular for a short time; then rejected, hated by enemies, and surrounded by friends who deserted Him at His point of greatest need; tortured to death; and alone when He most yearned to feel My Presence. It's time to rethink what it means to be spiritually formed, to live the life My Son lived. The truth of My story and the words of My love were alive in Him, not always as happy emotions but always as anchoring reality. He walked in truth. I call you to follow His lead."

"Father, I recently read something M. Scott Peck wrote: 'if the Gospel writers had been into PR . . . , they would have created the kind of Jesus three quarters of Christians still seem to be trying to create . . . portrayed with a sweet smile on his face, patting little children on the head, just strolling the earth with this unflappable, unshakable equanimity . . . But the Jesus of the Gospels . . . did not have much "peace of mind" as we ordinarily think of peace of mind in the world's terms, and insofar as we can be his followers, perhaps we won't either.' Is Peck right?"

"Deceivers deny it. Have nothing to do with purveyors of trouble-free Christianity, with teachers who claim to know the spiritual secret—whether through prayer or other means—of turning every misery into joy and every trial into blessing. For now, My plan is not to remove trouble; it is to sustain you through trouble, just as My Spirit sustained My Son in faithfulness through all kinds of difficulties. Never support in any way the message of people who believe they have advanced beyond the teaching of Christ [vv. 9–11], who invite you to live an easier life than My Son lived.

"Henri Nouwen didn't get everything right (no one does), but personal integrity required him to confess that 'life is a short time . . . in which sadness and joy kiss each other at every moment . . . Behind every smile, there is a tear. In every embrace, there is loneliness. In every friendship, distance.'"

"Father, what then am I to do when I feel terrible, when emptiness fills me, when loneliness suffocates my hope, when severe fatigue immobilizes both my body and mind?"

"Gaze on My incarnate Son. Watch Him live. Watch Him die. Watch Him live again. You endure nothing that He didn't endure. He remained faithful to My truth that is alive in you. Kierkegaard rightly said, 'This is the road we all have to travel . . . over the bridge of sighs to eternity.' My Son walked the narrow road over that bridge. You can too.

"Celebrate My Son's death and resurrection as the means through which My Spirit pours His life into you. You can now love like Him while you cross the bridge of sighs. Walk in the truth of My Son's difficult but purposeful and joyfully loving life, a life made available to you through His tortured death. And remember this: the joy and peace available to you in this world only comes when you live for the joy and peace of others and in so doing bring glory to Me as you advance My plan. My command (and it's nothing new) is that you *walk in love* through all life's troubles as My very human Son did with the same resources that are now available to you [vv. 4–6]."

"Father, I'm hearing echoes of what You're saying in Martin Luther's words about Your Son: 'He ate, drank, slept, walked; was weary, sorrowful, rejoicing; he wept and he laughed; he knew hunger and thirst and sweat; he talked, he toiled, he prayed . . . so that there was no difference between *him* and other men, save only this, that he was God, and had no sin.'

"I need to reflect more on what Luther was talking about and to more fully grasp Emil Brunner's wisdom, that 'The Son of God in whom we are able to believe must be such a One that it is possible to mistake him for an ordinary man.'"

"Remember My message to you in this letter: *Watch out!* The deep truth that God became a man, a real Man, is easily missed. And the deep truth that you can remain faithful to Me as He did—through all the disappointments, heartaches, and betrayals of life—even without an exhilarating sense of My Presence, is difficult to embrace.

"But the truth is true. He endured the wilderness before He enjoyed the Promised Land. So must you. There is no other route to joy. Deceivers deliver an appealing message, that I provide a way to walk around the wilderness, not through it. I don't. My Spirit is forming you to live like My Son, to walk in truth, to dance in love, to abide in Me, whether you feel My Presence or not, whether you live in hardship or blessing."

"Perhaps now, Father, I can be less frustrated by how troubled and empty I so often feel. Maybe now I can dance a little better even when I'm weary."

"To dance means to love. To love in this world means to feel pain and lament failure, to enjoy blessings and celebrate My felt or unfelt presence, but to never let the way you feel determine the way you relate. When you obsess over the way you feel, you are trying to find yourself; you are not pouring life into another. And, as My Son made clear, that is the path to death. An ego trip is a trip to nowhere.

"And yet even church leaders sometimes miss the deep truth of living the difficult life My Son lived, insisting instead on feeling what they want to feel, celebrating their value and demanding others do the same. Don't miss deep truth. Diotrephes did. I talk about him in My next letter. But I talk more about Gaius. He walked in truth even when it was difficult. Keep reading. Three more letters to go."

Love Letter Sixty-Four:
3 John

RELEASE LOVE BEFORE YOU JUDGE SIN IN ANOTHER

"Father, I think I get the story You tell in this next letter. But I don't get the point."

"Think of someone whose arrogant spirit offends you, someone who irritates you with how insensitive and demanding he or she can be."

"Just one?"

"Someone who more than others gets under your skin. Then tell Me what goes on inside you when that person comes to mind."

"Okay, I'm thinking of someone who is completely unwilling to face how he comes across, a man who is smugly sure of himself, never wrong; really nice until you get in the way of what he wants. I either want to avoid him entirely or find some way to let him know how self-righteous he is. I guess he's a Christian—I have no right to judge—but I see little humility or other-centeredness in how he relates. He sometimes comes across as caring and is full of God-talk, but bottom line is: he wants what he wants."

"You say you have no right to judge, but you do feel above him. You enjoy rehearsing his faults in your mind and sharing them with others who feel as you do about him. You judge him for wrongs that you do not see in yourself. And you measure him by a moral code you assume comes from Me.

"It's tragic to hate in My name, to criticize another, thinking you're loving Me by representing My justice. The great tragedy is not that someday you will die. The great tragedy is that you may die before you learn to really love. Think about the person you delight to judge, then listen to My message to you in this sixty-fourth love letter:

When you see something in another worthy of criticism, before you think further about that person's faults, resolve that your life will become an increasingly visible and humble demonstration of love."

"Father, the words of a Puritan prayer express what I'm aware of right now: 'It is a good day when Thou givest me a glimpse of myself.' Something good is stirring in my brokenness; I think it's the desire to love that You've put in me. But I'm still not hearing how You're saying that in 3 John."

"As long as you hold on to a superior, critical spirit, you will not hear My voice. The unknown Malcolm Hein put it well: 'There is little room for wisdom when one is full of judgment.' The writer Leo Tolstoy learned a lesson you are slowly learning: 'All, everything that I understand, I understand only because I love.' What you hear without loving is not worth hearing. Repent and listen.

"My church is made up of flawed people. You are one of them. In My sixty-fourth letter, through John I write to Gaius, a flawed but good man in a church that suffered under the influence of Diotrephes, a flawed and ungodly elder. Diotrephes would have gotten under your skin if you had been involved in his church. You've been studying this letter for some time now. Tell Me what you have understood."

"More facts than truth, I think. I see four people in this letter: John the apostle, who knew he was loved by Your Son; a good man named Gaius, to whom John was writing; Demetrius, a traveling teacher well thought of by John; and a local church elder named Diotrephes, a man caught up in himself, like the guy I was just thinking of. I've been trying to get inside the heads and hearts of these four men, hoping I might hear what You're saying to me through their stories."

"Tell Me what you've learned."

"Well, John was an old man obsessed with Your Son. In his gospel, John refers to Him as 'Jesus' 237 times. Matthew used that name only 150 times, Luke 89, and Mark 81. Even Paul in all his letters used the name 'Jesus' only 213 times. Seeing that added to my impression that John couldn't bear people thinking of Your incarnate Son as either less than God or less than man and, therefore, less than the point of everything.

"And, Father, it occurred to me that the same thing is happening in church circles today. Too many of Your followers see Your Son as pleasantly friendly rather than unapproachably holy, *as less than fully divine.* Others see Him as a Superman from Krypton who lived above the struggles and heartaches and frustrations of real people, *as less than fully human.*

"I like the way Dorothy Sayers put it: 'The people who hanged Christ never, to do them justice, accused him of being a bore—on the contrary, they thought him too dynamic to be safe. It has been left for later generations to muffle up the shattering personality and surround him with an atmosphere of tedium. We have very efficiently pared the claws of the Lion of Judah, certified him "meek and mild" and recommended him as a fitting pet for pale curates and pious old ladies.'

"Father, I'm more clearly seeing John as a man in utter awe of Your holy Son and, at the same time, overcome by the staggering privilege of profound intimacy with Someone so unapproachably perfect and yet so approachably full of welcoming love. John was unable to keep quiet about the new way to live made possible through Your fully divine and fully human Son. I want to share that inability."

"No degree of fellowship with Me enjoyed by My most devoted follower is beyond your reach. Between Me, My Son, and My Spirit, nothing good is impossible. One mark of real fellowship with Us is the power to love the person in your life whom you feel most justified in judging and to keep loving others, whether your Diotrephes changes or not. Don't aim too low in your journey toward spiritual formation. Never sell short what We are capable of doing in your life."

"Father, I gather You were asking Gaius to move further into the new way to live by releasing love into others rather than getting worked up over Diotrephes. From what You say about Gaius, I assume he was already hospitable, eager to welcome traveling teachers into his home, to spare them the ordeal of bunking down in one of the filthy inns that passed for hotels in the first century.

"You wanted Gaius to show hospitality to Demetrius, a man who gave up income to travel around to various churches encouraging Your people in Your truth. But doing so was going to be a bit of a challenge because John had already directly asked the same of the church, and Diotrephes had ignored the request and bad-mouthed the apostle. So for Gaius to welcome Demetrius would be a direct challenge to the authority of Diotrephes and might lead to that tyrant throwing Gaius out of the church. Do I have all that right?"

"You do. You've done your homework. Now hear what I'm saying to you. If My life is in you, and it is, you are capable of loving well even when the cost is great. Don't measure the risk. Instead, celebrate the privilege. Reveal My character to a watching world by releasing My love from your truth-filled heart in the presence of people who release the devil's hate from their lie-filled hearts and think they're serving My cause."

"Father, was Diotrephes a Christian?"

"Even those whom I lift high into heavenly places are capable of sinking low into devilish depths. You sink with them when you presume to stand above them in judgment. Hear what I'm saying to you through the lives of those four men:

❈ *Be like John.* Walk in the truth—the truth that My Son gives you His life so you can live a new way, a way that includes loving well when others don't.

❀ *Be like Gaius.* Concern yourself more with the well-being of others than your own, even when giving up self-protection entails imminent risk.

❀ *Be like Demetrius.* Continue teaching truth wherever you have opportunity. Don't be muffled by opposition.

❀ *Don't be like Diotrephes.* Only My Son belongs in first place. Life does not come by filling yourself. True life, what you most desire, comes when you empty yourself of pride. My Spirit loves to fill the empty soul with divine life."

"Father, I come away from this conversation with two thoughts ringing in my mind. One, it's hard to stop judging others because it's so reliably and immediately pleasurable. Two, You're calling me (and You've equipped me) not only to love others at any cost to myself but also to recognize and resist any influence or teaching that would weaken my vision of what's possible, my understanding of the radical kind of love that is in Your Son and is now in me, pressing for release."

"In My next letter, I spare no words in letting you see *both* the vileness of what you are up against and vulnerable to as you seek to live the new way of self-renouncing love *and* the seriousness of resisting My call to love and instead looking out for yourself. But don't be afraid. I am for you. My Son is with you. My Spirit is in you. My plan is on course. I always have people, though only a few, who live to display My love. Always remember: With Me, a few is an army. Victory is certain. Keep reading."

Love Letter Sixty-Five: Jude

KEEP YOURSELF IN MY LOVE AS YOU WAIT FOR MY PARTY

*F*ather, once again (will it never end?), You confuse me. In verse twenty-one of Your next-to-last love letter, You tell me to keep myself in Your love. Three verses later, You're telling me that it's You who keeps me from falling. Father, who does the keeping, me or You? And if it's a joint venture, who does what? What's my part and what's Yours?

"I'm asking these questions with some urgency. A mildly offensive comment, spoken yesterday by someone who loves me as few ever have, undid me. The comment wasn't all that bad, and I knew right then that it was more momentarily insensitive than mean-spirited. I wanted to offer instant forgiveness, to perhaps acknowledge that the comment did hurt but then to smile and speak warmly into the offender's beautiful heart with tenderness and love.

"But rather than my reaching into the other's beautiful heart, the painful words reached deeply into the ugliness lying deep in my not-so-beautiful heart. I was incensed. I felt small, unappreciated, not believed in, and severely judged. Talk about an overreaction. For the rest of the day, I simmered, I nursed my wound, I experienced the hurt, I sulked, I forced out a few acts of kindness, and I gave myself over to mindless television. Worse, I became my own psychologist. I tried to remember how my parents may have failed me so it could explain (and excuse?) why I'm still so sensitive to occasional slights. *If I can explain a problem, I can probably fix it.* That's how I sometimes think.

"Pathetic, isn't it? After sixty-four incredible conversations with You, after You've so clearly and patiently exposed my real problem of trying to find my life through others and so dramatically unveiled the real solution of Your love that actually found a way to both forgive me and put Your Son's life in me, I feel disgusted with myself. My self-loathing nearly immobilized me for an entire day.

"Father, I wanted to be able to easily forgive and, as You put it, to keep myself in Your love. But I didn't. I *couldn't*.

"I know I'm badly off base, but here's what I was thinking: Somehow You didn't do Your job. You didn't keep me from falling. And, Father, I fell hard, down deep into relational sin. I was useful to no one and useless to You. More than anything else, I hate grieving You and burdening others with my immaturity. What does it mean for me to keep myself in Your love, and exactly how do You keep me from falling?"

"Why do you suppose I led Jude to put aside his plan to write a review of the love story I'm telling and instead urge you to vigorously—with all the energy of a marathon runner, straining toward the finish line—stay committed to the story I've once for all entrusted to My people [v. 3]?"

"I don't know."

"Why do you think that through Jude I'm now denouncing the same perversions of My story that I already denounced through Peter [2 Peter 2] in similarly scorching language?"

"Father, I don't know. I wish I did."

"Why do you imagine I began My sixty-fifth letter by reminding you, yet again, that you're *called* to My party, *loved* as I love My Son, and *kept* as an engaged woman is kept by love for her wedding night? And why do you guess I end this letter with an invitation to dream of the day when you will stand, not shrink, in the presence of My glory and feel only joy, no shame, as you prepare to kick up your heels, to dance with the Star forever and with all His little stars?"

"Father, *I don't know.* But I'm listening."

"Then hear this:

My power is sufficient to keep you from falling off the narrow road. But on that road you will feel, more acutely sometimes than others, the unbearable ache of repeated failure to love, of always falling short of My glory. That ache either will be transformed by My Spirit into a consuming awareness of grace and into the joys of passionate hope, or it will seduce you into accepting a revised version of My story that promises to provide now the relief I promise later.

"Don't be surprised by your failure. Be surprised, staggered by My response. Only in worship will you keep yourself in My love. Only in brokenness will you know My power to keep you from falling, from sliding off the narrow road into the ditch that Satan disguises as the broad road, a good one, to all the satisfaction you want now. As you feel the unbearable ache of failing and being failed, I am able—if in brokenness you worship—to keep you persevering on the only road that will bring you into My Presence, full of joy and ready to dance."

"So You aren't irritated when I screw up like I did yesterday?"

"Your screw-ups provoke Me to again display My amazing grace, which brings Me great joy. But no, I don't want you to sin. I hate sin. I never excuse it. I only forgive it. But your failure provides you the opportunity to, once again, look bad in the presence of love, to celebrate the love you taste from others but fully enjoy only from Me. That's the gospel. That's My story. Contend for it with all your might [v. 3]. Don't let the ache you feel as you follow Me turn into faith-destroying frustration with yourself or with Me. If that happens, you will lose confidence in the story I am telling and be drawn into a disastrous but cleverly disguised and more immediately appealing version."

"What do You mean?"

"Everyone wants to feel good quickly. In this letter, I give examples of people who let that desire push them into the ditch of destruction that false teachers advertise as the road to life.

- ❀ Israel saw My power. I rescued my people from Egypt as I rescued you from Satan's kingdom. When hardships plagued their journey to promised joy, as they will yours, they lost confidence in Me and interest in My plan. They stopped believing. *They refused to wait* [v. 5].
- ❀ Some of My angels glimpsed pleasures enjoyed by others, by humans, that I had not made available to them. They cut their ties to Me to get what they wanted. What they got was a moment of pleasure and an eternity of misery. Had they stayed faithful to Me, their capacity for joy would have been filled to the brim in the day when I fully reveal My glory in the universe. *They refused to wait* [v. 6].
- ❀ The citizens of Sodom and Gomorrah, experiencing human desires that they could not satisfy without Me, abandoned themselves to corrupt desires that they could satisfy without Me, immediately and with momentarily consuming intensity. Had they turned to Me in believing trust, I would have kept them in self-control that would have brought them into the joy I created them to experience. But *they refused to wait* [v. 7].

"You must wait. That's My plan. But when the ache of living in this world seems unbearable, you will be attracted to the *way of Cain* [v. 11]. In a book called the Targum, My Jewish people depicted Cain as saying, 'There is neither judgment or judge; there is no other world.' There will be seasons when you will feel a nearly irresistible pull to find whatever satisfaction this world can provide, whether in church or in your culture. Cain was not surprised by My grace because he recognized only his disappointment, not his sin. He was indignant that life in this world could be so hard and felt justified in doing whatever made it easier. Much of what passes for My way is the way of Cain. Be on your guard.

"That same indignation, the arrogant notion that you deserve to feel better now, makes you vulnerable to the *error of Balaam* [v. 11]. Balaam not only was drawn more to money for himself than to ministry for Me [Numbers 22–24] but also found satisfaction (which he proudly demanded as his right) in leading others into the temporary but intense pleasures of sin [Numbers 31:8, 16]. Perverse pleasure loves company. Sinning together numbs the conscience. But the misery that follows can find no company. There is no fellowship in hell.

"And when following Me leaves you feeling less important than you want, you will be tempted to join the *rebellion of Korah* [v. 11]. His privileged place as a Levite wasn't enough for him. He rebelled against Moses, who held the position Korah craved, and he did so in the hope of replacing Moses [Numbers 16]. When your lust for significance erupts into discontent and into covetous rebellion against what you perceive as My low calling, remember Jeremiah's apt words to his insecure secretary, Baruch, 'Should you seek great things for yourself? Seek them not' (Jeremiah 45:5).

"False teachers offer short-term pleasure and long-term loss [vv. 12–15]. Like My children in the wilderness, they live with an undercurrent of constant complaint. They find fault with everything. Theophrastus, an ancient student of Greek character, captured the attitude of fault-finders in these words: 'When his mistress kisses him he says: "I wonder whether you kiss me so warmly from your heart." When he finds a purse in the street, it is: "Ah, but I never found a treasure."'

"Hidden beneath the happy smiles of blessings-now preachers is a spirit of discontent smothered by confidence in their false message (or by the money and power and acclaim it brings), a grumbling that though smothered drives their terrible theology. They bury their ache beneath their lies.

"I want you to feel your ache but to focus on My *call*, My *love*, and My *power* to *keep* you on the narrow road to My party. You're invited to My party because I love you, and I mean to get you there. Trust Me and wait. That's the message that began this letter.

"I end My letter through Jude by urging you to build yourself up in your holy faith and to pray in My Holy Spirit [v. 20]. Rehearse all that you know of My story, continually; and always enter more deeply into its plot by reviewing these conversations. And ask My Spirit to meet you where you are, whether nursing a grudge over an offensive comment or singing a hymn with joyful passion, and to do in you and through you what He most longs to do. You may not feel Him working or experience My Presence, but He is always providing the power to keep you walking this narrow road, and when you slip off, to get back on.

"No matter how badly you fail or are failed, remember, you are *called*, *loved*, and *kept*. And by rehearsing the story I am telling through My Son and by praying in My Spirit, you will keep yourself in My love. You will press on through the wilderness with the Promised Land in sight. You will enjoy whatever pleasures I provide now, knowing the pleasures you most desire will be available soon. And you will live fully in the place I assign you, knowing that what might appear to be a more significant place promises only illusory joy.

"Wait for My story's unimaginable ending. See it unfolding now. If you wait, you will not walk in the way of Cain; you will not make Balaam's error; you will not join Korah's rebellion. Instead, without grumbling or fault-finding, you will 'wait for the mercy' of My Son, your 'Lord Jesus Christ to bring you to eternal life' (v. 21), to the dance of love.

"And if you wait, if you resist the urge to numb the ache in your heart and let My Spirit transform your ache into the joy of hope, then you will never again glibly repeat the doxology that completes My sixty-fifth letter: 'To him who is able to keep you from falling and to present you before his glorious presence without fault and with great joy. To the only God our Savior be glory, majesty, power and authority, through Jesus Christ our Lord, before all ages, now and forever. Amen' (vv. 24–25)."

"Father, I want to sing that song with joy, from the center of my aching but hopeful heart."

"Get ready. I am about to unveil My Son as you've never seen Him before. He came. He's coming. And He'll come. Keep reading, one more letter."

PART SEVEN

The Promise Is Kept: Happiness Forever: Revelation

*T*he cartoon shows Agnes the dreamer telling her friend, "Tomorrow is a new day that brings the hope of prosperity and possible glee." Her dour friend responds, "It's not likely, though." And Agnes, speaking for much of Western culture and too much of today's church, indignantly declares, "If you realists would lighten up, existence would be a lot more fun."

Suggestion: if you insist on lightening up God's story, don't read Revelation. God is the ultimate realist. He *is* reality. In Him, brutal realism and breathtaking romance are not incompatible. They actually work together.

The love stories we're used to, the ones we enjoy watching on-screen and reading in novels, follow a moving but still lightened-up pattern: connection, estrangement, reconciliation; and sometimes the reconciliation seems rich and real. Sometimes it is. And our hearts are touched.

God's story, the truest love story ever told, is different, infinitely better, though it may not seem so at first. It begins as the others, with passionate connection. When Adam met Eve, the fire of love burned right away. And for a time, they got along well with God and each other. Then estrangement set in. But their estrangement was not caused by misunderstanding or miscommunication or emotional wounds from childhood or easily remedied character flaws. The root problem was ugly, inexcusable self-centeredness, a refusal to believe God and a resolve, on their own terms, to look after their own well-being as their highest ethic.

It followed that judgment, not therapy, was needed to effect deep and lasting reconciliation; not *arbitrary* judgment where an angry God thinks up the worst punishment possible but *inevitable* judgment, the unavoidable consequence of living selfishly: loneliness. Dorothy Sayers said it well: "If you want your own way, God will let you have it. Hell is the enjoyment of your own way forever." That's judgment. Cut yourself, and you bleed. Live selfishly, and relationships deteriorate. You end up alone, estranged from everyone, including yourself.

More sin—laziness, bickering, sarcasm, using sex for no more than personal pleasure—follows. The fruit of the flesh grows abundantly on the tree of the lonely, entitled self.

So God's story goes something like this: *connection, wickedness, estrangement, judgment, reconciliation.* The reconciliation is not based on sentiment or resolve, neither heart-tugging emotions nor determined efforts to get along. The reconciliation God brings about depends on purifying judgment that kills evil and enlivens the goodness of genuine other-centered self-abandoning love.

Realism, however, isn't immediately appealing. So with Agnes we say, if realists, God included, would just lighten up and talk less about judgment and more about warmth and kindness and wounds and healing and better communication and improved relational skills and real commitment, our Christian existence would be a lot more fun. And it would be, maybe for a long time. But reconciliation without purifying judgment, without pride-shattering brokenness and mind-altering repentance never results in secure intimacy. There's no dancing, at least not the kind that goes on in the Trinity, not the kind that directs other people to the party.

But realism is tough. It requires us to admit that God's story isn't always fun, and for now, it wasn't meant to be, not until the next life. His sixty-sixth love letter makes that clear, so clear that it sometimes takes a lot of faith to keep believing that the story we've signed up to tell is a terrific love story with a really happy ending.

Sometimes our faith takes a beating. It's then we're most tempted to edit God's story, to redline the judgment parts. We'd like to lighten it up a bit, make it more pleasant, delete some hassles and add better promises of more blessings. We want God's story to spell out effective strategies (believing prayer? daily obedience?) for making life good. And when things do get rough, we'd like God-honoring avenues (spiritual disciplines? spiritual direction?) that reliably produce rich experiences of God's presence, at least until our effective strategies kick in and things improve, allowing us then to dance better and enjoy life more.

Here's my point. If we reject realism, if we downplay or ignore the inexcusable and pervasive selfishness in us that makes divine judgment a pivotal chapter in God's love story, we're not going to like His sixty-sixth love letter. It just won't make sense. John's bizarre and bloody visions—especially the ones that graphically depict the wrath of the Lamb—which came to John while he was jailed on an island prison called Patmos, will seem like overkill, unnecessary to the goal of good relationships and a pleasant life and a lot of fun. Let's just love and get on with life. What's the problem? Why all this focus on judgment?

What John saw on Patmos was the unfolding of God's story, the unveiling of God's Son as He is, not as we might wish He were. John's visions reveal that what is happening as God's way of doing things is breaking into our way of doing things. The whole story was (figuratively) written on a scroll, an old-fashioned book-like document that told God's plan for reconciliation, His way of making everything new (Revelation 21:5). The sealed scroll, the unopened book, records all that's going on now in the middle of all the good and bad of life. It tells the story of how God is releasing us to love, how He's arranging for thorough reconciliation.

Hundreds of years earlier, Daniel saw a similar scroll, a preview of what God showed John. That scroll told the story of a coming time of unbearable distress (Daniel 12:2), *through* which, not *from* which, God would deliver His people. There was no promise of "prosperity and possible glee," not for this world. Realism isn't always fun.

In Daniel 12, I heard the strange promise that the "power of the holy people" would be broken (v. 7). I saw in that promise that any claim by God-followers to protection from trouble in this world would be exposed as groundless, but that through tough times, which produced humbling brokenness, His people would be "purified, made spotless and refined" (v. 10). Judgment, then reconciliation.

I heard, too, that people who God calls "wicked" would discount real-ism and hang on to false optimism, continuing on their merry way of making life work and perhaps even feeling spiritually alive but with no understanding of how God is telling His love story. Eventually, we're told the wicked will wake up to "shame and everlasting contempt" (v. 2).

When Daniel heard all this, he couldn't make sense of it. "I heard, but I did not understand" (v. 8). God's response seems terse: *Go your way, Daniel; this conversation is over. I told you before to close up and seal the words of this scroll until the time of the end. I know you don't understand all that I'm revealing to you. It isn't time yet. For now, leave the scroll unopened. The words are sealed until the time of the end* (vv. 4, 9).

Here's the big news: the time of the end is now! It began when Jesus came. Listen to New Testament writers. Paul: "The night is nearly over; the day is almost here" (Romans 13:12). Peter: "The end of all things is near" (1 Peter 4:7). John, in an earlier letter before he wrote Revelation: "This is the last hour" (1 John 2:18). And listen to Jesus Himself: "The time has come" (Mark 1:15).

Now here's the point: it's time to open the scroll, not just to hear about God's plan but to watch it unfold, to see it happening. And that's what the sixty-sixth love letter is all about. In visions, it's the unveiling of what God is doing right now through His Son. More to the point, it's the unveiling, the apocalypse, the revelation, the revealing of Jesus Christ, of who He is and what He's up to.

In God's last love letter to us, He opens the door into heaven and lets us see the story He's telling right now, in each of us and around us and through-out the entire world, in America, China, Iraq, New Zealand, France, everywhere. He lets us see what we cannot see with our natural eyes. In dis-turbing images and graphic pictures, we're given a symbol-laced glimpse into the cosmic love story of *connection* disrupted by *wickedness* followed by *estrangement* that requires *judgment* before *reconciliation* is possible. It's realism, raw and true.

But is it gospel? Is it good news? It certainly isn't fun. As we read Revelation, we must remain clear on one thing: *the party is already underway.* Followers of the Lamb can dance now. We can live like Jesus now, in this world as it is and in our relationships as they are, by embracing suffering without revenge or complaint as we tell God's story, by loving others whether they return our love or not.

Dancing like Jesus is not always fun. Too many dance partners step on our toes. Sometimes, because of our own clumsiness, we twist our emotional ankle or break a relational leg. And then we want so badly to get off the dance floor, maybe into shopping, sports, sex, or sleep. The new way to live is radical, and it's difficult. The old way—look out for yourself, love only when it feels good—is easier, more fun.

And we wonder, are the good guys winning? Is goodness defeating badness? It doesn't look like it, not in this greed-driven world. Does dancing with Jesus make a difference? Is it even possible? Will life ever work the way it should?

In the late 1800s, a Bible student named James Denney wrote some uncommonly perceptive words that have ongoing relevance. They're helping prepare me to read the sixty-sixth letter. The writing is old-fashioned, but the message is current:

> The question is sometimes asked whether the world gets better or worse as it grows older, and optimists and pessimists take opposite sides on it. Both . . . are wrong. It does not get better only, nor worse only, but both. Its progress is not simply a progress in good, evil being gradually driven from the field; nor is it simply a progress in evil before which the good continually disappears: it is a progress in which good and evil alike come to maturity, bearing their ripest fruit, showing all that they can do, proving their strength to the utmost against each other; the progress is not in good itself or in evil itself but in the antagonism of one to the other.

In other words, the battle is on. And we're on the front lines. Christ's kingdom, His way of relating is breaking into this world through us, through His followers, through the church. And Satan doesn't like it one bit. The more that good shows up, the more strongly evil fights back. The two kingdoms collide. That's the story of Revelation for twenty chapters. The last two are all about realized victory.

This final love letter may seem a strange way to end a love story. At first glance—and maybe a dozen more—its realism feels more disruptive than appealing, more confusing than comforting. But listen: "Blessed is the one who reads the words of this prophecy, and blessed are those who hear it and take to heart what is written in it, *because the time is near*" (Revelation 1:3; emphasis added).

And then, after John has seen the scroll opened, an angel tells him, "Do not seal up the words of the prophecy of this book, *because the time is near*" (22:10; emphasis added).

Now here's the clincher. God had told Daniel that when the time came, the scroll he was told to "close up and seal" would be opened. The seals would be broken. The unseen story would be revealed. And when that happens, *"those who are wise will understand"* (Daniel 12:4, 10; emphasis added).

As we prepare to see God's story unfolded before our eyes in living color, let's pray for wisdom. I want to be among the wise who understand the story that God is telling me in a new way in His last love letter. I long for wisdom. Life is too hard to navigate without it.

Now it's true, as Eugene Peterson points out in *Reversed Thunder*, that the first sixty-five letters tell me all I really need to know. There's nothing in the sixty-sixth I haven't heard before. But now I'm hearing it differently. I'm *seeing* truth. The Spirit uses the images and symbols and visions of Revelation to wake up my imagination, to help me visualize the words of Jesus and to be awed by the sheer brilliance of His way of doing things so that I'm moved to hold steady no matter how bad things get, to keep on doing what I can to bring His kingdom to earth—in spite of severe opposition and struggle and failure—until the party begins.

Prepare for the unveiling. The Spirit is about to remove the drape from a great work of art. There is none greater. We're about to *see* reality, the way things really are. The first sixty-five letters have positioned us in a front-row seat for the revelation of God's Son and of the righteously difficult but amazingly merciful story He's telling.

If realists would lighten up, existence would be a lot more fun. But nobody would dance. Not the way Jesus does. And life would be fun for a while, then empty forever.

The realism of Revelation lets us see that the dance floor is a battlefield. But it's where we learn to dance. It's where we see Jesus. I think I'm ready for the final dance lesson. I hope you are too.

Love Letter Sixty-Six: Revelation

REIGN WITH THE LAMB NOW,
AND YOU WILL SING WHEN THE LION ROARS!

*F*ather, I just read words from Francis Schaeffer that, I think, provide the right glasses through which to read Your sixty-sixth letter.

"Here's what he wrote: 'Both the Scriptures and the history of the church teach that if the Holy Spirit is working, the whole man will be involved and there will be much cost to the Christian. The more the Holy Spirit works, the more there will be personal cost and tiredness. It is quite the opposite of what we might first think. People often cry out for the work of the Holy Spirit and yet forget that when the Holy Spirit works, there is always a tremendous cost to the people of God, weariness, tears and battles.'

"These words encourage me, Father. After talking through sixty-five of Your letters, I still feel tired, at times more than ever in both soul and body. And I find that deep tears come more easily than deep laughter, especially when something touches me in a tender spot. And the battle raging in me and around me doesn't let up. If anything, it's getting more intense. Is this really the work of Your Spirit? Is it part of maturing? Is this one stretch of the narrow road to life?"

"When My Son's kingdom breaks into yours, expect a collision. When His way of relating confronts the world's way of relating, including yours, all heaven and hell break loose. The battle is on, a battle to the death and to life. The side that appears to be losing is winning and will soon win, visibly and decisively. My Son will see to that. And the side that seems now to have the edge, the side whose godless agenda is growing in worldwide support, loses *forever*."

"Father, I want to be fully on Your side. However victory looks in this life, that's what I want. I don't want to be a mediocre Christian. I don't want to think I'm maturing when I'm not. And don't let me treat weariness and tears and battles as evidence of immaturity if in fact they are really the spiritually forming work of Your Spirit. I'm afraid that if I make that mistake (and I think I have), I'll focus on getting more energy, fighting back tears behind sociable laughter, and avoiding battles with whatever violation of love might be required. Father, that's all just a pile of self-obsession.

"Whatever it takes—worse fatigue, more tears, harder battles—I want to go all the way with You. You've taught me a great deal through Your letters already. But now as we approach this last one, I find myself longing not for more knowledge (though there's so much I don't know) but for all that I've learned and have yet to learn to be 'taken up into my life' by the Holy Spirit. I want to love well no matter how tired I am. I want to love more like Your Son whether I'm crying or I'm fighting another battle.

"I'm drawn to that phrase, *taken up into my life*. I read that phrase, written by Kierkegaard, just last night. It resonated with me. But his next words scared me. He compared someone who learns Your truth but isn't gripped by it to a man who 'builds a great castle and lives in an adjoining shack.'

"Father, Your truth is a mansion. I want to live there every day, to never wander off, to explore every room and every hallway and every corner. As I walk through this world, I want to live in Your truth. 'In spiritual matters,' Kierkegaard went on, 'a person's ideas must be the building he lives in—otherwise, there is something terribly wrong.'"

"We've talked quite a bit. What do you now understand to be wrong with you?"

"Oh, Father, so much. A spirit of entitlement. My demand to be treated well that's so often stronger than my desire to treat others well—an it's-all-about-me syndrome. An addictive attraction to pleasure or relief however I can get it. Insensitivity to my impact on others and self-congratulation for how friendly and thoughtful and funny I can sometimes be and how helpful I am when it's convenient.

"I could go on. But I wonder if what most keeps me from going all the way with You is complacency. I think I quietly cherish the illusion that I'm really a pretty decent Christian. Maybe I believe that Your Son's kingdom has already done a nice job of breaking into my life and of breaking me. Father, I can be proud of even my humility.

"I don't want to buy into the kind of so-called *Christian* teaching that Kierkegaard despised, the kind that 'does not make known the Christian requirement—perhaps because it is afraid that people would shudder to see at what a distance from it we are living.' I don't know why this just now comes to mind, but in *The Diary of a Country Priest*, Bernanos thought it significant that Jesus did not say, 'You are the *honey* of the world,' but rather 'You are the *salt* of the earth.' Honey makes everything sweet. Salt bites as it heals and preserves from further decay. I've come to realize that real Christian teaching is more salty than sweet."

"If you see the distance between how My Son loves and how you love, you will know that His kingdom has more work to do. More salt must be poured on your wounds before you can do a good and loving job of pouring salt on others. You will not sing till you shudder. You will not stand strong in My holy Presence till, like John, you fall helpless before My Son. You will not live in My Spirit till you die to your flesh.

"You have been seeking Me for many years. You have heard Me speak to you in My first sixty-five letters. You are ready to read My final love letter to you. But don't merely read. Look! See! Listen!

❈ Prepare to *look* at the reality of My kingdom as it's coming right now into your life and into this world.

❈ Prepare to *see* My Son as you've never seen Him before.

❈ Prepare to *listen* as the story I tell reveals the movement of history that continually brings you to a crossroad where life-altering choices are required."

"Father, I want to look and see and listen. But the way You wrote this letter makes it difficult. The visions and images and symbols, for me at least, obscure more than they reveal. Why didn't You just describe in a straightforward way what You want me to understand?"

"I want you to do more than understand My story. I want you to be caught up in it, My truth taken up into your life. *Describing* reality either through clear narrative or direct teaching, what I have done mostly in My letters so far, reaches the mind with true truth. And that is needed, but it risks leaving you with a mere grasp of facts properly expressed in a statement of doctrine. *Picturing* reality in graphic images penetrates through, not around, your mind and into your imagination where true facts become living truth, experienced doctrine. Only then will My truth be taken up into your life.

"My final letter has the power to stir your depths as they have not yet been stirred. John saw reality. He saw what was happening in the invisible world as the visible world was pressing in on him. He saw that, right now, My Son is bringing His kingdom of a new way to relate into this self-obsessed world. There is more to reality than meets the naked eye. Only when you are gripped by what is happening in the invisible world will you live well in the visible world. I wrote this letter to sustain you through hard times with a vibrant awareness of what My Son is doing right now and what He yet will do."

"Father, I know some of the background for this letter. It's the content that puzzles me. Maybe if I get the background in my head, the content will reach my heart. As I understand it, Revelation is a personal letter from a pastor to churches he loved that were going through hard times. The apostle John was quite elderly when You inspired him to write it, somewhere in his mid-eighties. And he wrote it from Patmos, an island—really one big rock in the middle of the ocean—that Rome used as a jail for its political prisoners.

"The history I read indicated that Domitian, the insane, cruel emperor of Rome during John's last years, required everyone in the empire to bow before his image and repeat *Caesar Kurios*, 'Caesar is Lord.' John refused. He wouldn't bail out on You like that, so Roman justice branded him a seditious atheist and shipped him off to the island of Patmos to rot in the burning sun.

"I understand, too, that John wrote this pastoral letter as a prophetic encouragement to his fellow believers who were suffering badly under Domitian. John knew they were paying a terrible price for standing up to their evil culture. He knew, too, that trouble-avoiding compromise was more than tempting. What You revealed to him in all those visions, John wanted to reveal to the churches. He believed, apparently quite strongly, that if they saw what he had seen, they'd stay strong and faithful, no matter how hard things went for them in their lives. They'd live the new way in an old way culture.

"I found his greeting interesting: 'I, John, your brother and companion in the suffering and the kingdom and patient endurance that are ours in Jesus' (Revelation 1:9). I gather he realized that following Your Son as He brings His kingdom to earth means trouble and requires patience. So much for a honey-sweet message.

"But the way You had him write to his suffering friends really does puzzle me. Could you put in a few words what those Christians back then heard in this letter so I can hear it too?"

"Above everything else, My people then heard what I want you to hear now. And it's this:

Things are not as they seem. Evil, though widespread, is not winning. Faithfulness, though costly, is not futile. Affliction, though continuing, will end. The Lion's roar will soon be heard. Until then, reign with the Lamb. Live to love, not control.

"I wanted them, and I want you, to see the invisible but real movement of history. Despite corrupt politicians, rampant immorality, economic crises, natural disasters, disease epidemics, and widespread rejection of My Son, He is *right now* on the throne of the universe. He is moving history, according to My plan. Nothing happens without His permission. Nothing ever has. Nothing ever will.

"He is leading His bride through the desert toward the city. He is overcoming the *power* of evil with the *weakness* of love. The defeat at Calvary has already put Him in complete charge. And He is now supporting My people in persevering through great difficulties until He brings them all, everyone, to His wedding party in My home."

"Father, just briefly, could You show me how You're saying all that in this letter?"

"You've been sitting comfortably during our previous conversations. Sit up now on the edge of your seat. *Look* through the doors I open into the invisible world. *See* who's there and what's happening. And *listen* intently to everyone who speaks.

❀ In chapter 1, look at My Son as He revealed Himself to John who, when he saw My Son, was worshiping. Be still now and know that I AM God. My Son is God. My Spirit is God. See your Great High Priest wearing the golden sash, the belt for His robe, around His chest. In that day, a belt worn around the waist of a man's long robe meant there was work to be done. Wearing the belt around the chest declared the work is done. *It is finished.* Evil has been defeated. Your future is secure.

See His white hair of wisdom. No one is as brilliant. See His blazing eyes that burn through all pretense; His bronze feet that will not crumble under any weight; His voice that blocks out all other voices, the voice that His followers love to hear; the seven stars in His right hand, stars that decorated Rome's throne, claiming power that belongs to My Son; the sharp dagger coming out of His mouth ready to cut away spiritual cancer if you get close enough for surgery; and His face so bright that one look forever defines true beauty.

Look at Him. See Him. Fall down before Him. Then feel His right hand on your shoulder. Listen as He tells you not to be afraid. First you shudder, then you sing.

❋ In chapters 2 and 3, see My Son standing in the middle of your church. Listen to what He's saying to:

   ❋ *Ephesus* (and to you): you serve Me, you believe Me, but you do not love Me, not as you did at first. Your love for Me has grown cold;
   ❋ *Smyrna* (and to you): you live under *thlipsis*, under the crushing pressure of kingdom collision. I will not relieve the weight of opposition and struggle in this life. Stay faithful till My kingdom fully comes;
   ❋ *Pergamum* (and to you): you do good things every day. But you accommodate the godless culture around you in ways that you refuse to examine and confess;
   ❋ *Sardis* (and to you): you're religiously busy, but you're spiritually empty. Your church programs feed your ego. You look alive, but you are dead;
   ❋ *Philadelphia* (and to you): you feel weak. As your church world measures strength, you are weak. But you have not denied My name. You have kept My word. You are strong. Walk through the door I open for continuing service. What you do matters to Me and My kingdom; and
   ❋ *Laodicea* (and to you): self-obsession drives what you do. You believe you are doing well. Nothing matters more to you than that you feel good about yourselves. You nauseate Me.

   Look at your community and yourself. See My Son seeing you. Listen to what He says. Examine yourself in light of His words.

❋ In chapters 4 and 5, look through the open door into heaven. See the throne on which I sit. See in the middle of the throne a slain Lamb, not a fierce Lion. My Son is both, but He wins the victory through sacrifice, not control, not through the power of force. Until He roars to establish the victory His sacrifice has won, reign as a lamb with Him in your relationships.

Give up control. Sacrifice your well-being for a greater cause. You bring in My kingdom by reigning as a sacrificing lamb, not as a roaring lion.

❁ In chapters 6 through 11, look and listen with confidence: the Lion is roaring. Seven seals are opened. Evil self-destructs. *It's happening now!* Seven trumpets sound. Judgment spreads through the earth. *It's happening now.* It soon will happen more.

Reign with the Lamb who bears evil, and you won't tremble when the Lion destroys evil. Demand justice no longer. Expose injustice, but reveal love. It's a new way to live, the way of the Lamb. But know this: injustice will end. The Lion will roar.

❁ In chapters 12 through 20, see the sign of the woman clothed in light [12:1]; see Mary give birth to My Son, an infant who will one day rule all the nations with a scepter of iron [12:5]. Look again. See the dragon, Satan himself, fail in his effort to kill the woman and child. Then see him as he goes after you and all who name My Son's name, 'the rest of her offspring' (12:17).

See the dragon conscript two colleagues, the beast out of the sea (every political structure and leader opposed to My kingdom) and the beast out of the earth (every religious system and leader that promises a good life without My crucified Son as its provider). Then watch as the seven bowls of My Son's final wrath are poured out. See the two beasts thrown into everlasting fire [19:20]. See their followers die [19:21]. See Satan and his armies mobilize to wage war against My Son. See them hurled into the lake of fire by one word from My Son's mouth [20:7–10].

Never live in fear of the devil! Recognize him. Resist him. But know that My Son's power is greater than his. His doom is as sure as your life is secure.

❁ In chapters 21 and 22, look! All things are new [21:5]. Shalom: everything is as it should be. See My Son high and lifted up.

When Isaiah saw divine glory, he cried 'Woe to me!' (Isaiah 6:5). When you see My Son in that day, you will sing. You've already shuddered. You will shudder again. But then it will be time to dance, to laugh and sing as never before.

See what John saw that is soon to come—a new heaven and a new earth [21:10]. See the city of heaven come down to earth. See living water flow from My throne through the street of the Holy City [21:2; 22:1–2].

Listen to My Son: 'Behold, I am coming soon' (22:7). Demand nothing now. Endure everything now. He has come. He is coming right now. He will come again, soon. Wait. Persevere. Hope. Your destiny, eternal bliss; your every dream forever satisfied."

"Father, my heart is a reservoir of longing, a well of living water pressing to erupt. I'm weary. I cry. I do battle. *But things are not as they seem.* Father, I believe. Help my unbelief. Let me see Your Son. I can only say, with John, 'Come, Lord Jesus' (22:20)."

"My son, you've heard Me well. Francis Schaeffer was right. When My Spirit works, there is always tremendous cost to My people living in this time. But the cost can't compare with the gain. And the end is near. Keep looking. Keep seeing. Keep listening. *I'll see you soon!"*

Epilogue: The Story Everyone Needs to Hear

(IN SIXTY-SIX PARAGRAPHS)

*W*here are you? That was the question God asked Adam after he had made a mess of things and tried to cover it up. It opened Adam's ears to hear the beginning of an incredible story God would go on to tell.

And now He's told it, from start to finish, in sixty-six love letters. It occurred to me that the same question asked of us might open our ears to hear the whole story in a way that could keep us on the path to the party. So let me ask that question before I retell the story in sixty-six paragraphs.

Where are you right now? Any big challenges to your faith at the moment? Worried about where the world is heading? Concerned about personal matters? Feeling down for no discernible reason, tired, or more insecure than loved? Hiding loneliness or a sense of failure behind a friendly personality or a busy schedule or an air of competence? Is there anything you really want that God hasn't given you? And do the prospects for getting it look pretty slim?

Are you as bugged as I am by smiling Christians who assure you that if you have faith and pray hard that a loving God will turn things around for you, the way you want them, in this life? Is that the story God is telling?

I know you want to be happy. So do I. Everyone does. And here's the good news. A happy God, a very happy God, created you to be happy. And He has a foolproof plan to make you happy.

Funny thing, though. If we feel happy now without being grounded in His story, if our good feelings are rooted in something other than seizing our opportunity to be part of God's story as He tells it, then the happiness we feel works like an anesthetic. It numbs a pain lodged somewhere deep inside that we can neither bear nor eliminate. It blinds us to seeing how into ourselves we really are, and it keeps us from feeling really bad about it, which we should.

It doesn't sound like good news, but it is—and it's true: the happiness God gives in this life (not in the next) is discovered when we feel and embrace the profound disappointment that comes from living in a world that cannot satisfy our deepest desires and when we face and confess our entitled demand that we experience complete satisfaction now. It's then the Spirit of God puts us in touch with the hope from which springs the faith and love that keep us dancing into other people's lives. And that's our happiness, for now. I don't enjoy the process. It's not the way I expected to pursue happiness.

But maybe pursuing happiness isn't the point. If we let our desire for happiness become a demand, we'll have little interest in hearing the story God is telling. And if we're into our demand for happiness but want to preserve the illusion that we're following Jesus, we might make up a nice story about a nice God who wants nothing more than to give His kids a good time. God, we imagine, like so many foolish parents, tucks us into bed every night and asks, "Did you have a good time today?"

It's quite possible, you know, to believe that whatever happy feelings we enjoy, whatever positive attitudes we may have toward life, come from knowing God pretty well and living in His love when, in fact, those feelings and that happy attitude might be tied more than we think to our stories moving along according to our plans.

It would be a good idea when we hear God asking where we are for all of us to sit quietly enough and long enough to look squarely into the unpleasant reality that nothing, absolutely nothing that we're enjoying now is guaranteed to last; that things will get rough for all of us before we die; and that the happiness we rightly long for needs a better foundation than all the good things available in this world.

When we become even faintly aware of desires burning in our souls that are not satisfied and never will be in this life, either we move toward God and look eagerly for the path to the party He's planned, *or* we move further into ourselves and toward cynicism and despair. It's risky to get real. But it's riskier not to, at least in the long run.

If we feel the void we cannot fill and turn toward God, eventually we discover something beneath the void that surprises us. We find a longing we didn't know was there, a desire not only to be happy (though that's still there), a desire not to fill the void (though we still want it full), but a strong, clean-feeling desire to love someone other than ourselves, to live for a cause greater than our personal happiness.

And when we realize that God's love frees us to substantially satisfy that desire in this life and to fully satisfy it forever in the next, then we understand why God's story is gospel, good news. Then the story we hear from Him puts the *Hallelujah* in the "Hallelujah Chorus."

His story does include some tough chapters. It's brokenness over how into ourselves we are that gives us ears to hear everything God is saying. And it's repentance that gets the wax out. We hear about a party God is throwing for His Son and that empty, selfish people like us are invited. Until we get there, the anticipation becomes the happiness that keeps us on the path to the party and energizes us to do all we can, mostly by the way we relate, to persuade others to join us on the narrow road to more happiness than we ever dreamed was possible.

God's story is the story everyone needs to hear. And those who are honest enough to face what's missing and what's wrong in themselves are the ones who hear the story best. It's the only story that makes an examined life worth living, and it's the only story that delivers on its promise, though not on our timetable, to make us happy with a happiness that cannot be lost.

And now, with a brevity that will make a *Reader's Digest* condensed book look like a complete library of a prolific author's works, I want to present the story of God as best I can and as briefly as I can tell it in sixty-six short paragraphs. In order to showcase the story's ear-opening realism and its heart-awakening romance, I tell the story as if God Himself is the narrator and is talking directly to who He knows is listening.

Of course, He's already told His story in sixty-six love letters of varying lengths. I'm just repeating what I heard. Remember the simple outline already presented in the book. It will help you follow the plot:

- Part One: A Fall, a Promise, and the Story Begins
  Genesis Through Deuteronomy
- Part Two: History Gives Away the Plot
  Joshua Through Esther
- Part Three: Living in Mystery with Wisdom and Hope
  Job Through Song of Songs
- Part Four: A Word to the Foolish
  Isaiah Through Malachi
- Part Five: The Hero Takes Center Stage
  Matthew Through John
- Part Six: Clumsy People Take Dance Lessons
  Acts Through Jude
- Part Seven: The Promise Is Kept: Happiness Forever
  Revelation

THE STORY

PART ONE: A FALL, A PROMISE, AND THE STORY BEGINS
Genesis Through Deuteronomy

Long ago before time began, the Three of Us decided to create people like you whom We could enjoy as they enjoyed Us and the beautiful world We designed for their home. But your first parents foolishly decided there was more happiness to be found on their own without Me. Never underestimate the mess their decision made of everything and the mess your same decisions continue to make. And never underestimate My ability to clean up the mess and to bring everyone to Our party who wants to come. I have a plan. (Genesis)

I will do whatever it takes to fully restore My family and to have them with Me forever. My plan centers on revealing the lengths to which My love will go to bring you to My party. You walked away from Me, but when you realize who I AM, you'll want to come back. (Exodus)

You really have no idea how foolish you've become. You actually believe that you love well enough to win My approval. You don't.

Getting you to think right and love well is the toughest part of My plan. It will cost Me the death of My Son. (Leviticus)

And there's a price you must pay as well. I must let you realize that the mess your choices create puts the happiness you want out of reach. Humility comes hard to proud people. The return path to Me will involve suffering and misery. At times, you'll think it's the path to hell. It's not. Trust Me. (Numbers)

You're a slow learner. Before you learn to follow Me closely, you'll make an even bigger mess of things and get yourself in real trouble. You're a born lawbreaker, a natural sinner. But remember, you can't out-sin My love. (Deuteronomy)

PART TWO: HISTORY GIVES AWAY THE PLOT
Joshua Through Esther

You'll know My plan is working when you realize you're beginning to hate your selfishness more than your unhappiness. That realization gets the real battle underway, the battle against sin, against your natural inclinations. As long as you see unhappiness as your worst problem, you'll think I should treat you better than I do. But when you see how into yourself you are, you'll be amazed that I haven't crossed you off the invitation list to My party. (Joshua)

That realization won't come easily. You fiercely resist seeing how stupid and evil it is to live for yourself. Until you recognize that the way you relate to Me and to others is wicked, you'll see nothing that requires repentance. You should be surprised by blessings. Instead, you're stunned by judgment. (Judges)

Disappointments and disadvantages lead you to justify looking out for yourself and complaining when things don't go your way. Take heart. I have the power to work through everything that is difficult in your life in order to plant your feet on the road to joy. (Ruth)

The cancer of selfishness, however, has metastasized. It's spread throughout your entire soul. But I have the cure. Surgery is needed . . . without anesthesia. I force My plan on no one. You must be awake to cooperate with the process. (1 Samuel)

Surgery is always successful . . . if you stay on the table. Submit to My severe mercy, and you will learn to love. You'll sometimes still dance to hell's rhythm, but you will learn to dance to the rhythm of heaven, and that will make you a great person, more and more alive to My plan. (2 Samuel)

See to it that you don't fall for the devil's hellish lie: greatness is measured by a fallen world's standards. Neither money nor talent nor power defines greatness. Great people are people who love greatly. (1 Kings)

But you'll fail miserably. My plan takes that into account. Every failure presents an opportunity to bow low before My holiness and to stand tall in My grace. I give up on no one. (2 Kings)

My Spirit will work to detach you from depending for happiness on anyone or anything but Me. The satisfaction you now derive from *second* things will diminish. You will feel new extremes of emptiness that will make you wonder if My Spirit has stopped working. He never will. The emptiness you feel will slowly be transformed into a desperate thirst for Me, not for more second things. (1 Chronicles)

Real trust develops in the dark. When life makes no sense, when suffering seems random and over the limit, when your soul feels the weight of unbearable emptiness and fear, enter the struggle to trust. My kingdom is in sight. (2 Chronicles)

Through My Son and My Spirit, I am always with you. Though often unfelt and unrecognized, We are doing whatever it takes to make you whole and holy. That was My promise at the outset of this story. I aim to keep it. I *will* have you at My party. (Ezra)

Expect setbacks, big ones, in you, in your family and friends, and in your church. But keep taking small steps even when they seem to accomplish nothing. If it comes out of your love for Me, the smallest act of faithfulness and sacrifice is a great work. I see it. I will not forget it. I will use it. You matter to Me and to My plan. (Nehemiah)

Even when you wander far away from your home in Me, I'll be working behind the scenes to bring you back. There'll be plenty of opposition, plenty that will go wrong, whether you're in the far country or living in My community. But no one can thwart My plan, no one. You're on the winning side. (Esther)

PART THREE: LIVING IN MYSTERY WITH WISDOM AND HOPE
Job Through Song of Songs

You are not in control of either getting or keeping the blessings you desire. What comes into your life always comes with My knowledge and permission. What I allow is sometimes painful and often confusing. You will ask why and get no answer. Only in mystery will you discover humility and hope. (Job)

When you hurt, cry. A stiff upper lip will isolate you from Me. When good things happen, celebrate. Be thankful. And when nothing makes sense and you wonder if I even exist or, if I do, what kind of God I am, bring your honest questions to Me. With others who struggle and cry and laugh, bring all of yourself to Me, always. (Psalms)

Never relieve genuine confusion by coming up with formulas that provide the illusion of control—if you do this, you get that; if you pray like this, God will answer like that. In your confusion, fall before Me in reverence (you don't know enough to challenge Me) and follow Me with the wisdom I provide (you're simply not smart enough to chart your own course). (Proverbs)

Doing right doesn't always make things go right. That's a difficult lesson to learn. The spirit of entitlement that loves formulas and control is strong. I must lower you into the despair of humility—you are not in control—before I lift you into the delights of joy. I am in control. And I am good. My plan is on track. No matter how unhappy you become, never give up. (Ecclesiastes)

I love you. My Son loves you. My Spirit loves you. You taste Our love only a little compared to its abundance. Through everything that happens, We are drawing you closer to Us, forming you more like My Son. We are bringing you to Our party. We are bringing Our party to you. You will enjoy Our feast of love. (Song of Songs)

PART FOUR: A WORD TO THE FOOLISH
Isaiah Through Malachi

You really are very foolish. You cling to the belief that a difficult life is a worse problem than a selfish soul. Like a father with a foolish child, I must reward your foolishness with pain. But the pain I bring is always redemptive. It opens you to receive the comfort of forgiveness and the sure hope of becoming the person I created you to be. (Isaiah)

As you choose to obey Me, I will often seem absent. Following Me makes your life harder, not easier, than walking away from Me. For a time. And during that time, My Spirit will always provide what you need to press on to trust Me when everything falls apart. (Jeremiah)

When that happens, when your heart breaks, cry loud. Weep strong. Only in suffering will the depths of your demanding spirit be exposed. Only in suffering will you meaningfully abandon yourself to My hidden faithfulness. (Lamentations)

Only when you are so grieved by the raw evil of your demanding spirit that you're overwhelmed by the glory of My holiness will My love change you. Only when you recognize the evil energy in your relating will you be stunned by the beauty of My Son, a beauty you'll long to reflect. (Ezekiel)

You will not return to the happy days of naïve innocence. That's not My plan. Words cannot express what lies ahead. Life will become difficult. Dreams will shatter. I call you to imagine what lies *further* ahead. A new kind of happiness is coming. (Daniel)

You will be most happy when you love most like Me. When those who hate you treat you terribly, you will begin to understand how I love you. You hurt Me deeply. I am not unaffected by your rejection. But I will not abandon you. I cannot. I love you. (Hosea)

To be formed like My Son means to love like that, to love those who pound nails into your hands and feet. *Wake up!* Realize that's what you most want to do. *Lose hope!* Stop depending on life to work, on others coming through for you. *Pray right!* Pray for My will to be done, not yours. (Joel)

You sometimes think you're further along than you are. Your lack of sacrificial love is hidden behind exciting worship. But is it worship at all? Real worship generates real change. Do you worship? (Amos)

It's easy to focus on how others need to change more than you and to think you're honoring My justice when you hold them accountable. I will take care of all that's wrong in others. Make it your priority to concern yourself with what's wrong in you. (Obadiah)

You naturally want to see people punished who threaten your comfort. When My plan involves letting someone off the hook who has treated you poorly, you'll want to take matters into your own hands. I will never cooperate with your desire to protect yourself from enemies you refuse to love. That desire will lead you off the path to the party. (Jonah)

Don't make it your goal to get others to live right. Focus rather on walking with Me, doing what is just, and loving others. Don't listen to preachers who encourage you to value the blessings of life over the forgiveness of sins. Only forgiven people forgive others and live justly with them. (Micah)

You don't need to get rid of your enemies. I will defeat every enemy who stands in the way, not of your comfort but of your joy. (Nahum)

But My plan to defeat your enemies will not square with your understanding of how I should go about the battle. Don't ignore the struggle and confusion that will erupt within you as you watch Me fight for you against your enemies. You must tremble before you trust and struggle before you sing. (Habakkuk)

My plan to profoundly change the way you relate will frustrate you. You'll think I'm asking too much. You'll be tempted to settle for superficial change that comes more easily. You should know by now that change without brokenness and repentance falls far short of the change I have in mind. (Zephaniah)

But no matter how little deep change you see in yourself or others, keep doing My work. Build My temple. You are that temple. Your soul must be cleansed of every trace of self-interest. Only I, the Lord of Hosts, can clean out the filth and restore My temple as the house of worship. (Haggai)

Am I doing it? Yes. Can you see it? Not always. But things are not as they seem. My church looks more like a shopping mall than a holy temple. And yet good things are happening and are about to happen that soon you will see. Until then, live as a prisoner of hope. My plan is on course. (Zechariah)

You see so little now, so little of what is still wrong within you. When I open your eyes, you will see your foolishness and My faithfulness. Keep your eyes closed, and you will face Me as your judge. Turn toward Me in repentance and worship, and real life will begin. (Malachi)

PART FIVE: THE HERO TAKES CENTER STAGE
Matthew Through John

Never think that I changed from the angry God of the Old Testament to the loving God of the New. I am the same, always. I tell one story of a God who hates sin but loves you. The love in My love story now becomes plainly visible to all with eyes to see. My Son, the eternal God, Second Person in Our community of Three, comes to change everything, to make all things new, including your heart. He has taken charge. He's the King of the coming kingdom. His mission: to expose and destroy self-centeredness and to bring Our way of doing things into you and your world; to get heaven into you and to bring more of heaven into others by the way you relate. (Matthew)

My Son modeled a new way to relate, the only way that has the power to bring into every relationship the sheer delight We've enjoyed since before time began. In your world, so filled with pride and greed and selfishness, only humble servanthood and sacrificial suffering will bring change. My Son came to serve you and suffer for you. The King of kings became the Suffering Servant. It's a radically new way to live. Soon you will wake up to realize it's the only smart way to live, the only good way to live, the only way to bring heaven's kingdom to earth. (Mark)

My Son served and suffered with single-minded passion to see My plan carried out, to bring My family home. A perfect person orders his life around one supreme and noble purpose; he aims his life in one good direction from which he never veers. My Son, the only perfect Person who ever lived, wanted nothing more than to reveal Me and to spread My life throughout the world at any cost to Himself. You are destined to become just like Him. That's My plan. (Luke)

To enjoy Me, live like Him. There's no other way to experience joy in our relationship. Worship before Bethlehem's manger. What humility! Watch My Son live. Listen to Him speak. What beauty! What wisdom! Fall down at the foot of the cross. What love! What a climactic turning point in history! Stand before the empty tomb, then move into your world on a mission. What a privilege is yours! What power is available to carry out your mission! My Son revealed the way We do things. Give when no one gives back. Love when no one returns love. Forgive when no one deserves forgiveness. Suffer in the place of others rather than making them pay. That's the way of the kingdom. (John)

PART SIX: CLUMSY PEOPLE TAKE DANCE LESSONS
Acts Through Jude

Meet with other followers of My Son to better learn the full message of this new life and to tell it to the world. Depend on your new power to suffer on behalf of your new mission as you develop into a new kind of community with a new and living hope. The party is underway. *Start dancing.* (Acts)

Listen to everything I say through My Son and My Spirit. Get clear on the message you've been privileged to hear, enlightened to embrace, and called to tell. As you seek wisdom, remember this: *clarity comes through the cross*. The death and resurrection of My Son guarantees the success of My plan. (Romans)

The more My story grips you, the more you'll long for things to go better than they do. You will get discouraged. You'll feel excited one moment and down the next. Your community will disappoint and frustrate you. Be patient. Stay the course. I will accomplish My purpose in you and in My church. I will carry out My plan for the world through you and through My church. Keep telling My story. (1 Corinthians)

It will get difficult. When expectations don't match reality, you'll feel betrayed. Your spirit of entitlement dies slowly. But it will die. Live to know My truth. Know My truth to live it. The more you see what's going on in you and in this world and the more you realize what depths of selfishness remain in My people (yourself included), the more you'll be immersed in tears and filled with hope. Change is needed. Change is coming! (2 Corinthians)

With hope comes freedom. You can live. You can breathe.

Everything is forgiven. But freedom is easily abused. You are free to love, not to indulge your whims. You are free to depend on My Spirit to become all you were meant to be. You are not free to change simply by exerting willpower. It won't work. Live in My Spirit. Keep in step with His rhythm. There is no greater freedom. (Galatians)

You are free to love. Love not only *like* My Son but also *for* My Son. You are now part of a community that represents Him. You are His body on earth. Live to *complete* Him by loving. You are His temple in the world. Live to *reveal* Him by loving. You are His bride for whom He gave His life. Live to *delight* Him by loving. Celebrate the heights of privilege to which I have brought you. (Ephesians)

Hold nothing back. Give Me everything. You'll lose nothing of real value. To live is Christ. The attitude that ruled My Son can now rule you. The yearning to know Him will eventually eclipse all other desires. Through My Spirit, you now have the power to live a new way, the way of love. Dance! Sing! Real life is yours. (Philippians)

But don't make the mistake of so many whose desire for happiness becomes a demand. Don't expect to experience in this life the joy that will be yours when My Son returns. Engagement provides the anticipation of complete joy. Marriage is its consummation. My Son is in you now as the *hope* of glory, not its *experience*. Don't live to feel full. Live from the truth of a fullness that you will one day fully enjoy. (Colossians)

My Son will return. Cling to that hope as if your life depends on it. It does. Without that hope, My plan is a sky hook, a grand deception better ignored than embraced. With that hope, My plan is your anchor in rough waters, the promise of a safe harbor where you're expected. Never turn away from Me. Keep serving Me with all your strength. And wait. Wait patiently, expectantly, longingly, for My Son to return. His coming is your hope. (1 Thessalonians)

Interpret all that's happening now in the light of what's coming then. Judgment is coming, the end of selfishness, and the destruction of evil. Community is coming, the reunion of family, satisfaction of every desire, and the eternal party of love. Until then, keep active. You have work to do. (2 Thessalonians)

My enemy will try to stop you any way he can. He will trick many, even church leaders, into twisting My story to accommodate and not destroy your pride. He will change My story from truth that requires submission into an opportunity to feel the excitement of creating truth for yourself, to come up with "special knowledge" available only to the elite and enlightened. Hold fast to the truth I tell you. It will be a battle. Fight for truth. It's a good fight. Guard everything you've heard from Me in My love letters to you. Risk everything on what you know to be true. (1 Timothy)

Listen to those whose way of life validates My truth. Seasoned saints have this in common: they've paid a price to follow My Son, and they all believe it was worth it. Take confidence in what they say. Find strength in their example. Keep walking the narrow road with the few who have found it, who know it leads to the life I created you to enjoy. A party awaits. (2 Timothy)

The party has already begun. You can dance to heaven's music now by revealing the *beauty of grace* that became visible in My Son's first coming. Keep living the new way of grace until the *beauty of glory* fills the earth when My Son returns. Grace is not for beautiful people. They see no need of it. Reveal the beauty of grace to the ugly. Remember you were one of them. But no more. You are now beautiful in My Son. You can change. So can they. Withhold My good news from no one, not even Cretans. (Titus)

The life I offer changes everything. Real life dramatically transforms every person and every relationship into something beautiful. But your confidence in its power will be tested. In your efforts to relate well, to dance in love, you will kick the shins of others, and others will step heavily on your toes. You must remember that you have wronged Me more than you have wronged others and more than others have wronged you. Deal with them as I deal with you. (Philemon)

It will not be easy. Real love is costly. You'll be tempted to back off, to shrink back, to settle for less than offering true community. It's easier to water down My command to love, to simply get along as best you can and enjoy whatever pleasures are available. I call you to so much more. And you can respond. Right now, My Son is standing at My side as your guarantee that you are forgiven for loving so poorly, you are understood in all your hurts and struggles, and you are equipped to follow Him through every dark night. Don't be among those—and there are many—who shrink back. With My Son as your advocate, you can press on. Do it! (Hebrews)

And don't prattle on to others about My good news unless you're living the good news in the way you relate: by listening more than making your point and by showing compassion to irritating people. You are on a mission that requires you to relate to others with their potential for happiness more in mind than your own. Complete your mission, and you will be rewarded. (James)

My plan will fulfill all your dreams. Soon. In a little while. But you must realize that I live above time. My perspective is infinitely wider than yours. As you experience time, it's purification now but pleasure forever. First, the slow development of holiness. Then when holiness is complete, complete happiness. Every good thing will be yours to enjoy. Soon! (1 Peter)

Waiting is hard. Many will make fun of your pie-in-the-sky understanding of My story. They want everything now. Prove them wrong. My nature is in you. Live a life that can be lived only by those who know there's more coming than pie. It's a full banquet. Nibble now until you're seated at My table. Your place is reserved. (2 Peter)

You've never seen Me. You've never laid eyes on My Son. You've not felt His literal embrace. And, therefore, you've never experienced the fullness of unmixed joy that is My Spirit. But you've had tastes. You taste the reality of real life every time you love others for Our sake and theirs. By loving, you can enjoy communion with Me now in this life until our union is complete in the next. (1 John)

I want you to love, to relate in real life to real people: young people who live more in the felt moment than in My enduring truth, older folks who wish things wouldn't change, and the great majority of people who do their best to manage their everyday lives without compromising their values or surrendering their visions for a good life. Live in the real world as a real person. You feel down, you pay bills, you get lonely, you enjoy golf. My Son was a real person, a boy who lived with a mother and dad, a young man who learned a trade, an adult who danced at a wedding, cried at a funeral, prayed when things got rough, and died for a cause He believed in. My Son lived the real life I call you to live, *divine energy visible in common humanity.* (2 John)

It was that energy that kept Him loving in a world of people who didn't. When you see something in another that's worthy of criticism, before you respond to that person's faults, check out your own life. Is divine love energizing your attitude and the words you want to say? (3 John)

Always keep My story in the forefront of your mind. I've invited you to My party. I've equipped you to love. I've anchored you in hope. You'll face terrific opposition as you live to tell My story. Keep My story alive in your mind, and I'll keep you dancing on the narrow road. Keep moving. Keep waiting. My plan will soon come to a spectacular climax. (Jude)

PART SEVEN: THE PROMISE IS KEPT: HAPPINESS FOREVER
Revelation

Trust Me. Things are not as they seem. My Son is right now bringing His kingdom to earth. The collision of kingdoms, the resistance of everything opposed to My plan, is the source of all the upheaval in the world. My Son will judge severely. The forces of evil will be destroyed. And He will bless abundantly. My story is about to end in the eternal day of a new way to live in a new world. Can you hear the music? The party is underway. It won't be long till My Son makes everything new. And then you'll really dance! (Revelation)

Sources Cited

Prologue
N.T. Wright, quoted from an interview appearing in *Christianity Today*, January 2007, Vol. 51, No. 1, page 40.

PART THREE: LIVING IN MYSTERY WITH WISDOM AND HOPE
Love Letter Eighteen: Job
Soren Kierkegaard, *Provocations* (New York: Plough Books, 2007).

PART FOUR: A WORD TO THE FOOLISH
Love Letter Twenty-Four: Jeremiah
Rhonda Byrne, *The Secret* (New York: Atria Books/Beyond Words, 2006).
Soren Kierkegaard, *Provocations* (New York: Plough Books, 2007).

Love Letter Twenty-Five: Lamentations
The Weight of Glory by C. S. Lewis © C. S. Lewis Pte. Ltd. 2001.

Love Letter Thirty-Two: Jonah
The Problem of Pain by C. S. Lewis © C. S. Lewis Pte. Ltd. 1940.
A Grief Observed by C. S. Lewis © C. S. Lewis Pte. Ltd. 1961.

Love Letter Thirty-Four: Nahum
Martin Luther, *A Commentary on Saint Paul's Epistle to the Galatians*, 1833.

Love Letter Thirty-Eight: Zechariah
Mother Teresa, *Come Be My Light*, Brian Kolodiejchuk, ed. (New York: Doubleday Religion, 2007).

PART FIVE: THE HERO TAKES CENTER STAGE
Love Letter Forty-One: Mark
The Lion, the Witch and the Wardrobe by C. S. Lewis © C. S. Lewis Pte. Ltd. 1950.

PART SIX: CLUMSY PEOPLE TAKE DANCE LESSONS
Love Letter Forty-Four: Acts
Peter Kreeft, *The Philosophy of Tolkien* (Fort Collins, CO: Ignatius Press, 2005), 72.

Love Letter Forty-Five: Romans
G. K. Chesterton, *Orthodoxy* (New York: NuVision Publications, LLC, 2007).
Garrett Green, *Imagining God* (Grand Rapids, MI: Wm. B. Eerdmans, 1998), 151.
Collected Letters by C. S. Lewis © C. S. Lewis Pte. Ltd. 2000.
James T. Como, *Remembering C. S. Lewis* (Fort Collins, CO: Ignatius Press, 2005), 97.

Love Letter Forty-Six: 1 Corinthians
C. S. Lewis quoted in *When Heaven is Silent* by Ronald Dunn (Fort Washington, PA: Christian Literature Crusade, 2008).

Love Letter Forty-Seven: 2 Corinthians
Mere Christianity by C. S. Lewis © C. S. Lewis Pte. Ltd. 1942, 1943, 1944, 1952.

Love Letter Forty-Eight: Galatians
John Owen, *The Holy Spirit* (Carlisle, PA: Banner of Truth, 2005).

Love Letter Fifty: Philippians
Thomas Chalmers, *The Expulsive Power of a New Affection*, http://parishpres.org/documents/The%20Expulsive%20Power%20of%20a%20New%20Affection.pdf.

Love Letter Fifty-One: Colossians
R.C. Lucas, *The Message of Colossians and Philemon* (Downers Grove, IL: IVP, 1980).

Love Letter Fifty-Two: 1 Thessalonians
Leon Morris, *New Testament Theology* (Grand Rapids, MI: Zondervan, 1990), 86.
Tim Farington, *A Hell of Mercy* (New York: Harper, 2009).

Love Letter Fifty-Three: 2 Thessalonians
Dante, *Divine Comedy* (1306).

Love Letter Fifty-Seven: Philemon
Martin Luther, quoted in *1 and 2 Timothy, Titus, and Philemon* by H. A. Ironside (Grand Rapids, MI: Kregel Academic & Professional, 2007).
Alexander Smellie, *On the Hour of Silence* (1906), 396.

Love Letter Fifty-Eight: Hebrews
Martin Luther, *The Evangelical Repository and Bible Teacher* (1880), 144.

Love Letter Sixty-Two: 1 John
Dietrich Bonhoeffer, *Who Am I?* (Minneapolis, MN: Augsburg Fortress, 2005).
John Owen, *The Holy Spirit* (Carlisle, PA: Banner of Truth, 2005).

Love Letter Sixty-Three: 2 John
The Business of Heaven by C. S. Lewis © C. S. Lewis Pte. Ltd. 1984.
M. Scott Peck, *Further Along, The Road Less Traveled* (New York: Touchstone, 1998), 160.
Henri Nouwen, *Out of Solitude* (Notre Dame, IN: Ave Maria Press, 2004).
Emil Brunner, *The Mediator* (Cambridge, UK: Lutterworth Press, 1934), 341.

Love Letter Sixty-Four: 3 John
Leo Tolstoy, *War and Peace* (New York: Signet Classics, 2007).
Dorothy Sayers, *The Greatest Drama Ever Staged* (Hodder and Stoughton, UK: 1938).

PART SEVEN: THE PROMISE IS KEPT: HAPPINESS FOREVER
Love Letter Sixty-Six: Revelation
Agnes cartoon by Tony Cochran. Published by ArcaMax, © 29 June 2009.

Dorothy Sayers, *The Divine Comedy, Part 2: Purgatory* (New York: Penguin, 1955).

James Denny, *The Epistles to the Thessalonians* (1892), 313.

Eugene Peterson, *Reversed Thunder* (New York: Harper, 1991).

Soren Kierkegaard, *Provocations* (New York: Plough Books, 2007).

George Bernanos, *The Diary of a Country Priest* (New York: Avalon, 2002).

Weekly Reading Guide

Suggested approach: Each week read the chapter(s) from *66 Love Letters* on Sunday. Then the rest of the week, read as much of the corresponding book(s) of the Bible as God leads you.

WEEK	SCRIPTURE	WEEK	SCRIPTURE
1	Genesis	27	Amos & Obadiah
2	Exodus	28	Jonah & Micah
3	Leviticus	29	Nahum & Habakkuk
4	Numbers	30	Zephaniah & Haggai
5	Deuteronomy	31	Zechariah & Malachi
6	Joshua	32	Matthew
7	Judges & Ruth	33	Mark
8	1 Samuel	34	Luke
9	2 Samuel	35	John
10	1 Kings	36	Acts
11	2 Kings	37	Romans
12	1 Chronicles	38	1 Corinthians
13	2 Chronicles	39	2 Corinthians
14	Ezra & Nehemiah	40	Galatians
15	Esther	41	Ephesians
16	Job	42	Philippians
17	Psalms	43	Colossians
18	Proverbs	44	1 & 2 Thessalonians
19	Ecclesiastes	45	1 & 2 Timothy
20	Song of Solomon	46	Titus & Philemon
21	Isaiah	47	Hebrews
22	Jeremiah	48	James
23	Lamentations	49	1 & 2 Peter
24	Ezekiel	50	1 & 2 John
25	Daniel	51	3 John & Jude
26	Hosea & Joel	52	Revelation

About the Author

$\mathcal{D}$r. Larry Crabb is a well-known psychologist, seminar speaker, Bible teacher, author, and founder/director of NewWay Ministries. In addition to various speaking and teaching opportunities, Dr. Crabb offers a week-long School of Spiritual Direction and a weekend conference, entitled *Life on the Narrow Road*. He is also Scholar in Residence at Colorado Christian University and serves as spiritual director for the American Association of Christian Counselors. His many popular books include *Inside Out*, *Finding God*, *Connecting*, *Becoming a True Spiritual Community*, *The PAPA Prayer*, *SoulTalk*, and *Real Church*.

For additional information, please visit
www.newwayministries.org.

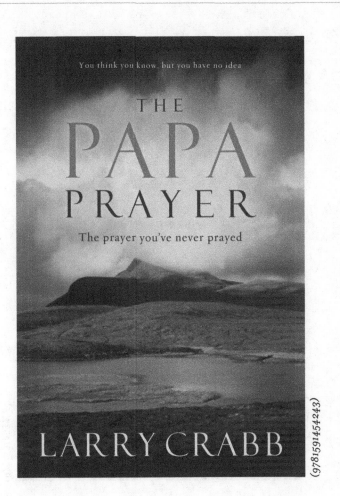